ENGLISH PRINTING, VERSE TRANSLATION,
AND THE BATTLE OF THE SEXES,
1476–1557

Women and Gender in the Early Modern World

Series Editors: Allyson Poska and Abby Zanger

In the past decade, the study of women and gender has offered some of the most vital and innovative challenges to scholarship on the early modern period. Ashgate's new series of interdisciplinary and comparative studies, 'Women and Gender in the Early Modern World', takes up this challenge, reaching beyond geographical limitations to explore the experiences of early modern women and the nature of gender in Europe, the Americas, Asia, and Africa. Submissions of single-author studies and edited collections will be considered.

Titles in this series include:

Women, Imagination and the Search for Truth in Early Modern France
Rebecca M. Wilkin

Hermaphrodites in Renaissance Europe
Kathleen P. Long

Salons, History, and the Creation of Seventeenth-Century France
Faith E. Beasley

From Wives to Widows in Early Modern Paris
Janine M. Lanza

*Intertextual Masculinity in French Renaissance Literature
Rabelais, Brantôme, and the Cent nouvelles nouvelles*
David P. LaGuardia

English Printing, Verse Translation, and the Battle of the Sexes, 1476–1557

ANNE E. B. COLDIRON
Florida State University, USA

ASHGATE

© Anne E. B. Coldiron 2009

All rights reserved. No part of this publication may be reproduced, stored in a retrieval system or transmitted in any form or by any means, electronic, mechanical, photocopying, recording or otherwise without the prior permission of the publisher.

Anne E. B. Coldiron has asserted her moral right under the Copyright, Designs and Patents Act, 1988, to be identified as the author of this work.

Published by
Ashgate Publishing Limited
Wey Court East
Union Road
Farnham
Surrey, GU9 7PT
England

Ashgate Publishing Company
Suite 420
101 Cherry Street
Burlington
VT 05401-4405
USA

www.ashgate.com

British Library Cataloguing in Publication Data
Coldiron, A.E.B. (Anne E. B.), 1959–
English printing, verse translation, and the battle of the sexes, 1476–1557. – (Women and gender in the early modern world)
   1. French poetry – Translations into English – History and criticism 2. English poetry – French influences 3. Man-woman relationships in literature 4. Women in literature 5. Marriage in literature 6. Sex in literature 7. Translating and interpreting – England – History – 16th century 8. Translating and interpreting – England – History – To 1500 9. Book industries and trade – England – History – 16th century 10. Book industries and trade – England – History – To 1500

   I. Title
841'.008

Library of Congress Cataloging-in-Publication Data
Coldiron, A.E.B. (Anne E. B.), 1959-
  English printing, verse translation, and the battle of the sexes,1476–1557 / by Anne E.B. Coldiron.
    p. cm. — (Women and gender in the early modern world)
  Includes bibliographical references and index.
  ISBN 978-0-7546-5608-1 (alk. paper)
  1. French poetry—Translations into English—History and criticism. 2. English poetry—French influences. 3. Man-woman relationships in literature. 4. Women in literature. 5. Marriage in literature. 6. Sex in literature. 7. Translating and interpreting—England—History—To 1500. 8. Translating and interpreting—England—History—16th century. 9. Book industries and trade—England—History—To 1500. 10. Book industries and trade—England—History—16th century. I. Title.

PR131.C66 2009
841.008—dc22

2008018068

ISBN: 978-0-7546-5608-1

Printed and bound in Great Britain by
MPG Books Ltd, Bodmin, Cornwall.

Contents

List of Figures	*vii*
Acknowledgments	*ix*
Preface: To the Reader: Between the Sheets	*xi*

1	Introduction	1
	Contexts, Part I: Early Printing in England	2
	Contexts, Part II: Translation	4
	Contexts, Part III: Translated Poetry and English Poetics	6
	France, Romance, and the *Querelle*; or, Gender, Genre, and Mode in Early Printed Poetry	7
	An Alternative to Courtly, Romance, and Clerical Discourses: Features of the Poems	10
	The Present Book: Chapters, Case Studies, and Approaches	16
2	"The Mireur and Maistresse" of "Intelligence": Christine de Pizan's Translated Authority in Early English Print	21
	Survey of Translations of Christine's Works in Early English Print	21
	Taking Advice from a Frenchwoman: Printers, Paratexts, and Presentational Strategies in the *Moral Proverbs*	38
	First Take: Christine and England	40
	Second Take: "Oure" Elders, Christine's Authority, and Caxton's Presentational Strategies	44
	"Taking" the *Proverbs* Themselves: The Relation of Content to Paratexts	52
	Third Take: Authority, Fame, and the Early Chaucerian Canon	56
	Outtakes and Postscripts: The *Morale Prouerbes* in the Sixteenth Century	65
3	"La Femme Replique": Debating Women in English Translation	69
	Wynkyn de Worde's *Interlocucyon*	70
	Sympathy Reframed: An Ovidian Dido as Chastity Warning	85
	Dangerous Beauty, Or the Ugliness of *The Beaute of Women*	97
	Conclusion	111
4	Framing Misogamy: The Prologue and Prohemye to *The Fyftene Joyes of Maryage*	113
	"The Prologue of the Translatour"	117
	"The Prohemye of the Auctour"	123

	Woodcuts, the Lost Epilogue, Misogamy and Misogyny	136
	Conclusion	139
5	Translating Marriage Complaints	141
	Voicing the Woman's Side: *A Complaynt of them that be to soone maryed*	144
	Copland's Acrostics (Para)textual Histories, and Printers' Interventions	158
	"Th' instrument is not in point": Impotence, Wifely Sexuality, and Late Marriage	165
	Conclusion	171
6	Misogamy and Translation at Henry VIII's Court: Heywood's *A Mery Play*	173
	The Contexts	174
	Misogamy and the Translation	177
	Johan and Literary History	188

Appendix 1: The "Letter of Dydo to Eneas"; The Beaute of Women — 193

Appendix 2: The Paratexts to the *Fyftene Joyes of maryage* — 207

Appendix 3: The Marriage Complaints — 215

Bibliography — *237*
Index — *253*

List of Figures

English images are taken from the Early English Books Online database and are used with the permissions of Proquest/UMI, Inc., the Folger Shakespeare Library, the British Library, the Pierpont Morgan Library, and the Harry Elkins Widener Collection of the Houghton Library, Harvard University. French images are taken from Gallica, the digitization project of the national libraries of France, and are used with the gracious permission of the Bibliothèque nationale de France.

2.1.	Christine de Pizan, *[Les Cent Histoires de Troye]* *L'épître de la déesse Othéa* (Paris: [Pigouchet], c. 1500), Aiii. (Gallica BnF Notice No. FRBNF31117543).	32
2.2.	Christine de Pizan, *C. Hystoryes of Troye*, tr. R. Wyer (London: Wyer, [1540? 1549?]), [A7].	33
2.3.	Christine de Pizan, *Morale Prouerbes of Cristyne* (Westminster: Caxton, 1478), [Ai].	46
2.4.	Christine de Pizan, "Morall prouerbes of Christyne," in *The Boke of Fame* (London: Pynson, 1526), [E4].	61
2.5.	Christine de Pizan, "Morall prouerbes of Christyne" in *The Boke of Fame* (London: Pynson, 1526), [E5].	63
3.1.	Anon., *Interlocucyon* ... (London: de Worde, 1525). Title page.	73
3.2.	*Prouerbes of Lydgate* (London: de Worde, c. 1510?). Title page.	75
3.3.	Anon, *Seyinges of Salomon and Marcolphus*. (London: de Worde 1529). Title page.	76
3.4.	*Complaynt of a louers lyfe*. (London: de Worde, c.1531). Title page.	77
3.5.	*Interlocucyon* ... (London: de Worde, 1525). Title verso.	79
3.6.	Octavien de St. Gelais, tr. Anon., "Letter of Dydo to Eneas," in *The Boke of Fame* (London: Pynson, 1526), Fol. [F3v].	87

3.7	Octavien de St. Gelais [*Épîtres d'Ovide*] (Paris: A. Vérard, c.1505), p. 72. (Gallica BnF Notice No. FRBNF31046494).	90
3.8	Octavien de St. Gelais, *S'ensuyt les XXI épistres d'Ovide* (Paris: Vve. J Treperel, c. 1520–1525), p. 63. (Gallica BnF Notice no. NUMM71774).	91
3.9	Anon., *The Beaute of Women* (London: Fawkes, 1525), Title page.	99
5.1	Pierre Gringore, tr. R. Copland, *A Complaynt of them that be to soone maryed* (London: de Worde, 1535). Title page.	147

Acknowledgments

A version of the latter part of Chapter 2, "Taking Advice From a Frenchwoman," appears in Caxton's Trace: Studies in the History of English Printing, ed. William Kuskin (University of Notre Dame Press, 2006). A version of part of Chapter 4 was published as "Paratextual Chaucerianism," Chaucer Review 38.1 (2003): 1–15. An early version of part of Chapter 2 won the South Central Modern Language Association's Center for Humanities Research Prize (Texas A&M University) for best essay of 2001 ("Technology as Translation: the Case of Caxton and Christine de Pizan," SCMLA, Tulsa, OK, Nov 5, 2001); thanks to the Center for this recognition and support. Thanks to the British Library, the Pierpont Morgan Library, the Huntington Library, and the Widener Library of Harvard University for permission to use images from books held in their collections, and thanks to UMI/ProQuest for permission to reproduce those images from the EEBO database. Special thanks to the Bibliothèque nationale de France for permission to print images from the Gallica project.

The staffs of the Folger Shakespeare Library, the Library of Congress, and Special Collections of the Hill Memorial Library at Louisiana State University provided sustained expertise and encouragement. The Louisiana Board of Regents, the LSU Office of Research, and the LSU College of Arts and Sciences provided essential long-term funding. Thanks to graduate students Elizabeth Cowan, Erica Daigle, Alexandra Reuber, Sarah Brandeberry and Liz Jackson; Jennifer Terry's precise, imaginative, thoughtful work created the Appendices. Thanks to seminar participants at the Attending to Early Modern Women Conference, 2006, for lively comments, and especially to Jane Donawerth. Thanks to my new colleagues at Florida State University for a very warm welcome.

So many scholars and friends have helped me with this book that even a simple list exceeded the space available here; I'm hoping that having your own copy won't disappoint you. For humane patience, tact, and hard work, thanks to Erika Gaffney, Whitney Feininger, Meredith Coeyman, Diane Casti, Heather Dubnick, and the other readers and editors at Ashgate Press. For his wit, encouragement, perceptive advice, and affection, most special loving thanks to Nicholas Crawford.

Preface

To the Reader: Between the Sheets

This book is a recovery project, bringing to new light a body of early printed poetic translations about women, marriage, and gender relations. Popular in their day, most of these translations about women were likely never thought of as great literature. They are certainly not pleasing to modern sensibilities. In fact, the poems treated here are little read, rarely mentioned, hard to obtain, and, once obtained, hard to read, if not "unreadable" in several senses.[1] Not only are the physical texts of these poems held in restricted archives and digitized in restricted databases, their unfamiliar typefaces and their language and orthography, unglossed by editors, feel rough and strange to most modern readers. Despite a strong transhistorical interest in the poems' themes—"woman questions" and the battle of the sexes—their historical distance from us can seem very great. Even poems on topics of such enduring interest can fall out of fashion; what is unread is soon unedited, then becomes inaccessible, and over time reaches a state of unreadability. That state invites a recovery project such as this one only if the material has some value worth the new reader's time—your time. I hope here to explain to you, the new reader, why it is worth my trouble and your time to approach these old poems about women.

What is to be gained from such a recovery project? The simplest gain is to know more about what was actually printed and read in the early Renaissance and thus to read beyond a canon of "usual suspects"—beyond, that is, the works most often edited and discussed in modern times. Access is next: in order to give modern readers easier, less costly, unrestricted access to these little-known poems about women, I have transcribed most of them in Appendices 1, 2, and 3. Third, this book aims to render the poems readable (that is, more easily comprehensible)

---

[1] They are literally unreadable to many since they are available in rare copies held in archives; they are available on Early English Books Online (EEBO) only to readers with access to large or wealthy libraries. The selected readers who have such access then find the poems in their original blackletter typefaces, difficult because unfamiliar to modern eyes. These texts may in fact have been available in their first printings to a considerably less elite readership—a wider and more variably composed readership—than they are now. The choice to print transcriptions is thus based in part on what could be viewed as a political effort to improve long-term access, beyond the confines of archives and corporatized databases. On the implications of and some solutions for the unreadability of early modern literature, see my "A Readable Earlier Renaissance," *Literature Compass* 3.1 (2006): 1–15.

by providing basic, introductory information about their contexts, the people associated with them, and the English and French literary traditions with which they connect. In many places, the book explains and glosses the poems themselves. Finally, an important reason to read on is that these poems change what we know and tell each other about the history of literature on women and about English literary history in general. The poems invite new kinds of reading because they perform unusual mediations between cultures, between languages, between media, and indeed between the genders.

Like the wider corpus of early printed translations of which they form a thematic subset, these poems mediate in several senses. As translations from French, they stand between two languages, two cultures, and two literary systems that were rapidly diverging and yet still powerfully engaged with one another. Any translation is an interpretation, of course, but my effort here is to read the poems both as cross-cultural interpretations and also as palimpsests or footprints of dynamic contacts between Franco-Burgundian literature and English literature. In doing this, the book's first, best model is the work of Anne Lake Prescott, whose studies of the presences of French literature in England are nuanced, extensive, and profound. Margaret Ferguson, Deanne Williams, Karen Newman, Ruth Morse, and others have also illuminated the connections between French and English cultures and literatures. Like the work of these scholars, this book reads across literary cultures and steps outside older models of influence to understand textual transmission in sites apart from the *translatio studii*—for these are not the old Latin-derived high-culture works we usually think of when we think of Renaissance translation. Unlike the work of these scholars, this book takes up some different aspects of these connections, looking particularly at the importance of printing technology, at an earlier era, and at works further outside the main canon. To make these poems more readable, in short, I take up some new questions about their English-French cultural mediation and about what Karlheinz Stierle famously called "the co-presence of cultures" that I find in them.

Another crucial aspect of these poems' dynamic "between-ness" is their motion across media. These poems are mostly born into late-medieval manuscript circles or as early French imprints, but they appear in English in early print in rapidly widening distribution. This move between media has tremendous implications at every level of interpretation, and this book tries to capture as much as possible about what happens "between the sheets." That is, here we shall read not only between the lines, as literary interpreters, but also between the pages, as textual interpreters: making literary and interpretive sense of the material-textual evidence of the books themselves and the generative, dynamic processes of textual transformation revealed there. Each case study takes particular imprints in their material-textual detail. Even more than particular footnotes here show, this book owes a debt to the work of such scholars as Julia Boffey, Martha Driver, A. S. G. Edwards, Lotte Hellinga, and, most recently, Alexandra Gillespie. My case studies focus closely on the printers' interventions, especially in their paratexts and presentational strategies, which are essential to making these poems readable and, more broadly, are essential to the creation of early English literary culture. Just as any translation is an interpretation, any imprint or edition manifests its producers' interpretations and understandings of the work. And just as translations move the themes and poems *between* cultures, the printers studied here move the poems *between* whole systems of script and print production, distribution, and reception. This book, then, reads early English printed poems on their pages for their mediating power—for the cross-cultural, cross-media, and literary-interpretive agencies they reveal.

All this mediating work—between French and English, between script and print—has fairly obvious implications for our critical narratives of periodization. It probably goes without saying that this book, like much recent work from such scholars as A. C. Spearing, James Simpson, David Aers, Kent Cartwright, and others argues for continuity between "medieval" and "Renaissance." But the book does not argue for transition as the only or even the most salient aspect of that continuity. Rather, it argues for literary change as something that is perfectly linear only when viewed in hindsight; when examined, as I try to examine it here, as an evolving series of uncertainties, literary change turns out to be a matter of contingencies, opportunities, whimsical changes of fashion—much more like what contemporary media and theorists, modifying Lucretius, call the "clinamen" or what chaos theorists would call "flocking behavior," or a matter of what economists and sociologists following Malcolm Gladwell would call "tipping points." In other words, it becomes clear in a recovery project like this one that the canons and critical narratives of traditional literary history are nearly so neat as to be impossible or tautological. Real literary change is messy, involving dead ends, unconnected likenesses, strange failures of appropriation (as in Chapters 2 and 6), alongside inexplicable fads and wild popularities, as in Chapters 3, 5, and especially 4. The cooperating agents of those rapid and unpredictable changes were the early printers and translators (very often, as in most cases treated in this book, the printers were also translators). Neither agent of literary change can be best understood apart from the other, and so this book also argues for the interactive and multiplying powers of what I call the transformational arts of early English print. By *transformational arts*, I mean the technical and aesthetic experiments in language and media that the first two or three generations of printers used: first, the mediating arts of verbal translation in reconfiguring themes, forms, genres but also the media experiments in typefaces, border designs, visual translation, illustration, *mise-en-page*, commendatory and fictional framing, and even the acts of binding, presentation, and distribution. These textual transformational arts, including both translation and printing, form the basis of the English literary Renaissance, but they forge changes and continuities unpredictably. Although the poems treated here stand between what we have categorized as two distinctive periods, and although they are certainly transitional in some ways, as I point out frequently in the book, these poems reveal the uneven, imperfect, and yet generative processes of textual transmission at work in a most formative phase of English literary history.

Finally, most obviously, because of the themes of the poems chosen for treatment, this book is about early modern mediations of a very fundamental and persistent kind of difference. This book treats poems about what happens, does not happen, should happen, or must not happen *between* men and women. This book's chosen poems explore relations between the sexes and the norms men set for women and for each other as they deal with women. The poems contain direct arguments, dialogues, and apostrophes between men and women, and the book reads these in terms of their position between French and English literary systems and between script and print production. The poems also stand in a scholarly gap between the thriving discussions of late-medieval poetry on women and gender and the equally thriving discussions of early modern literature and gender; the former generally end with Christine de Pizan, and the latter generally begin with the mid-sixteenth-century pamphlet wars. This book itself stands between those discussions and is also necessarily in implicit conversation with the work of many scholars like Diane Bornstein, Lori Walters, Linda Woodbridge, Joan Kelly Gadol, Constance Jordan, Betty Travitsky, and Wendy Wall (whose *Imprint of Gender*, although it takes up a later phase of printing, matters to this book more than specific citations can indicate). In other words, what is on both sides of the scholarly gap also, if indirectly, informs this recovery project.

From these intermediating positions—between script and print, between France and England—the poems end up forming an alternative set of discourses on women and gender relations. These poems turn out to have been quite unlike the romances so popular in both medieval and Renaissance literature, in both script and print, and unlike the courtly and Petrarchan poetics so well studied in the scholarship on both periods. These non-elite, widely distributed poems take a different tack. They develop a distinctive set of poetic conventions for writing *between* media and *between* cultures about marriage, love, and sex—about what passes between women and men. This is an important part of the book's recovery project: identifying, illustrating, and making readable the unusual mediating characteristics of this uncourtly, antiromance, alternative line of poetry.

In the introductory Chapter 1, I first explore the contexts of these mediating experiments in poetry. Chapter 1 treats the context of early print culture (what I have elsewhere described as the francophone public sphere of early English print), the context of French-English relations in that sphere, the contexts of translation and literary-historical backgrounds. Chapter 1 also explains in some detail the characteristics of the poems taken as a whole—that is, it describes what features and conventions we can identify as forming this alternative discourse on gender relations. Only then does Chapter 1 describe how each remaining chapter's cases illustrate different aspects of this alternative line. Chapter 2 revises our views of the translated authority of Christine de Pizan. Chapter 3 studies three cases of a dialectical impulse in the poems: the *Interlocucyon with an argument betwyxt man and woman*...(1525); the one-sided epistolary arguments of the *Letter of Dydo to Eneas* (1526); and the one-sided, proscriptive arguments of the *Beaute of Women* (1525 and 1540). Chapter 4 studies an enduringly popular misogamist satire, *The Fyftene Joyes of Maryage* (1509). Chapter 5 studies a pair of complaints that extend the marital discussion into a sort of debate, the *Complaynt of the To*

Soone Maryed (c.1505) and the *Complainte of the To Late Maryed* (c.1505? and c. 1535). Chapter 6 offers a new view of John Heywood's translated verse farce, *Johan Johan* (c. 1535). The poems here are chosen as revealing cases, and since each case tends to be revealing in its own way, this book follows where the cases lead instead of trying to force their considerable range and variety into a single argument. Because these case studies demonstrate different things, no one chapter includes all the features and characteristics of the alternative line of poetry identified in Chapter 1. Instead, the larger picture emerges through a consideration of the variety and range of these cases' dynamic mediations of difference. Thus the Preface's title: what matters most here is what happens between men and women, between French and English, between printers and readers (from blank sheets to filled books), between script and print.

This book is emphatically not an argument for the literary greatness of these poems, even though some of them are fairly successful aesthetic experiments that simply did not turn out to be central in the long-term canon. Instead, it is a demonstration of a way of recovering and rereading the past that I hope will prove useful even beyond the themes of gender selected here. The book is also, finally, an argument for the poems' several challenges to literary history. The poems help to complete the history of "woman questions" in English poetry and the history of the media revolution and evolution after Caxton. They demonstrate that modern editorial practice obscures a great deal of the meaning that it is possible to recover from the actual pages. They illuminate new aspects of the importance of translations, especially translations from French, and they reveal some distinctive, French-affiliated alternatives to courtly, romance, and Petrarchan modes of poetry about women. They challenge our notions about poetic genres and forms, about literary authorship, and about periodization. This book aims to make such variously challenging poems more readable without eliding historical distance. That is, I hope that the book itself might mediate between these strange old poems and you, their new reader.

Chapter 1
Introduction

Yf ther be yll women and rebell
Shrewed dispytous and eke felonyous
There be other fayre and do full well
Propre gentyll lusty and joyous ... (ll. 301–5)

—*The Complaint of the Too Late Married*, tr. Robert Copland, c. 1505

Those who write against women and marriage, says the male speaker of this complaint, are "Tryfelers" (l. 266), "lyers" (l. 268), and "bastardes" (l. 296); the speaker dismisses such traditional antifeminist and misogamist authorities as Theophrastus, Jean de Meun, and Mathéolus. Poems disputing the usual misogynist line had occupied a secure if beleaguered position in French gender discourses since Christine de Pizan's famous *querelle de la Rose / querelle des femmes*. And in England, by the mid-sixteenth century, printed pamphlets debated "woman questions" in prose. However, a century after Christine's *querelle* and a half-century before the English pamphlet wars on gender, a complex, contentious literature about men, women, sex, love, and marriage was reaching English readers in early printed translations. These French-born poems seem to have been less secure and possibly more beleaguered in their new English milieu, judging from patterns of publication and the printers' efforts to naturalize them.

Furthermore, these poetic translations are decidedly uncourtly and often sexually frank. The above-quoted *Complaint*, for example, features some scopophilic stanzas approving of female sexual desire and some graphic lines lamenting the speaker's own impotence: "But comynge to a bed delycyous / For to holde the spere in a full hande / It plyeth and fayleth for wyll not stonde" (ll. 200–202). Sexual problems and delights, marriage as an unnatural imprisonment, the economic burdens of family life: the early printers publish some provocative material about gender relations that stands quite apart from the better-known courtly and romance-related poetry taken from the continent.

In identifying this alternative line, this book explores a gap in our literary scholarship that is both chronological and generic. Although there are many excellent studies of courtly and romance literature and much scholarship about early theological and didactic writing on (and usually against) women, the many noncourtly, nonclerical, popular poems treating gender issues are less well understood. Likewise, although there is plenty of fine scholarship about gender discourses in later-medieval manuscript culture and likewise about "woman questions" in the Elizabethan and Stuart periods of print, much less is known about what came between. An early phase in the history of English literature on gender has gone relatively unmapped, and it is a crucial one. Right between what we have periodized as "medieval" and "Renaissance" (or "early modern"), this moment of information revolution determines what English readers will come to expect in poetry. Since that information revolution was created by a cross-cultural traffic in technology, ideas, and aesthetics, these poetic translations were more important in the printers' output than our current critical canons would suggest. This book asks how these poems come to take their place in the receiving early print culture and finds that they apparently had significant commercial potential but needed, and received from the early printers and translators, strong aesthetic and ideological interventions.

Outside the technological constraints and literary conventions of manuscript culture, yet acutely aware of such conventions, the early printers and translators enjoyed a certain free space, an experimental phase in the new medium. Understanding the poems on gender as part of this early phase of media experiment means examining specific early imprints in light of their visual and material presentation in print and what it implies. The particular features of this moment—especially the printers' technological interventions, their powerful connections with France and the rest of the francophone continent, and their heavy reliance on translation—shape this alternative strand of poetry about gender. Before introducing the characteristics of this alternative poetry, I introduce its special informing contexts: the world of early English printing, its francophone foundations, and the prominence of poetic translation in it.

Contexts, Part I: Early Printing in England

From the time of Caxton's press, a new English literature came forth out of foreignness and in the swirling energies of a media revolution. In the "marketplace of print," as Alexandra Halasz calls it, much faster distribution of a greater number of texts became possible for the first time, and increasing literacy meant that new readerships had access to a rapidly expanding body of texts. Any new information technology creates a sudden content vacuum, and the early printers in England filled theirs with all kinds of material. They printed prose and poetry, practical and fictional works, tracts and manuals: a proliferation of kinds and formats and contents and styles. In the relatively unregulated space after Caxton (1476) but before the charter of the Company of Stationers (1557), this proliferation meant both instability and opportunity of several kinds. This marketplace, this site of aesthetic and economic opportunity, also became, conceptually at least, a "public sphere of early print," and what matters most here is that English printed poetry first went "public" in a foundationally foreign, thoroughly francophone subculture.¹ As I have detailed elsewhere, the entrepreneurial frontier of early English print relied most heavily on French and Burgundian printing technology, French and Burgundian book design and aesthetics, francophone workers, and texts in French. Thus the new English poetry is, in most ways, French-born. In fact, more than 100,000 lines of early printed poetry were translated from French before 1558, a number that is about six times greater than the number of lines translated from Italian. The early print record thus opens for our consideration many things that our canons and criticism have largely overlooked. That English Renaissance literature finds its first mass distributions in a francophone matrix has broad implications for literary and cultural studies—and here, specifically, for the appropriation of gender discourses.²

Caxton, Wynkyn, Copland, Pynson, Wyer, and others among the first, second, and third-generation francophone printers in England imported many works on women, sex, love, and marriage. These early printers were usually also translators, and they rendered the works about women in English verse for a rapidly expanding readership. Of course, these topics had long been treated in manuscripts throughout Europe, including those circulated in medieval England and Scotland; as Francis Utley's work shows, some were vernacular, many in Latin.³ Much later, by the mid- and late-sixteenth century and into the early seventeenth century, "woman questions," or arguments about women, marriage, and gender relations, were printed in prose treatises and pamphlets.⁴ But between these two better-known phases, something special happens in the history of "woman questions." The technology of printing puts such material relatively quickly before a

---

¹ For details, see my "Public Sphere/Contact Zone: Habermas, Early Print, and Verse Translation," *Criticism* 46.2 (2004): 207–22. "French" here refers not only to what we now call France, but to the wide sweep of French-speaking cultures across upper Europe, to include Burgundy, parts of what are now Belgium and Alsatian Germany, Luxembourg, and various regional varieties of "French," such as the Poitevin, Angevin, Touraine, and Lyonnais. "France" and "French" are necessarily catchall terms here, but the francophone, then as now, includes considerable variety.

² From those broader implications, and from the large corpus of early printed verse translations from French, this book selects one especially intriguing thematic set: poems about women, sex, love, marriage, and gender relations. The present book forms one part of a larger, long-term study of the role of early printed translation and cultural appropriation of French materials has in the development of English poetry.

³ Alcuin Blamires, ed., *Woman Defamed, Woman Defended: An Anthology of Medieval Texts* (Oxford UP 1992), provides an array of important primary texts. Francis Utley, *The Crooked Rib: An Analytical Index to the Argument about Women in English and Scots Literature to the End of the Year 1568* (Ohio State UP, 1944) treats manuscript as well as some early printed materials in English. Paul Meyer, *Romania* VI (1877): 499–503, presents a good list in French to supplement Jules Gay, *Bibliographie des ouvrages relatifs à l'amour, aux femmes, au mariage...*, 2nd ed. (Paris: J. Gay, 1864).

⁴ Bornstein, ed.; Utley; Jordan; Woodbridge; Henderson and McManus; and many others.

widening readership. The printer-translators apparently perceived this readership as innocent in certain ways, as readers whose sensibilities had to be cultivated, whose habits of reading had to be trained, whose purses had to be opened.

To reach this readership, the printers often chose to translate French works about sex, marriage, love, and women. We should not underestimate either the commercial motivation behind this choice of a perennially saleable topic or the direct practicality of the choice. Because these printers were nearly all francophone and well connected to the continent, they had good access both to the latest continental printing gear and to the most popular French-language texts. They thus had the ability to transform both the linguistic and the material forms of those texts, and they recreated French gender discourses in self-consciously literary forms. Their deliberately literary treatments, however, are not idly belle-lettristic. The printers often strenuously repackaged the imported material on gender, changing emphasis, reillustrating, censoring, exaggerating, omitting, and adding material. They used the paratextual spaces vigorously, even aggressively: woodcuts, titles, prefaces, epilogues, acrostic poems, *mise-en-page*. Their paratextual work, often even more than the work of verbal translation in the poems themselves, reshaped this popular, sometimes controversial material. Since paratexts, as Gérard Genette and scholars following him have shown, function as presentational spaces that code and determine an audience's relation to a work, paratexts are essential in the printers' reaching, cultivating, and opening the purses of the new readership. And since any translation is an interpretation, a differential analysis of versions will highlight the early printer-translators' particular interpretations of a work. Furthermore, a parallel analysis of differences between French and English paratexts can directly highlight the printer-translators' calculations of the distance between French and English readerships concerning gender topics. In this way, we can measure cultural distance to explore the gender topics, and we can use the gender topics to measure cultural distance (and this book aims to do both). By comparing poems and their paratexts across the Channel, this book looks directly at the printer-translators' efforts to address cultural distance and to reshape and re-present French gender poems for the new English reader.

Contexts, Part II: Translation

Again, because most of the early printers in England were also francophone translators, translation from French was key for the importation and development of gender poems in England. These translations offer us both general and specific insights; they form a wide-ranging record of precise moments of cultural contact. In them we see how specific cultural ideas and tropes about gender were given literary expression for a new readership. Often we can also see in these poems and paratexts how certain ideas about gender do *not* translate; how certain topics (seduction, betrayal, female sexual desire) can be comfortable in one literary system and less comfortable in another; how the category of "the literary" (like the categories "women," "gender," or "beauty") does and does not cross cultural barriers. In fact, these translations remind us how any topic or concept, even if general and widely accepted, is nevertheless embedded in specific practices and historical moments. Beyond this embeddedness—this specificity and localization—a longer, literary-historical view of translation measures how (and how readily) literary themes, genres, forms, and movements cross national borders over time and how cultures resist, appropriate, or mutually colonize one another. A translation can be read for its illumination of specific differences between two works, but it may also illuminate differences between two authors, two genres, two literary histories, or, most broadly, two literary systems or even two cultures. Each translation thus records cross-cultural contact at multiple levels, which may be synchronic or diachronic. Each translation, in other words, manifests a nonliteral but literary and aesthetic version of Mary Louise Pratt's "contact zones."

As manifestations of contact, and beyond the transfer of content, literary translations involve aesthetic friction between elements necessarily unlike in the two traditions concerned. Always already different, a translation signals that aesthetic choices have taken place about things like form, voice, and tone. Such choices depend on the translator's assumptions about a new, imagined literary audience and what will suit that audience. So in any translation pair—the translation and its prior analogue in another language—we can read for aesthetic difference, for formal friction. In doing so, we can uncover assumptions about audience as well as implicit claims about literary value, authority, and authorship. These are no small matters, and every poetic translation bears traces of such prior choices, assumptions, and claims. Thus, every translation can teach us more about the literary system as a whole—indeed, more about two literary systems—than would be discernable in a monoglot analysis. Translation study is thus a marvelous analytic tool for literary-historical study.

When we look, as this project does, at particular translations—at what was translated, how, by whom, in what contexts, with what reception—we find some new information about early modern gender discourses (to be treated below) and some fairly serious challenges to the usual accounts of literary history.[5] Some of those challenges are theoretical: translation changes what we mean by *author* and puts pressure on what we mean by *originality*, *text*, *form*, and *genre* and especially alters what the aesthetic particulars in any given form or genre may mean. Intertextuality, imitation, canons and reception, reader response: so much of what we talk about in criticism takes on new meaning when we consider literature in translation.

Early printed translations from French, of which these poems on gender form a significant part, issue specific challenges to currently accepted literary history. For instance, the pedagogically useful period boundary at "Renaissance" crumbles when we read an early print record in which thriving translations from French

---

[5] For my fuller analysis of this point, please see "Translation's Challenge to Critical Categories," *Yale Journal of Criticism* 16.2 (Fall 2003): 315–44.

manuscripts create continuity, not discontinuity, with the previous age. Likewise, the useful, widely accepted idea that Petrarchism creates English Renaissance poetry must be enriched and modified in light of the record of early print. Most early printed poems in English—these poems on gender in particular—are decidedly not Petrarchan, nor are they, as one might expect, Petrarchan in French translation. As important as Petrarchism would become in the literature of later sixteenth-century England (and certainly in our canons and criticism), the first 75 years of printed poetry in England do not contain a single sonnet or a single Petrarchan lyric except Morley's translation of the *Trionfi* (and Chaucer's translated Petrarchan lyrics inset in the *Troilus*). This fact about translation and early print promises to expand significantly what we have told each other about Renaissance poetry since Burckhardt. Here this matters especially because Petrarchan discourses have loomed large as an often troubling set of dominant tropes about women and gender relations. Yet their actual presence in the early English sixteenth century was restricted largely to manuscript readerships. Other kinds of poetry on gender thrived among the unevenly known but almost certainly larger and more varied readerships of early print. For these readers, the print record shows us that before Petrarchism had its English day, what seems actually to have dominated were romance and courtly works, misogynist clerical works, and the alternative line of poetry identified and introduced in this book. This in no way diminishes the importance of Petrarchism to English poetry, but it significantly alters what we know about the canon of poetry on women, sex, love, and marriage.

Contexts, Part III: Translated Poetry and English Poetics

Although there is also a great deal of early prose translation from French, this book focuses on poetry, where the translators' interventions most (and most deliberately) shape the developing literary sphere. Translation of poetry must concern itself with much more than content since *what* is said in poetry is usually less important than *how* it is said. Since poetry derives its meaning not primarily from bare statement but from the artistry with which it is constructed, the poetic translator's work is necessarily more complex than that of the prose translator. Not that content and statement are unimportant here: indeed, this book treats the content of what is translated as key; but in poetic translations, more than in prose, translators and printers must make decisions about form, which further involves decisions about the decorum of form and content and about shaping and presentation. In prose, the conveying of content is the main goal, and departures from content are relatively few or at least relatively clear in rationale. Constraints of form rarely require changes to the substance of a prose translation, for instance, and any such changes are easy enough to identify and explain. In poetic translations, however, the translators' (and here, the printers') work involves more complex negotiations of elements likely to be radically different in the two languages. Genres, forms, point of view, voice, tone, sound effects, lineation, syntax, intertextuality, and visual presentation on the page—all these moving pieces must be considered in their relations to one another.

To choose, for instance, to translate a work out of French tetrameter couplets into pentameter rhyme-royal stanzas changes more than the rhythm and rhyme of each line (although it certainly does that, usually involving *chevilles* and other amplifications that will cause shifts in emphasis and meaning). Such a formal choice would require the creation of something like a verse-paragraphing strategy and an understanding that stanzaic units move a narrative forward with a different pacing and aggregation. Such a choice would entail an enhanced formality of presentation for best coherence with the statelier rhythm and literary history of rhyme royal. Here it matters a great deal that the printer's technical support of the rhetoric of this versification choice would also be required, through such means as spacing, lineation, and *mise-en-page*. This simple example shows that what one form conveys in one system will necessarily turn out not to be what the new form conveys within the new system. This fact, of course, opens up a rich hermeneutic space for translators, readers, and critics. Choices like these, but usually more complex, enter the early modern translators' and printers' calculations as they create literature in the new print medium.

Translations of poetry, in short, offer a special opportunity to observe specific literary decisions and tendencies as they play out in the early phase of a revolution in media technology. The first English translator-printers' verse translations reveal what English readers were taking in, what literary habits were being formed, as the new technology accelerated and altered the national poetry's development. These printer-translators move poems about gender relations between languages and cultures, but also between media—that is, between whole systems of literary production, distribution, and reception.

France, Romance, and the *Querelle*; or Gender, Genre, and Mode in Early Printed Poetry

It is commonplace with medieval roots: since the days of the troubadours, or at least since the courts of Eleanor of Aquitaine, France has supposedly been the sophisticated center of all things related to love, courtship, marriage, and sex. For our purposes, beneath the truism are at least these affiliated truths: (1) a very large body of romance and "courtly" poetry dealing with gender has come to England from France in both manuscript and print; (2) a distinctive alternative set of discourses about gender also comes from France in early print; and (3) France is indeed the originating site of the world's longest running literary dispute about women, the *querelle des femmes*, but its uptake in England is uneven, dispersed, and subtly transmuted. Romance and courtly literature and the *querelle* are already well known to us, so this book aims its attention instead at the alternative line of poetry about gender. As distinctive as that line is, it is nevertheless reliant on—and in some ways defiant of—the dominant romance and courtly discourses of late-medieval France. The alternative line is also connected, though more loosely, to the *querelle des femmes*. That is, each of these better-known French-based discourses stands as a sort of background against which the book's main topic, the alternative discourses of early print, can be usefully understood.

Beginning with the *querelle de la Rose*, Christine de Pizan in 1399 instigated debates among the leading intellectuals of the late fourteenth and early fifteenth centuries about the nature of women and writing about women. Christine questioned the content and values of misogynistic literature—including the foundational romance, the *Roman de la Rose*, as well as courtly tropes of seduction, clerical treatises on marriage, and negative exempla on women. She first pointed out certain problems of literary interpretation inherent in the misogynist tradition. Since the authors of the tradition are all men, she questions how complete their perspectives can be. How reliable is the authority of an unmarried cleric writing misogamist works? In another vein, she declares that using a persona does not absolve an author of responsibility for misogynist violence or scenes of rape and seduction. The *querelle* also raises questions about literary exemplarity: If exemplarity is to be a favored mode, can we not use examples of "good women" and "bad men" as well as the other way around? Are not exemplary history and historiography malleable in the writer's hands, in other words?[6] Does a male-authored literary tradition record anything useful or just about women and women's experience? And how would a female-authored canon differ from it? Christine directly raises these and other hermeneutic issues around women and literature in the context of the *querelle de la Rose*, and her own oeuvre can be read in terms of these questions. It is perhaps a measure of her influence that we now take these questions as perennial, essential, basic; when she raised them, they were radical, inflammatory.[7] Christine's challenge aims at the same genres and tropes of literature about women—romance, courtly seduction literature, and clerical misogynies—that the early printers in England, a century later, would find important and commercially viable enough to translate for the new English public.

Clearly, Christine's arguments in the *querelle* did not reduce the viability of courtly and romance literature in or outside of France, and much of what the early English printers did take up and translate turns out to have only oblique roots in the *querelle*. Yet certain details in the early printed corpus itself testify broadly to the ongoing importance of these French literary questions. Christine's prose and poetry, as Chapter 2 demonstrates, is powerful in England in the new milieu

---

[6] Boccaccio's exemplarities in the *De Casibus* and the *De Claris mulieribus* differ, and Christine's exemplarities in the *Epistre Othee* differ further still. Chaucer, writing at roughly the same time as Christine, raises similar questions in the content of the *Legend of Good Women* and the *Wife of Bath's Tale*, but Christine's *querelle* is specifically and overtly literary-critical, whereas Chaucer is slyly metatextual. An added point of interest here is how the English printer-translators add Chaucerian-style framing stanzas for some of this material, even when there is no Chaucerian substance in the poems themselves. See Chapter 4.

[7] See Hicks; Hult; Ellis; Bornstein; et al., and the critical works discussed in Chapter 2.

and medium. And we can hear echoes of Christine in, for instance, the *Complaint* quoted above, as the speaker dismisses the very authorities Christine has discredited in the *querelle*. But such imprints were not intended as protofeminist literary criticism. Early English readers of print did receive a large early body of gender discourses from France. But outside the relatively elevated, intellectual-coterie context of Christine's *querelle*, in the open marketplace of early English print, these discourses are only indirectly connected to the *querelle*, as we shall see.[8] France may have been the originating site of an important dispute about women in literature, but the early printers in England took up French poetry about gender rather than the well-known French critical commentary around it.

Where sex, love, and marriage are concerned, French works, it seems, were a good commercial bet for the printers: many of these verse translations about gender were reprinted and reissued over the years. French romances, in prose and poetry, were extremely popular in English print. These included, to mention just a few examples, Caxton's version of the *The Book of the Knight of the Tour Landry* and such early printed "revival" translations as a *Roman de la Rose* and the *Lai de Lanval*. Alain Chartier's *La Belle Dame Sans Merci*, long attributed to Chaucer, was translated by Richard Roos in the fifteenth century and printed by Pynson in 1526. *L'amant mal traite de samye*, the *Ypomédon*, and Pierre Gringoire's allegorical *Chateau d'Amours* appeared in English translations in this early period. The very popular *Appolonius of Tyre*, on which Shakespeare's late romances build, was perhaps one of the most widespread and enduring romances of the early modern period; it, too, came to early English readers from a French version. There is also a fair amount of poetry that is not "romance," generically speaking, but still uses the themes, tropes, and ideologies of late medieval romance. The "Complaint of Venus" and "Complaint of Mars" (Chaucer's translation from Oton de Graunson) are two such shorter poems that deploy romance modes and conventions. The very popular "Complaint of the heart through-perced with the looking of the eye" is another short translation made up of romance and courtly topoi that was put into early English print. This broad appropriation of romance and courtly literature from France is important for many reasons, not least because it maintains a continuity between script and print cultures and readerships, creating a common discourse on gender issues.

But that was not the only kind of literature that flourished in early print. The courtly, romance, and Petrarchan traditions and images are so familiar and so much discussed that we tend to overlook gender poetry in other modes, a tendency I seek to adjust here. A very different kind of poetry about gender came from France, too. Anti-idealizing, not Petrarchan, containing critiques of the courtly and inversions of courtly tropes and images: it is this alternative literature on which the present book concentrates.

---

[8] This is not primarily the private-public distinction it sounds like, however, because Christine published her own works in multiple script copies and supported herself with the proceeds and patronage. She was "published" in script and was prominent in French letters.

The print record reveals that competing and even contradictory strands of discourse about women found a robust and enduring readership. By comparison with the relatively accessible romance-related works, these other translations may prove odd and difficult for modern readers, but for Renaissance readers they formed a viable alternative discourse on gender topics. Their contraventions of romance modes are fascinating and in some sense connect English poetics with the *querelle*. (After all, the *querelle* itself begins with Christine's protofeminist salvo against misogyny in the *Roman de la Rose*, not only against the clerical misogyny of Valerius and Mathéolus and the classical misogyny of Theophrastus and Ovid.) Not that this alternative, antiromance/noncourtly strand of poetry follows Christine; some poems treated here do attack the courtly patterns that Christine recognized as dangerous to women, but many poems here recycle and reconfirm the very misogynist sources Christine deplores. Not fully protofeminist except in fugitive bits, the translations do offer alternative modes of writing about women that counter certain aspects of romance literature and ideology. In some cases the poems take the language and imagery of the romance and courtly traditions and invert or subvert them. In other cases, the works use misogynistic ideas or commonplaces to puncture courtly or romance-idealized images of women. Occasionally, the works challenge the very structures of patriarchy that underpin courtly poetry and clerical misogyny alike.

An Alternative to Courtly, Romance, and Clerical Discourses: Features of the Poems

Each chapter here takes the form of case studies of particular works. Before describing the individual chapters and cases ahead, each of which illustrates only its own particular part of the wider overall picture, I would like to suggest now the general features and outlines of that overall picture. The alternative strand of gender poetry treated here—these noncourtly, antiromance, un-Petrarchan, and nonclerical translations—share some specific characteristics. These poems consistently feature (1) working-class protagonists; (2) dialectical and catenary rather than episodic or interlaced structures; (3) a focus on economics and an association of women and poverty; (4) a reconfiguration of marriage and courtship that is against romance and courtly norms; (5) a focus on bodily embarrassments and unpleasantness; (6) inversions of and allusions to romance-courtly literary conventions, sometimes resulting in satiric or parodic style, but always within the printers' efforts to position even earthy gender material as literary; (7) women's speech, agency, and sexuality that are just as problematic as in the mainstream courtly and romance traditions but here sometimes treated as positive or at least given a different prominence and value; and (8) a stringent reshaping of the translations by means of new paratexts, presentational strategies, and changes of poetic form.

These eight overall features of the alternative line of poetry identified here are not to be thought of as an organizing device for the book. Indeed, no case study in the chapters ahead treats all these features, and each chapter discusses only the most striking, relevant features of its cases. Overall, however, the early printed poetry identified in this book tends to share these features, so they warrant brief introductory discussion here:

1. The translations usually focus on working-class or middle-class protagonists and speakers, presenting a less elevated view of gender relations than that found in mainstream romance or courtly works. They base gender relations outside the court and its conventions, and they are not set in romance-allegorical landscapes. The "woman" is not a "lady" in these works.[9] The men in these works are common husbands and laborers, not lords, knights, or courtiers. Men and women work and struggle alongside one another in urban or village settings, as in the *Fyftene Joyes of maryage* or Heywood's play *Johan Johan*, and in decidedly nonluxurious domestic scenes. The *Castle of Labour*, for instance, a long poem including an allegorical dream-vision, follows a working man and his wife as they try to avoid poverty. The settings move from the couple's simple bedroom, to the workplace and town marketplace, and then back to the home. After learning from a series of personifications about the importance of hard work, they find the "castle of rest" in a plain fireside scene complete with dog, table, and wife stirring a pot of dinner. ("Rest" in this image is for the man who sits by the fire, not for the woman who cooks over it). No knights or ladies inhabit this translated *Castle*.[10] The poems treated here use similar protagonists and settings in shorter forms.

2. These verse translations do not usually use the episodic or interlaced narrative structures of romance. They rely chiefly on dialectical and catenary structures instead. Debates and arguments occur within many of these poems, and the "too soon" or "too late" marriage complaints treated in Chapter 5 form a dialectical pair looking at two sides of one central gender question: when and whether to marry. Directly dialectical is *The Interlocucyon, with an argument, betwyxt man and woman, to see which is the most excellent*. Despite its English-added paratexts, a hybrid dream-vision and *chanson d'aventure* frame, it is an exemplary rhetorical debate-poem. The *Fyftene Joyes of maryage* stories are so radically catenary that some critics have been confounded by trying to read the work as one long narrative in which the unnamed protagonists ("husband" and "wife" or "man" and "woman") are the same throughout. But plot details mean that the stories must be read as a series of examples varied so as to highlight the multiplicity of satiric "joys" in marriage. The work is a string of stories about any-

---

[9] Queen Dido is the exception, but her challenge to romance-courtly literature, and to epic and historiography, forms a critique of Aeneas and masculine-heroic ideals; it is not based on her status as a queen or on her "ladylike" qualities.

[10] This work, Barclay's translation of Pierre Gringore's very popular *Chasteau de Labour*, is a fascinating poem with double framing devices. Its several thousand lines and scores of woodcuts make it too long for treatment in this book.

husband and any-wife, not a chronology of episodes. In just this way, the *Hye Way to the Spittal Hous* and *The Shypp of Fooles* estates satires (too long for treatment here) deploy their critiques by way of a string of varying examples.

3. These translations often focus on economic problems in gender relations, usually associating women with poverty and loss. This tendency shows strongly in the early translated estates satires. For instance, when Robert Copland versifies the prose estates satire *Le Chemin de l'hôpital* in English, he adds a section at the end asking why there are no women among the many classes of foolish, wretched, destitute folk on the estates-satiric *Hye Way to the Spittal Hous*:

> Copland
> Yet one thyng I wonder that ye do not tell
> Come there no women this way to swell[?]
> Porter
> Of all the sortes that be spoken of afore
> I warraunt women enow in store
> That we are wery of them euery day
> They come so thycke that they stop the way
> The systerhod of drabbes, sluttes, and callets
> Do here assorte / with theyr bagges and wallets
> And be partener of the confrary
> Of the mayteners of yll husbandry
> Copland
> A lewd sorte is of them a surety...

Although not previously distinguished in the poem, many bag ladies, ignorant, bad householders, the slovenly sisterhood, and worse are here singled out in the English version only; indeed, so many poor women are headed for the hospital of wretched fools that they clog the road. In a different vein, marrying outside one's class is one sure way to board the translated *Shypp of Fooles*.[11] Marrying across class lines is a particular problem for the woman speaker in the *Complainte of the to soone maryed*, treated in Chapter 5. More often, the man is the one warned that love and marriage lead to poverty, labor, and trouble, as in the *The Castle of Labour* (where the man is so warned, but where the woman ends up working as the man rests by the fire) or in the *Fyftene Joyes of Maryage*, the subject of Chapter 4. Some poems examine the unpleasant economic consequences of love and marriage for both men and women, sometimes reducing amorous encounters to mercantile exchanges. The English versions occasionally intensify this effect, as when, in the woman's long soliloquy in the *Complainte of the to soone maryed*, the amorous courtly epithet "mon grant tresor" is rendered in English as "Is this to be my paye?" Likewise, at the center of the *Too Soon* complaint is an economically

---

[11] Alexander Barclay's translation from a French version of the immensely popular pan-European phenomenon, Sebastian Brant's *Narrenschiff*, focuses several sections on women and gender issues in these lines; unfortunately, it is much too long for treatment here.

motivated inversion of the *carpe diem* seduction trope: after an intimate scene, the newlywed man urges his wife to hurry back to work to recover the wages they have lost while dallying in bed. The new bride responds vociferously, and with a parallel economic complaint, to the effort to persuade her out of bed and back to work.

4. In addition to this emphasis on money, the translations counter any idealization of courtship and marriage by focusing on its anticourtly, antiromance, and antiromantic aspects. Marriage, if not the end of courtship and romance— "end" in both senses, "goal" and "termination"—was clearly an institution that was to be understood separately from love in these poems.[12] When these works treat premarital courtship, they render it an economic transaction, a danger, or as a brief pleasure before the long hardships of married life. In one case, the *Complaynt of the too late maryed*, also treated in Chapter 5, youthful courtship is represented as an extended phase of wastefulness filled with venereal disease, greedy lovers, promiscuity, brawling, arrests, and the betrayals of friends. Likewise, as Chapter 4 explains, the paratexts to the *Fyftene Joyes of maryage* baldly state that premarital courtship is part of the entrapment system that leads to marriage, which brutally deprives individuals of their natural liberty. John Heywood's *A Mery Play* (also known as *Johan Johan*), treated in Chapter 6, translates the classic adulterous triangle of French farce, in which no rosy view of either marriage or courtship can survive. Part of the dismantling of marriage as ideal involves the economic emphasis as well. In some poems, if a wife warms up to a husband, she only wants to trade for a new dress. The trading of sex for goods goes on outside marriage, too. The *Shypp of Fooles*, for instance, displays both greedy wives who thus bankrupt their husbands and also husbands who pimp their wives for money. Women's sexuality is not euphemized into courtly "grace" or "favor" in this line of poetry. These translations unflinchingly anatomize the uncomfortable juncture between sex and economics within marriage, and they reduce courtship or "dalliaunce" to its barest, instrumental bones.

5. These translations focus, sometimes graphically, on bodily discomfort and embarrassments and on sexual failures of various kinds. Impotence, disease, promiscuity, wife-beating, body odors, flatulence: these translations are decidedly uncourtly in that they refuse to euphemize or to avert their gaze from indelicate or unpleasant physical aspects of gender relations. This is especially true in the *Fyftene Joyes*, the *Complaints* of marriage, and Heywood's *A Mery Play* or *Johan Johan*. In that early Tudor play, a long soliloquy laments, among other things, the wife's flatulence, and the husband declares his wish to beat her until she loses control of her bowels. The digestive-bodily emphasis spills over into the printers' paratexts as well. For instance, printer-translator Robert Copland creates an original acrostic for the *Complaints* pair that self-deprecatingly jokes about his own rhetoric as flatulence. In a more serious vein, the anonymous translator

---

[12] In that sense at least, these poems can be seen as "courtly": marriage had its economic rationales, separate from romantic attachments.

and printer Richard Pynson adds disturbing phallic imagery to the new woodcut and a punning phallic warning to the new epilogue of the *Letter of Dydo*, treated in Chapter 3. Also part of a more serious attention to the bodily is the deliberate suppression of some lengthy French praise of women's bodies and a deliberate expansion of verses regulating, coercing, and policing the woman's body, found in *The Beaute of Women*, treated in Chapter 3. The bodily can be a source of broad humor, of course, but it also here presents a clear contrast to romance and courtly discourses about gender relations.

6. In conjunction with such anti-idealizing content, these poems often use satiric or parodic style and, in particular, techniques and figures that signal the reader to read against the idealizing grain. For instance, the *Castle of Labour* relies on some techniques of allegorical romance (a long dream-vision sequence, personification, prosopopoeia), but the protagonists and settings are so clearly anticourtly that the title has to be seen as, if not parodic, certainly subversive of courtly modes of narration and allegoresis. In this work, the forms of high-medieval dream-vision contain a working-class nightmare. The central, title trope of the *Castle of Labour* parodies and subverts the many late medieval and early modern Castles of Love, Knowledge, Pleasure, Sapience, and so on. Likewise, the satiric title of the *Fyftene Joyes of maryage* punctures religious idealizing titles like the *Fifteen Oes* or the *Fifteen Joys of the Virgin*. Its mocking French style and staccato prose rhythms are largely lost in translation to a more decorous English pentameter; the translators seem to shrink from the rowdy aesthetics of French gender satire. However, animal imagery is used frequently in these poems to figure the condition of people in love or married: the bear trapped in the pit, the fish in the net, the bird in cage. As the figurative language suggests, in this strand of gender discourses, love and marriage do not elevate—they imprison and dehumanize.

7. Although the woman is not a "lady" in this alternative line of poetry, the stasis of the courtly pedestal and the itemizing method of the Petrarchan and troubadour blazon do find some rough equivalents. Here, however, the point of such methods is not idealization or epideixis.[13] Women's beauty is put on explicit display and her body parts are broken up into sets for scrutiny and regulation in *The Beaute of Women* (Chapter 3). Female beauty is morally dangerous there, and the English translation keeps a French refrain that repeats "Beauté sans bonté ne vaut rien" [beauty without goodness is worth nothing]. The speaking, moving, sexually powerful, good woman is about as rare here as in the courtly tradition. In fact, the trouble with women in many of these works is that they so incorrigibly do insist on speaking, spending money, having sexual desires, socializing with friends, and not staying home. However, there is one case treated here in which a woman with desires of her own is portrayed more favorably. The graphically

---

[13] Whether we see these as harmful, as, for example, Nancy Vickers does, or more neutrally and available to women writers and in mutuality, as, for example, Gordon Braden does, the Petrarchan tropes emphasize the beloved's desirability and the lover's suffering. In this alternative line of poetry, the picture is more ambiguous.

described love object—the sexy, amorous wife in the *Complaynt of the too late maryed*—is a silent but kindly and blameless foil to her husband's impotence. She "casts a begginge legge" over him in bed one morning, but he cannot perform; she shows him her breasts and tries to initiate sex, but "the spear will not stand." Equally remarkable are the numerous speaking women here, especially those in the *Interlocucyon*, the *Letter of Dydo*, the complaint poems, and Heywood's farce. These women, although probably all ventriloquized by male printers and translators, speak more-and-less eloquent, more-and-less successful, protofeminist arguments. As Chapter 2 explains, the terms set by Christine in the French *querelle des femmes* do not make their way into these English-speaking women's parts. Yet there is probably more, and earlier, granting of women's strong voices here than we might have thought. Overall, the same "chaste-silent-obedient" assumptions still ground the works, but because these poems differ so much in technique from the mainstream courtly-romance-Petrarchan traditions—and because they aim at a wider audience—they open a different discursive space for effective female speakers.

8. The printers and translators create deliberately literary frames for these works, often with paratexts—prologues, proems, epilogues, colophons, titles—woodcuts, and *mise-en-page*. They clearly viewed the poems as malleable, revisable, interpretable works. They just as clearly acted on the poems in ways we now would call "literary." Often, the printer-translators change the poetic form of a work, thus changing its implications and repositioning it in literary history. They feel free, too, to play with tone, versification, lineation, and stanza patterns. The printer-translators excise material, add material, suppress or tone down certain features; they embellish, they redirect attention, or they admonish the reader (in some cases, the female reader). Often the translators and printers reveal a self-consciousness about their actions, alternately promoting or hiding the Frenchness of their wares, conventionally apologizing for their own imperfections or blaming their source authors. They try to place their poems in literary lines: sometimes implicitly in a French line, as with the addition of a *chanson d'aventure* frame or a *demande d'amour* soliloquy in a rondeau verse form, or explicitly in an English line, with dream-vision framing, or labored pentameters, or easily recognizable allusions to Chaucer. They are acutely aware of their new English reading public, and what they do in translation and printing reveals their sense of that audience. They both accommodate and shape the literary sensibilities of the new readership for English poetry.

Overall, in different ways and in different literary genres—epistle, exemplary narrative, allegory, didactic poem, estates satire, farce, complaint, debate poem—these translated poems offer alternatives to and implicit critiques of the more dominant romance and courtly English discourses.

The Present Book: Chapters, Case Studies, and Approaches

The present book analyzes particular poems as case studies in early modern translations of gender poetry. First of all, because these alternative poems are so little known, the book provides basic interpretive summaries, explanations of the main topoi at issue, and readings of selected passages. Where works are more familiar, such groundwork is not as necessary, but this book is deliberately heavy on the interpretive and factual spadework and deliberately light on the high theoretical analysis. I trust future readers to see, as I do, the many critical and theoretical potentials in these works and to have the space and time, as I do not, to explore them more fully. Second, and also because most of these works are so little known and hard to read in their original typefaces, I have provided transcriptions in the Appendices. These largely preserve original spelling and punctuation in order to acknowledge rather than elide historical distance.[14] Fortunately, the works of Christine de Pizan, the *Interlocucyon*, and *Johan Johan* are easily available in good modern editions. But the unfamiliar works, either unedited or in obscure editions—the *Letter of Dydo*, the *Beaute of Women*, the paratexts to the *Fyftene Joyes of maryage*, and two long marriage *Complaints*—appear in the Appendices in the order in which they are discussed in the book itself. Third, I have selected shorter poems that I hope will illustrate in a reasonable space the overall features described above as well as the considerable range and variety of the translations. This means leaving out some fascinating, important, long works like the *Castle of Labour* translation, concentrating on briefer glimpses of the common themes and features. Finally, instead of trying to coerce this suggestive material into making one argument, I treat these rich, varying works as separate revealing cases of a lesser-known, early alternative line of poetry about gender.

Chapter 2, "The Mireur and Maistresse" of "Intelligence": Christine de Pizan's Translated Authority in Early English Print, treats Christine de Pizan, a late medieval author whose work was taken up much more in early English print than is generally known. Despite the assertions of some recent critics, I find that Christine was not suppressed or ventriloquized in England. On the contrary, she was appropriated as an authoritative voice, and in almost all cases her authority to advise was preserved, publicized, and praised. The record of early print also reveals, however, that while we know her now as an early feminist, her early modern English fame was greater as a political advisor, a mythographer, and an authoritative wisdom-writer. The evidence for her unusual position in the English literary system is the subject of the first part of Chapter 2, a survey of the six major English translations of her work printed before 1550. The second part of the chapter takes up one specific, now-little-read work of Christine's wisdom literature, the *Prouerbes moraulx*, in its three appearances in England. While the content of

---

[14] Exceptions: I have used "s" for long s and have expanded certain common abbreviations within square brackets. Where texts are very uncertain or illegible, I also enclose best guesses in square brackets.

this work is not focused primarily on gender issues, what we see in the two early printings of it is an effort to frame Christine as a wise, authoritative adviser. Early printers Caxton and Pynson advertise her authorship even as they twice selectively reposition the poem as part of the founding canons of English literature.

In early sixteenth-century England, Christine was not particularly known as a feminist literary debater, as she had been known in early fifteenth-century France. Although Bryan Anslay's translation of the *Cite des dames* sees print in 1521, and although a good range of her other work was available in early English print, the printers never directly pick up the fully developed elements of the *querelle*. They do, however, translate works that derive indirectly from the *querelle*. Some of these use Christine's tactics and arguments, and some quote her opponents and repeat filtered versions of their views. All are shaped as specifically literary in some way. The rest of the present book returns only infrequently, therefore, to those transmuted, recontextualized elements of the *querelle* that do find their way into early printed poetry. There is little direct influence here, and no one openly carries the *querelle* forward in early English print. In an alien English literary system, Christine's points occasionally resurface in different kinds of texts, in different modes and methods, often obliquely in the voice of a female speaker, in the alteration of a verse form, or in a new paratext. So the material on Christine founds the rest of the book only indirectly, and not in the usual sense of influence. Indeed, a matter of interest is how influence models do not account for the uneven afterlives of such a writer, who was clearly understood in England as authoritative, but whose best-known, most subversive, most canon-challenging ideas do not find their way into widest circulation.

Chapter 3, "'La Femme replique': Debating Women in English Translation," begins with an early printed gender debate poem, the *Interlocucyon betwixt a man and a woman*. As Diane Bornstein shows, this long poem may be our only open link between the literary *querelle* that Christine started in France in the early fifteenth century and the latter-sixteenth- and early seventeenth-century prose debates in England about women. Available in two modern editions, this translation of Guillaume Alexis's *Debat de lomme et de la femme* looks rather different in its English version and contexts. The woman gets the longest and last word, ending the *Interlocucyon* with a 52-line catalogue of Very Bad Men.

The next work treated in Chapter 3 is another woman's complaint against bad men or, rather, against one particular bad man: the *Letter of Dydo to Eneas*. An anonymous translation of Octavien de St. Gelais's version of Ovid's *Heroides* VII, this work presents a critique of the romance-heroic male as a long poem in the woman's voice. Like Christine's *Morall Prouerbes*, this work appears in English verse in Pynson's Chaucerian collection *The Book of Fame*. Dido's letter, however, is a one-sided debate, addressing the absent Aeneas in her suicide speech, in effect providing a lyric expansion on one resonant instance of what the woman in the *Interlocucyon* had deplored in her final catalogue. Because this version of the *Letter of Dydo* has never been edited, I provide a full transcription in Appendix 1.

Chapter 3 ends with another one-sided "debate" about the nature and value of woman, the *Beaute of Women*. This is an odd poem about which we know very little; my research indicates that it was probably cobbled together from selected elements of two or more French analogues. This three-part poem begins with a mostly-original prologue in praise of women that uses elements of the many French *Louenge des femmes* poems (some titled *Blason des femmes*, *Louenge des dames*, and so on). The second part of the work itemizes women's physical beauties in narrowly prescriptive sets (for example, three parts of a woman should be curved: her eyebrows, her neck, the small of her back). The third, admonitory part of the poem moralizes about women's beauty and insists that women join goodness to their beauty. Unlike *The Letter of Dydo* and the *Interlocucyon*, which feature prominent female speakers, the *Beaute of Women* shows woman not as a speaking subject with agency, but as in its lewd title woodcut, as a body-object, utterly silenced and then fragmented. This work is transcribed in Appendix 1.

The alternative line of poetry about marriage is so interesting in terms of literary translation and printers' interventions that it warrants three separate chapters here. Chapter 4, "Framing Misogamy: the Prologue and Prohemye to the *Fyftene Joyes of maryage*," explores the longest and one of the most popular antimarital works of the early modern period, the satiric *Fyftene Joyes*. Like its French source, the *Quinze Joyes de mariage*, this early poem offers a compendium of topoi of later English gender discourses. Marriage is a trap, a prison, a subversion of natural human liberty. Marriage involves disgusting bodily processes, economic hardship, noisy children, nosy neighbors. Marriage is a misery, in short, and in this poem, it is largely so because of the nature of wives. Women are portrayed as shrewish, promiscuous, greedy, sexually insatiable or frigid, wasteful spenders, excessive consumers. Although the husbands are hapless and unsympathetic characters, the poem's misogamy is almost entirely based on misogyny. The misogyny, moreover, is unmitigated in translation. An epilogue available in French apologizes to women readers and promises to write the woman's view of marriage next. The extant English copies do not have such an epilogue; because the lines of textual transmission are not clear—we do not know whether the printer had access to one of the French versions with an epilogue—this may or may not indicate the printer's assumptions about the gender of the English readership.

The English printers do, however, retain a frame containing arguments against marriage that do not rely on misogyny. In a remarkable anticipation of terms we more usually associate with eighteenth-century "enlightenment" discourses, the prologue connects individual domestic liberty with the liberty of the political subject. The printers also devote much energy to positioning this satire in a literary line: they change the French prose into pentameter couplets, and they add an additional, openly (and interestingly) Chaucerian frame to this non-Chaucerian work. Since these paratexts are available only in blackletter text on microfilm and in two rare copies and one fragment, I have transcribed them in Appendix 2.

Chapter 5, "Translating Marriage Complaints," treats an innovative pair of translations, the *Complaynt of them that be to soone maryed* and the *Complaint of the to late maryed.* Here, too, issues in nonaristocratic marriage are worked out in a specifically literary effort. The translator and printer work to create a dialectical pair, adding important French elements to the English literature on the topic. The "Too Soon" complaint features two female speakers, a wife and her mother, ventriloquized by a male husband persona. The wife, who speaks the central nine stanzas of the poem, is an eloquent witness to how bad marriage can be for women, especially where economics are concerned. The "Too Soon" also features several strongly anticourtly moments, some reminiscent of the *Castle of Labour* and the *Fyftene Joyes*. In the "Too Late" companion complaint, a chaste, beautiful wife makes repeated sexual advances to her aged husband. Described in detail, she is not the insatiable or promiscuous unsatisfied wife typical in the misogamist tradition: this desiring wife remains faithful, he remains impotent, and the lament is not against her or against female sexuality. Instead, the male speaker laments that he did not marry her while he could still perform sexually. Single life is described in negative, anticourtly terms, and both complaints emphasize the economic and the bodily. These poems stand in marked contrast to, say, the "Complaint of the Heart and the Eye" translation, the poems in *The Court of Venus*, or other early modern lovers' complaints. They are transcribed in Appendix 3.

Chapter 6, "Misogamy and Translation at Henry VIII's court: John Heywood's *A Mery Play*," studies the only Tudor drama to translate a French sexual farce. (That glaring lacuna of literary history—only one translation from a tradition that includes several hundred plays of enduring popularity—is intriguing but may finally be inexplicable.) Sex, marriage, and the church were not idle issues at the Tudor court circa 1533, when this play was published by John Rastell, brother-in-law to Thomas More. The chapter brings relevant historical context from both sides of the channel but finally cannot declare this a *traduction-à-clef*. Heywood was the chief court dramatist, writer of interludes, humanist question-dramas, epigrams, and more; he was a relative of printer John Rastell. Despite such connections, his effort to import a very uncourtly French sexual farce did not succeed either at court or later in wider theatrical contexts, as far as we know. Curiously, too, the play itself is quite skillful, and Heywood's interventions render the cuckolded husband more serious and sympathetic, while not in any way toning down his cowardly misogyny, his wife's baseness, or the cuckolding priest's hypocrisy. Heywood alters certain French literary conventions and shows himself sensitive to cultural difference, but this fascinating play is finally anomalous, both in literary history and in terms of Heywood's largely humanist oeuvre.

Instead of proving one thing, then, the cases selected for treatment here reveal an array of possibilities outside those we usually read and study. However, within each case study, the theoretical approach or method is fairly consistent: I use the comparative new historicism here, with an additional attempt at what Roger Kuin calls "critical tact."[15] In general, the belief that grounds this method is that we

---

[15] See Kuin's *Chamber Music: Elizabethan Sonnet Sequences and the Pleasure of Criticism* (Toronto: University of Toronto Press, 1998) for a virtuoso demonstration of

are better equipped to understand early modern English literature if we read it in its full, polyglot, international context, and especially here, if we examine the francophone origins of its early printed poetry. More specifically, critical tact means that each poem will require different comparative-historicist treatment and that no one formula or theory will work equally well in all cases. For instance, in understanding Heywood's translation of French farce, the different conventions for naming characters in French and English theatrical traditions are important, but in translations of Christine de Pizan, the political histories of the two nations during the Hundred Years' War are what matter. In a similar way, the poetics of the early acrostic and certain facts about French book production are essential to understanding what Copland attempts in his paired complaints, but the *Fyftene Joyes* translation requires instead attention to Chaucerian allusions and methods of framing literary narrative. This seems an obvious matter of common sense, but it means that even in such a thematically focused selection of poems, no one theory or method will work to illuminate all the unpredictable, poem-level contacts between the two literary systems. I have resisted the urge to theorize and have tried not to stomp in the vast minefields of anachronism possible here. Because poetry is concerned, always, with aesthetics and form, I have attended to the sound of the verse in both languages and to the reader's encounter with the variant visual pages. Above all, I have tried to suggest, rather than to anatomize or prescribe, the critical and literary-historical possibilities in this corpus because I trust future readers to continue discovering its rich potential. If we look past edited, modern canons, the print record shows us some distinct alternatives in play in the rapidly developing literary system of early print.

This early phase of printing originates the slow earthquake of a media revolution from which Western culture is still rocking; from a certain view, our own Internet revolution is but one of its aftershocks. The present book explores a little-studied but controversial part of the alien, trembling land we call the past. These verse translations on gender were printed in that early moment of opportunity and instability, well before censorship laws and literary categories were fully fixed, just before France and England had quite given up colonizing each other, decades before the debates on women had settled into prose treatises, and long before critics and readers had started deciding what to canonize as "Renaissance poetry."

---

critical tact. Comparative historicism is fully explained in my "Towards a Comparative New Historicism: Land Tenures and Some Fifteenth-Century Poems," *Comparative Literature* 53.2 (Spring 2001): 97–116.

Chapter 2
"The Mireur and Maistresse" of "Intelligence": Christine de Pizan's Translated Authority in Early English Print

Survey of Translations of Christine's Works in Early English Print

Recent critics such as Jane Chance, Dhira Mahoney, and Jennifer Summit have claimed that Christine was repressed, ventriloquized, lost, or deauthorized in England, but considerable, interesting evidence exists to the contrary.[1] (Caxton, for instance, calls Christine "the mireur and maistresse" of "Intelligence" in 1478.) While two manuscript translations in particular damage Christine's authority, a larger body of her work in wider circulation in English print venerates her. The main culprits in her English deauthorization are Thomas Hoccleve and Stephen Scrope. Hoccleve's translation of the *Epistre au dieu d'amours* has long been understood as distorting her critique of misogyny,[2] and Scrope's translation of the *Epistre Othea* deliberately misattributes authorship to men, as Chance shows. But other recent claims about the suppression of Christine's voice in England are based on inaccurate or incomplete evidence. One scholar's claim that Pynson's imprint of the *Morall Prouerbes* deauthorizes Christine, for instance, ignores Pynson's titles and running heads, as illustrated in the second section of this

---

[1] In "Gender Subversion and Linguistic Castration in Fifteenth-Century Translations of Christine de Pizan," in *Violence Against Women in Medieval Texts*, ed. Anna Roberts (Gainesville, Fla: University of Florida Press, 1998), pp. 161–94, Chance concludes that translators "silenced her by excising her authority and her authorship" (172). Precisely the opposite happens in many early printed translations of Christine, as we will see in the discussion below of the *Morale Prouerbes* translation and editions. Chance treats Anslay's translation of the *Livre de la Cité des Dames*, Stephen Scrope's translation of the *Epître d'Othée*, certain manuscripts of the *Fais d'Armes/Fayttes of Armes*, and Hoccleve's antifeminist translation of the *Epistre au dieu d'amours*. Summit's dissertation and book, "The Goose's Quill: The Production of Female Authorship in Late Medieval and Early Modern England" (Baltimore: Johns Hopkins University, 1996) and *Lost Property: The Woman Writer and English Literary History 1380–1589* (Chicago: University of Chicago Press, 2000), pp. 61–71, agree, adding, however, in a section entitled "Lost in Translation," an important emphasis on changed contexts. P. G. C. Campbell may have started this persistent line of thinking in "Christine de Pisan en Angleterre," *Revue de littérature comparée* 5 (1925): 659–70.

[2] Diane Bornstein, "Anti-Feminism in Thomas Hoccleve's Translation of Christine de Pizan's *Epistre au Dieu d'Amours*," *English Language Notes* 19 (1981): 7–14.

chapter. Likewise, the claim that neither the manuscript nor print versions of the English *Boke of the Body of Polycye* acknowledge Christine's authorship is not correct: she is acknowledged in both, as quoted and explained below, though not as obviously or effusively as in Caxton's *Morale Prouerbes of Crystyne* and not as lengthily as in the preface to one of the English versions of her *Fais D'Armes*.[3] This chapter, then, seeks in part to adjust the record and in part to reflect on what it means that Christine actually comes out better in English print among increasingly non–French-speaking, nonaristocratic readers than she did in a bilingual English courtly manuscript context.

Martha Driver's analysis of the English and French woodcuts in Wyer's *Othea* imprint, for instance, offers a new way of thinking about gender in the early print world. She contextualizes the representations of Christine in terms of typical sixteenth-century printing practices.[4] Driver finds that "the economics of the business of printing" finally has more to do with the printers' suppressions of authorship (not just Christine's) than gender (139), and that typical printers' habits of self-promotion from our perspective look like gendered acts when they were probably mainly self-promotional or commercial decisions. Additionally, my survey suggests that there was economic and cultural capital to be had in printing Christine (and in translating works on gender). Three generations of English translators and printers introduced Christine to the new English reading public very respectfully, and sometimes nearly fulsomely. Known, read, and authoritative in early modern England, Christine was nevertheless deracinated and therefore valued and positioned differently on the two sides of the channel. Truly a major writer in France, she was a niche writer in England, and not exclusively or even especially in the early-feminist niche in which we now place her. The new medium of print first allows wider audiences to read and to join discussions of gender issues, but the English translations of Christine in early print set the terms of gender discussion in ways we are less likely to appreciate without a comparative-historicist view and an eye to print production methods. Not generally antifeminist, as is often claimed, these translations validate and elevate her work and usually name her as author.

---

[3] Dhira Mahoney, "Middle English Regenderings of Christine de Pizan," in *The Medieval Opus*, ed. Douglas A. Kelly (Amsterdam: Rodopi), pp. 405–27. Relying on Campbell, she does not mention Caxton's epideictic colophon poem in his imprint of the *Morale Prouerbes of Crystyne* in 1478 and implies that Pyson's re-edition of it in 1526 erases her authorship by titling the collection *The Boke of Fame*; this misses the fact that Pynson's reprint retains Christine's name in the title and running head, "The Morall Prouerbes of Christyne," in 1526. For details of Christine's visible presence in *The Book of Fame*, see the second section of this chapter. Mahoney also follows Campbell (666–8) in saying that "in neither [translation of the *Corps de Policie*] is Christine acknowledged as author" (407), which is not the case.

[4] Driver, "Christine de Pisan and Robert Wyer: *The .C. Hystoryes of Troye*, or *L'Epistre d'Othea* Englished," *Gutenberg Jahrbuch* 1997: 125–39.

But they necessarily place her in a rather curious English discourse context. Cristina Malcolmson demonstrates that:

> [T]he Tudor courts were familiar with the idea of a "city of ladies" in a limited but definite way, and that manuscripts of her works ... were available in the royal libraries .... Christine's work and the concept of the "city of ladies" most likely provided the Tudor courts with an unidentified, generic defense of women ....[5]

This is surely so in the powerful aristocratic circles Malcolmson studies here. But, like most scholars' focus on clerical works and prose treatises about gender, this focus on the script presence of the *City* at court (a court still bilingual and thus still resonating with medieval French images and themes) overlooks the large, new, English-only literary system developing after Caxton and the different context it forms for Christine's works (and for other works on gender).

This point affects not only our understanding of Christine's reception in England but also the way her work was and was not like the other works on gender treated in this book. The newly expanding English literary system quickly filled with numerous printed literary translations from French about gender issues, but how many new readers had the full clerical or court context for literary works on gender? Some probably did, but many surely did not. So the translations on gender topics in script could more easily assume knowledge of the socioliterary dialectic Christine began, while the translations in print might have lost, by loss of readerly context—or may appear to have erased— the protofeminist potentials in these earlier translations of Christine's own works. For example, the woman speaker refuting male misogyny—what Christine was, literally, in life—may be undercut in Hoccleve's script translation of the *Epistre au dieu damours*; yet the woman speakers refuting male misogyny in the printed *Interlocucyon* debate poem and in other indirect dialectics (discussed in Chapters 3, 4, 5, and 6) have all sorts of paratextual and presentational explanatory efforts thrown up around them, apparently for the new readers' benefit. While no *querelle* documents are translated or printed in early modern England, one crucial aspect of the *querelle*, its intensive literariness, may show up obliquely in the fact that so many of the early gender imprints are poems, not prose arguments, which would come later. On the other hand, despite the printing of the *Cyte of Ladyes* in 1521, none of Christine's direct arguments forms the main thrust of English gender discussions. One can at least say that the difference between Christine's earliest authority in English print and the subsequent mutations (and mutings) of the feminist dialectics she originated may result from this uneven context for the *querelle* in England. A concomitant factor may be the prevalence of misogynist works popular in early print, issued by printers like de Worde and Copland. It is the English context, then, more than the

---

[5] "Christine de Pizan's *City of Ladies* in Early Modern England," *Debating Gender in Early Modern England, 1500–1700* (New York: Palgrave MacMillan, 2002), pp. 15–35; p. 16.

translations of Christine themselves, in which shifts of meaning and value occur. Although these early translations do elevate Christine's position and put her work before a broadening English public, the many subsequent verse translations from French disperse the complex gender dialectics she originates, and her powers end up not deauthorized, as we usually think, but decontextualized, which is a different thing, with different causes and effects.

How much did translation aimed specifically at the new print reader have to do with the continuance or disappearance of Christine's ideas in England? How did printers' actions affect her authority and reputation? Are misogynist translators or money-grubbing, self-promoting printers responsible for differences in the French and English contexts for women's writing and feminist literary debates? Or are they simply responding to conditions around them? Such questions probably have no final answers, but it is at least demonstrable that, contrary to what we have previously thought, Christine was deracinated but not categorically deauthorized in early modern England.

The early printed translations of Christine's works treated here are as follow:

1. *Morale Prouerbes of Cristyne*. Tr. Anthony Woodville. Westmestre [sic]: Caxton 1478. STC 7273. Re-edited and printed in *The Boke of Fame*. London: Pynson, 1526. STC 5088.

2. *Fayttes of Armes and of chyualrye*. Tr. Caxton. Westminster: Caxton 1489. STC 7269.

3. *The Booke ... called the body of polycye...* Tr. unknown. London: John Skot, 1521. STC 7270.

4. *Boke of the Cyte of ladyes*. Tr. Bryan Anslay. London: H. Pepwell, 1521. STC 7271.

5. *C. Hystoryes of Troye* [Epistre Othea]. Tr. R. Wyer. London: Wyer, [1540? 1549?]. STC 7272.

6. *[Letter of Cupid.]* Tr. and abridged by Thomas Hoccleve, c. 1402. Printed in Thynne's Chaucer (1532) and subsequent editions; STC 5068, 5069, 5070.

Maureen Quilligan has convincingly argued for the importance of Christine's *auctoritas* in the early modern European romance and for her important interventions in the longer tradition in terms of women's writerly authority.[6] English printers also accepted her *auctoritas* outside the allegorical romance genre, as the translations' titles clearly indicate, positioning her prominently as an authoritative writer of proverb and wisdom literature, of military history and theory, of political theory, and of mythography. The list suggests that Christine was appropriated as a serious moral writer beginning in 1478 with Caxton's printing of Anthony Woodville's translation of her *Prouerbes moraulx*. Indeed, Caxton composes a rhyme-royal colophon poem for that edition, praising her high authority:

---

[6] Quilligan, *The Allegory of Female Authority* (Ithaca, NY: Cornell UP, 1991).

Of these sayynges Cristyne was aucteuresse
Whiche in makyng hadde suche Intelligence
That therof she was mireur & maistresse
Hire werkes testifie thexperience
In frenssh languaige was writen this sentence
And thus Englished dooth hit rehers
Antoin Wideuylle therl Ryuers

Go thou litil quayer, and reco[m]mand me
Unto the good grace, of my special lorde
Therle Ryueris . for I haue enprinted the
At his co[m]mandement . folowyng eury worde
His copye / as his secretaire can recorde
At Westmestre . of feuerer the .xx. daye
And of kyng Edward / the xvii yere vraye

Enprynted by Caxton
In feuerer the colde season[7]

When in 1526 Henry VIII's King's Printer, Richard Pynson, re-edited and printed the work, he took care, just as Caxton had done, to make her authorship visible in the title and running heads, contrary to what some scholars have claimed.[8] Pynson placed her 100 verse proverbs alongside the poetry of Chaucer and Lydgate, but titled under her name, in a collection he called *The Book of Fame*. These early translations neither suppress nor ventriloquize Christine, instead foregrounding in paratexts and by means of publication context her instructive *auctoritas*. (The second section of this chapter compares the versions of the *Morale Prouerbes* in greater detail.)

In 1489, Caxton printed his translation of the *Faits d'armes et de chevalerie*, Christine's 286-page treatise on the art, science, legality, and ethics of warfare. Twenty known English copies are extant, a remarkable survival number greater than that of Caxton's *Aeneid*. Judging from marginalia, marks of ownership, and other details of provenance, the work was read and known in Tudor England.[9]

---

[7] Caxton conventionally enough accords higher authority to Christine as author than to her translator, Anthony Woodville, the Earl Rivers, despite his arguably higher social status. N. F. Blake, *William Caxton and English Literary Culture* (London: Hambledon, 1991, p. 143) thinks that the first stanza is by Rivers and the second by Caxton because of rhyming words and vocabulary; I attribute both to Caxton since the first stanza refers to Rivers in the third person: "This wisdom ['sentence'] was written in French, and (thus Englished) Anthony Woodville Earl Rivers doth rehers it."

[8] Mahoney 407 following Campbell 666–8; Summit.

[9] A.T.P. Byles, ed., *The Book of Fayttes of Armes and of Chyualrye* (London: Oxford University Press, 1932), pp. xxxi–xxxvi.

Here again, Christine's authority is taken seriously, and for an explicitly male readership: Caxton tells us in his epilogue that Henry VII asked him to translate and print it "to thende that every gentylman ... & all manere of men of werre captayns / souldiours / vytayllers & all other shold haue knowledge how they ought to behaue theym in the fayttes of warre & of battaylles" (epilogue; Byles, ed., p. 291, lines 11–16). Caxton names Christine as author several times in the text and translates her authorial prologue fully. Byles's survey of manuscripts shows that the line of texts that does suppress her authorship is not the English line—French printers Antoine Vérard and Philippe le Noir follow the B-group manuscripts in suppressing it, but Caxton's text follows the A-group.[10] It would be nice to know whether Caxton had the deauthorizing B-group manuscripts available to him and chose the authorizing A-group versions instead. On the other hand, regardless of Caxton's agency or choice, Christine's authority as a military historian does in fact reach English readers in print.

Caxton's *Fayttes of Armes* has several kinds of interest for Renaissance scholars. Book historians notice its Caxton 6 typeface (with cut flourishes) and its interesting imposition problem in quire O. Furthermore, it is a mature Caxton imprint, displaying coherent concepts of spacing, layout, and paraph usage and consistent signatures and wood initials.[11] Historians and historicists note Christine's discussion of aspects of the Hundred Years' War (for example, in Book I, Chapter v), of particular contemporary battles (for example, Roosebeke, 1382, and Hasbain, 1408), and of strategies for the more recent technologies of warfare (for example, springalles, mangonelles, rybawdekins, lead pellets, gunpowder). Berenice Carroll and Renate Blumenfeld-Kosinski have argued that Christine is a peace theorist as well as a military historian in this work, viewing war as a last resort.[12] Christine's work is synthesized from several works, including Vegetius's *De re militari*, Honoré Bonet's *Arbre des batailles*, Frontinus' *Stratagemata*, Valerius Maximus's *Facta Dictaque Memorabilia*, and some anonymous contemporaries. Because of her method, some modern critics have dismissed its originality or its authorship, but syncretic compilation was a well-accepted kind of authorship, as A. J. Minnis and others have demonstrated.[13]

Christine's creation as a whole is more humane than its compiled parts. For example, unlike Bonet, she argues against killing prisoners in battle. Like him, she restricts the classes of people who can justly be taken prisoner: commoners only

---

[10] Byles, ed, pp. xv–xxvi; on French imprints, pp. xxvi–xxviii.

[11] Byles, ed., xxx–xxxi.

[12] A position she develops in the *Livre de la Paix*. Carroll, "Christine de Pizan and the Origins of Peace Theory," in *Women Writers and the Early Modern British Political Tradition*, ed. Hilda Smith (Cambridge UP, 1998), pp. 22–39; Blumenfeld-Kosinski, "Christine de Pizan and the Political Life in Late-Medieval France," in *Christine de Pizan: A Casebook*, ed. Barbara Altmann and Deborah McGrady (New York: Routledge, 2003), pp. 18–19.

[13] See also, Byles, ed., pp. xli–xliv, on the originality of the work.

if they aid the enemy, no blind or disabled people, no madmen, and no scholars.[14] Often Christine's work seems eerily relevant to our own times: on the need to exhaust all other possibilities before going to war, she writes, "That whiche may be bought [that is, with money] ought not to be bought with mannys blode," quoting one of her patrons, Charles V of France (II.xi; Byles, ed., p.129, 1.4). This survey does not seek to analyze the differences, most quite subtle, between Christine's French and Caxton's English versions of the work, but one point is worth mention. Caxton revises Christine's unflattering references to England, specifically on the wrongful English holding of French fortresses and on the wrongful English breaking of truces.[15] As we know, Christine had a low opinion of the English.[16] Caxton prudently promulgates a version of her theory of war and peace rather less likely to be inflammatory or insulting and more likely to be acceptable to English readers. There seems to have been no need to suppress her gender: it is instead her Frenchness and her anti-English sentiments that invited revision.

In 1521 John Skot prints his first book, *The Boke of the body of Polycye*, a translation of Christine's *Livre du corps de policie*, an extensive political-theory treatise based on the metaphor of the body politic.[17] Only two printed copies of this work are extant, one on vellum and one on paper, but both are in English. As Robert Lucas points out, this work "a connu un sort inhabituel: celui d'être plus populaire en Angleterre que dans son propre pays. Il ne fut jamais édité en France ...."

---

[14] In the chapter "Whether a [sic] english scoler or of som other enemyes lande were founde studyeng atte the scoles in parys myght be taken prisoner or not," Christine explains that scholars studying in Paris "haue forsaken the world and all other pleasirs for loue of science / So shulde he be wel ful of unkyndness that shulde doo eny euyll to them ...." (III. xix; Byles ed., p. 226 lines 32–4) and further states that since the time of Charlemagne, there has been an international community of scholars under the protection of the learned French kings and that their safety should be guaranteed (III. xix). France, in Christine's view, should remain a civilized place, and that means welcoming an international community of scholars—even English scholars visiting in time of war.

[15] Caxton writes, "... that som of his enemyes held and kept from him wrongfully" for "que les anglois a t[o]rt tenoient" (II. xi, Byles, ed., p. 128 ll. 24–5); and, instead of "et mesmement les anglois en ont aucune fois vse contre les francois quant treues estoient" becomes "where namely it hath be som tyme vsed" (IV. iv, Byles, p. 251, line 2).

[16] Christine's *La Lamentacion sur les maux de la France* describes the dreadful state of the nation; in the *Ditié de Jeanne d'Arc*, she calls Henry V's claim (reasserted at the treaty of Troyes in 1420) to the French throne illegitimate and Charles VII "the cast-out child of the legitimate king of France." Trans. Renate Blumenfeld-Kosinski, from Angus J. Kennedy and Kenneth Varty, eds., *Le Ditié de Jeanne d'Arc* (Oxford: Society for the Study of Medieval Literatures and Language, 1977); quoted from *Selected Writings of Christine de Pizan*, ed. Blumenfeld-Kosinski (New York: W. W. Norton, 1997), p. 253. See also note 39 below for part of Blumenfeld-Kosinski's translation of the *Ditié* (1429).

[17] Robert Lucas, ed., notes nine French manuscripts, one English manuscript (CUL Kk I 5) on paper, fifteenth century, and a lost manuscript from Burgundy; *Livre du Corps de Policie* (Geneva: Droz 1967), pp. xliv–l.

[... knew an unusual fate: that of being more popular in England than in its own country. It was never edited in France].[18] There is also one English manuscript of the work, which is not identical to the printed version.[19]

The interplay between the Tudor context for the printing and the work's promonarchical positions may help to explain its relatively greater appeal in early English print. Christine says she gets her metaphor from both Plutarch and John of Salisbury, but she is a more conservative monarchist than Salisbury, rejecting his controversial views on just tyrannicide. Kate Langdon Forhan explains thoroughly the contextual differences in Salisbury's and Christine's writing of the metaphor of the body politic. Salisbury writes the *Policraticus* in 1159, when "a king of tremendous promise and energy sat upon the throne of England ... [and] a whole generation of highly trained, able, and articulate administrators ... would transform the kingdom."[20] Christine, however, wrote her treatise around 1408, in the context of the latter Hundred Years' War, when:

> France hovered on the brink of civil war. The growing disability of Charles VI trapped France between the two powerful personalities of his brother, Louis, Duke of Orleans, and his uncle Philip Duke of Burgundy. The crisis was partly resolved with the assassination of Louis ... and the eventual exoneration of his assassins on the grounds of tyrannicide (Forhan 40).

As Blumenfeld-Kosinski points out, Christine writes during a period of triple crisis for France: the English occupation and war, volatile civil war and unrest, and the Great Schism (1378–1417). No wonder she rejects the idea of just tyrannicide. Her treatise on the body politic then finds new relevance, and its first and only early printings, in England in 1521. In that year, Edward Stafford, Duke of Buckingham, claimant to the throne, was executed for treason, the same year Henry VIII was named Defender of the Faith after writing the *Seven Sacraments* and in the midst of papal intrigues and maneuvering with the Holy Roman Empire. Recall, too, that this is just after Henry's showy rivalries with François I (the Field of Cloth of Gold; the *lit de justice*, the royal library at Fontainebleau outclassing even Henry's very tony bowling lanes in Whitehall). These years saw alternating trade treaties and battles with France. Charles V became Holy Roman Emperor at Aix-la-Chappelle in 1521. France seemed to offer a model of the extreme cultural success a monarchy could achieve, but the history of monarchy, like literary history, took two different courses in the two countries. Forhan elsewhere explains

---

[18] Lucas, ed., p. li. Lucas's edition of 1967 seems to have been the first one separately printed in French, though at least eight French manuscripts are extant, and Maurice Roy includes the *Livre* in his *Oeuvres de Christine*.

[19] Diane Bornstein, ed., *The Middle English Translation*.

[20] "Polycracy, Obligation, and Revolt: The Body Politic in John of Salisbury and Christine de Pizan," in *Politics Gender and Genre: The Political Thought of Christine de Pizan*, ed. Margaret Brabant (Boulder, Colo: Westview Press, 1992), pp. 33–52, p. 34.

how the utterly fragmented French polis of Christine's day makes the solidly monarchist positions in her *Livre du Corps de Policie* look less conservative and more pragmatic, offering real solutions for pressing problems of political chaos.[21] In the work's original context, France was falling apart; in the translation's context, England was competing with France, struggling to catch up, but coming together, or so it looks 500 years later.[22] One can imagine that the *Boke of the Body Politic* might have had special appeal or authority in Henrician England. Certainly, Henry would have approved of her denial of the concept of just tyrannicide. In any case, the Frenchwoman's relatively conservative position is given an authoritative voice on important questions of nationhood, governance, and the body politic in the mid-Henrician years.

Here again, Christine's gender seems to be no problem in the new context, and here even her nationality is not much of a problem, contrary to what some scholars have claimed. The English printer preserves her visible authority, printing her epilogue with the title "Here Christine cocludeth [sic] her booke."[23] Skot's edition, though it differs some from the English manuscript, retains references to France and retains Christine's self references:

> Nowe I am come blessyd be our lorde to the ende that I entended./ that is to saye it hath lyked our lorde to gyue me power to make an ende of thys
> presente booke whiche I beganne at the heede of
> the body after the wrytynge of Pultarque [sic] that   [P3v]
> is to knowe of the polycye whiche is vnderston[t]e by the pryn
> ces to whome I moost humbly requyre / and fyrste to the [c]here
> of all the moost noble kynge of Fraunce / And afterwarde the
> prynces and all other of his royall bloode / that the dylygent
> laboure of wrytynges of theyr humble creatre [Christ]ine / as wel
> in this presente dede as in her other dedes suche as they be or
> may be that it myght be to them agreable. And yf so happen
> that by ygnoraunce as a woman of lytell knowlege make fau
> [t]e in ony of these thynges before rehe[rc]ed / that of theyr grace
> she myght be pardoned. And that the entente of her good wyll
> whiche entendeth not but to all goodnesse and to [y]e ende of her
> werke may be pardoned. And yet I pray for a rewarde of them
> that [b]en lyuynge and theyr noble [successoures] the kynge / and
> other prynces of Fraunce that for remembraunce of my sayen

---

[21] Kate Langdon Forhan, *The Political Theory of Christine de Pizan* (Burlington, VT: Ashgate, 2002), pp. 45–75, 87–102. Forhan also illustrates how the intellectual background of Christine's moment inflects the treatise: the contrast to Nicolas Oresme, for example, highlights certain aspects of her thinking that might otherwise seem unremarkable.

[22] Blumenfeld-Kosinski, pp. 9, 16–18; Forhan, *Political Theory*, pp.1–26 and passim.

[23] The manuscript reads, "Here Christine concludith her boke" (Bornstein, ed, p. 192).

ges in tyme to come whan the soule is out of my body to haue
me in mynde in theyr deuoute prayers ... [lineation preserved].

She further asks her royal and noble readers for the reward of their prayers for her soul after her death. The standard paratextual humility topoi work for Christine in both languages. Just as striking is the English prologue, which translates her self-justification vividly:

If it be possyble that of vyce myght growe ver
tue [/] it wyll please me well in this partye to be
passyoned as a woman lyke as many men hol
den oppynyon that nature of woman can [nat]
kepe vnder seylence the abundauce of hyr [cou]
rage. Now come hardely and shewe out by many clere ryuer[es]
and crystall sprynges / and by the vnstauchable fountaynes
of my courage / whiche can nat hyde for to cast out the desyres
of vertue. O vertue a thynge noble and deyfyed how dare I
be so bolde and auaun[t]e myselfe to speke of the whiche I know
right well that myne vnderstandyng can nat quyckely com
prehende ne vnderstande clerely ne declare ... [A1r; lineation preserved]

The English manuscript, CUL Kk.1.5, also preserves Christine's authority in both prologue and epilogue, although the manuscript translation differs somewhat from the printed version.[24] There is, in short, no effort in English, either in manuscript or print copies of this work, to stanch her writerly fountains.[25]

Another serious work, the *C. Hystoryes of Troye*, came out from an important third-generation English printer, Robert Wyer, probably in 1540.[26] There had already been two English translations in manuscript of Christine's 100-story *Epistre Othea*, at least 47 fifteenth-century French manuscripts, and at least four (but likely as many as seven) French editions in print before 1534.[27]

---

[24] See Bornstein, ed., pp. 22–6, for tabulation of the differences among versions. The English manuscript translation, for instance, marks the prologue as Chapter 1, but it begins with Christine's gendered humility topos, as the printed translation does. See also pp. 39 and 192–3 for specific differences in passages discussed here.

[25] Karen Green might disagree, since she reads Christine as a maternalist rather than a purely monarchist political theorist, contrasting her with Hobbes and creating a feminist critique of Hobbes using her ideas; "Christine de Pizan and Thomas Hobbes," *Philosophical Quarterly* 44 (Oct 1994), pp. 456–75.

[26] Some scholars think 1549–50. P. B. Tracy, "Robert Wyer: A brief analysis," *The Library* 6th series 2 (1980): 294–303, p. 300, cited in Driver, 125. Gabriella Parussa, ed., *Epistre Othea* (Geneva: Droz, 1999), says 1530 without explanation (p. 29).

[27] Parussa, ed., p. 29, note 53, and pp. 87–108 on manuscripts.

Jane Chance finds Scrope's manuscript translation, circa 1450, "immasculating," meaning that Christine's female voice and presence are removed and masculinized.[28] Her evidence is persuasive. Certainly Scrope's translation, like the other B-group manuscripts, suppresses Christine's authorship. Anthony Babyngton's manuscript translation famously calls Christine a "full wyse gentle-woman of Fraunce" but then ambiguously says that she had the manuscript copied by learned men—which she, in charge of a scriptorium, could well have done; yet Babyngton casts her more as patroness than author. However, suppression of authorship and immasculation do not seem to motivate the early English printed version of this work. The printed version is a different text. While it does not announce her authorship as do the other imprints studied here, it does not suppress female authority and in fact foregrounds it. Especially considering Martha Driver's evidence about how typical it was for printers to supplant original authorship, Christine's authority outside the *Othea* (and female authority within the *Othea*) remain remarkably strong. I say this because of the nature of the work itself and also because of its genre, presentational strategies, and narrative framing devices. Let me be more specific.

The *Epistre Othea*, a major mythography, is set up as a sort of protofeminist Troy Book *Moralisé*—it pretends to be the goddess Othea's words to young Prince Hector. Indeed, Christine had chosen its exegetical format—text, illumination, gloss, allegory, and inscription—placing her work deliberately in the line of self-glossing mythographers like Macrobius, Fulgentius, Bernardus Silvestris, and Pierre Bersuire. In most French versions, both print and manuscript, the format is elegant. Early printed versions, those of Pigouchet and Le Noir, for example, feature slender typefaces and detailed woodcuts, laid out symmetrically and consistently so that each page has the coherence of high-medieval commentaries. The English effort to imitate that authoritative format in print is considerably cruder, as Driver's plates illustrate. As is typical in English imprints, the cuts are thicker and include less fine detail, but here the effort to distinguish type size and face is also less effective (see Figures 2.1 and 2.2). Even with an inferior technical capability, the English printer makes a real effort to preserve the format of text-and-exegesis. Although the English pages are less skillfully produced, the format immediately tells the reader that this work is a high, serious mythography with commentary. Metatextuality and an exegetical format do not in themselves guarantee *auctoritas*, but with that format, Wyer signals *auctoritas* to English readers.

Wyer's readers would find a triple dose of female *auctoritas* beneath the visual signal: not only Christine's own format—expensive, with woodcuts for each story—and not only her hermeneutic apparatus, but a narrative frame in which she, the female author, presents the wisdom of Troy that the reader is supposed to take to heart. Likewise, within that frame, the powerful female persona, the Goddess Othea, delivers the specific wisdom that the story's fictional prince is supposed to take to heart. Inside the tales, too, gender issues come up repeatedly,

---

[28] *The Epistle of Othea*, ed. Curt Bühler, EETS (London: Oxford UP, 1970).

Mais la ou prudence est despitee toutes choses contraires ont seigneurie. Et a ce propos dit Salomon en ses prouerbes.

¶ Si intrauerit sapientia cor tuum et scientia anime tue placuerit consilii custodiet te et prudentia seruabit te. Prouerbiorū secundo capitulo.

ij Glose.

d Je ot(h)ea que attrepance est sa seur/ laquelle il doibt aymer. La Vertu dattrempance Trapemēt peult estre dicte seur et est semblable a prudence. Car attrempance est demōstrāce de pru dence/ et de prudēce sensuyt attrempāce. Pour ce dit q̃ il la tiēne pour samie. ce q̃ sēbla blement doibuēt faire tous bons cheualiers desirans le louyer dōne aux bons. Si cōme dit le philo sophe nomme democritus.
Attrēpance amodere les Vices/ et parfait les Vertꝰ

Texte

Et ie te dis que souuenir
Ten doibt com silz fussent passees
Sach es quilz sont en mes pensees
En esperit de prophecie
Or enten et ne te soucye
Car riens ne diray qui nauienne
Sauueu nest/ orten souuiengne.

ij Texte.
e T a celle fin que tu saches
Quil te fault faire/ et que tu faces
A toy les vertus plus propices
Pour mieulx paruenir aux premisses
De vaillance cheualereuse
Et tout soit elle auentureuse
Encor te diray qui me maine
Jay vne mienne seur germaine
Remplie de toute beaulte
Mais sur toute especialte
Est doulce/cope/ et attrempee
Ne iamais dire/nest frappee
A riens fors mesure ne pense
Cest la deesse dattrempance
Si ne peulx sa par elle nom
Auoir de grant grace le nom
Car selle nen faisoit le pois
Tout ne te vauldroit pas sept pois.

a.iii

ij Allegorie.

¶ A Vertu dattrem pance q̃ a proprie te de limiter les saperfluitez doit auoir le bon espe tit. Et dit sainct augusti au liure des meurs de le glise q̃ loffice de attrepance est restraindre et appai ser les meurs de concupiscēce qui nous sont cōtrai res et nous des tourner de la loy de dieu. Et aussi despiter delices charnelles et lon enge mondaine. A ce propos par le sainct pierre la postre en sa premiere epistre.

¶ Obsecro vos tāq̃ aduenas et peregri nos abstinere vos a carnalibꝰ desiderijs que militant aduer sus animam. Prima petri secūdo capitulo

Fig. 2.1   Christine de Pizan, *[Les Cent Histoires de Troye] L'épître de la déesse Othéa* (Paris: [Pigouchet], c. 1500), Aiii. (Gallica BnF Notice No. FRBNF31117543).

¶The .vi. Allegorie.

Ged the workes of mercy, for misericorde or mercy hath many intercessours: it is impossible but that the prayers of many shuld not be exaulted. And to this purpose speketh our lord in the Gospell. Beati misericordes quoniam ipsi misericordiam consequentur.

¶The .vii. Hystorie.

Make not thy Goddesse,/ of blynde Venus
Ne of her Appyer promyse, take none

¶The .vii. Texte.

none hede
her to pursue, it is nothe tra-
uaylous
Not honourable, but full of qua-
rynge bytwe.

¶The .vii. Glose.

Venus is a Planet of the Ayre, of whom the fryday hath his name, and the metall whiche we call Coper to her is attrybued. Venus gyueth influ- ence of loue, and of bayaut myndes, and there was a Lady so named, whiche was quene of Cypres. And for somoche as she excelled all other in beautie and Iolitie, and was right Amourouse also not constant in one loue but abandoned to many, they called her the Goddesse of loue. And bycause that the gyueth inſlu ence of luxurie saith Othea to the good knyght that he make not of her his god desse: that is to vnderstande, that vnto that vice he ought not to abandone his body nor his entent, and to this purpose sayth

Fig. 2.2 Christine de Pizan, C. Hystoryes of Troye, tr. R. Wyer (London: Wyer, [1540? 1549?]) [A7].

as Sandra Hindman and Gabriella Parussa have shown.[29] It is another instance of Christine's womanly self-insertion into important literary canons: just as the *City of Ladies* offers a protofeminist alternative to *the City of God* and other medieval allegories, the *Epistre Othea* offers a protofeminist alternative to one of the central myths of Western culture, the legends and myths of Troy, written by a woman, with wisdom given by a goddess to instruct a prince and with exemplary women figuring prominently in the stories. Without rehearsing the concentric feminine circles of this framed narrative, we can still see that the *C. Hystoryes of Troye* assumes and promulgates female authority on several levels: textual, paratextual, thematic.

Christine de Pizan, then, is brought to early Tudor England as a serious, learned writer, authoritatively female, but not exclusively or even especially as a feminist writer. But what about the works translated into early English print that are most familiar now, her *Cite des dames* and her *Epistre au dieu d'amours*, which have led us to canonize her largely as an early feminist or prefeminist writer? We now read both these works as protofeminist, and their content strongly supports that reading.[30] But these two works originated as a response to—and staked a main dialectical position in—a particular literary and social debate, the *querelle de la Rose*. In reading the English translations, then, we need first to gauge the degree of decontextualization at work between the two audiences with respect to this informing originary discussion (quite apart from the translators' agencies). We need to understand, in other words, that we have not two but four interpretive contexts to consider: the English and the French versions as we read and discuss them now in the context of twenty-first-century feminism, the French version as created in the originating context of the *querelle*, and finally the English printed versions translated for an early modern audience without that originating context and also without benefit of our own contemporary feminism or feminist theory.[31]

---

[29] Hindman, *Christine de Pizan's "Epistre Othéa": Painting and Politics at the court of Charles VI* (Toronto: Pontifical Institute of Mediaeval Studies, 1986), especially pp. 23, 40–41, 56–7, 59, 70, 92–93, 97, 99, 129–30, 187. See also index *s.v. women*.

[30] Despite some good arguments to the contrary: see, for example, Sheila Delany, "'Mothers to Think Back Through': Who Are They? The Ambiguous Example of Christine de Pizan," *Medieval Texts and Contemporary Readers*, ed. Laurie A. Finke and Martin B. Schichtmann (Ithaca, NY: Cornell UP, 1987), rpt *The Selected Writings of Christine de Pizan*, ed. Renate Blumenfeld-Kosinski (New York: W. W. Norton and Co., 1997), pp. 312–28.

[31] Not to mention the more general historical contexts: Christine writes first in late-medieval France, that is, from a France in the final horrors of the Hundred Years' War with England, and in a manuscript world where she controls production and readership to a much greater degree than can be said of most writers. By the time of the Tudor translations, Henry VIII had designs on the continent, having occupied considerable French territory and married off his sister Mary to Louis XII of France; of course, Christine could not control posthumous versions of her own works, much less the contexts into which they fell in the age of mechanical reproduction.

We may tend to assume our own feminism as a natural context for any works about gender—which it could not have been—or to assume an English readership as well-versed in fifteenth-century literary arguments as Christine's first readers were. Our first challenge, then, is to remove anachronistic assumptions so natural or transparent to us. (The other side of the challenge is to imagine and apply certain elusive, variable assumptions about gender that are now lost to us.) Since Christine was known in England as a serious writer with considerable *auctoritas*, it may be useful to ask how the works that are overtly concerned with gender were positioned in Renaissance England. That is, how did a nonfeminist England, at war with France, using a radically new means of production, come to receive the *City of Ladies* and *The Letter of Cupid*? Did her authority extend to gender topics, as we modern feminists assume it would have done; and, more to the point, how did English readers receive her works about gender relations without the deep originating context of the *querelle de la Rose/querelle des femmes*?

The *querelle* began in the late fourteenth century with questions of literary interpretation and gender relations: Either the *Roman de la Rose* is a harmless romance, an allegorical fiction about a lover's pursuit; or perhaps a dangerous, influential piece of misogyny that ends in a violent rape fantasy; or, indeed, it is antiexemplary, a subtle critique of misogyny created with juxtaposition, with multiple and unreliable narrators, and with what post-Robertsonians might call an ironic use of persona. Can an author viably denounce his own protagonists' immoralities? Does the nature of intertextuality absolve an author of responsibility for quotations or allusions to objectionable content? Had women been authors, would the content of books be so heavily misogynist? Do women write and read differently? These enduring questions began as the *querelle de la Rose* among Christine de Pizan and a group of leading intellectuals who were also politically important people: Jean de Montreuil, Provost of Lille; Pierre Col, Canon of Paris; Gontier Col, royal secretary; Jean Gerson, Chancellor of the University of Paris, later, Guillaume de Tignonville, Provost of Paris; and Isabeau de Bavière, Queen of France. Their arguments broadened over time into the *querelle des femmes*, socioliterary debates about the nature of women and their roles in society and the nature of writing about and by women. In France, these works were available in multiple manuscript copies (indeed, Christine assembled them and had them copied, and the Queen of France received a copy). Not only were the texts of the *querelle* writers at issue but also the *Roman de la Rose* itself as well as the *Lamentationes* of Mathéolus (in Latin but also in the influential fourteenth-century French translation of it by Jean le Fèvre de Resson); the *Livre de Leesce* of le Fèvre, his own reply to Mathéolus; the *Miroir de Mariage* of Eustache Deschamps; Christine's *Epistre au Dieu damours*; and numerous treatises, commentaries, narratives, and other works following from and alluding to these (such as Martin le Franc's *Le Champion de Dames*, Christine's *Cite des Dames*, and works by others who refer to all or to several of these[32]). As a result, Christine was well known in her day and in the centuries that followed, not only as a prolific writer but also as the chief figure in these well-known long-running debates about literary interpretation and the social and literary position of women.

In sixteenth-century England, however, this was not at all the case: the *querelle* finds uneven uptake at best. Although there are English manuscripts of the *Roman de la Rose*, and although Chaucer's translation of it is important in early print, the other voices of the *querelle*—even Mathéolus's infamous *Lamentationes*—do not make it into early English print.[33] What parallel debate there was in England was relatively restricted to clerical and script coterie readerships; it was not, in other words, the recopied, rehashed, long-running, oft-studied public debate originating with Christine. Not that there was no antifeminist discourse in England: the revived works of Lydgate and the printing lists of, for example, Robert Copland and Wynkyn de Worde provide ample instances. Despite Chaucer's suggestive prefaces that recapitulate or invite many of these same questions, the socioliterary and interpretive terms of the *querelle* were simply not as familiar in England.

So even the *Cite des Dames*, with its elaborated protofeminist themes, was in this sense speaking alone and out of context in English. The *Cite* still works in translation as a protofeminist utopia, but its feminist hermeneutics cannot bounce as far without the complete contextual backboard. In England, the *Cyte of Ladyes* must have been more readily associated with or compared with such works as the *City of God* or the various allegorical cities, castles, and ships that were the sites of extended moral arguments in early English print. Yes, taking up the *pioche d'inquisition* is still a groundbreaking feminist act, whether on French or English turf. (In English, Anslay renders *pioche d'inquisition* "the pycoys of thyne vnderstandynge," ch. viii [Ddi], which is not exactly the same kind of hermeneutic tool.) And in any language, the *City of Ladies* directly challenges aspects of patriarchy and their literary and social consequences. But in early English print, it might have been understood not so much as a central manifesto in the *querelle*. It might have been better understood as one among many serious moral works, as an allegory on women's societal roles from the pen of the author of the *Faytts and Armes*, the *Boke of the Bodye of Polycye*, the *C. Hystoryes of Troye*, and the *Morall Proverbes*. To historicize in terms of genre might mean that "City" is the operative term, and "Ladies" the application or variant term (we now, I think, foreground the "Ladies" more). The work must have then had a flavor more

---

[32] See Eric Hicks, ed., *Le Debat sur le Roman de la Rose* (Paris: Honoré Champion, 1977) and Joseph L. Baird and John R. Kane, eds, *La Querelle de la Rose: Letters and Documents* (Chapel Hill, NC: University of North Carolina Press, 1978).

[33] At least one later translation alluding heavily to the *Lamentationes* was printed: the *Quinze Joyes de Mariage*, the topic of Chapter 4. These allusions may indicate some familiarity with at least the names Mathéolus (as a bigamist) and Theophrastus (as a misogynist and misogamist). Mathéolus in fact garners sympathy in the *Fyftene Joyes*. On the general presence of Christine in Tudor England, see Malcolmson.

general and didactic than we detect in it now. Perhaps both the *querelle* in early fifteenth-century France and feminism in the twenty-first century form happier ideological contexts for Christine's works on gender than anything the translators could draw on in sixteenth-century England.

Likewise, but with more dubious results in terms of *rezeptiongeschichte*, the *Letter of Cupid* in its Tudor context looks less like an opening salvo and direct challenge to courtly misogyny in the debates about the *Rose*, as it had been in France, than it does a piece of nostalgia for Ricardian courtliness. After all, Christine's near-contemporary Chaucer and his follower Hoccleve had given some small English echo to part of the *querelle* in its moment: Chaucer translated the *Roman de la Rose* (the work against which Christine first wrote) and in the prologue to the *Legend of Good Women* has the God of Love chastise the persona Geoffrey for antifeminism, raising the same question about an author's responsibility for promulgating misogyny that Christine had raised in France. Chaucer's Wife of Bath's Prologue and Clerk's Tale also take up fairly closely the socioliterary issues in the *querelle*, although not in a series of public critical exchanges among powerful parties. A generation later, Hoccleve translates Christine's *Epistre au Dieu damours* but removes her main arguments against the *Roman de la Rose*. (Here is a real site of suppression of female authority and of Christine's antimisogyny, as Bornstein, Chance, and Fenster and Erler have demonstrated.[34]) In other words, there already had been a contemporaneous English uptake of France's literary *querelle*, relatively slight but nevertheless at least partly following its lines (though in the case of Hoccleve, appreciably distorting its protofeminism).

That early appropriation of the *querelle* does not seem to have remained vibrant in England. A century or so later, when Thynne's printed collection of 1532 included both Chaucer's *Roman de la Rose* and Hoccleve's translation of Christine's *Letter of Cupid*, the *querelle* had become in England merely an echo of an echo. While the *querelle* enjoyed a faint Tudor reprise, it was, relatively speaking, a lost or faded context for English readers of print.[35] Not that "woman questions" were not being posed in England—just that the long, specific, high-powered literary debates with which Christine was publicly identified in France were not public identifications for her in England and were certainly not a salient context for her work. If this is a loss of authority, which it may be, it comes about because of something much more complex than any one translator's work: an erosion or slippage in contexts between cultures. The other large gap or slippage in English context, outside the scope of this chapter, is a problem of categories across cultures. Despite the efforts of Isabella Whitney in the 1570s and of Speght

---

[34] Bornstein, "Anti-Feminism," note 2 above; and Chance, "Gender Subversion," note 1 above; Thelma Fenster and Mary C. Erler, eds, *Poems of Cupid, God of Love* (Leiden: E. J. Brill, 1990), especially pp. 159–74.

[35] But see Malcolmson on the availability of the *City of Ladies* in Tudor manuscript circles. Again we find that the readerships of script and print, while not easily separable, do not fully overlap.

and Lanyer in the early seventeenth century, the category "professional woman writer and book-producer" was not operating much in England. It would take two centuries before Aphra Behn would make the category viable in England as it had been in France since Christine.[36] How did readers without that "bookwoman" category place her in the English system? A "full wyse gentyl woman of Fraunce" is how Babyngton handles it, but Christine looks more anomalous in England than she did in France, where she was already anomalous enough. In other words, Christine was not deauthorized but was deracinated on several counts—gender, yes, but even more than that, out of her intellectual context, out of her originating dialectic, out of her times, out of her national place.

Any translation is, of course, a deracinated interpretation, a necessarily partial and filtered appropriation. Any translation also registers the sensibilities of an audience; more precisely, a translation tells how the translator imagines, calculates, or predicts an audience's sensibilities. The translations of Christine register the early printers' and translators' calculations of the sensibilities of the early Tudor print readership. Printers and translators like Woodville, Caxton, Pynson, Wyer, Skot, Pepwell, and Anslay clearly calculated that English readers of print would accept Christine's *auctoritas*, even while printers like Wynkyn de Worde and Robert Copland (and, yes, Pynson and Wyer, too) are simultaneously churning out crude misogynies. The early marketplace of print, to use Alexandra Halasz's term, was at least open to both sides of "the woman question," though the balance certainly tilted in the misogynist direction. Since Christine's authority was not lost or suppressed, although she now looks deracinated and anomalous, might this involve a certain paradoxical liberation, the escape of the emigrant or the floating signifier? The context lost in translation here may in fact allow Christine to be taken up selectively as a serious prolific writer of prose and poetry across genres and topics. To English readers, because she was not known as primarily a feminist debater, and because the category "woman book-creator" did not yet exist, she could be read as a military historian, strategist, and ethicist; a political theorist; a mythographer and culture critic; and a dispenser of authoritative moral wisdom for an expanding early Tudor print readership.

Taking Advice from a Frenchwoman: Printers, Paratexts, and Presentational Strategies in the *Moral Proverbs*

Christine's authoritative *Prouerbes moraulx* offers a case of serial textual transformation that reveals in greater detail how her work was appropriated and

---

[36] Helisenne de Crenne, Louise Labé, and the DesRoches sisters are the most often cited, but French canons are extensive, with French women, especially widows, active early in the sixteenth-century printing trades as well. Jane Donawerth mentions a classical woman writer whose similar position as a foreigner resulted in a certain kind of freedom from native strictures: Aspasia, writing in the fifth-century BCE.

reshaped in English translation. An important French manuscript copy of her works (c. 1401–1410) was brought to England in the latter part of the fifteenth century and was known among a small circle of influential English readers; the *Prouerbes moraulx* was translated from the copy and then printed twice in English, in 1478 and 1526. The three appearances of Christine's proverbs in England reveal three distinct positions that the author and her work held there and indicate the translator's and printers' roles in the re-evaluation and repositioning process. The case is especially intriguing because the three texts of the work cross cultures and span script and print media. Translation, of course, is never just about "re-languaging" content. This case reveals that the printers' presentational strategies perform a "translation" as well since they radically transform the reader's approach to these texts. In other words, the three incarnations of Christine's proverbs not only move the text from French to English languages and cultures, but they translate most powerfully between script and print media and audiences.

The 101 pithy couplets that make up the *Prouerbes moraulx* first came to English readers in BL MS Harley 4431, a French manuscript personally supervised by Christine but English-owned during the late fifteenth century by the family of Anthony Woodville, Earl Rivers. Next, in 1478, William Caxton printed Woodville's translation of the verses as *The Morale prouerbes of Cristyne* (STC 7273), and in 1526 Richard Pynson printed an edited and reformatted version, "Morall Prouerbes of Christyne," in the Chaucerian anthology *The Boke of Fame* (STC 5088). In both French and English, the proverbs advise on social mobility and individual aspiration, on personal comportment, on handling money, on speech and silence, and on relations among classes. Although a few telling translation changes are worth note, the bare content of the proverbs changes little among incarnations. However, changes in the contexts and paratexts among these incarnations alter significantly what that bare content implies, suggesting shifts in the value English printers assumed English readers would find in Christine's proverbs. While the French manuscript instructs a bilingual, cosmopolitan, elite readership from a fairly restricted point of view, Caxton's imprint attends to and even directly addresses changing structures of textual and social authority. Then, 48 years later, Pynson's imprint raises questions about literary canonicity and individual fame, themes hardly noticeable in the text's first incarnation. Proverbs are generally considered an inflexible, even static genre—inherited wisdom resistant to change—but their serial transformations in this case challenge that view, showing them to be highly fluid and subject to interaction with the changing paratexts. This essay examines each incarnation of Christine's moral proverbs in turn, revealing how each version's presentation distinctively "takes" her advice to be "taken" by English readers.

First Take: Christine and England

As we have seen, a significant body of Christine's writing was available in various forms to fifteenth- and sixteenth-century English readers. Christine had complex personal and literary connections to England. Her son, Jean du Castel, served the Earl of Salisbury and later Henry IV in England, and Henry invited Christine to England as a court poet. Christine refused Henry's offer, and several of her works express anti-English sentiments and horror at English actions during the Hundred Years' War. It is important to remember that during Christine's lifetime, much of northern France was English-occupied territory, sometimes brutally occupied. Despite her own understandably negative attitudes toward England during a time of protracted conflict between the countries, the reception history records that her work reached a bilingual and in many respects bicultural coterie of aristocratic readers on both sides of the channel.

The shared concerns of this readership—and the surprisingly limited effects of cultural difference—show up in the materiality and provenance of the first incarnation of the *Prouerbes moraulx* in the manuscript now called BL Harley MS 4431. This beautifully illuminated book of Christine's works in poetry and prose is one among many extant manuscripts collecting Christine's works.[37] Several pieces in Harley 4431 were read and translated in early modern England.[38] The manuscript itself was physically "Englished," deracinated and repatriated, pulled back and forth between the two nations during the latter decades of the fifteenth century, part of territorial struggles and marital connections that are typical of English-French relations in the early modern period. Harley 4431, a presentation copy of the works of Christine dedicated to Isabeau de Bavière, Queen of France, was taken to England by John, Duke of Bedford in about 1425, part of the gains of his regency. He gave it to his second wife, Jaquette de Luxembourg. When Bedford died, she married Sir Richard Woodville; their son Anthony became the owner of the book and the translator of the *Proverbes moraulx*. After Anthony

---

[37] A good basic list can be found in Maurice Roy, ed., *Oeuvres poétiques de Christine de Pisan*. (3 vols; Paris: Firmin-Didot, 1886–1896), I. v–xxv; see also Kennedy, pp. 121–3, for a list of the 252 extant mss containing at least one item by Christine, and passim under each individual work's listing. BL Harley 4431 contains items now canonized (*Livre de la Cité des Dames, Cent Ballades, Livre du Duc de vrais amants*) and items now infrequently read (the *Jeux a vendre*, the *Dit de Poissy*, the *Oroyson Nostre Seigneur*, for example, and the *Prouerbes moraulx*). She is clearly a much more "major" European author than most canons have reflected.

[38] See Roy's manuscript stemmata, pp. xxi–xxiii, and note 2 above. This is not to say that all the English translators used this manuscript—they surely did not. But Roy's stemmata show that this manuscript contained items more generally available to English readers of the period.

Woodville's death in 1483, Louis de Bruges obtained the book.[39] But in being "taken" back and forth between French and English contexts in manuscript, the advisory *Prouerbes moraulx* does not really change tone or color. The content of some of Christine's other works would have been received quite differently by the houses of Valois and York/Lancaster (the *Ditié de Jeanne d'Arc*, for example, which does not appear in Harley 4431[40]), but the *Prouerbes moraulx* does not take up the topical matter of international conflict and thus would likely have reached the similarities between the two-sided audience more than their differences. In this incarnation, the *Prouerbes moraulx* would stand comfortably alongside other advice books and conduct books made for young aristocrats, works like Christine's *Enseignements moraulx a son fils* (indeed, these two instructive works are adjacent to one another in this and other manuscripts). It is fairly safe to assume that this manuscript enjoyed a limited and homogeneous readership, but the limits are class- and coterie-based, certainly not language- or nation-based, as we, so largely monoglot and mononational, might now assume. The physical book and the *Proverbes moraulx* it contains, in other words, are "taken" across national boundaries with little resulting interpretive dissonance, certainly less than a Deleuzian model of textual *déterritorialisation* might predict.[41]

The deterritorialized content seems quite conservative: the proverbs progress quickly from general virtues to specific practical advice on social and moral matters.

---

[39] By 1676, Henry, Duke of Newcastle, owned it and passed it to the Harley collection via his granddaughter's marriage. More details of provenance are in Paul Meyer, "Note sur le manuscrit offert par Christine de Pisan à Isabeau de Bavière (Musée Britannique Harley 4431)," in Roy, ed., III.xxi–xxiv.

[40] Blumenfeld-Kosinski's prose translation of the *Ditié* (1429) captures some of the mocking, angry tones of Christine's anti-English sentiment:

And so you English, lower your horns, for you will never find good game! Don't carry on with your nonsense in France! You are check-mated, something you wouldn't have thought possible recently when you seemed so threatening; but then you were not yet on the path where God cuts down the proud. You thought you had already conquered France, and that she would be yours forever. Things have turned out differently, you false people! You'll have to beat your drums elsewhere if you do not want to taste death like your companions whom the wolves may well devour, for they lie dead in the fields. And may it be known that she [Joan of Arc] will cast down the English, there will be no getting up, for this is the will of God who hears the voices of the good people whom they [the English] wanted to harm! The blood of those forever dead cries out against them, God will no longer stand for this, but condemn [the English] as evil—this is decided. ... As for the English, whether one laughs or cries about it, they are done for. One will mock them in times to come. They have been vanquished! And all you lowly rebels who make common cause with them [the Burgundians], now you can see that you should have gone forward rather than backward and become the serfs of the English (pp. 258–60).

[41] The Deleuzian notion of deterritorialization in translation does not really apply as well to such a bicultural readership. See Deleuze and Guattari, *Kafka: Pour Une Littérature Mineure* (Paris: Éditions de Minuit, 1975).

Prudence, reason, temperance, courage, justice, faith, charity, and hope, in that order, each get a couplet. The personified virtues are very lightly allegorized:

> Prudence apprent lomme a viure en raison,
> La ou elle est eureuse est la maison
> Esperance conduit les fais humains
> Mais ne tient pas ses promesses a maîns.

> [Prudence teaches people to live in reason; where she is, is a happy house .... Hope conducts human affairs but does not keep her promises to many.][42]

Several couplets explain the consequences of a lack of certain virtues: without faith, no creature can please God; without charity, one cannot be acceptable (couplets 6, 7). One next expects a catalogue of lightly personified parallel vices, but practical advice about social relations follows instead. The other most frequent themes, in both languages, are prudent lifestyles, proper behavior, handling money, and personal advancement in general and at court. Both versions advise on how to avoid all kinds of trouble here and in the hereafter.

It is perhaps surprising to find few proverbs about relations between men and women from an author elsewhere so deeply concerned with gender. The author clearly knows that Harley 4431 will have women readers, particularly the Queen of France, to whom it is presented. But the *Proverbes moraulx* itself seems to address a mixed readership. One couplet (83) says women should be quiet; but other couplets advise that "people" should be prudently quiet. Another couplet warns men and women not to spend too much time alone together whispering, or their reputations will be harmed (61). One couplet aims at men who speak ill of women (81). This point intersects with some of Christine's wider purposes since it is precisely against slanderers of women like Mathéolus, the Roman writers, or Pierre Col, whom she engages in the *querelle des femmes*. Beyond this, there is little gendering in the *Proverbes moraulx*, and its initial manuscript context points the advice mainly at aristocrats of either sex and either nationality. Often, where the French is general and could be aimed at a mixed readership, the English adopts a specifically gendered pronoun, usually masculine but sometimes feminine (see couplets 33, 40, 71, 79, 92, 96, 99, 101). In a few places Christine uses a gender-

---

[42] Numbers given here are couplet numbers, not line numbers. Because Maurice Roy, *Oeuvres complétes*, edits the *Prouerbes moraulx* from BNF 605, French passages here are taken from the somewhat less authoritative transcription by William Blades of BL Harley 4431, the manuscript Woodville used (*Les Prouerbes moraulx, as composed by Cristyne de Pisan* ... {London: n.p., 1859}). A recent edition by Jean-François Kosta-Théfaine regularizes spelling, adds punctuation, expands abbreviations, and includes an intelligent introduction, "The *Proverbes moraulx* de Christine de Pizan," *Le Moyen Français* 38 (1996): 61–78. English passages (except my translations) are taken from Caxton's version of 1478 (STC 7273).

neutral pronoun, and Woodville uses "he" or "man." Given the frequent use until very recently of the "universal masculine" (in which "men" stands for "people" and "he" for "he or she"), this probably would not have been read as an exclusion or suppression of women by most readers in 1478, as it is by many twenty-first-century readers. Of course, this is the very problem with the universal masculine: it marks the erasure of feminine difference and the subsuming of "she" into "he." Christine does not surface the subsumed feminine in the grammar of the *Prouerbes*, although that is indeed her project at the level of content in several other works. While Christine's care in, for instance, the *City of Ladies* or the *Three Virtues* is to locate female virtue or to argue that virtue finds an equally happy home in women's lives and legends, her care in the *Prouerbes moraulx* is to advise more generally. Nation, language, and gender, then, do not provide axes of difference for the proverbs as presented in Harley 4431; the content of this work stands comfortably in general instructive and courtesy genres for both French and English readers.

The real action here, in fact, is not to be found in the content of the *Prouerbes moraulx*. The composition of the volume—a single-author collected works—asserts what turns out to be the most important, most enduring element of the *Prouerbes moraulx* taken up in English incarnations: Christine's authorship and authority to advise. Christine's authority is depicted repeatedly in the sumptuous miniatures placed throughout the book. The miniature that concerns us most here is on folio 259v, where the *Proverbes moraulx* begins. This famous illumination depicts Christine in her most usual pose, at a desk with a book, instructing a group of four men, one in monk's robes. Despite a minimalist incipit, "Cy commencent proverbes moraulx," her authorship and authority to give advice are much on display in this first script context to come before English readers. Christine's authority to advise is an essential feature of her authorship more generally. It is constitutive of the *Epistre Othea*, with its framing device of an advisory goddess; it is crucial to the political works like the *Livre du corps de policie* and her writings about and to King Charles; and of course its assertion is the founding premise of the *Liure de la cite des dames* and the *Enseignements moraulx* and *Proverbes moraulx*. Asserting this authority—thereby credibly inserting herself into patriarchal canons—is perhaps her central aim and achievement, as Maureen Quilligan and others have demonstrated.[43]

---

[43] Quilligan, "The Allegory of Female Authority: Christine de Pizan and Canon Formation," in *Displacements: Women, Tradition, Literatures in French*, ed. Joan DeJean and Nancy K. Miller (Baltimore: Johns Hopkins UP, 1991); and more fully developed in *The Allegory of Female Authority* (Ithaca, NY: Cornell UP, 1991). See also Jennifer Summit, *Lost Property* (Chicago: University of Chicago Press, 2000), pp. 62-107; and Patricia A. Phillippy, "Establishing Authority: Boccaccio's *De Claris mulieribus* and Christine de Pizan's *Le livre de la cité des dames*," in *The Selected Writings of Christine de Pizan*, ed. Blumenfeld-Kosinski, pp. 329–61.

However, while Christine's authority to advise, an aspect of her authorship so prominent in the Harley 4431 manuscript, seems quite secure in the hands of the English re-presenters of her work, it nevertheless seems vulnerable to the ruptures of the new media and contexts. (After all, female textual authority is arguably one area of cultural difference between France and England in this period.) Christine's advice-giving *auctoritas* does survive the various translations—of language, of medium, of readership—to which it is subjected in early English print, but the printers "take" her advice such that subtly different aspects of it are emphasized. It makes sense that the early printers should attend to questions of authority and authorship: the new medium threatens disruptions to *auctoritas* and to hierarchies of authorship. Woodville's translation (c. 1478, printed by Caxton) involves both a cross-channel "Englishing" and a rupture into a broadening and less homogeneous group of English readers of printed books. In Harley 4431, the presentation of Christine's authority emphasizes her learnedness and her ability to impart wisdom (even to men, even to clerics). Woodville, Caxton, and Pynson each clearly get this point and try variously to convey it, but her authority finds different expression as it intersects differently with their own respective concerns.

Second Take: "Oure" Elders, Christine's Authority, and Caxton's Presentational Strategies

Caxton's imprint is an ambiguous measure of Christine's cultural capital in early modern England. It stands alone, four leaves in folio, with a certain singularity, if not "aura," in the usual sense.[44] On the one hand, the *Prouerbes moraulx* was apparently perceived as commercially viable, as a commodity desirable enough to succeed by itself. On the other hand, the work loses force and authority without the printer's investment in a "complete works of Christine" volume. Yet one could argue that the "works" concept, like the "prolific female professional writer" category, was not developed in Caxton's England as it had been in France—or at least was not tested in the marketplace before Pynson's Chaucer imprints (discussed below).

BL Harley 4431 was a "works" volume available to Caxton through Woodville; single-author "works" volumes were widely available in French print (as Tchemerzine's ten volumes show); and Caxton printed heavily from French material. Thus, while the idea of a "works of Christine" volume would have certainly been possible for Caxton, he perhaps did not perceive such a volume as a likely profit maker. Did he perceive her authorship as less prominent than Chaucer's

---

[44] Walter Benjamin's terms, of course, are created for political and economic milieux very different from those surrounding Christine's texts. "Kleine Geschichte der Photographie," 1931, introduces the idea of aura, more fully articulated in "Das Kunstwerk im Zeitalter seiner technischer Reproduzierbarkeit," 1935; ed. Hannah Arendt, trans. H. Zohn, *Illuminations* (New York: Schocken Books, 1969).

(who was less prolific in multiple genres than Christine, but who was already seen as the greatest English poet)? Or did Caxton see her as he saw Chartier—a major French author whose works he chose to produce piecemeal, perhaps not wanting to risk the costs of a large production on a French author? Or did the genre of the *Prouerbes moraulx* make it a work in the small, single-production category, something like the *Dictes and Sayenges* or his other shorter didactic titles? Impossible to say for sure, but Caxton does overtly support Christine's authority, so the lack of a "complete Christine" volume does not necessarily imply Caxton's diminished sense of her *auctoritas*.

Caxton tries to preserve in certain ways the particular aura of the French manuscript, even in a new era of mechanical reproduction. His Typeface 2 and his *format allongé* do attempt a certain "handwritten-ness" and even expand the manuscript's outer-margin space. (See Figure 2.3, an image of the first page of *The Morale Prouerbes of Cristyne* 1478.) The manuscript's individual rubrication of couplets and generous spacing between them are not idle luxuries; rather, they suit the literariness of the work. These script production values stress the couplet as the work's chief unit of poetic discourse and encourage a separate reading of each aphorism, which supports the non-narrative, nonthematic, nearly random arrangement of the proverbs' content. These signifying production values, however, to which Caxton had access in Harley 4431, are lost to print—lost, perhaps to print economics. Caxton sets the work as an unbroken stream of pentameter verse, presenting these 202 lines as a narrative unit, though they do not in fact work as narrative. In this imprint, Caxton either seriously misreads the work or, more likely, shows little interest in the rhetoric of spacing and lineation. Again, this in itself does not indicate a diminished English reception of Christine's work but rather illustrates the printers' mixed efforts at translating literary meanings—meanings so often implicit, contextual, and paratextual—between media with very different production values.

The loss of the miniature that depicts Christine giving advice is also ambiguous: its absence seems at first glance to diminish her *auctoritas*. The printer compensates by asserting her authority in other ways,[45] by translating the signifying visual cues of the miniature into verbal additions to the text. The title names her as author, first. Most important, Caxton's colophon stanzas advertise and explain Christine's

---

[45] A patron-translator of Woodville's status in England at that time would surely have helped the perceived status of the volume. Woodville's sister, Elizabeth, married King Edward IV in 1464. By 1473 Woodville was Chief Butler of England and one of the guardians of the Prince of Wales. Woodville himself was betrothed (in 1478, between marriages) to Margaret, sister of James III of Scotland. When Edward died in April 1483, Woodville was protecting the Prince; he was intercepted and executed without trial by June of that year, and was later called "the noblest and most accomplished victim of Richard III," *DNB s.v.* Anthony Woodville. (Woodville's niece Elizabeth married Henry VII, unifying the houses of York and Lancaster.)

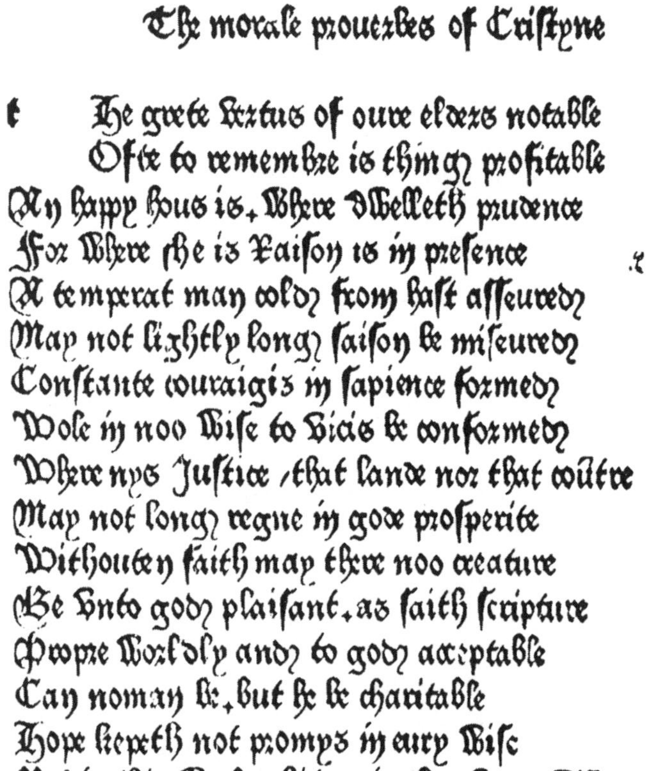

The morale prouerbes of Cristyne

The grete kertus of oure elders notable
Ofte to remembre is thyng profitable
An happy hous is, where dwelleth prudence
For where she is raison is in presence
A temperat man colde from hast assured
May not lightly long saison be miseured
Constante couraigis in sapience formed
Wole in noo wise to vicis be conformed
Where nys Justice, that lande nor that coultre
May not long regne in gode prosperite
Withouten faith may ther noo creature
Be vnto god plaisant, as saith scripture
Propre worldly and to god acceptable
Can noman be, but he be charitable
Hope kepeth not promys in eury wise
Yet in this world hit guieth many awise
In grett estat ligth not the gloire
But in vertu whiche worth is memoire
A cruell prynce gronded in auarice
Shulde his peuple not truste, if he be wise
Piupnyng in tyme and wisely to refreigne
Maketh oon welthy & in estat to reigne
Nob preyse nob blame comunely by vsance
Sheweth folye and noo maniere constance
A prynces court withoute a gouerneur
Beyng prudent can not leste in honneur

Fig. 2.3   Christine de Pizan, *Morale Prouerbes of Cristyne* (Westminster: Caxton, 1478), [Ai].

auctoritas, and they also show us more precisely which questions about authority in the new print era were most on Caxton's mind in making this imprint.

Caxton's deceptively simple colophon appears at the end of Woodville's translation, and it bears repeating and further analysis here. After Christine's 101 aphoristic couplets, these rhyme-royal stanzas explain the roles of the various parties responsible for this book (it is worth repeating here):

Of these sayynges Cristyne was aucteuresse
Whiche in makyng hadde suche Intelligence
That therof she was mireur & maistresse
Hire werkes testifie thexperience
In frenssh languaige was writen this sentence
And thus Englished dooth hit rehers
Antoin Wideuylle therl Ryuers

Go thou litil quayer, and reco[m]mand me
Unto the good grace, of my special lorde
Therle Ryueris . for I haue enprinted the
At his co[m]mandement . folowyng eury worde
His copye / as his secretaire can recorde
At Westmestre ... of feuerer the .xx. daye
And of kyng Edward / the xvii yere vraye

Enprynted by Caxton
In feuerer the colde season

Caxton's care to expand the explicit and to alter the traditional "go little book" topos highlights some of the issues surrounding authorship that were in flux in the early print period. Explicits had long served "closural" and "identificatory" functions in the script age, and the early printers showed no sign of giving up this useful space. In fact, their colophons often reveal an understanding of the enhanced possibilities for the explicit as a space in which to create metatext or to draw heightened attention to their own acts of printing while providing specific identifying detail about the particular imprint. This case is no exception: Caxton gives place, date, regnal year, and even seasonal detail ("the colde season") as well as details about the genre, author, translator, secretary, and printer. He also adds some timely, significant changes. For example, the "go little book" topos or apostrophe to the quire is usually the prerogative of the author. It had long served not only as a mark of closure but as a number of other things: a kind of validation of the book's integrity as a whole entity; for a poem, the "go little verse" and for a letter the "go little bille" work in the same way at the smaller scale. These closural topoi give notice of a work's destination and sometimes a reminder of its origin. In this closural space, all kinds of rhetorical or metatextual gestures could conventionally be made. The apostrophe to the quire, related to and overlapping with the lyric envoi,[46] could conventionally contain praise of the patron, more or less disingenuous humility, subtle complaints of the purse, a mini-résumé of an author's other works, or a variety of matters topical or occasional. Apologia, disclaimer, lament, self-presentation, retraction, supplication, and more: all could find appended space in the "go little book." Aware of these conventional possibilities, Caxton manipulates them meaningfully, as he manipulates other paratexts like prologues and epilogues.[47] Here he uses the conventional space to articulate and to clarify the relations among this text's author, translator and patron, secretary or scribe, and printer.

Christine de Pizan, meanwhile, gets top billing as "authoresse." To a twenty-first-century reader, "authoress" might seem an insult, but in 1478 this was unusual praise to give a woman in England, awarding her high *auctoritas*, that very serious power of logos.[48] Furthermore, Christine is "the mirour and maistresse" of "Intelligence," so much intelligence in "makyng" had she. "Makyng," too, accords significant power to Christine as *auctor*: "makers" were the real poets (from *poein*), not just light versifiers, but like Chaucer, writers of literature to be taken seriously. The word "mirror" implicitly places her as an instructive authority in the medieval *speculum* tradition; thus, the new English reader is to heed, not just read, her words. Moreover, Caxton praises her work's "sentence," its meaningful, serious content. (His choice of rhyme-royal verse implicitly accords the work a more elevated status, as well.) "Sentence" is famously contrasted with "solas," just as *fructos* and *flores* or "aut prodesse, aut delectare" are traditionally juxtaposed, but here Caxton does not mention any pleasant or light qualities of the *Prouerbes*. Instead, he notes that Christine has written other "werkes" as well, and they "testifie th'experience"—experience, of course, being an important characteristic of a proverb writer of either gender.

---

[46] On the envoi and medieval epistolary conventions, see Camargo, pp. 98–120 and LeBlanc *passim*. On the envoi in terms of metatextuality and closure in lyric poetry, see Coldiron, *Canon* pp. 46–56 and 71–5.

[47] For Caxton's prologues and epilogues, see Norman F. Blake, *Caxton's Own Prose* (London: Deutsch, 1973) or Nellie S. Aurner, *Caxton: Mirrour of Fifteenth-Century Letters* (London: Allen, 1926, rpt NY: Russell and Russell, 1965), pp. 223–96. Selections are available in W. J. B. Crotch, *The Prologues and Epilogues of William Caxton* (EETS o.s. 176, London: Oxford UP, 1928).

[48] On the relatively few learned women granted such status in the early modern period, see Elizabeth Guild, "Women as *Auctores* in Early Modern Europe," in *The Cambridge History of Literary Criticism, III: The Renaissance*, ed. Glyn P. Norton (Cambridge, England: Cambridge UP, 1999), pp. 426–32; or the essays in *A History of Women Philosophers: Medieval, Renaissance, and Enlightenment Philosophers, AD 500–1600*, II, ed. Mary Ellen Waithe (Boston: Kluwer Academic Press, 1989); and in Jean R. Brink, ed., *Female Scholars: a Tradition of Learned Women before 1800* (Montreal: Eden Press Women's Publishing, 1980) and Patricia H. Labalme, ed., *Beyond Their Sex: Learned Women of the European Past* (New York: NYUP, 1980).

With the word "experience," these stanzas join an important late medieval epistemological debate, familiar to us now mainly through Chaucer's distinction in the *Wife of Bath's Prologue* between "experience" and "authoritee." Critics have long understood that Chaucer has the Wife of Bath claim experience as an alternative (feminine) epistemology, replacing the traditional (masculine) epistemology of deriving *auctoritas* from the texts of older makers. Ambiguities in Chaucer's "Wife of Bath's Prologue" and "Wife of Bath's Tale" have prevented critical agreement about whether and to what extent the feminine epistemology of "experience" is undercut, satirized, or devalued there with respect to "authoritee."[49] Here, however, the verses Caxton adds do not make "experience" feminine-identified. They imply rather that Christine commands both epistemologies: her authority—her authorship—is exemplary, and her authoritative qualities of intelligence and "sentence" are supported, not undercut, by the alternative epistemology of "experience." Chaucer's "Wife of Bath's Tale" is based, through a line of medieval antifeminist satires, on Mathéolus's *Lamentationes*, one of the works against which Christine argues in the *Livre de la Cité des Dames* and the *Epistre au Dieu damours*. Entirely without irony or subversiveness, then, and presenting a notion quite opposed to the "experience" of La Vieille or Alison of Bath, Caxton's praise of Christine's "experience" removes her from that side of the *querelle*, in a sense vindicates her, and displays her authority to instruct in a different, arguably broader, debate.[50] Caxton's praise is geared primarily to the genre and quality of the work, not to her gender—he does not, in other words, call the verses sweet, pleasing, delightful, or soft. Nor does he mention her as an afterthought: Caxton does not undermine in any way her *auctoritas* or mark it as different from that of a male author of proverbial wisdom (though he does grant her an "experience" appropriate to purveyors, of either gender, of this kind of verse). Unlike the subversions and silencings that some critics have found in other early modern English men's translations of Christine's work, here it is clear that her authority as learned writer is not in question. In fact, Caxton's colophon stanzas

---

[49] Among relevant discussions of the *Wife of Bath's Tale* in terms of the experience-authority dichotomy: Lee Patterson, "'For the Wyves love of Bathe': Feminine Rhetoric and Poetic Resolution in the *Roman de la Rose* and the *Canterbury Tales*," *Speculum* 58 (1983): 656–95; and Barrie Ruth Strauss, "The Subversive Discourse of the Wife of Bath: Phallocentric Discourse and the Imprisonment of Criticism," *ELH* 55.3 (Fall 1988): 527–54. La Vieille's words in the *Roman de la Rose* present exactly the kind of lewd "experience" that Christine rejected: "Mais je sai tout par la pratictique:/ Esperiment m'en ont fait sage," 12804–5.

[50] Quilligan does not discuss this specific point but explains persuasively how Christine inserts herself (authoritatively) into the canon. On Christine's relation to literary history, see, among many others, Phillippy; Lori Walters, "The Woman Writer and Literary History: Christine de Pizan's Redefinition of the Poetic *Translatio* in the *Epistre au dieu d'amours*," *French Literature Series* 16 (1989): 1–16; and Renate Blumenfeld-Kosinski, "Christine de Pisan and the Misogynistic Tradition," in *Selected Writings*, ed. Blumenfeld-Kosinski, pp. 297–311.

and title perform verbally the assertion of *auctoritas* accomplished visually in the manuscript miniature introducing the *Prouerbes moraulx*.

The verses simultaneously address a parallel concern of Caxton's historical moment: the rapidly changing economies and roles and concomitant shifts of authority involved in making printed books. Caxton explains that the wisdom ("sentence") was written in French and that "thus Englished," Anthony Woodville, Earl Rivers, "rehearses" it. This looks utterly traditional at first glance, using one of the most common verbs in the fifteenth and sixteenth centuries used to describe the act of translation, "to English." (Notice that one does not generally "françaisiser" or "gedeutschen" or "españolar" a work, but one can "English" it, then as now, the noun for our language slipping flexibly into a verb.) Seeking a word to rhyme with Rivers, Caxton finds "rehers," which turns out to add to our sense of the hierarchies at work here. This word tells us that a translation is a rehearsal, a reiteration or repetition, a secondary thing—again affirming the primacy and status of Christine's authorship. Except for Christine's gender (which in Caxton's presentation is less important than her impeccable authority), the author-translator-text relationships are so far traditional. That Caxton's patron, however, is also his translator and copytext-provider renders this set of bookmaking relations unusual and threatens the older set of relations: most commonly in the script age, patrons commissioned translations or made translations themselves and commissioned scribes or secretaries, illuminators, and bookbinders. In the later print age, patrons still commissioned translations, or commissioned printers saw to the translations themselves. Even among these multiple, shifting, and overlapping roles (many early English printers were also translators, for example), in the authorial-function food chain circa 1478, translator is still a lower position than either author or patron. But here we have a case of one individual, Woodville, occupying both the higher-status social position of patron (and brother-in-law to the king[51]) and the lower-status functional position of translator. The disruptions occasioned by the new means of production—new roles, new functions, new economies, new representations of what efforts have gone into the making of a book—create a conflict between social and functional status. Caxton faces an untraditional problem (that of placing his own actions as printer) in these seemingly traditional rhyme-royal verses. In the first stanza, the relative status of the author, Christine, and the translator, Woodville, is clear. That functional hierarchy trumps the social hierarchies involved: although the Earl Rivers (a.k.a. Anthony Woodville) is Caxton's patron, commissioner of the volume, and Christine's social superior, Anthony Woodville (a.k.a. the Earl Rivers) is still only the translator, a rehearser. Caxton's solution is to rank Christine first, as author, and Woodville (à Rivers) well beneath her, as translator. Then in stanza 2's commendation of the patron, Caxton names him not as Anthony Woodville but as "special lorde." Caxton

---

[51] See note 41 for information on Woodville's position. In contrast, Christine was the daughter of Tomas de Pizan, astrologer and physician to Charles V; she was the widow of a well-placed royal secretary, Estienne Du Castel.

praises each authorial function but uses simple tropes to articulate and separate them. An extended trope of transition, anadiplosis, allows Caxton to overlap the key functions, to elide the common name, and to build to a stress on the lordship: translator, Anthony Woodville, Earl Rivers, special lord (patron). That solution still separates Woodville's roles as translator and patron but places them in a neat, nearly chiastic structure, an implicit anti-metabole. In altering the traditional formulas, these carefully orchestrated lines negotiate the delicate problem of a misalignment of (old) social and (new) literary hierarchies.

Caxton also alters the traditional claims of a translator's fidelity to suit his new literary economy. Such claims of "following every word" accurately are usually in this period—and indeed in the preceding centuries back to St. Jerome—made by the translator. For medieval translators, fidelity to a source text was seen to be a moral and spiritual duty, more important, or so they said, than even translation's pragmatic, culture-preserving, or culture-building work. In this case, the typical move would be for Woodville to claim fidelity to Christine's text, or for a secretary or scribe to ventriloquize that claim of translatorial faithfulness. Here, however, the claims to fidelity do not attach to the translator but instead are quietly displaced onto the printer himself, with Earl Rivers's unnamed secretary as witness to Caxton's fidelity to copytext. Declaring the fidelity of the printed text to the script copytext is a slick substitution: in the age of the new medium, the implicit analogy is that the printed text will be to script copytext as translated poem had been to source poem, which is to say, a faithful rendition, accurate in detail and true to the spirit of the original. Thus, the printer's responsibility in the new world of presses is made analogous to the translator's high moral duty in the older world, that is, to preserve and transmit a culture of letters (*translatio studii*) but also faithfully to bring a primary or higher-value "original" to new readers.[52] In this case, Caxton slips something radical, or at least something new in 1478, into the traditional fidelity topos: it is now the translator's script, not the author's, to which a strict, word-for-word fidelity is claimed. Thus, in Caxton's brief sleight of hand, Woodville's translation takes on a value analogous to that of an "original," and Caxton's actions as printer take on the importance and trust of accurate

---

[52] Discussions of translation have focused, until our century, on fidelity: Cicero, *De optimo genere oratorum* 14 and 23; Horace, *Ars Poetica* 133-4; Jerome's letter to Pammachius; Boethius's second commentary on the *Isagoge* of Porphyry; *et al.*; for a short history of the concept as related to early modern poetic translation, see Coldiron pp. 17–20 and 24–5. Rita Copeland persuasively writes of the rhetorical and hermeneutic functions of medieval translation. Karlheinz Stierle ("*Translatio studii* and Renaissance," in *The Translatability of Cultures*, eds Wolfgang Iser and Sanford Budick {Stanford UP, 1996}, pp. 55–66) moves the discussion forward with useful distinctions between vertical and horizontal translation and between medieval and Renaissance translation practices; Christine's own practice, however, under Stierle's rubric, would make her a "Renaissance" and a "horizontal" translator. On Christine's disruptions of the *translatio studii*, see Walters, Quilligan, and Phillippy.

transfer and faithful representation that had long been the conservative province of translators. (We might wonder whether fidelity as a textual value becomes, as the print era progresses, less a moral duty of translators and more a commercial function of printers, owed and answerable not to church or patrons but to buyers and readers—an instance of larger social and ideological shifts in the period.) Caxton's reassuring, familiar format and the familiar claims would have helped everyone— readers, writers, apprentices, patrons, perhaps the printer himself—understand the multiple role reassignments involved in the new systems of literary production. Here we see a printer portraying his actions as transformative, as representational in nature, as a reshaping that was evidently conceived as potentially risky and suspect, subject to error, fault, failure, or bad faith. Like the risky and suspect transformations of translation, the new transformations of printing apparently needed the support of such reassuring claims.

"Taking" the *Proverbs* Themselves: The Relation of Content to Paratexts

The first couplet of Woodville's translation, compared with Christine's first couplet, shows the translator making changes consonant with the printer's claims. The first couplet creates a hierarchical context for inherited *auctoritas* more openly than the French original does. The English begins:

[T]he grete vertus of oure elders notable
Ofte to remember is thing profitable

Unremarkable by itself, but Christine's French version begins:

Les bonnes meurs et les sages notable [sic]
Rementeuoir souuent sont proufitable [sic]

Roughly, Christine begins by saying that good morals or manners and notable wise people often are profitable to remember. Woodville, on the other hand, says that it is a profitable thing often to remember the great *virtues* (not *meurs* [morals-manners]) *of* (not *et*) and *our* (not just any) notable *elders* (not *sages*).[53] Woodville adds an awkward extra syllable to these lines, but, more significantly, he adds a possessive genealogy of virtue. The translation changes mean that these are not just any sages

---

[53] This speculative interpretation may well be overreading or misreading: as Jane Donawerth reminded me in private correpsondence, "the deconstruction of the 'of' phrase-modifier into an 'and' of balanced substantives is a poetic figure common in the sixteenth century, and might have been read back into [the] 'of' phrase." An anonymous reader points out that Woodville's "oure" sometimes enjoyed similar flexibility; I would further say that the "oure" could be one more trace of that lingering biculturalism in aristocratic sectors of France and England.

but our own elders, whose virtues, not only whose wisdom, we (English) readers naturally inherit. Woodville opens with a familial implication, a rhetorical "we" that places the new English reader not in a cosmopolitan, aristocratic coterie but as the child of a tradition, defined now by nation and language, not class, and about to receive instruction in "our" heritage of virtue (a heritage "Englished," despite the high French visibility of the title). Woodville's claim to the Frenchwoman's advice as "oure" heritage recalls England's claims to the French crown and to French lands, claims Woodville himself sought to enforce in several overseas campaigns. The claim also recalls the provenance of the French manuscript he used to make the translation: Woodville's "oure" comes at the end of almost a century of efforts to "English" Harley 4431, as noted above. The "oure" could also be a faded trace of that centuries-old biculturalism among French and English aristocrats. In any case, with their presentation and pronouns, Woodville and Caxton "English" the work's instruction for good, absorbing its wisdom into "our [English] elders' virtues."

The interpretive implications of this are several: in nationalizing the readership, the "oure," this imprint would also seem to expand the relevance of some of the proverbs across class lines, though from this distance we cannot be certain about the socioeconomic status of a group as amorphous as a readership. The proverbs themselves exhibit a concern for navigating changing hierarchies of social authority, just as the paratexts exhibit a concern for changing textual authorities. Even without certainty about the exact constitution of the readership, we can reasonably speculate that some of this social advice, commonplace or abstract in script, would have taken on a new relevance for new readers in Caxton's context. For instance, when Caxton "takes" the advice to a broader readership, several verses about money and class could become practical, more than theoretical, advice. "Necessity pouerty and indigence / ... cause many great inconvenience": such "inconvenience" feels more urgent when one is part of the "many" experiencing it instead of reading about it from a secure economic position. Other proverbs about money that might ring differently to readers with daily economic concerns: "He is proudent | that maketh pourueyance / For thyng to come bifore er falle the chance" (17), or "Great pain to change condicion in age" (34); or "Borne ful many an heuy charge" (43, adding a mild, merchant-class pun in the English?). In manuscript, the couplets' potential impact is limited by their applicability to a coterie readership; their potential impact is expanded in print.

Likewise, a few proverbs that encourage upward mobility through hard work would have a different resonance for those more likely to be experiencing upward mobility:

> Often is seen a man in Indigence
> To hygh estat comen by his diligence (76)

And:

> Grete diligence with a good Remembrance
> Dooth a man ofte to hygh honneur auance (14).

Other proverbs caution against the difficulty, uncertainty, and dangers—moral and practical—of social advancement:

> Whoo wole him self to greet estat enhance
> Muste byfore be acqueinted with suffrance (35).

Even after paying one's dues:

> Seruice in court is noo seur heritage
> Hit faileth ofte with litle auantaige (84).

With ever-expanding layers of "service" at the turn of the sixteenth century, a wider readership could find new relevance in such a couplet. Practically speaking, the risk of high climbing is a commonplace fall:

A meene estat is better to entende
Than hygh climmyng lest that oon sone descende (94).[54]

Although individual challenges to social hierarchy are in this view both possible and desirable, unmitigated advancement is not the ideal. Social advancement at every rank, from indigence to courtly favor, is fraught with troubles in this view. Several dangers are involved in advancement. First is the traditional danger to the soul from wrongful acquisition:

> Worldly richesse for to wynne wrongfully
> Dooth in dangier bringue the soule & body (48).

Christine (in the language of Woodville) cautions traditionally against pride (18) and overconfidence (21) as well. Furthermore, "Faueur gileth" and can deceive your moral judgment ("and many a tyme hit tourneth / The Right to wrong | & wrong to right retourneth," 36).

---

[54] This idea, like others in the Morale Prouerbes, is a commonplace, picked up in various forms by Barclay, Heywood, Greene, W. Wager, Davies, Minsheu, Dyer, Spenser, Barnabe Rich, W. Spelman, Haughton, and others. See Tilley s.v. climb. Christine's version is the earliest attribution in English print, though Tilley does not note its existence. Tilley does include Woodville's translation of the Dictes and Sayinges, 1477. His omission of Christine is an instance of the suppression of female authority in the canon that is unrelated to the actions of early translators/printers.

Alongside such seemingly conservative advice on the mixed nature of social mobility come hints of a progressive empathy for the poor and a critique of the rich and powerful that surpasses a traditional "blessed are the poor" idea. One proverb notes that little love is lost between classes:

> Selden is seen eny faueur to be
> Bitwix oon riche . and oon in pouerte. (68)

This problem, however, is blamed squarely on a failure of sympathy on the part of the rich: the well-fed simply will not give credence to the pains of the hungry:

> He that is fed & has his hertis luste
> What peigne the hungry hath . he wole not truste. (31)

The proverbs' cautionary emphases could be read as opposing the increasingly mobile world into which they are translated by Caxton and Woodville.

Yet finally, a few subtle alterations in the Woodville/Caxton imprint may imply a shift away from three-estate thinking about hierarchies of authority toward more contemporaneous concerns for social mobility and subjects' agency:

> Where nys Justice | that lande nor that cou[n]tre
> May not long regne in gode propserite. (5)

Here, Woodville has added the goal of national prosperity to that of national greatness and longevity in Christine's proverb, which reads:

> Pays ou lieu ou iustice ne regne
> Ne peut longtemps durer tant soit gra[n]t regne (5)

Among such traditional advice-to-princes proverbs, one finds advice that the prince's relation to the people is crucial. More precisely, the prince needs the people's approval, as the Tudors would come to understand so clearly:

> A benigne prince of gode condicions
> Draweth many oon to his opinions. (24)

In this couplet, Woodville changes what Christine has said that the prince needs: in French, a merciful and moral prince draws the hearts of the subjects and others:

> Prince ou il a clemence et bonnnes moeurs
> De ses suges et dautres trait les cuers. (24)

Woodville changes her emphasis on the love of the subject and others for the prince (*trait les cuers*, draws the hearts [of his subjects and others]) to an emphasis on the thinking of the subject. In Woodville's version, the desired result is drawing a more general "many oon" to the Prince's opinions. By removing *dautres*, Woodville removes Christine's quiet connection between foreign and domestic policy. More significantly, the relation between the English subject and monarch, unlike that between the French subject and monarch, is now a rational, not an emotive, one.

In any case, Woodville and Caxton promulgate Christine's practical advice for social relations among rulers and ruled, among high and low ranks, but it resonates differently in print than in the private script copy. There is advice here not only for princes and courtiers but also for middling sorts, aspirers, savers, spenders, young, old, women, and men. However, this potential of the proverbs for speaking to a variety of readers may not have been fully actualized until the proverbs were brought before an expanding print readership.

In summary, Caxton's paratexts recompose and preserve Christine's advisory authority even as they attend specifically to problems of authority and hierarchy raised by the new print medium. At the same time, the proverbs themselves directly advise a broadening potential readership on social inequalities, economic success, and individual aspiration in a more socially mobile world. Texts and paratexts connect: the proverbs advise on socioeconomic imbalances and disruptions that resemble the disruptions caused by sliding, colliding social and functional hierarchies of authority in the new print medium.

Third Take: Authority, Fame, and the Early Chaucerian Canon

In 1526, almost a half-century later, Richard Pynson reprinted an edited version of Caxton's text of Woodville's translation of Christine's proverbs. He places the proverbs in a collection that raises questions about individual fame and literary canonicity. The production of the volume displays Christine as a Chaucerian; connects her to the early English high canon; and, here again, shows that for these early printers, her gender in no way excluded her from systems of literary authority. The collection also rebalances the thematic emphasis of the proverbs toward its own overall theme of fame or reputation, and the placement and page layout of the "Morall Prouerbes" in the volume invite speculation about how Pynson perceived the literary properties of this work.

French-born Pynson, king's printer to both Henry VII and VIII, was responsible for including the proverbs in the Chaucerian compilation *The Boke of Fame* (STC 5088). The eight items in the *Boke of Fame*, in order, are Chaucer's *House of Fame* (A2–C3) and *Parliament of Fowls* (C4–D2); Alain Chartier's *La Belle Dame Sans Merci* (in Richard Roos's translation, here attributed to Chaucer, D2v–E3v); Chaucer's ballade on fortune that we now call "Truth" (E4); Christine's proverbs (E4–E5); the anonymous "Complaynt of Mary Magdalen" (E5–F3v); the "Letter of Dido" (F3v–F5, an anonymous English translation of Octavien de St. Gelais's version of the Ovidian epistle); and the Proverbs of Lydgate, titled *Consulo Quisquis Eris* (F5v–F6). The six extant copies of *The Boke of Fame* are bound together with *Troilus* and *Canterbury Tales*. Julia Boffey calls this "a comprehensive three-volume anthology of Chaucer's writings," which we can infer was Pynson's fairly significant effort to publish the first "Works" of an English poet, despite *The Boke of Fame*'s non-Chaucerian items.[55] Thus Christine's proverbs, first presented in a single-author collection, then printed to stand alone in Caxton's slender folio, are here re-re-presented among seven other pieces in an anthology ostensibly assembled on the basis of theme—the theme of fame—but marketed as part of a larger collection created on the basis of Chaucer's authorship. Pynson surely knew that neither of the book's ostensible principles of collection is perfectly borne out in the contents: neither theme nor authorship, in other words, explains the selections perfectly. The mixed principles of collection make it harder to assess the relation of Christine's proverbs to the whole, but the details of orthography, page layout, and binding do offer some grounds for speculation. Pynson's reprinting of Christine's proverbs in this curious book shows us additional values perceived in her text and presented to English readers.

First, the proverbs as presented here participate in early Tudor construction of an English literary canon. Pynson was not operating on a strict, modern idea of authorship: the *Boke* was marketed and titled as Chaucerian; but, as Forni and Boffey remind us, several pieces in the collection are attributed specifically to other authors (Christine and Lydgate). The volume perhaps "reflects the end of the fifteenth-century manuscript tradition of circulating Chaucer's minor poems in anthologies" (Forni 428). I would add that by 1526 the idea of a single-author printed "complete works" had been thriving for some time in France, though it was new to England; Pynson, like other early English printers, was actively engaged in bringing French texts and French literary and publishing habits to England. Regardless of the degree of literary intentionality involved in Pynson's editorial work in this volume, the results were in fact canon forming. Apparently, Pynson saw—and thus his readers would have met—Christine de Pizan and her proverbs as "Chaucerian," whatever that meant in 1526.

Although we do not now generally see Christine as Chaucerian, Pynson's epilogue to the *House of Fame* gives us a good idea of what he, at least, thought "Chaucerian" meant and thus what values guided his selection of items for the volume:

> ... whiche worke [the *House of Fame*] as me semeth | is craftely made | and digne to be writen & knowen: for he toucheth in it right great wysedome and subtell underst~dyng | and so in all his workes he excelleth in myn opinyon | all other writers in Englysshe | for he writeth no voyde wordes | but all his mater is full of hye & quicke sentence | to

---

[55] Boffey, "Richard Pynson's Book of Fame and the Letter of Dido," *Viator* 19 (1988): 339–53. Kathleen Forni, however, rejects the idea that Pynson was trying to create a canon: "I believe that [the Boke of Fame] was not an incipient single-author edition, but was modelled on ... eclectic vernacular anthologies" (433), and it would thus be "anachronistic to view this edition as an early attempt at canon formation" (434).

whom ought to be gyuen laude & praise | for his noble makyng and writyng... Also here foloweth another of his works [*Assemble of Foules*] (Ciii).

Not only does "Chaucerian" here mean pithy, wise, subtle, and densely packed with value, it means the best of *English* poetry in particular. Elsewhere Pynson explains that Chaucer was the "flour of peotes [sic] in our mother tong" (D2v). This national-literary consciousness—already a traditional matrix for and use of Chaucer in the fifteenth century, as Seth Lerer has amply demonstrated—is here promoted in print. Pynson evidently perceived these qualities—"sentence," *gravitas*, noble making, and a national exemplarity—in Christine's work as well.[56] Stylistic "Chaucerianism" in the *gravitas* of Christine's proverbs we may grant, and just as Caxton attributed "sentence" to her work, Pynson's placement of it in this collection indicates that Christine's perceived status remained high.

As much as the new context "translates" Christine into an elevated position alongside the English National Poet, it also alters again the implicit thematic of the proverbs themselves. The proverbs treat the theme of fame much as they intermittently address so many other general themes of human social life (social relations, personal behavior, handling money, getting along). Reading these proverbs out of context, in other words, one would not first think of "fame" as their main theme. But in *The Boke of Fame*, this theme attracts more attention than it would have done previously and, theoretically speaking, more "relevance" (as explained by cognitive linguists[57]). Several proverbs present what would have been in 1526 an older approach to the themes of fame and reputation: a *contemptus mundi*, traditional advice to renounce the things of the world, including the opinion of others, and to focus only on the soul's afterlife (proverbs 48, 51, and 90, for example). On the other hand, several proverbs also present what would then have been a newer approach, something like a humanist attitude toward fame, what is called in hindsight a "Renaissance" ideal of reputation.[58] Not that the period boundary is rational or real in this case, just that the long paradigm shift from what

---

[56] Boffey further explains the "Chaucerian" coherence of the volume and points out similarities in style and flavor: "[A]ll the apocryphal poems in the volume constitute responses to, or extensions of, the main themes of the canonical works"; she remarks that Christine's proverbs "reiterate and amplify" Chaucer's (340–41).

[57] Adrian Pilkington, *Poetic Effects: a Relevance Theory Perspective* (Amsterdam: J. Benjamins, 2000), building on the foundational work of Dan Sperber and Deirdre Wilson, *Relevance: communication and cognition* (Oxford: Blackwell, 1986).

[58] On Christine as a humanist, see Earl Jeffrey Richards, "Christine de Pizan, the Conventions of Courtly Diction, and Italian Humanism," *Reinterpreting Christine de Pizan*, ed. Richards (Athens, Ga: University of Georgia Press, 1992), pp. 250–271. Richards does not treat the *Prouerbes moraulx*, though there are a number of "humanist" ideas therein: Proverb 63 is pro-learning (as befits the author of the *Chemin de longue estude*), and Proverb 77 makes a distinction between opinion and knowledge. The final couplets of the piece may exhibit a tension between the renunciatory and glory-seeking imperatives.

we now call "medieval" to what we now call "Renaissance" literature involves a concomitant, messy ideological shift of focus from heavenly to earthly fame. Proverb 9, for instance, elevates a nearly classical idea of the glory and memory of virtue above even "greet estat" or rank:

> In greet estat ligth not the gloire
> But in vertu whiche worth is memoire.

Likewise, Proverb 33 is concerned with truth and renown:

> His Renon shal be good & long lasting
> That hath the fame of trouth in his deling.

Proverb 49:

> Better honneur is to haue & a good name
> Than tresor riche . And more shal dure the fame

makes explicit the concern for enduring renown. This English translation has added the idea of enduring fame to Christine's rather simpler, more traditional distinction between good name and ill-gotten gains:

> Mieulx vault honneur bonne grace et bon los
> Quauoir flourins mal acquis dire los.

In other words, there is slightly more *exegi monumentum* than *contemptus mundi* here, and when placed in a collection on "fame," such a then-current issue—perhaps more on the minds of Pynson's readers—may have appeared the more evident. Just as the theme of social mobility, while in fact no more central to Christine's work than her other themes, seemed more salient in Caxton's imprint than in the script coterie context, the motif of reputation or fame would have seemed more prominent in the Pynson production.[59] The mixed principles of authorship and theme of the *Boke* certainly indicate aspects of the "taking" of Christine's advice in early English print.

There is, however, some intriguing and highly speculative evidence in the volume's production details of a possible vacillation in Pynson's thinking about how Christine's advice was to be presented. Pynson creates a uniform blackletter typography and double-column layout for this collection of reprints. Figure 2.4 shows this to be a more crowded, more economical page layout than Caxton's

---

[59] The full theoretical and interpretive implications of collection principles are outside the scope of this chapter. See especially Richard Katz, *The Ordered Text* (New York: P. Lang, 1985); D. Fenoaltea and D. Rubin, *The Ladder of High Designs* (Charlottesville: University of Virginia Press, 1991).

format allongé, one that does not at all seek to imitate the aura of the manuscript original. The book necessarily involves catchwords, several quires, and woodcuts, clearly requiring more labor to produce than Caxton's simple four-leaf folio. Most of Pynson's changes to the proverbs are minor and orthographic in nature, although he does improve the meter and meaning in a few places.[60] Changing Caxton's title, *The Morale Prouerbes of Cristyne*, to the *Morall Prouerbes of Christyne* seems inconsequential, yet it does preserve her visible authorship.[61] Despite Pynson's larger project and his attention to orthography, the lack of spacing and his willingness to orphan couplets at column and page breaks show him to be no more interested than Caxton had been in the couplet as a unit of poetic discourse (see Figures 2.3 and 2.4). Elsewhere in *The Boke of Fame* Pynson

---

[60] His spelling changes may be clues to general changes in English orthographic habits between 1478 and 1526 or, more likely, to differences between Caxton's and Pynson's house styles. Pynson uses uppercase letters only at the beginning of lines, while Caxton's type 2 allows uppercase R and I within the line. Caxton has some caesura marks, but Pynson adds | to most lines, without an obviously discernible metrical principle. Some spelling changes in the Pynson imprint are consistent: *wyll* instead of *wole*; *it* instead of *hit*; *honour* instead of *honneur* (perhaps moving away from French forms; likewise *labour* instead of *labeur*). Some of the changes indicate semantic attention to the text: Pynson corrects Caxton's erroneous *cautele* to *cautelte* at couplet 32 and fixes word order as well. Caxton's couplet 32 reads:

Falsehede is not to cautele soo applied
But by some folkis somtyme hit is aspied

Pynson's reads:

Falseheed is nat to cautelte so applyed
But by some folkes | it is somtyme espyed

Likewise, in couplet 35, Pynson changes the word enhance to advance. Instead of Caxton's "Whoo wole him self to greet estat enhance / Muste byfore be acqueinted with suffrance," Pynson's text improves the sense with "Who wyll hym selfe to great estate auaunce / Must afore | be acqueynted with suffraunce." In couplet 40, Pynson changes Caxton's "He that secheth often other to blame / Yiueth right cause to here of him the fame" to "Giveth right cause | to here of hiselfe y` same." "Ful many an heuy charge" becomes in 1526 "Full many a heuy charge." In one instance, Pynson's text alters the meter. In couplet 94, "A meene estat is better to entende / Than hygh clymmyng lest that oon sone descende," the second line's decasyllable loses one syllable with "A meane estate is better to entende / Than high clymbyng | lest one sone discēde."

[61] Chaucer's verses on fortune are announced (fol. E3v) as "certayne morall prouerbes of the foresayd Geffray Chaucers doyng," and Christine's proverbs follow Chaucer's on E4–5. The announcement could be read as an effort to attribute authorship of Christine's proverbs to Chaucer, but it seems intended to apply only to the ballade "Truth" itself and in my view does not in any way deauthorize Christine, given the titling on E4.

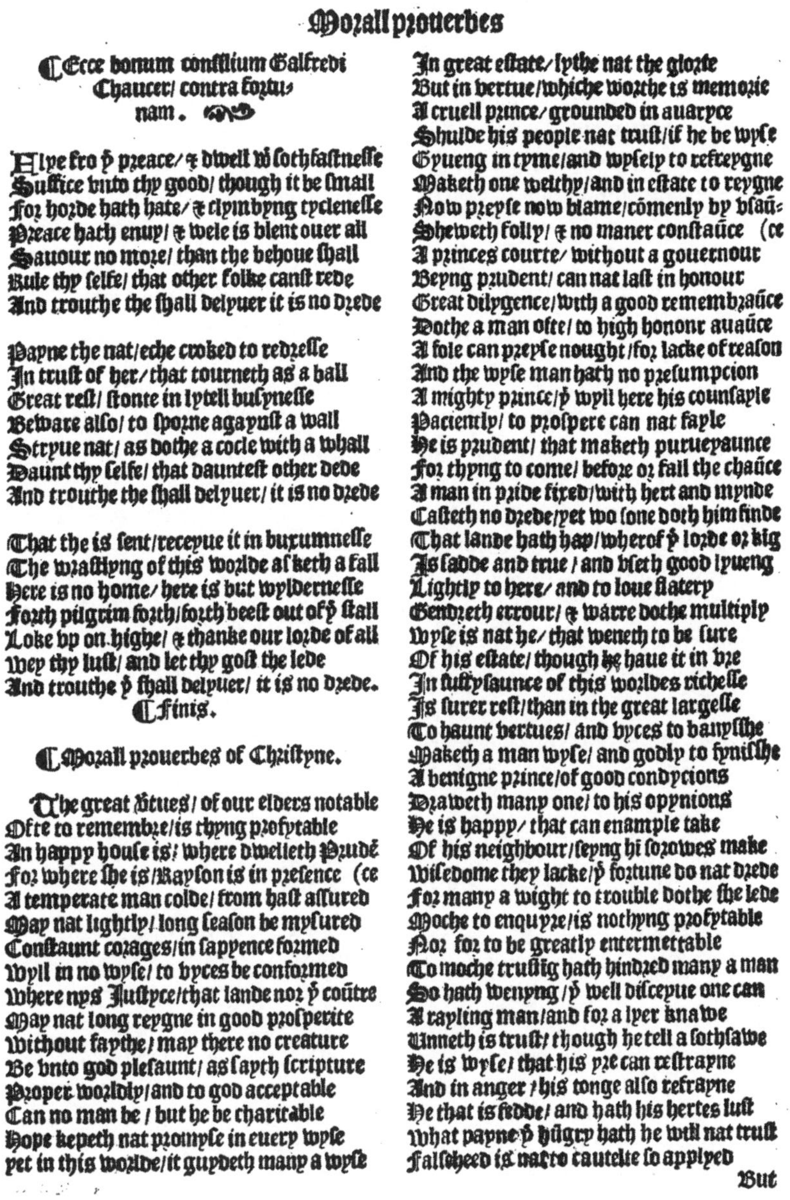

Morall prouerbes

Ecce bonum consilium Galfredi Chaucer/ contra fortunam.

Flye fro þ preace/ & dwell wt sothfastnesse
Suffice vnto thy good/ though it be small
For horde hath hate/ & clymbyng tyclenesse
Preace hath enuy/ & wele is blent ouer all
Sauour no more/ than the behoue shall
Rule thy selfe/ that other folke canst rede
And trouthe the shall delyuer it is no drede

Payne the nat/ eche croked to redresse
In trust of her/ that tourneth as a ball
Great rest/ stonte in lytell busynesse
Beware also/ to sporne agaynst a wall
Stryue nat/ as dothe a cocle with a whall
Daunt thy selfe/ that dauntest other dede
And trouthe the shall delyuer/ it is no drede

That the is sent/ receyue it in buxumnesse
The wrastlyng of this worlde asketh a fall
Here is no home/ here is but wyldernesse
Forth pilgrim forth/ forth beest out of þ stall
Loke vp on highe/ & thanke our lorde of all
Wey thy lust/ and let thy gost the lede
And trouthe þ shall delyuer/ it is no drede.
Finis.

Morall prouerbes of Christyne.

The great vtues/ of our elders notable
Ofte to remembre/ is thyng profytable
In happy house is/ where dwelleth Prude
For where she is/ Rayson is in presence (ce
A temperate man colde/ from hast assured
May nat lightly/ long season be mysured
Constaunt corages/ in sappence formed
Wyll in no wyse/ to vyces be conformed
Where nys Justyce/ that lande nor þ coūtre
May nat long reygne in good prosperite
Without faythe/ may there no creature
Be vnto god plesaunt/ as sayth scripture
Proper worldly/ and to god acceptable
Can no man be / but he be charitable
Hope kepeth nat promyse in euery wyse
Yet in this worlde/ it guydeth many a wyse

In great estate/ lythe nat the glorie
But in vertue/ whiche worthe is memorie
A cruell prince/ grounded in auaryce
Shulde his people nat trust/ if he be wyse
Gyueng in tyme/ and wysely to refreyne
Maketh one welthy/ and in estate to reygne
Now preyse now blame/ comenly by bsau-
Sheweth folly/ & no maner constaūce (ce
A princes courte/ without a gouernour
Beyng prudent/ can nat last in honour
Great dilygence/ with a good remembraūce
Dothe a man ofte/ to high honour auaūce
A fole can preyse nought/ for lacke of reason
And the wyse man hath no presumpcion
A mighty prince/ þ wyl here his counsayle
Paciently/ to prospere can nat fayle
He is prudent/ that maketh purueyaunce
For thyng to come/ before or fall the chaūce
A man in pride fixed/ with hert and mynde
Casteth no drede/ yet wo sone doth hym finde
That lande hath hap/ wherof þ lorde or kig
Is sadde and true / and vseth good lyueng
Lightly to here/ and to loue flatery
Gendreth errour/ & warre dothe multiply
Wyse is nat he/ that weneth to be sure
Of his estate/ though he haue it in vre
In suffysaunce of this worldes richesse
Is surer rest/ than in the great largesse
To haunt vertues/ and vyces to banyshe
Maketh a man wyse/ and godly to fynishe
A benigne prince/ of good condycions
Draweth many one/ to his oppnions
He is happy/ that can enample take
Of his neighbour/ seyng hi sorowes make
Wysedome they lacke/ þ fortune do nat drede
For many a wight to trouble dothe she lede
Moche to enquyre/ is nothyng profytable
Nor for to be greatly entermettable
To moche trustig hath hindred many a man
So hath wenyng/ þ well discryue one can
A rayling man/ and for a lyer knawe
Vnneth is trust/ though he tell a sothsawe
He is wyse/ that his pre can restrayne
And in anger / his tonge also refrayne
He that is sadde/ and hath his hertes lust
What payne þ hūgry hath he wyll nat trust
Falsheed is nat to cautelie so applyed
But

Fig. 2.4 Christine de Pizan, "Morall prouerbes of Christyne," in *The Boke of Fame* (London: Pynson, 1526), [E4].

breaks couplets and stanzas between columns and also between pages. Evidently he was not concerned with the capacity of visual presentation to support poetics or, rather, had not chosen to use page layout to support literary significance, as mid- and late-century printers would do.[62] The page layout of the "Morall Prouerbes," furthermore, invites inquiry about Pynson's sense of their "fit" in the volume as a whole, his sense of what Christine's literary value would be for English readers. It may be that at some point during the production of *The Boke of Fame*, Pynson envisioned Christine's proverbs as the last item in the volume but later saw fit to add other items. This would indicate both Pynson's real literary appreciation of the closural and metatextual properties of this work as well as another elevation of Christine's status.

What follows here is my highly inferential speculation about what the odd layout of the last page of the "Morall Prouerbes" may imply. There is probably no evidence that can decide these questions, but I have not seen them raised elsewhere in these terms. Boffey and Forni each remark on the odd column layout on the second page of the "Morall Prouerbes," in which the left-hand column contains 25 lines, continued at the top of the right-hand column for 25 lines (24 and a space; see Figure 2.5). Both columns on the lower half of the page are devoted to the "Complaynt of Mary Magdalen." Forni mentions that this layout may have resulted from the removal of Caxton's colophon stanzas since their regnal years and printer's identifications were obsolete in the new context. She suggests that the woodcut for "Magdalen" was inserted to replace Caxton's verses (431). I discuss the results of any such replacement below but here speculate that the layout might indicate instead a change of plan at some intermediate stage of printing. The final page of this *Boke*, F6r, ends with a very similar column division, 24 lines on left and right, the layout of a "last" item, followed by "Imprinted at London in Fletestrete by Richarde Pynson | printer to the kynges most noble grace." The last page of the "Morall Prouerbes," that is, is laid out as if it were to have been a final page for the volume. Boffey is surely right to think that Pynson's work in creating this collection of reprints may have been "more opportunistic than innovative" (341), and in such a case it is possible that the "Morall Prouerbes" might have been

---

[62] Printers of, for example, Du Bellay's *Antiquitez* (Paris, 1558), in which an architectural page layout works with varying meter in the sequence, or Spenser's *Amoretti* (London: Ponsonby, 1595), in which printing one sonnet per page emphasizes the singularity of each sonnet and slows the reading experience, much as final hexameter lines force a reader's attention to each stanza of the *Faerie Queene*. At midcentury in France, the Estiennes were already implicitly connecting typography and poetics, as did Watson in the 1582 *Hekatompathia*. F. Joukovsky's edition of Du Bellay's poems, *Les Antiquitez; Les Regrets* (Paris: Flammarion, 1994), preserves and discusses this aspect of the text. See also Coldiron, "How Spenser Excavates Du Bellay's Antiquitez," *JEGP* (*Journal of English and Germanic Philology*) 101.1 (January 2001): 41–67, on these layouts. Earlier English printers seem to stress economy of layout and content rather than the aesthetics of the page and its intersection with poetics.

The cōplaynt of Mary Magdaleyne

Humylite is a thyng cōmendable
He is a fole/ that dothe his charge enhaūce
Upon promyse/ without other substaunce
It syteeth nat a man to diffame
For vpon hym selfe/ shall retourne ẏ blame
For to forgete a gyste or curtesy
Sheweth ingratytude euidently
Sured maner/ and fewe wordes well set
In women dothe ryghtwell / where they be
Seruyce in court is no sure heritage (met
It fayleth ofte/with lytell auauntage
He that spurneth a nall with violence
Unto hym selfe/dothe most grefe and offēce
To tourne to iape an iniury or a wrong
Is great wysedome to be vsed among.
Goodly reasons nat well taken ne cōstrude
Semeth floures cast among beestes rude
A wretchfull man or one in gelousye
Aught haue no trust/for often they wyll lye
Cruell spekyng in a mater heynous
Asketh answere angry and dispytous
There can no good endure season ne space
But onely suche/ as come by goddes grace
Idell pleasures vsed custumably   (thy
Be harde to chaūge tho they be blame wor

He that loueth euell tales to reporte
To make debate/ semeth well his disporte
Necessyte/pouert/and indigence
Causeth many great inconuenyence
A meane estate is better to entende
Than high clymbyng / lest one sone discēde
Right to release somtyme is no dotage
So that it be for a more auauntage
In well doyng/ hauyng a true renoun
Bryngeth a man to good conclusyoun
Forgetyng god/ for this worldes richesse
Sheweth no faith/but slouth & gret latches
There is nothyng so riche I you ensure
As the seruyce of god our creature
Lytell baylleth good ensample to se
For hym that wyll nat the contrary sye
Though that dethe to vs be lamentable
It to remembre/ is thyng most conuenable
Thende dothe shewe euery worke as it is
Wo may he be/ that to god endeth mys.

¶ Thus endeth the morall prouerbes/
and here foloweth the complaynt
of Mary Magdaleyne.

My lorde is gone/ẏ here in graue was laid
After his great passyon/and dethe cruell
Who hath hym thus agayne betrayd ?
Or what man here about can me tell ?
Where he is become/the prince of Israell
Jesus of Nazareth/my goostly socour
My parfyte loue/and hope of all honour

What creature hath hym hens caryed ?
Or howe might this/so sodainly befall ?
I wolde I had here with hym taryed
And so shulde I haue had my purpose all
I bought oyntmētes / full precious & ryall
Wherwith I hoped his corps to anoynted
But he this gone/ my mide is dispoynted

Plōged in the wawe of mortall distresse
Alas for wo/ to whom shall I complayne
Or who shall deuoyde/this great heuynesse
Fro me/ wofull Mary Magdaleyne (yne
My lorde is gone/alas who wroght this tre
This soden chaūce percech my hert so depe
That nothyng can I do/but wayle & wepe

Whyle I therfore aduertise/ and beholde
This pitous chaunce/here in my presence
Full litell marueyle/though my hert be colde
Consydryng lo/ my lordes absence
Alas that I/ so full of neglygence
Shulde be foūde/bycause I come so late
All men may say/ that I am infortunate
                                    Cause

Fig. 2.5   Christine de Pizan, "Morall prouerbes of Christyne" in *The Boke of Fame* (London: Pynson, 1526), [E5].

at some earlier point intended to end the volume until further opportunities arose in the form of the subsequent items. Indeed, the last couplets of Christine's poem are appropriately valedictory for such a terminal position:

Though that the deeth to vs be lamentable
Hit to remembre is thing most conuenable

Thende dooth shewe euery werk | as hit is
Woo may he be . that to god endeth mys.

The lines carry a subtle metatextual self-reference, inviting attention, at the end of a "work," to the quality of that work. At some point after setting the two balanced columns (saving four lines for a colophon), but before setting the colophon, Pynson may have decided not to end the volume with these lines but instead to add (and set) the subsequent items, "The Complaynt of Mary Magdalen," "The Letter of Dido," and Lydgate's proverbs. The initial plan of the volume's contents would have been *House of Fame*, *Assemble of Foules*, *Belle Dame Sans Merci*, "Truth," and, as finale, Christine's "Morall Prouerbes." In such a plan, Christine's general advice would have completed a Chaucerian gallery of meditations on reputation, choices in love (especially women's choices), and fortune. If we speculate that the plan of the volume changed, we may find evidence here of a loosening of both the criteria for its collection—authorship and theme—since Christine's advice is in fact followed with two anonymous (female) laments and capped with counsel from the Monk of Bury. Imagine a moment of decision at which Pynson has set the "Morall Prouerbes" with that final, balanced-column page layout and is ready to finish setting the page with a closural colophon. Then, for whatever "opportunistic" reason, he sees fit to make a longer volume. Christine's proverbs, first envisioned as closural, may then have served as a stimulus or transition into the particular additions, and with Lydgate's, would have provided balance, a practical-moral frame. Christine's final verses treat the endings of things, an idea now taken up not for its closural function but to introduce the two "death-songs." The voices of Magdalen and Dido then present negative exempla of "ends." Each poem represents itself as a woman's final lament before dying, making poetic and antiexemplary sense of their excessively passionate, woeful, and famous endings. The volume then closes with further cautionary proverbs from Lydgate about how to conduct oneself while still living, introduced as "A lytell exortacion howe folke shulde behaue them selfe in all côpanyes."

If my admittedly very speculative explanation for the odd page layout is correct, Christine's wisdom was initially taken up for its closural and metatextual value but was finally used as a kind of hinge for the volume. As the volume "turns" toward its close, the proverbs not only "reiterate and amplify" Chaucer's moral wisdom, as Boffey says, they also close the Chaucerian-authored pieces and frame, with Lydgate's advice, the latter half of the *Boke*. In an advisory female voice, they introduce the two famous examples of female passion, one sacred, one secular, just as in her own *Epistre Othea*, framing female wisdom introduces sacred and secular exempla. Chaucerian poetry about fame, then, is framed and "centered" with Christine's advice.

The layout and quire construction may or may not imply such an evolution of Pynson's plan for the *Boke*'s contents, and the proverbs' role in any such change of plan is necessarily imaginative. But whether Christine's "Morall Prouerbes" figured in Pynson's plan for closing the *Boke* or were simply envisioned from the start as a (literally) central item in it, Christine's authority and authorship remain strong here. She is placed with Chaucer and Lydgate in an important volume. The removal of Caxton's colophon does, however, remove all reminder of the translator's work (as well as the work of the previous printer, witnessing scribe, and patron). Pynson's presentation remystifies or at least de-archaeologizes the origins of Christine's text, collapsing the multiple roles involved in the text's transmission that Caxton had taken such care to elucidate. It is not that Pynson is shy about his role in the volume: he is willing to announce his work in making the *Boke* in his own colophons, as in his "enuoy de limprimeur" following the *Belle Dame Sans Merci* and in his almost chatty prose epilogue following the *House of Fame*. But here, while Christine's authorship is still secure, the carefully articulated layers of participation in the text—the genealogy of the text, so clear in Caxton's imprint—are elided. Christine's Frenchness is fully absorbed into "oure" Englishness under a specifically Chaucerian rubric. The appropriation of "Frenchness" into "Englishness" is complete in this presentation, and it is connected with an early effort to establish a national poetry, the collected works of the "flower of the mother tongue." To a much greater degree than theme or content, the idea of the *Boke* and its paratexts connect Christine's authorship to English literary fame. Her authorship was relevant for Pynson's audience around 1526 in ways that it had not been for Caxton's audience of 1478 or for the readership of BL Harley 4431 circa 1405.

Outtakes and Postscripts: The *Morale Prouerbes* in the Sixteenth Century

The impulse to collect and publish pithy moral advice does not disappear after Pynson. The actions of these early printers on Christine's text in some ways represent or even predict trends to follow. *The Morale Prouerbes of Cristyne*, along with the *Dictes and Sayinges of the Philosophres* (1477), also translated from French by Anthony Woodville, form the earliest examples printed in England of what would become a very widely printed kind of verse literature, proverbial or epigrammatic verse.[63] Such verse—gnomic, memorable, useful couplets grounded in social experience and inherited beliefs—found broad audiences throughout the period.[64] Later collections of verse proverbs include seven editions of William Baldwin's *A treatise of Morall Phylosophie, contaynyng the sayinges of the wyse, gathered and Englyshed* ... (in four books, and later in seven books; editions appeared in 1547, 1550, 1552, 1553, 1555, 1556, and 1557)[65] and, of course, John Heywood's copious epigrams, *Two hundred Epigrammes, upon two hundred prouerbes, with a thyrde hundred newely added and made* ... (Berthelet, 1555). Like so many earlier Tudor writers, Heywood also translates from French (his *Mery Play* is the subject of Chapter 6 to follow).

Although such imprints were important throughout the period, the verse-proverb habit in England did not find itself restricted to wisdom collections alone. Verse proverbs like Christine's made their way individually and in small clusters into all kinds of imprints aimed at broad and varied readerships. Some of these can be seen as part of a prevalent mode in early English verse that I am calling elsewhere "low georgic"—not Virgilian or even Hesiodic georgic, but practical literature designed to guide and advise on matters of daily living.[66] Even Tottel's

---

[63] See J. S. Gill, "How Hermes Trismegistus was Introduced to Renaissance England," *Journal of the Warburg and Courtauld Institute* 47 (1984): 222–5. For a structural analysis of proverbs, see Alan Dundes's classic essay, "On the Structure of the Proverb," in *The Wisdom of Many: Essays on the Proverb*, eds Alan Dundes and Wolfgang Meider (New York: Garland, 1981), pp. 43–64. For still-valuable general background to proverbs, see Grace Frank, "Proverbs in Medieval Literature," *MLN* 58 (1943): 508–15, or David Heft's dissertation, "Proverbs and Sentences in Fifteenth-Century French Poetry" (New York University, 1941), or the 12-page abridgement of it (NY: Washington Square, 1942). See Meider, *International Proverb Scholarship: An Annotated Bibliography, and Supplements*, for further resources; Tilley for sixteenth- and seventeenth-century proverbs; Whiting for earlier proverbs; and Philippe Moret's excellent long historical survey of the French traditions, *Tradition et Modernité de l'aphorisme* (Geneve: Droz, 1997), especially pp. 21–83.

[64] Early collections after Christine's include the satiric imprints of 1492 and 1529, known as "Solomon and Marcolphus," and the proverbs spoken between King Boccus and Sydracke. De Worde makes two editions of *The prouerbes of Lydgate* (1510? and 1520?) and two of *Stans puer ad mensam* (1510? and c.1520), of which I. Redman at Southwerk makes another printing. Ostensibly a book of table manners, the *Stans puer ad mensam* is a book of instruction for youth that is not unlike Christine's *Enseignements moraux*, which sometimes appeared with or near the *Prouerbes moraulx* (in BL Harley 4431 and BNF 605, for example).

[65] On which see Curt F. Bühler, "A Survival from the Middle Ages: William Baldwin's Use of the 'Dictes and Sayings,'" *Speculum* 23 (1948): 76–80.

[66] Examples of this "low-georgic" mode in which verse proverbs are found include an early and often reprinted book of hawking (*The bokys of haukyng and huntyng and also of cootarmuris and here now endeth the boke of blasyng of armys translatyt and compylyt togedyr*, 1486; later imprints appear in 1496, 1518, 1547, 1550, 1556, and 1558); *A glasse for housholders* (R. Grafton, 1542); and *A werke forhousholders ... Gadred and set forth*

Songes and Sonets has a series of proverbs ("It is no fire that gives no heat," 24 lines of proverbs beginning on fol. T1v). Proverbial mode is also important, it seems to me, in the captioning of woodcuts and in the *impresas* and mottoes of the emblem tradition. Not directly related to the foundational imprint under discussion here, and not strictly "proverbial" in the sense of the other examples mentioned here, still such pithy couplets make a point, memorably. Christine's proverbs antedate the Erasmus craze, too: the first *Adages* in English were published in 1539 (STC 10437). It is clear that English verse proverbs, beginning with Woodville's translations from French, enjoyed a wide dispersal and steady currency throughout the period and were seen as valuable or appropriate for a range of publications. Gender and gender relations, of course, were among the many general topics treated in proverbial literature; a Frenchwoman's authority helped inaugurate the mode in English print.

Furthermore, these numerous verse proverbs import not just content but the habit of aphoristic verse, and they disperse the habit of the pithy couplet through a number of printed venues and kinds. Verse proverbs may set an early taste for the Euphuistic style so favored in the later Renaissance and may be related to a more general formal tendency during the period toward poetic compression, what Alastair Fowler has called the "epigram shift." Verse proverbs may also prepare for the impulse in the Renaissance sonnet to close with a summative or "turn-away" couplet. Caxton's early printings of verse proverbs translated from French probably helped condition readers to this lasting English stylistic habit.

In any case, each text of Christine's proverbs available to early modern English readers appears to have had slightly different perceived value. Clearly, the editions of 1478 and 1526 appropriate Christine's advice for wider and less homogeneous distribution than was possible in manuscript. Caxton's and Pynson's respective presentational strategies affirm Christine's authorship for a widening readership, but each early imprint appropriates slightly different aspects of her advisory authority for the new literary systems developing in England. The differences in presentation among these three appearances of the proverbs let us see the changing value and emphasis this work was to have for English readers. The two printers'

... Newly corrected ... with an addicion of policy for housholdying (de Worde, 1530, and five subsequent editions in 1531, 1533, and 1537). The seven editions of John Fitzherbert's book of husbandry printed between 1523 and 1555 contain verse proverbs but also include other verses translated from French, part of a more general uptake of French practical verse during the period. The many shepherd's calendars in which verse proverbs appear offer multipurpose guidance to English readers and also form the basis of later Renaissance literary forms. Several early shepherd's calendars (STC numbers 22410–12, for example) include proverbial verses, one of which echoes Woodville's opening genealogical gesture: "A fewe of the prouerbes of our predecessoures, ryght engenyous and cautelous...These prouerbes be good to merke" (44 lines, sig Y3–4). Certain less directly didactic books also include verse proverbs of the sort Caxton's Christine imprint initiated. *Howleglas*, the jestbook, and the *Temple of Bras*, a Chaucerian collection, also include proverbial verses, despite their primarily ludic or nondidactic purposes.

presentational strategies parallel the concerns of their respective moments and thus subtly highlight certain features of the proverbs: the authoritative and singular advisor, Christine, whose proverbs speak to shifting structures of authority (1478); and the "Chaucerian" Christine (1526), whose proverbs on individual fame join the early English literary canon as it is being formed.

Chapter 3
"La Femme Replique": Debating Women in English Translation

Long before the notorious, mid-sixteenth-century English "pamphlet wars" debating the nature of women, several poetic translations printed in the 1520s brought the topic before the English reading public. This chapter takes up three long French-born poems on the topic, selected to show the considerable range of the printers' and translators' interventions. The *Interlocucyon, with an argument, betwyxt man and woman* ... (1525), translates a witty, sophisticated gender-debate poem; the *Letter of Dydo to Eneas* (1526) is a paradigmatic complaint against a man's betrayal; and the *Beaute of Women* (1525, 1540) is a proscriptive, didactic poem that anticipates certain features of later printed prose conduct books. Although these poems apparently found healthy readerships, even the one that is best known now, the anonymous *Interlocucyon*, is not often read now even among scholars.[1] In each case, questions about women's worth are posed in explicit or implicit contrast to assumptions about men's worth. And in each case the translators and printers make significant interventions—both visual and verbal—changing the implications of the French material.

The present chapter offers a comparative reading of the French and English versions of the *Interlocucyon* debate and then considers two of its near-contemporaries, the *Letter of Dydo to Eneas* and the *Beaute of Women*, as one-sided arguments, near-debates, or monologues. These translated poems join the long, pan-European discussions about the nature and goodness of women, but each handles French material very differently. The *Interlocucyon* features a formal debate between a man and a woman, but the woman's part includes a long, final speech indicting an antiexemplary catalogue of bad men. The paratexts added to the English version advertise this poem's inflammatory gender-debate content and try to position that content in specifically literary traditions. The *Letter of Dydo* amplifies and personalizes the voice of the woman in the *Interlocucyon*, speaking the woman's side of a prototypical gender problem, the betrayal of a woman by

---

[1] Michel-André Bossy, for instance, has demonstrated several specific links between this poem and Christine de Pizan's *Epistre au dieu d'amours*; see "Woman's Plain Talk in *Le Débat de l'omme et de la femme* by Guillaume Alexis," *Fifteenth Century Studies* 16 (1990): 23-41; see pp. 23, 29, 32, 34, and 40n27. See also Bornstein and Bawcutt as discussed below and notes 2 and 3. Beyond Bossy's and Bornstein's specific links, this poem does not revisit Christine's literary-hermeneutic arguments but instead depends on more traditional and broadly dialectical elements debating the nature of women.

an untrustworthy man. The *Letter*'s betrayer, Aeneas, is also protoypical, at once an exemplary nation-founding hero of Tudor mythography and here a negative exemplum of perfidy. This one-sided poem features a highly sympathetic, Ovidian Dido and, like its French and Latin sources, gives no voice to Aeneas at all. Yet the poem's paratexts and the printing context for the poem utterly change the meaning of the translation itself. The speaking woman's indictment of male perfidy is here reframed to promote female chastity and to restrict female sexual desire. Finally, in contrast with the powerful female speeches in the *Interlocucyon* and the *Letter*, the *Beaute of Women* not only speaks exclusively in a male voice but also issues proscriptive, reifying pronouncements about how women must be silent—and how they are supposed to look and act. The heavily moralizing, misogynistic content of the poem does not seem unusual or noteworthy until we see the complete, cross-cultural printing context. Then we can see how the printers' actions variously "translate" this material on gender, taking it rather far from its prior meanings. Unlike what scholars have previously thought, this poem turns out to have been made from a composite of French sources; where the printer and translator of the *Letter of Dydo* uses the paratexts to reframe the poem's meaning, the *Beaute of Women* translator-printer acts as a *compilator* or *cento*-writer who shifts the meaning of the material by means of selection, omission, and juxtaposition.

This chapter, then, examines what the voicing of "the woman's part" of gender debates—or the silencing of the woman's part—achieves in these translations and how the printers' actions matter. The poems bring only some elements of the old *querelle* to English readers in the new culture and medium. In these poems, the printers' interventions matter at least as much as the content of the translations; that is, the paratexts matter as much as the texts. The printers' interventions change how the nature of women is characterized and interrogated, and they do so particularly by changing the meaning, value, and prominence of female speech in these poems.

Wynkyn de Worde's *Interlocucyon*

The *Interlocucyon*, early and traditional as it is, never elevates gender debating to the interpretive level of Christine's *querelle*. Yet in its English context—that is, alongside such related, contemporaneous verse translations as this chapter treats—its implications seem nearly protofeminist. One of Wynkyn de Worde's many imprints about women and gender relations, this work is a translation of *Le Débat de l'homme et de la femme* written by Guillaume Alexis in about 1460 and printed at least seven times in French before 1530.[2] Unlike most of Wynkyn's other output,

---

[2] Alexis, *Le debat de lome et de la fe[m]me* (Lyon: Pierre Mareschal s.d. [v. 1490]); *Le debat de lhomme et de la femme* (Paris: Trepperel 1493); *Sensuyt le debat de lomme et de la femme* (Paris: Jehan Trepperel, s.d. but probably c. 1500); *Le debat* ... (Paris: Guillaume Nyverd, s.d. [v. 1520]); *Le debat* ... (Paris: s.n., s.d. but c. 1520); Another (Paris: s.n. s.d.,

however, this little book is notable for giving the woman the last, longest word. Well before Gosynhill's *Schole House for Women* and *Mulierum Paean* break out the traditional arguments into separate he-said/she-said treatises, this work voices a male and female speaker in direct debate, flinging stanzas at each other inside one poetic work. The work's early appropriation of French gender discourses, and particularly its amplified female interlocutor, anticipates the better-known English debates of the mid and late sixteenth century.[3]

Bossy and Diane Bornstein have provided excellent, foundational readings of this work, well worth brief review here. Bornstein summarizes the positions of the two speakers:

In the debate both the man and the woman base their arguments mainly on scriptural authority. The man begins with Eve to demonstrate the evil of women. In turn the woman counters with the Virgin Mary, an example she uses several times ... The man uses all the traditional anti-feminist jibes: women paint their faces and waste money on

---

c. 1525), fuller bibliographical details, pp. 127-131 in *Oeuvres Poétiques de Guillaume Alexis, Prieur de Bucy*, eds Arthur Piaget and Émile Picot (Paris: Firmin Didot, 1896–1908; rpt SATF 1968), I. 121–44. The English translation is *Here begynneth an interlocucyon, with an argument, betwyxt man and woman* ... (London: Wynkyn de Worde, 1525), facs. rpt., ed. Diane Bornstein, *The Feminist Controversy of the Renaissance: Guillaume Alexis, An Argument Betwixt Man and Woman (1525); Sir Thomas Elyot, The Defence of Good Women (1545); Henricius Cornelius Agrippa, Female Pre-Eminence (1670)* (Delmar, NY: Scholars' Facsimiles and Reprints, 1980); Piaget and Picot also reprint the English poem, pp. 145–55. Priscilla Bawcutt explores a Scots translation written in the Aberdeen Sasine Register II. 480-1 (1502–1507) and explains that "the two works [in English and Scots] were translated independently" from the French (40), offers information about dating and authorship, and clarifies several readings. She finds that this abbreviated, reordered version "appears more misogynistic than the French work. It not only displaces the woman's climactic speech from its final position, but ends with the man's denunciation of female trickery" (39); "An Early Scottish Debate Poem on Women," *Scottish Literary Journal* 23. 2 (Nov 1996): 35–42.

[3] Diane Bornstein, ed., pp. v–vii and xi, places the work in the venerable line of "woman question" publications, between classical or medieval tracts and Renaissance prose treatises—between, on the one hand, Jerome, Theophrastus, Mathéolus, Deschamps, Boccaccio, Christine de Pizan, and Map, and on the other, Gosynhill's pamphlets, Elyot's *Defence of Good Women*, the *Prayse of All Women*, the *Treatise of Nobilitie and Excellencie of Woman Kynde*, and several others. See also, Blamires, Wright, Utley, especially pp. 339–41, and Gay; Linda Woodbridge, *Women and the English Renaissance: Literature and the Nature of Womankind, 1540–1620*. (Urbana and Chicago: University of Illinois Press, 1984); Pamela Joseph Benson, *The Invention of the Renaissance Woman* (University Park, Pa: Pennsylvania State UP, 1992); Katherine Henderson and Barbara McManus, *Half Humankind: Contexts and Texts of the Controversy about Women in England, 1540–1640* (Urbana and Chicago: University of Illinois Press, 1984); Lloyd Davis, ed., *Sexuality and Gender in the English Renaissance: An Annotated Edition of Contemporary Documents* (New York: Garland, 1998).

clothes; they deceive men, flatter, and lie; they speak too much, scold, gossip, contradict men, and reveal their secrets; they are avaricious ... The woman ... [enumerates] the virtues of women: they are chaste, religious, and merciful; they are good nurses and mothers; and they are generous patrons when they own property. (viii)

Bornstein points out that "for most of the debate the woman is on the defensive" until the long final section in which "she cites a series of negative male examples ... men are aggressive, violent, deceitful, and ungrateful; they often act as murderers, tyrants, criminals, and war mongers; instead of slandering women, who are their mothers and nurses, they should be grateful to them" (ix). Bossy, writing about the French version, explains that while Alexis's oeuvre is generally antifeminist, this work defends women, even though it appears to debate the question (23–5). The long final section's unanswered condemnations of men and the French version's verbally adept female speaker create this unusual result.

In their content, the French and English versions differ very little. But even while preserving similar content, the English version makes meaningful changes to the French text. Paratextual changes, for instance, may not alter a work's content, but they matter a great deal in how French poems are conveyed to English readers. In the *Interlocucyon*, the printer and translator create a complex and specifically literary set of frames for the English debate. Visual paratexts also imply certain interpretive shifts.

First, in the verbal paratexts, the translation passes itself off as an English work: there is no mention of a source or of the French version. (In Lawrence Venuti's terms, it is an "invisible" translation, pretending to be a native; this debate is to be understood as English.) While most extant French imprints include in the title or colophon Guillaume Alexis's name and status as a monk (the "Prieur de Bucy"), Wynkyn de Worde's edition bears no author's name. Many of Wynkyn's other translated imprints are invisible in the same way, so this suppression of Frenchness and of authorship is not unusual in this printer's output.[4] Second, Wynkyn's habit, like that of many early English printer-translators, was to adopt not only texts but layouts, page design, woodcuts, book design, typefaces, and so on; this imprint is no exception. The English *Interlocucyon* does include two woodcuts, and Wynkyn may have taken the overall design concept from one of the many French imprints of Alexis's *Débat*.[5] The title cut Wynkyn uses (Figure 3.1; cover illustration)

---

[4] I think Martha Driver's point about printer Robert Wyer, explained in Chapter 2, regarding the tendency of early printers to suppress source authorship, extends to Wynkyn as well.

[5] It might not be possible to determine with certainty which one. The title cut to the edition of c. 1490 (Lyon) shows a courtly interior scene between an aristocratic man and woman. The title cut to the first Paris edition by J. Trepperel, c. 1493, offers a typical border design with large-lettered inscription moving clockwise from bottom left. The second Trepperel edition, Paris c. 1500, seems to me the best candidate for the imprint imitated by the English printers: the title cut features two factotum figures separated by a tree. An

Fig. 3.1   Anon., *Interlocucyon* ... (London: de Worde, 1525). Title page.

is clearly a composite of common factotum elements (that is, interchangeable and often reused figures), each of which appears elsewhere. For instance, the factotum woman shown here is the one Martha Driver brilliantly reveals in *The Image in Print* as an "everywoman" figure (64–74). The man shown here also appears in the title cut of another gender-related debate not treated in this chapter (*The Seyenges of Salomon and Marcolphus*, 1529) as well as in *The complaynt of a louers lyfe* (c. 1531) and the *The Prouerbes of Lydgate* (c. 1510?).[6] This figure is thus an interchangeable "debating" figure, a variation on the "everyman" and other figures Driver establishes as visual types created by De Worde's use of factotum and composite images (61–74). Bornstein thinks the title cut to the *Interlocucyon* signals the printer's understanding of the work as antifeminist (vii). I think it signals instead his normal practice of reusing visual elements and of using title images to advertise content. In this case the title image is a very literal advertisement that the work is a male-female debate. Clearly, the female figure in debate position places the poem as one of his several "woman question" publications. What is less certain is whether the title cut's reused male figure might further place the *Interlocucyon* in another topic area of interest to De Worde's readers—common or proverbial wisdom. Did De Worde calculate that customers would recognize these reused factotum images as signals of genre and theme, or were these simply the figures at hand? It is probably not possible to know at what point such images' associations with a theme or genre actually render them functional signals to a readership, but the frequent reuse does suggest that Driver's "everywoman" and perhaps also this advisory male debater might well have been taking on such functions in the 1520s.

What is more provocative than the thematic signals the printer may or may not be sending to the reading public is an irregularity in the title woodcut. Several colleagues have suggested to me that the blank banderole, a speech or identity banner, above the woman's head is a sign that she is silenced, but I would argue the contrary: blank banderoles were common above early composite factotum cuts, as Driver and Gillespie have shown. Sometimes banderoles indicated a rank or a name, but here they seem to indicate figures in conversation, as for instance in other debate poems or in some works like Pynson's *Calendrier des bergiers* (1506, fols. G4–G8), where the speaking parts are actually given in the banderoles. Furthermore, the woman has both a speech banner and a speaking hand gesture, while the man, who does have a speaking hand gesture, has clearly had his speech banner obliterated by two pieces of border design that are asymmetrical, obvious

---

undated Trepperel and a Paris edition by Nyverd c.1520 are missing their title pages. A Paris edition of 1530 has the famous clerk-at-desk woodcut as its title, like the one Wynkyn uses as a title-verso cut) and two other cuts within showing a man with a sword speaking to a woman. See the notes to Piaget and Picot's edition, and Tchemerzine I.74–8.

[6] See Martha Driver, *The Image in Print* (London: The British Library, 2004), especially pp. 62–3; see Alexandra Gillespie, *Print Culture and the Medieval Author* (Oxford UP, 2006), pp. 147–9 and Figure 20. This figure also appears in STC 22408.

Fig. 3.2   *Prouerbes of Lydgate* (London: de Worde, c. 1510?), Title page.

Fig. 3.3   Anon., *Seyinges of Salomon and Marcolphus* (London: de Worde, 1529). Title page.

"*La Femme Replique*" 77

Fig. 3.4   *Complaynt of a louers lyfe* (London: de Worde, c.1531). Title page.

additions. Other uses of this same debating man (see Figures 3.2 and 3.3) do allow him his speech banner. Notice that the speech banner is intact in the *Prouerbes of Lydgate* (c. 1510); obliterated in our gender debate, the *Interlocucyon*; intact in the *Salomon and Marcolphus* debate (c. 1529); and obliterated in the *Complaynt of a louers lyfe* (1531). While I have been unable to collate the figures, a close examination of the differences among these debating men indicates that the *Interlocucyon* and the *Complaynt* debater, each with a banderole obliterated with border design, are apparently printed from the same woodcut as that in the *Prouerbes of Lydgate*, where the speech banner is intact. But the *Salomon and Marcolphus* debater is a different figure: the plants at his feet, the rocks in front of his left foot, the fold of his hat, the shape of the beard and hair, and the angle of several folds in the gown all show that Marcolphus, with his banderole intact, is not printed from the same woodcut as the other figures. This may be a reason to consider redating these imprints: the *Prouerbes*, intact, would still come first, followed by the *Interlocucyon* and *Complaynt*, both broken, and then finally the Marcolphus figure, if it were to have been recut to solve the problem of the broken banderole in the *Interlocucyon* and the *Complaynt*. In any case, different blocks could have been used within one edition of the same text; since so few copies exist, any such reconstruction is speculative.

Beyond speculation about dating these imprints, what interpretive sense can we make of this irregularity? Was this suppression of male speech deliberate on De Worde's part at all—or might the inserted, asymmetrical border design have merely been used to try to cover a problem with the woodblock or in the printing process? Was it really a selling point for De Worde's book that the woman silences the man on the title page? If the block used for the *Interlocucyon* in 1525 had been accidentally broken at or near the banderole, this silencing of male speech with the floral border was a matter of practicality, only fortuitously representing La Femme's overwhelming final tirade. If we assume, on the other hand, that the printer intentionally replaced the man's banderole with border design, we must also assume that the printer's wish to represent an important feature of the poem—the woman's final, 52-line speech that does in fact silence the man—was worth the cost of a new woodblock. And yet, the unlikeliness or lack of proof of such a printer's motive does not in any way diminish the effect of that image. Regardless of its original cause, the title cut to the *Interlocucyon* is a very direct, specific representation of poetic content. Whether by chance of a broken block or by design, that important final element of the French debate poem, the woman's long unanswered catalogue of bad men, is not only translated verbally but is represented visually in this irrregularity in the title image.

The next woodcut in the work, the famous and often reused image of the cleric-at-desk (Figure 3.5), however odd it seems to modern readers at first glance, may be a visual gesture to the authorship, genre, and literary history of the French source. Again, De Worde reuses this image frequently enough that it becomes, if anything, a general signal of writerly authority. In this case, though, it seems to carry a more specific connotation. The French versions generally mention Alexis as author in

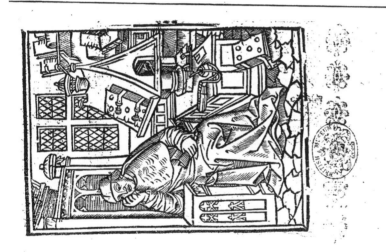

⊕ Hen Phebus triumphat/ most ardēt was & shene
In the hote sommer season/for my solace
I lay downe to rest me/where in this case
Under the vmbre of a tre/bothe fayre & grene

⊕ As after ye shall here/a stryfe there began
Whiche longe dyd endure/with great argument
Bytwyxte the woman/and also the man
Whiche of them coulde pyoue/to be moost excellent.
    ⊕ The man.

⊕ The fyrst whiche I here: was the mā that sayde
Adam our forfather/by womans shewde councell
To ete of an apple/was pytously betrayde
Well happy is he/that with you dothe not mell.
    ⊕ The woman.

⊕ Ihesu of a mayden/and vyrgyn his mother
Was incarnated/to redeme that man had loste
Set thou this one/now agaynst the other
And woman is more excellent/in euery coste.
    ⊕ The man.

⊕ Do women in to deuyls/neuer was transformed
But women in to aungels/full ofte hath ben fygured
For they? pryde in hell cruelly to be burned
Unhappy is he/that hath one to his make.
    ⊕ The woman.

⊕ More than to men/for they? chastyte
Hye our dere lady/thaungell spoted
Sayenge the son of god/in her conceyued sholde be.
    ⊕ The man.

⊕ Ioseph by woman/was put in pryson
And iohn was slayne by womans treason

A.ij.

Fig. 3.5 *Interlocucyon...* (London: de Worde, 1525). Title verso.

colophons or titles, if not by name, then as the Prieur de Bucy. While there is no mention in the English version of Alexis or of any French author, with this monk figure at the threshold, there is a suggestion of the clerical or scholarly tradition of "woman question" treatises, perhaps in the line of Mathéolus or Jerome. This dual-woodcut presentation carries an introductory sense, signaling readers first that the work is a gender debate in which the woman dominates strongly, and next that the work may have clerical origins or misogynist topoi.

Although the poem itself fulfills entirely the title cut's promise that the woman's part of the debate will overpower the man's, and although the male speaker's part of the poem fulfills the verso cut's promise of clerical misogyny, the poem's verbal frame—a frame added by the English translator—adds a third, rather more complex implication. The new English framing speaker overhears the man and woman debating as if in a *chanson d'aventure* or in a (day)dream-vision poem. The new verbal frame thus positions the work differently still: this will indeed be a debate, with male misogyny silenced in the end by female speech, but the poem will also locate itself against the courtly rather than the scholarly tradition. The English-added frame begins:

> When Pheb[us] reluysa[n]t / most arde[n]t was a shene
> In the hote sommer season / for my solace
> Under the umbre of a tre / bothe fayre [&] grene
>   I lay downe to rest me / where in this case.
>
> As after ye shall here / a stryfe there began
> Whiche longe sys endure / with great argument
> Bytwyxte the woman / and also the man
> Whiche of them coulde proue / to be moost excellent.
>
> The man.
> The fyrst whiche I herde: was the ma[n] that sayde
> ...

At this point the actual debate begins. After 49 quatrains (the last 11 of which are spoken by the woman), the translator adds these lines to end the poem:

> The auctor.
> Of this argument / the hole entent
> I marked it / effectually
> And after I had herde / them at this discent
> I presed towardes them / incontynently
> But when they sawe me / aproche them to
> Lest I wolde repreue / theyr argument
> Full fast they fledde / then bothe me fro
> That I ne wyst / whyther they went
> Wherfore now to iudge/ whiche is moost excellent

I admyt it / unto this reders prudence
Whyther to man or woman / is more conuenyent
The laude to be gyuen / and wordly [sic] magnyfycence.

The *chanson d'aventure* frame is also, of course, French-born. Related to the medieval dream vision (even though this speaker never actually admits to falling asleep), this frame places explicit responsibility on the readers to draw their own conclusions ("I admyt it unto this reders prudence"). Both the dream-vision and *chanson d'aventure* frames allow the narrating or authorial speaker a safe distance from the topic and the appearance of neutrality. So the translator frames Alexis's bare debate with a revised authorial persona—not the author named in the source or even the Prieur de Bucy implied in the inner woodcut, but a quasicourtly "Auctor" persona. This "Auctor" strongly reframes the debate of the title cut's bourgeois factotum figures as if they were courtly speakers in a romance encounter.

The mixed signals of these paratexts—the gender-debate woodcut, the clerical-line woodcut, the courtly-literary framing device, the forensic format and versification—open the work quite curiously in English. Except that they each represent the work as in some way "literary," the paratexts do not really reflect a coherent presentational strategy for this work. Like other early printer-translators, Wynkyn, an active intervener in and repackager of French gender discourses, may have been experimenting with representational strategies for the material. Printers and readers in 1525 were still setting out the horizons of expectation for the new English poetry, and poems on gender, as this one suggests, proved to be a frequent site of experimentation.

In addition to these visual and verbal translations, the translator (who may also be Wynkyn de Worde) intervenes with a new set of versification strategies for the *Interlocucyon*. As with so many English translations from French, the short French lines of the source—*octosyllabes* in this case—are rendered in longer English lines. However, this translator shows little metrical skill. The lines turn out as approximate, irregular pentameters, despite the labored and clumsy marking of caesuras in nearly every line. Several stanzas in the final section are closer to tetrameter, and, as in the above passage, some lines are short and some (the poem's final line, for instance) are hendecasyllabic or longer. This change is typical in early verse translations from French to English: instead of allusive, abstract, compressed, epigrammatic French lines, we find specific, verbally textured English lines, often with doubling or amplification. The body of the *Interlocucyon* is made up of quatrains in crossed rhyme (*abab*), not *rimes plates* (*aabb*) as in Alexis's poem. This results in a slower pace and a woven rather than a stacked or epigrammatic effect.

Alexis's stanzas are really remarkable—the repeated "ia" rhyme in the third line of each quatrain is very difficult to sustain. The English translator wisely chooses instead to vary his rhymes throughout the work, giving himself much more flexibility. However, this means that the snappy phonetics and the spirited dueling refrains of the French debate are missing from the start, losing most of the French version's rhetorical play and point. This loss is considerable, and when read in its full contexts, this aesthetic difference changes the balance and meaning of the gender debate. The opening lines, as edited by Picot and Piaget, will illustrate:

> LOmme commence.
> Adam jadis, le premier pere,
> Par femme encourut mort amere
> Qui tresmal le consilia:
> Bien eureux est qui rien n'y a.
> La femme respond.
> Jhesus de femme vierge et mere
> Fut fait homme, c'est chose clere;
> Aussi nous reconsilia:
> *Malheureux est qui rien n'y a*[7]

In English, the corresponding stanzas are:

> The Man.
> The fyrst whiche I herde was the Man that sayde:
> Adam our forfather by Woman's shrewde councell
> To ete of an apple was pyteously betrayde.
> Well happy is he that with you dothe not mell.
> The Woman.
> Jhesu of a mayden and vyrgyn his mother
> Was incarnated to redeme that man had loste
> Set thou this one now agayne the other
> And Woman is more excellent in every coste

Specificity (the apple), adverbial additions ("pyteously"), and doubling ("mayden and vyrgyn") are entirely typical changes in translating from the shorter French to the longer English line. The English version, especially with 10- and 12-syllable lines like these, loses the punchy rhythms of the *octosyllabe* couplets.

Moreover, the English version drops the complex cross-stanza wordplay in which the woman repeats but revises the man's words in exactly the same verbal pattern, effectively flinging them back at him in a nearly stichomythic style. In French, the third line verbs (*consilia/reconsilia*, and in other stanza pairs, for instance, *adulteria/maria, ydolitria/humilia, on n'y/ supplia, spolia/employa*) tighten the verbal connection between stanza pairs, sharpening the tension between

---

[7] [The man begins. Long ago, Adam, the first father, incurred bitter death because of a woman who advised him very badly; happy is he who has no part in it (i.e. relations with women). The woman answers. Jesus was made man through a woman virgin and mother, that's clear; so it reconciles us: unhappy is he who has no part in it.] Thanks to Nancy Vine Durling for helpful suggestions on the translations for early French poems.

assertion and contradiction. The woman picks up the man's rhyme schemes as well, using whatever rhyme he selects for the *aa* couplet in her own *aa*. The refrains powerfully reinforce this effect: *Bien heureux qui rien n'y a / Malheureux qui rien n'y a*, sustained throughout the poem, forms an important structural counterpoint lost entirely to the English. The rhyme scheme is in fact not just *aabb*; it is *aabb aabb ccbb ccbb ddbb ddbb* and so on, a showy, heightened performance indeed.

Also lost with these parallel refrains is a piece of fifteenth-century intertextuality: the lines imitate almost exactly a double-ballade refrain set in Villon's *Le Grant Testament*.[8] English readers may not have had the same full, immediate mental access to those lines as French readers might have had; I suspect that a translator who added *chanson d'aventure* framing stanzas would have known them. Yet if the translator were aware of this echo, either he did not think his English readers would be aware of it, or he did not think it was worth the effort to convey—that, or such specifically allusive intertextuality is not something that is finally possible to convey in another literary tradition.[9] We shall see later in this chapter that sometimes translators bring French refrains straight into English verse without translating them at all, but Alexis's flashy, allusive refrains did not come across intact. In any case, along with the sound-play of the dueling refrains, the poem's gesture to (and joining of) the community of French readers and poets is gone. The poem can no longer signal itself as part of the Villon family or signal to the subculture of late-medieval readers for whom gender debating was a staple poetic art.

Furthermore, the removal of the dueling refrains and answering rhymes from the English also removes rhetorical power from the woman speaker, who in the French version is the one we end up wanting to listen to, waiting to see how she will cap him *this* time. The verbal suspense and interest of the poem, in other words, rest with the energy of this remarkable female speaker, and the English woman, while offering almost exactly the same content in her rebuttals, does not come across as a particularly adroit interlocutor.

Michel-André Bossy, however, points out that compared with its own literary milieu, the French poem actually features a relatively plain-speaking female persona.[10] Here is a case where a comparative historicist method can clarify distinctions that are otherwise lost. In Bossy's view, the French female speaker's plainness relative to the flashy French rhetoric of Alexis's literary world works out as an implied advantage for the woman. Too much verbal cleverness could substantiate charges of being *cauteleuse* [sneaky], flattering, lying, and verbally

---

[8] Piaget and Picot, eds., identify the allusion, pp. 121–2. Bossy, pp. 23–4, reminds us that it could have been Villon who borrowed it from Alexis. It seems likely that this was a commonplace, nearly proverbial refrain line.

[9] One deep loss of context may in part explain some of the verbal differences: could English readers have brought the long-echoing traditions of the Occitan and Provençal *tenzone* to their reading of gender debates in the same way French readers might have done?

[10] *Passim*, with some convenient examples on p. 31.

manipulative. If she is a plain-speaker, she exonerates herself of those charges with each unornamented stanza. She is much plainer in English, but the advantage of plain-spokenness is lost when it is placed in a relatively flattened English context: *rhétoriqueurs* were not wildly popular in England (as they were in France), so instead of looking honorably plain, she risks seeming simply dull. The English poem is much less verbally entertaining overall, which by the end renders its protofeminist content less persuasive. In translation, then, she has lost both the advantage of relative plainness and any advantage a verbal dexterity could have given her in English.

In the remarkable final section of the French poem, the woman speaks 52 lines of nonstop couplets defending women and (mostly) attacking men. Titled "La femme replique" in both French and English versions, this final section lets the translator's cloak of invisibility slip, revealing its French origins. It is notable that the visibly French origin pops out just at the moment the woman's speech dominates. This final section gives the woman the last word—many last words, in fact. In French scholarship on the poem, there has been some question about whether or not this final section might simply be another poem grafted on here; its couplets in French make a real break with the flashy stanzaic dueling of the rest of the poem.[11] The content is very close between versions, but at this key point, the translation of rhyme matters: the English translator turns this final section's French couplets into eleven more *abab* quatrains, just like the rest. The new English rhyme scheme thus makes for a more coherent result, unifying the woman speaker's long final section with the rest of the poem. What had seemed a postscript in French seems in English like the woman speaker's complete takeover of the form and content of the poem. Here we see another frequent habit of the early translator-printers: striving for a formal consistency in the English literary product, they often select one English verse form and stick with it, regardless of variations in the French source. In some cases this ruins certain effects of the French, but here it changes the woman's final speech from an afterthought to a more seamless part of the whole—from tacked-on coda to triumphant finale.

In its French milieu, the *Débat* does not stand out so much in terms of its rhetorical performance (such was the French emphasis on verbal effects) but is one admittedly flashy example among many *débat* exercises.[12] In suiting its less flamboyant English context, the poem may lose rhetorical sparks, but it is a special link, as Bornstein shows, between medieval and Renaissance treatises on women, and it is an unusually direct and profeminist gender debate for its English readership. Likewise, in the context of Alexis's oeuvre, it is more exercise than sincere expression. Alexis cannot be thought of as having a feminist or even protofeminist sensibility, but he did create an effective, rhetorically interesting female speaker.

---

[11] Piaget and Picot, eds, pp. 122–3.
[12] See Paul Meyer's list in *Romania* 6 (1877): 499–503. See also Utley, p. 54.

However, in the English context of Wynkyn's printed output (since we do not know the translator's identity), the poem looks decidedly literary and protofeminist. It displays negative male exempla and men's culpable behaviors and gives the woman a much more real, effective, and integrated voice than she finds in other contemporary imprints debating gender issues.[13] The woman's side of the *querelle* is voiced relatively little in early English poetry (compared, that is, with French poetry). In the *Interlocucyon*, at least, the verbal and visual interventions of the printer and translator not only import the speaking woman from France, but they make a clear effort to render her voice even more prominent and effective.

Sympathy Reframed: An Ovidian Dido as Chastity Warning

Where the *Interlocucyon* ends with the woman's voice cataloguing the problem of bad men, the *Letter of Dydo to Eneas* (1526) consists entirely of a woman's specific accusations against one singularly bad man, Aeneas. It is a one-sided

---

[13] Compare, for instance, De Worde's imprint from Lydgate, *The payne and sorowe of euyll maryage*, c. 1530 (STC 19119) or the works treated in Chapter 4. One oblique complication to this matter of speaking women is found in the English suppression of two French stanzas about women and the priesthood:

L'Omme.
Dieu ne voulut oncques femme estre
Ne quelque femme faire prestre
Pour chanter le Per omnia :
Bien eureux qui rien n'y a.
La Femme.
Premier de femme voulut naistre
Le seigneur de tous le maistre
Qui les prestres sanctifia :
Maleureux qui rien n'y a.

[The Man: God did not want to be a woman nor for any woman to be made a priest, to sing the Per Omnia (that is, the Per omnia saeculorum); happy is he who has no part in it. The Woman: The Lord of all, the master who sanctified the priests, chose first to be born of woman. Unhappy is he who has no part in it.]
Piaget and Picot explain the omission this way: "Il semble en effet que le traducteur ait subi l'influence de la Réforme ... s'il est difficile d'expliquer la disparition de la strophe 4, il est permis de supposer que les mots Per omnia au v. 11 auront embarrassé le poète anglais" (145 n1). [In effect, it seems that the translator may have felt the influence of the Reformation—if it is difficult to explain the disappearance of the fourth stanza, one may suppose that the words Per omnia in line 11 will have troubled the English poet.] Since the poem was printed about 1525, it could be that the stanzas were seen as controversial, but there is no real evidence either way. However, the whole Pauline question of women speaking is also suppressed here, which seems to me more important.

argument, the "she-said" part of a he-said/she-said dialogue in which male and female are mutually and agonistically constructed. Where the *Interlocucyon* offers biblical examples of bad men—Cain/Abel, Judas/Reuben, Judas Iscariot, and the Apostles who betrayed Christ—the *Letter*'s classical example of Aeneas on his way to Rome had particular power in Renaissance culture as a founding myth of the Tudor dynasty. Where the *Interlocucyon* featured factotum anywoman-anyman figures in debate and presented both sides of the argument in more or less parallel terms and forms until the ending, the *Letter of Dydo* focuses on this resonantly paradigmatic couple by erasing the viewpoint of the culpable man and giving the accusatory female speaker full and sympathetic voice. Like its French and Latin antecedents, this epistolary poem is addressed mostly to the absent Aeneas, with asides to the reader and to Anna, the sister. Yet, as we shall see, the paratexts surrounding the poem reduce that female voice and its potential critique to an exemplum that warns young women against unchaste behavior. Because the paratexts effectively contradict the message of the translation itself, and because this poem is the first Ovidian Dido in English print, the *Letter of Dydo* makes an especially intriguing addition to early modern debates about gender.

Pynson's imprint of 1526 is an anonymous translation of an extremely popular French Dido poem, itself a translation of Ovid's *Heroides VII* made by Octavien de Saint Gelais. Saint Gelais's version was very widely disseminated in dozens of manuscripts and early imprints (Julia Boffey points out that at least four known readers of the French manuscripts were women, p. 344 n24). One of Vérard's early editions of Saint Gelais's text, including Latin phrases from Ovid printed in the margins, was probably available in early sixteenth-century England. Pynson's considerable connections with Vérard support that probability (345–7; see also Winn *passim*). But while copies of Vérard's and the Trepperel editions of this work might have been available to Pynson, there is no real evidence of it as a specific copytext for the *Letter*. In fact, the striking woodcut (Figure 3.6) is not traceable to Vérard, as are so many Pynson cuts (Boffey 346).

The translation and its paratexts stand at one side of a long history of interpreting Dido, worth recalling briefly here. The two main traditions, the historical or "chaste Dido" line and the passionate or unchaste Dido line, develop the Virgilian story differently, as John Watkins, Diane Purkiss, Barbara J. Bono, Julia Boffey, and others have shown.[14] The "chaste Dido" line, from Servius's

---

[14] Watkins, *The Specter of Dido*; Purkiss, "Marlowe's *Dido Queen of Carthage* and the Representation of Elizabeth I," in *A Woman Scorn'd: Responses ot the Dido Myth*, ed. Michael Burden (London: Faber and Faber, 1998), pp. 151–67; Bono, *Literary Transvaluation: From Virgilian Epic to Shalkespearean Tragicomedy* (Berkeley: University of California Press, 1984), especially pp. 83–139. For the variety of medieval traditions, see Julia Boffey, "Richard Pynson's Book of Fame and the Letter of Dido," *Viator* 19 (1988): 339–53; p. 344 n21; and on the many medieval Latin versions, p. 351 n46 and p. 352 n48. See also Adrianne Roberts-Baytop, *Dido, Queen of Infinite Literary Variety* (Salzburg: Inst. f. Englische Sprache und Literatur, 1974) and Timothy Crowley, "Arms and the Boy:

Fig. 3.6 Octavien de St. Gelais, tr. Anon., "Letter of Dydo to Eneas," in *The Boke of Fame* (London: Pynson, 1526), Fol. [F3v].

commentary on Aeneid I–IV, including Macrobius, church fathers following Tertullian rather than Augustine, and Christine de Pizan's *City of Ladies* I.46 and I.55, emphasizes Dido as the chaste widow of Sychaeus who offers herself in public self-sacrifice. The "passionate Dido" line tends, instead, to read a moralized Virgil in something like this oversimplified way: Dido represents extreme passion, Aeneas represents logical nation-founding, and the former must be rejected if we are to have an empire. More and less ambiguous versions of this basic idea accord Dido greater or lesser sympathy (one thinks here of the way Christine de Pizan's Dido differs from Boccaccio's Dido). Ovid's *Heroides*, however, founds a much more sympathetic line of Dido versions by giving her a significant, solo voice and by presenting Aeneas as an ungrateful, untruthful betrayer tainted with moral cowardice. Most critics would place Chaucer's version in the *Legend of Good*

Marlowe's Aeneas and the Parody of Imitation in Dido, Queen of Carthage," forthcoming in *ELR*.

Women in this Ovidian line (at least for its tone, despite its ambiguous framing and use of third-person narrative). The Ovidian line asks how we can glorify a man who arrives in tatters on the shore of a great city, is rescued and reoutfitted by the queen, but repays his benefactress by seducing her, promising to marry her, and leaving her (pregnant in some versions) in the middle of the night. The version of Octavien de Saint Gelais is strongly Ovidian, as is its English translation.

When the woman's side of the question is heard in this way in the early modern period, it attacks more than just one bad-male betrayer—it potentially challenges the whole system of patriarchal nation-building so important in Tudor self-definitions (as well as the heroic-romance tradition in literature). After all, Aeneas is not, in most legends, the prototypical bad man but the prototypically great one, the founding hero of the Roman Empire, the hero of the chief myth of civilization building available to Tudor England. This troubling conjunction of politics and gender may recall an earlier moment in French history, the one detailed by Nancy Bradley Warren in an analysis of the early modern English reception of Christine de Pizan, Joan of Arc, and Margaret of Anjou.[15] That moment was Octavien de Saint Gelais's cultural location, roughly speaking, but this early English Dido poem, printed in a very different time and place, likewise gives prime attention to the contested, uneasy place of the feminine in nation formation.

To print such a troubling exemplum in 1526 seems to have called up the printer's most strenuous paratextual efforts, efforts that alter, even invert, the meaning and value of the poem. Saint Gelais's prologue, in both manuscript and later printed editions, is an obsequious, multipurpose homage to the monarch (originally Charles VIII, but very slight changes would allow it to be used for nearly any monarch). Richard Pynson, King's Printer to Henry VIII, a person not uninterested in—and not a disinterested party to—myths of empire, does not adopt that laudatory prologue, which would have served well. Instead, Pynson reframes the poem anew as if to suppress its implicit critique of empire and its open critique of male adventuring. Pynson's paratexts, and the larger publication context for the volume—a pseudo-Chaucerian *Boke of Fame* focused on female examples—utterly change the meaning of the hypersympathetic Ovidian Dido, turning her into a chastity lesson for young women. The medieval habit of exemplarity persists in print, and the translator's paratexts perform a rereading of the poem that matches in strength the rereadings of medieval exegetical commentators. While both the translation itself and Pynson's new woodcut do maintain and even heighten the power of Dido's voice, the other framing paratexts and the wider printing context create a "backlash," undoing the protofeminist work of the poem.

First, the woodcut: The early French woodcuts differ strikingly from Pynson's remarkable cut. Figures 3.7 and 3.8 show two early French images illustrating

---

[15] Warren, "French Women and English Men, Joan of Arc, Margaret of Anjou, and Christine de Pizan in England, 1445–1540," *Exemplaria* 16.2 (Fall 2004): 405–36.

Saint Gelais's poem.[16] In the first, Dido is shown looking into a mirror. This cut illustrates a moment of private reflection before or during the poem's ostensible utterance and highlights the speaking persona's interrogation of her own identity and situation. (This woodcut captures more literally what Derrida called "dipossession speculaire" in the opening section of *De la Grammatologie*, that self-reflection in awareness of self-alterity, the dispossession of the self.) Another early French woodcut, Figure 3.8, shows an exterior scene near the city, with a speaking factotum Dido and a speaking factotum Aeneas. Beyond their names in the banners, nothing in the figures indicates a special status for either one, as factotum cuts sometimes did—no crown here for Queen Dido, no sword and shield for hero Aeneas. This cut does, however, make the absent Aeneas present as a listener to Dido's poem, which is largely in the second person and addressed to him. By re-embodying Aeneas visually on the page, this illustration undermines a signal feature of epistle: the genre implies but deliberately does not depict or award any personhood to the silent, absent letter-recipient (outside, that is, the voiced perspective of the epistolary speaker). A third French woodcut not shown here is a flashback cut that illustrates a moment of inset narrative within the poem rather than illustrating the immediate occasion of the poem. That image shows Dido both as queen (she is crowned) and as lover (embraced by Aeneas), vividly depicting a happier moment recalled in the poem and thus focusing the reader's attention not on the moment of the poem's speaking but on the loss being narrated and lamented. That image was printed in 1534, almost a decade after the *Boke of Fame* (but "nouuellement," according to the title page) and so might not have been available to Pynson. But these samples do show how much Pynson's choice of illustration stands apart from the general range of early printed French images. Given Norman-born Pynson's connections with French printing and his use of other Vérard woodcuts, it is clear that many woodcuts, including a range of factotum figures, were available to him, not the least from Wynkyn de Worde's considerable stock (on which he drew elsewhere).

However, Pynson eschews the factotum and instead illustrates the English translation of Saint Gelais with the woodcut in Figure 3.6, a single block cut. The cut is untraced at this writing, but it might well have been created for this specific use. Here we see an uncrowned Dido, hair streaming, impaling herself on a giant phallic sword, pyre at the ready nearby, with Carthage—and thus her queenship—in the background. This image is much like many of the common portrayals of Dido in late-medieval French manuscripts, including those containing Saint

---

[16] Figure 3.7 [*Epîtres d'Ovide traduites en français par Octavien de Saint Gelais*] (Paris: Verard, c. 1505), fol. 72. Figure 3.8, *Sensuyt les XXI epistres d'Ovide* ... (Paris: [Vve. Trepperel], c. 1525], fol. 63. Not shown, *Les XXI Epistres Douide translatees de latin en francoys Par Reuerand pere en dieu Monseigneur Leuesque Dangoulesme* ... *Nouuellement reueues* ... (Paris: Guillaume de Bossozel, 1534), marked Fo. xxxviii (fol. 73).

Fig. 3.7   Octavien de St. Gelais [*Épîtres d'Ovide*] (Paris: A. Vérard, c.1505), p. 72. (Gallica BnF Notice No. FRBNF31046494).

"La Femme Replique"

Mais puis que iay perdu ma renõmniee
Et le bon bruit dont ie faz estimee
Pouure peule du surplus ie feray
Quant paroles ou escriptz ie perdray
Or donc enee tu sen vas a grant erre
Habandonnant et dido et sa terre.
Ainsi sera portee par mesme vent
Ta foy promise et ta voille en auant
Or as emprins dresser ton nauigage
En esperant y auoir aduantaige
Et de querir les lieux ytaliens
Qui pas ne sont encor en tes liens
Plus ne te plaist cartaige la gentille
Ne le pays ne sa terre fertille.
Les choses faictes et seures tu deffuis
Et les furtiues tu les quiers et poursuis
Mais ou sont ceulx a ton aduis ence.

Ad vada mean
dri consinit essu-
glos.

Nec qui a te no-
stra sperem prece
posse moueri·

Atloquor verso
nouimus ista deo.

Fig. 3.8   Octavien de St. Gelais, *S'ensuyt les XXI épistres d'Ovide* (Paris: Vve. J Treperel, c. 1520–1525), p. 63. (Gallica BnF Notice no. NUMM71774).

Gelais's version.[17] Pynson's printed image in fact immediately recalls the Dido of French medieval manuscripts, or it would for readers of print familiar with such manuscripts. For any reader, this image heightens the intimacy and trauma of the Dido story since it depicts her final self-silencing as a personal matter that is taking place far from the polis. Most of the manuscript's images of Dido's suicide I have seen so far depict scenes very like these, but nearly all feature some kind of blood dripping or gushing from the wound, and most feature witnesses nearby, usually with horrified, anguished faces. The walls of Carthage are usually quite prominent in these manuscripts. Pynson's small space and economical double-column format meant that a small woodcut would have to omit detail, but it seems clear that the creator of the cut takes his concept from such an illumination. Even without the manuscripts' detailed, colorful gore, Pynson's choice of image heightens sympathy and horror for Dido beyond that of most of the extant French printed images.

As for the translation itself, Julia Boffey's excellent analysis of the differences between the French and English versions need not be rehearsed in detail, but her main points are important to recall. Boffey points out that the anonymous translator's French was not the best; the translator goes beyond the commonplace translators' disclaimers in unusually sincere, apologetic detail in the prologue. "To translate Frenche I am nat redyest / No mervayle is sithe I was neuer yet / In those [par]ties where I might la[n]gage gete" (53–5). Boffey notes that the translator pads the lines awkwardly, often misunderstands French words or phrases, and generally weakens the effect of the French (347–50). We might be glad, then, that the translator shortened the work from 430 to 242 lines. These reductions "[highlight] Dido's innocence and [give] prominence to the central fact of Aeneas's perfidy" (349; see also 350–1). It is a "declassicizing" version—here I would add, of an already declassicized version, since Saint Gelais omits many of Ovid's classical allusions and back-stories. The English version—"an obvious and consistent tampering with the moral implications of the story" and "a bowdlerized legend of Dido"—omits the scene of seduction in the cave and Dido's pregnancy, yet makes "Aeneas' faithlessness ... seem more heinous than in the versions of Ovid and Chaucer" (351).

Just what is the trouble with Aeneas in this version? Without the telos of Rome, this would be a familiar, even banal story: a faithful, sympathetic woman has fed, nursed, nurtured, and loved Aeneas, not to mention resupplying his ships and men, and he breaks his vow to marry her, and leaves—to found Rome. This poem, however, creates a picture of Aeneas and his goal that differs slightly from other versions. "The thynges well done and sure ye dispice / Thyngs vncertayne ye

---

[17] These include BnF ms fr 232; ms fr 233, ms fr226, ms fr 235; Lyon ms Richelieu 229, and a Latin ms of Virgil, BL ms Kings 24; all these are available on bnf.fr, the website of the Bibliothèque nationale de France. I have not been able to examine all the scores of medieval French manuscripts extant that contain images of Dido. Thanks to Malcolm Richardson for mentioning the cross above one of the buildings in Pynson's woodcut, which may carry an anachronistic or proleptic religious implication.

sertche and enterprise" (24–5), says Dido. The short attention span of the empire founder, always seeking the next challenge, whether political or sexual, could raise the spectre of Henry VIII:

> Certe[n]ly as by your dedes I perceyue
> Other louers in recompence ye haue
> And if ye haue faithe of another lady
> She shalbe deceyued as well as I (29–32).

Yet this Aeneas is a mere empire-imitator: The time may come, says Dido, "That ye shal bylde a mighty stro[n]g tour / And a cyte Cartage to resemble" (35–6). Even if so, she says, "ye may happe gouerne all Italy / yet shal ye neuer haue spouse nor wife / Kynder than me" (40–42). Aeneas is fundamentally unkind (65–7) and "A droppe of trouthe in hi[m] I can not finde" (68), "trouthe" here in the chivalric sense of *troth*, the Gawain-sense of keeping one's pledges. It seems impossible for him to have been born of Venus:

> ye were...
> ... borne i[n] rockes i[n] thornes or among breers
> Among tygres [&] wolves cruell and feers
> There were ye borne [&] lyued without norture
> For without mercy ye arte of thy nature (70–75).

Aeneas, prototype of epic glory and nation-founding, ancestor (according to Tudor myths, anyway) of Troynovant, appears shallow, cruel, and untrustworthy in this condensed, one-sided critique. Aeneas' very genealogy is in question, a genealogy that bears on English nationhood as it was imagined in the early sixteenth century.

However, the English translator and printer are careful not to print a deliberately subversive critique-à-clef of Henry VIII or the Tudor myth. Instead, they put their revision to a specifically gendered, didactic purpose. Boffey points out how the publishing context of this work matters: "This particular version of the Dido story, with its warning against duplicity, neatly fits the pattern of exemplary moral instruction with which the *Boke of Fame* is stamped" (352). Indeed, Pynson's *Boke of Fame*, as we saw in Chapter 2, is a powerful shaping context for a number of female-connected and French-affiliated translations. Yet here this warning against male duplicity does not warn men to reform. The negative exemplum of male perfidy is not intended to debate the question of male/female worth or to defend women, as such exempla were handled in the *Interlocucyon*. Instead, the contexts created by the printer and the translator—that is, the volume's general theme of female reputation and the translator's specifically admonitory epilogue—strongly refocus Dido's *Letter* on a demand for female chastity and virtue.

The English reframing of Dido begins, as so many other translations from French begin, with a prologue's overt literary motions and a self-disclosing translator-persona. The translator is, conventionally, a rejected lover who typically feels inadequate to the task (lines 43–7 and 50–56). Jane Donawerth has suggested in private correspondence that this translator might be a woman; she notes the absence of specific gender references in the prologue and the translator's self-comparison to Dido. In fact, this translator identifies so strongly with Dido that there is a physical reaction:

... [I must write] this rufull songe
Of poore Dydo/forsaken by great wronge
Of false Ene/who causeth my ha[n]d to shake
For great furye/that I ayenst hym take

Ah false vntrouth/unki[n]de delyng [&] double
My ha[n]de quaketh / whan I write thy name (ll. 18–23

These lines and the admonitory epilogue could support Donawerth's idea of a female translator for this work—a woman warning women against bad men. It has been my sense that one of the organizing methods of *The Boke of Fame* is to use a range of exemplary and antiexemplary women's voices in cautionary works about reputation: Christine, Mary Magdalen, Dido, the Belle Dame, and, if Donawerth is correct, even the voice of this translator.[18] In addition to the translator's vivid identification with and sympathy for Dido, the Prologue's nine rhyme-royal stanzas are explicitly and playfully literary, hunting in vain for Muses to invoke. (This Muse-hunt in fact resembles a witty passage in the *Fyftene Joyes* prologue we will see in Chapter 4.) There is weeping at Helicon (29–32). Juno is, in a small pun, dismayed (33). Nor can Niobe, Myrra, Byblis, Medea, and Lucrece help, though they would be fine muses for a woman's voice lamenting bad men (36–9). Venus is partial to Aeneas, so the translator turns to Celeno, "full of enuyous yre" (49), presumably ire against a translator who dares to versify, yet is not worthy to bear the inkhorn of real poets. Donawerth notes that this reference to Selene, the moon goddess who can shine only by reflected light, may also point to a female translator. Either way, like so many verse translations from French, this one creates a deliberately literary, self-conscious frame for the work, one that makes translation visible, yet displays the potentially jealous relation of translation to authorship. In this it resembles some of the complex translators' prefaces of the later sixteenth century such as those of Florio, who similarly genders translation and original, or of Tyler or Chapman. Like other early printed examples, this translator's prologue also does some back-story work, reminding readers of Aeneas' seven years of wandering after Troy and his bedraggled arrival in Carthage. This supplementary

---

[18] We have no proof of the translator's gender, though the work of Krontiris, Hannay, Prescott, and others on women and translation shows that there were more active women translators in the sixteenth century than we have thought; because of such scholarship, the idea of a female translator of Dido is no longer impossible.

background implies that the translator imagines an audience who will need this informative gloss.

After the self-disclosures and lettered muse-hunting, the translator makes a strong opening statement about the virtue of plain-speaking and the honest expression of emotions:

> Folke disc[om]forted / bere heuy cou[n]tenau[n]ce
> As ye haue cause / so order your chere
> But yet some folke / whiche vse disseblaunce
> Wolde say/other meanes moche better were
> That is to say / good cou[n]tenau[n]ce to bere   5
> Wha[n] ye haue cause / of thought or heuynesse
> That folke [per]ceyue nat your grefe [&] distres
>
> But as for me / me thynke playnnesse is best
> After your chere / to shewe your wo
> Shewe outwarde / what ye bere w[ith]in your (brest   10
> Sithe ye of force / must chuse one of the two
> Eyther among the dissemblers to go
>
> Or els be playne / chose after your lust
> But playnnesse is the waye of parfyte trust

This explains Dido's lament in terms of emotional sincerity—it is good to tell one's true feelings, and Dido has, the translator says, good cause to lament. But the reader must also choose either to be a dissembler or to be truthful: to be of Aeneas' party or of Dido's. Like the *chanson d'aventure* frame of the *Interlocucyon*, this frame directly poses an ethical choice for the reader. This emphasis on "playnnesse" has stylistic implications as well. The original English prologue in rhyme-royal stanzas is not perfectly plain, but like the simple couplets in the body of the poem, it does avoid excess ornament. The result is a very simple, readable poem but also a strong statement against falseness that maps gender and style onto "truth" in a notable way. Here stylistic ornament is equated with male duplicity, and stylistic simplicity is equated with female emotional honesty. The poem's plainspoken condemnation of male duplicity is then no surprise following this prologue.

Yet, after the poem, the translator's epilogue urges women not to express their (sexual) feelings. "Playnnesse" may be all right for a suicide swansong and for explaining the decorum between that topic and the simple literary style in which it is expressed, but the translator's final word on the matter undercuts this stated preference for sincerity and simplicity. Women, the translator says, must be cagier in love than Dido was:

> Lenuoy of the translatour.   245
>   ye good ladyes/whiche be of tender age

> Beware of loue/sithe men be full of crafte
> Though some of the[m] wyll [pro]myse mariage
> Their lust fulfylde/suche [pro]mise wylbe last
> For many of them / can wagge a false shaft   250
> As dyd Enee / cause of quene Dydose dethe
> Whose ded[s] I hate [&] shall duri[n]g my brethe
>
> And if that ye wyll you to loue subdue
> As thus I meane / vnto a good entent
> Se that he be secrete / stedfast and true   255
> Or that [i.e. before] ye set your mynde on hym feruent
> This is myn aduyse / that ye neuer consent
> To do y[e] thing / whiche folkes may reproue
> You in any thyng/y[t] ye haue done for loue.

Here the translator veers away from the long poem's condemnation of Aeneas, of duplicity, of perfidious men in general, and, by implication, its critique of patriarchy and nation-founding. Unlike La Femme's final word about bad men in the *Interlocucyon*, here the final word on bad men is a warning to young women. Donawerth remarks that a female translator might be offering here a sadder-but-wiser sisterhood. Certainly, the translator gives Dido a strong, sympathetic voice in the text itself, but the epilogue warns women against men who "can wagge a false shaft" (of course, that does not only mean their tongues; this phrase also reprises the phallic suggestion in the woodcut). Instead of warning men to stop wagging their false shafts, here women are warned never to do anything for love that could harm their reputations. Reinforcing a sexual double standard, the epilogue barely avoids blaming the victim.

As the sixteenth century progressed, Dido would be further reframed, voiced, unvoiced, and staged. In poetry, Thomas Feylde (1527) and the *Connaissance d'Amours* (1528) take up Dido very soon after Pynson does, as do Badius and Brandt in the next decade. Briefer treatments from Wyatt in Tottel's *Songes and Sonets* (1557), from Humphrey Gifford, or from Henry Chettle, do not resonate as much as Isabella Whitney's "To an Unconstant Lover." Turberville's *Heroicall Epistles* offer a full Ovidian set in 1567. In drama, John Ryghtwyse makes a Latin Dido play in 1527, and in 1564 there is an anonymous neo-Latin play. William Gager's play of 1583 rejects the Ovidian Dido, and he equates the chaste female monarch with the strong state—a sensible revision for his late-Elizabethan moment. Christopher Marlowe takes more risks, as usual, in *Dido, Queen of Carthage*. As Diane Purkiss says, Marlowe "refuses to admire pious Aeneas, and uproots moralizing meanings that understand the story as a tale of renunciation of love for the sake of empire" (166). It is not until the *Heroinae* of 1634 that George Rivers will use historical consciousness to debunk the Dido story entirely, explaining that it was chronologically impossible for Dido and Aeneas to have been alive at the same time. It is beyond the scope of this chapter to trace the history of Dido in the

Renaissance, of course. This first Ovidian Dido in Engish print, however, reveals how the printer and translator handled the difficulty of placing this story's implicit protofeminist critique before a widening Tudor readership.

Dangerous Beauty, Or the Ugliness of *The Beaute of Women*

The ongoing argument about women's value finds a third trajectory in a very odd translation, *The Beaute of Women*. Where the *Letter of Dydo*, like the finale of the *Interlocucyon*, gives voice to a woman speaking of bad male behavior, the *Beaute of Women* silences the woman entirely and places two kinds of female exemplarity, moral and physical, in tension. Where the *Interlocucyon's* woman refuses to accept blame or responsibility for what bad men have done, and where the *Letter of Dydo's* paratexts caution women to protect themselves against false men, the *Beaute of Women* assumes a male perspective and relocates the debate about the value of women in the woman's body and being. This is not exactly news in the history of misogyny. This translation, though, marks an extreme in that history since it first defines women's beauty in certain particular, physical ways (for example, high forehead, arched brows, small feet) and admonishes women to join goodness to their physical beauty. The poem makes the question of women's value almost completely proscriptive, and the poem's male voice specifies both the physical traits and the moral virtue required of women if they are to be considered beautiful. The work is dialectical only in that it poses two sides, physical and moral, of "how women ought to be." The woman's view is not represented at all; this is no male-female dialectic. Rather, the poem presents an idea of the feminine that specifically must not "talk back." A quiet woman is the only beautiful kind:

> [W]omans beaulte requireth thyrdely
> That stedfastly with out oultrage 50
> She kepe as dyscrete co[n]tynually
> Symple answer euer in her language

and later,

> [W]oll that the woman set her besy cure 90
> To maynteyne in hyr selfe a low laughyng
> To laugh ouer hygh besemeth no creature
> Even a woman's sneezing should be quiet (ll. 97–100).

As in the other poems studied here, an important part of the translation that is taking place between French and English is paratextual, formal, and stylistic. Unlike, say, the work of the printer-translators treated in Chapters 4, 5, and 6, whose interventions seem to take a more consistent slant on their material, this work seems to have been produced under a contradictory strategy, if it can be called a strategy at all. Perhaps, as may have been the case with *Dydo*, the translator and the printer did not understand the work in the same way. Or perhaps, as seems to have been the case with the *Interlocucyon*, the printer and translator were still experimenting and had not stabilized their concept for the work.

The *Beaute*'s source has never been precisely traced, and I propose here that it is in fact a composite translation that is heavily revised, reordered, and repackaged. There are other such composite translations—Chapter 5, for instance, studies another, more seamless case of a translator piecing parts of two works together in a new English frame—but the *Beaute* translation's unevenness also reveals a profound uncertainty and ambivalence about "woman questions."

The racy title cut is a first indication of a highly charged English response to the issue of female beauty. Figure 3.9 shows the remarkable title page to R. Fawkes's (or Faques's) edition of 1525 of the *Beaute of Women*. (An edition of c.1540 by Robert Wyer also uses this title cut; since there is no modern edition of the poem, my transcription is in Appendix 1). In the full title and also in the text, the translator and printer clearly announce this work's French origins: *Here foloweth a lytell treatyse of the Beaute of women newly translated out of Frenche in to Englyshe*. Sex and Frenchness seem to have been good selling points, judging from this title page, but the erotic beauty of this nude woman is dangerous, apparently: she plays the lute, an *A* adorns her plumed hat (perhaps for *amour* or *Amor* [vincit omnia]; the "A" would have entered this title cut into several long conversations about beauty, sexuality, and morality. [19]), a devil-jester stares at her genitals, and the image is surrounded by this inscription: *Peccati forma femina est et hortis con[d]icio* (untraced). Although the printer puts this highly charged image of a certain kind of female beauty and sexuality on the title page, the translator is clearly much less comfortable with the French poem's frank, erotic specifications of women's beauty. Within the poem, the Frenchness of the sources is still highly visible, but the elaborate French praise of women is muted and reduced, and the erotic elements are suppressed. The printer flaunts the erotic aspect of the work's topic and advertises its French origins but does not specify its sources; the translator, on the other hand, conventionally swears to follow the "sentence" of the French, yet strongly selects and eliminates the praises of women as well as the eroticized material that the printer displays.

The translation seems to be a reordered, revised, sharply condensed composite of two works, the *Louenge et Beaulte des femmes*, attributed to Jean Dupont-Alais, and an anonymous imprint, *Sensuyt la louenge et beaute des Dames*.[20]

---

[19] The expression, from Virgil's *Eclogues* X.69, is also spoken by Venus in the Roman de la Rose (l. 21332), who asks Fair Welcome to help the Lover. This "A" also follows the one worn by Chaucer's Prioresse (*Canterbury Tales*, GenPro 162), another figure for whom traditional or courtly beauty is an ambiguous attribute.

[20] This latter work is not listed in the BnF catalogue or in the BLC at the time of this writing. I found it in the microfilm series "French Books Before 1601." *Sensuyt la louenge et beaute des Dames* (Toulouse: Nicolas Vieillard, n.d); but the colophon reads, "Cy finist la

Fig. 3.9   Anon., *The Beaute of Women* (London: Fawkes, 1525). Title page.

Like most of the French sources available to printers in England, there were several versions of these works (and there probably were others no longer extant). It is often impossible to ascertain, without the luck of marginalia or provenance records, exactly which versions and copies the English printers used, so what follows here must be taken as provisional and speculative. However, structural, formal, and verbal resemblances support some of the bibliographic clues we do have. In order to pinpoint the English printers' and translator's interventions, I describe briefly here the common elements in the French imprints that could have been available to Fawkes, the printer, before 1525.

The *Louenge et Beaulte* attributed to Dupont-Alais consists of two long "louenge" sections powerfully praising women, followed by a shorter, epigrammatic "beaulte" section in which the female body is anatomized. The first "louenge" section consists of 23 stanzas of ottava rima, the second "louenge" section is 126 lines of couplets, and the third "beaulte" section contains 23-line stanzas, *aab*, with lines of three or four syllables. The poem opens cursing those who have spoken against women:

> Mesdisans, crevez de douleur,
> Oyans la louenge des dames:
> A vous n'appartient rien de leur:
> Mauditz soyez de corps et d'âmes
> Fuyez vous en, paillars infames
> Car comme la cire au feu fond
> Aussi la grant vertu des femmes
> Voz malices confond.
>
> Dames sont le jardin fertile
> Racine dhumaine nature
> Larbre convenable et utile
> De terrienne nourriture
> Dames font la douce pasture
> Ou il convient tout homme paitre

Louenge & beaulte des Dames. Nouuellement Imprimee a Tholoze par Nicolas Vieillard." "Nouuellement" implies an earlier imprint. Another Vieillard imprint, The *Blason des femmes*, uses the same typeface and title cut, dated 1538; I was unable to examine originals, but apparent breaks and blotches in the cut of 1538 suggest that the *Louenge* may have been printed first. The other *Louenge et Beaulte des femmes* (s.l., s.d), in octavo, eight folios; BnF Rés. Ye-2983, has what resembles a Trepperel-style cut (not Trepperel, but in that format); the wide inscription around the edge is like that of the title cut to the English *Beaute*, though the words are completely different. Another copy was probably the one edited by Anatole Montaiglon, *Receuil de Poesies françoises des XVe et XVe siecles....* (Paris: P. Jannet, 1857), VII. 287–301. Montaiglon describes a different cut in detail; the imprint is in quarto, ten leaves, 24 lines per page, and thus different from the Lotrian imprint of 1527, from the undated BnF catalogue imprints, and from the Vieillard imprint.

> Et toute humaine creature
> Loger, fructifier, et naistre.
>
> Dames font lentretenement
> Du monde et tout le secours
> Ung pillier ung soustennement ...²¹ (Montaiglon VII, 287–8)

This is an even stronger statement of woman's power and value than Christine de Pizan or La Femme in the *Interlocucyon* gave. It also renders woman as a pastoral landscape, fertile pasture where all humanity may graze. The praises continue for 23 stanzas, using other images to assert that women are the source of all human good. Note that there is no religious rationale here, something the English translator will add lavishly to his epideictic prologue. Women, in this French poem, are sources of delight and pleasure that are figured as wealth: "le trésor de riches amours," "bijoux et joies d'hommes," common images from courtly poetry. Women, the poem continues, are important in the political sphere, the key to benevolence, the cause of all good enterprises, the honor of the provinces, the fear of those who wound honor. They can perfect the imperfect, and "n'ont pouvoir de meffaire" [are incapable of misdeeds]. It gets better: "douceur immortelle ... richesse inestimable ... ung soleil rayant ... ung miroir de bons ... un roy ... une etoile ... une fleuve dont toutz vertus yss[u]ent" [immortal sweetness .... inestimable richness ... a shining sun ... a mirror of good things ... a king ... a star ... a river from which all virtues flow]. Celestial, terrestial, ethical, political, and sensual goods are logged to woman's praise. The value of women, in the French source, in other words, is not merely sexual or domestic, and not cast in terms of value only to individual men, but rather to humanity and the to world broadly conceived.

Parallelism is a favorite technique in the French poem, as in this chorographical stanza:

> Dames sont ung ciel de liesse,
> Ung paradis de courtoises
> Ung droit abisme de largesse
> Ung doulx vergier de noble vie
> Ung manoir plein de melodie
> Un mur de ferme contenance

---

²¹ [Slanderers, die of sorrow, hearing the praise of women: none of theirs belongs to you: Cursed be in body and soul! Flee! Flee from it, you infamous rogues, for as wax melts in the fire, so the great power of women confounds your wickedness. [n.b. rhyming-play in fond-confond; "paillard" has a negative sexual connotation]. Women are the fertile garden, the root of human nature, the proper, useful tree of earthly nourishment; women constitute the sweet pasture where all men are to be fed and where every human creature must lodge, and grow/ripen, and be born. Women are the continuation and help of the world, a pillar, a support ... .]

L[a] vie de pitie fleurie
De foy, damour, et dastinence.²²

This stanza's zooming camera shot from the heavens to the well-walled happy manor home with its firm walls of continence and abstinence, and singing within, idealizes women and the enclosure of women. Yet the garden in which the female body is imaginatively enclosed here is something other than *locus amoenus* or *hortus conclusus*: wise speaking, sweet thinking, quick courage, attractiveness, and loving language are the "natural" attributes of women. (The positive French garden, too, takes on a decidedly negative and biblical resonance in the inscription on the title page of the English translation.)

A needless *occupatio* stanza then states that the worth of a worthy woman surpasses all expression and defies all epistemologies:

Bouche ne peut monstrer ne dire
Entendement ne sens comprendre
Ne cueur penser ne main escrire
Ne parchemin ne livre prendre
Ne nul hault chemin entreprendre
Sentement ne science d'ame
Ne tous clercs du monde aprendre
La valeur d'une vaillante dame.²³

More follows, and while no trace of irony is detectable in the tone—or is there a hint in the reference to clerics?—such heaping hyperbole somehow comes to feel suspect or even insincere. One final catalogue is worth special mention because it is one that the English translator will invert:

Dames valent mieux mille fois
Que Tulles en son beau langage
Ne que Hector le Troyannais
Ne Hercules en vaisselage
Ne que Absolon en son courage
Ne que Priam en sa richesse

---

²² [Women are a heaven of joy, a paradise of courtesies, a great abyss (endless depth) of generosity/largesse, a sweet orchard of noble life, a dwelling full of melody, a wall of firm strength (also Huguet II.477, contentment), a path (Robert VI, Huguet VII. 467, from via; alt., "life," but the chorographia favors "path") adorned with sympathy/piety, of faith, love, and continence/abstinence.] Durling points out that "astinence" could also mean "disinterestedness," in certain contexts; correspondence, 2006.

²³ [No mouth can show or tell, no understanding or sense can comprehend, no heart can think, nor hand write, nor high path undertake, nor feeling nor knowledge of the soul nor all the clerks of the world teach, the worth of a worthy woman.]

> Ne qu'en sens Salomon le sage
> Ne qu'Alixandre en sa largesse
> Se ung hom avoit la bonte
> De David et magnifiance
> Et de Narcisus la beaute
> Et d'Abraham l'obedience
> Et de Job la grant pacience
> Et d'Achilles le hault vouloir
> Pour avoir sa benevolence
> A peine le pourroit valoir.[24]

Women surpass even the most exemplary classical and biblical men, and even a man with the best qualities would hardly deserve women's benevolence. After reading so much misogynist literature contemporary with this poem, one has the odd experience of not being able quite to believe this laudatory excess; one rereads for irony, for the twist that will reveal the poem's satiric place in Mathéolus's camp.

The second section, long couplets of similarly rich praise, has no apparent twist, either, though it is quite remarkable for its concrete descriptiveness of the earthly paradise. In this it is unlike much other late-medieval French poetry, which leans to abstraction rather more often than to concreteness. Pearls and rubies, but also unicorns, dolphins, and sturgeon, all kinds of textures, colors, odors: but woman surpasses all these wonders. In fact, death and our current fallen world is preferable to being without woman:

> Quant Dieu auoroit tout cecy fait
> Pour enrichir lomme et complaire
> Et femme luy voul[s]ist soustraire
> Il en despriseroit sa vie
> Et plustost luy prendroit envie
> De la mort ou de n'avoir riens
> Que destre roy de tant de bien
> Sans avoir femme en sa richesse
> Qui est le tout de sa liesse
> Et son corps vault mille foys plus
> Que tout ce qui est dit dessus.

---

[24] [Women are worth a thousand times more than Tully (Cicero) with his beautiful language, than Hector of Troy, than Hercules with his valor [Huguet VII.406], than Absolon with his courage, than Priam with his wealth, than Solomon the wise with his wit, than Alexander with his magnanimity. If a man had the goodness and magnificence of David, the beauty of Narcissus, the obedience of Abraham, the great patience of Job, and the high will of Achilles—he could hardly be worthy of her benevolence.]

Cy fine la Louenge des Dames.
Sensuit la beaute des femmes.²⁵

This is a remarkable coda to the creation and fall story, the story most reliably used to blame women for, well, everything. Here, Paradise is fabulous, but Adam would give it all up or die rather than do without woman, who is his real joy; her body is worth a thousand times any paradise. The English translator suppresses this passage entirely, even while retaining certain other elements of both "praise" sections.

The third section, on "beaulte," begins with this announcement just under the title: "Belle femme doit avoir" [(a) beautiful woman must have]. Three-line stanzas follow this, telling what the beautiful woman must have, each set cryptically titled, "Troys longs," "Troys noirs," "Troys courtz," "Trois gros"—implying that she must have three long things, three dark things, three short, and three fat. Also, she must have three low, three soft, three dimpled, three wide, three small, three simple, and three dangerous things in order to be beautiful. Some of these demands are still commonplaces used by advertisers: "Molz cheveux, / Molz genoulx, / Et molle mains" (soft hair, soft knees, soft hands). Others have lost their cultural power: fat forearms, for instance, are not now commonly thought beautiful, nor are dimpled knuckles a requirement for female beauty. All of this, is of course, heteronormative, and the lists of "threes" reminds us how fluid and contingent—how arbitrary—are such aesthetic demands. In any case, this "beaulte" section falls oddly after those long, eloquent praises of women in the previous section. The "threes" seem shallow, brusque. They miss the point of all that came before, deflating and undermining it. Women may be the gardens of the world and the honor of all creation, but still they must have small feet to be beautiful.

A numerological or calendric interpretation of this poem might be interesting—23 stanzas of praise, an insufficiency completed by the eternal hour of the earthly paradise in the next section (itself containing calendric surplus, 53 couplets), then the three-line, three-syllable, "threes" of women's beauty, completing the tripartite larger work. Although French poets, especially those influenced by the *rhétoriqueurs*, played such elaborate games with the numbers, letters, and patterns of poetry, the English translator is not in time with such a structural principle.

For our purposes, the French poem stands as a general template for the English, a template from which the English departures are significant. The English translator follows the tripartite template and retains part of the formal alternation between parts. The three parts here, however, are a prologue, a section codifying women's

---

[25] [When God would have done all that to enrich and satisfy and please man, and had He wanted to take woman away from him, he (man) would despise/scorn his life, and he would sooner want death or to have nothing at all, than to be king of so much wealth without having woman among his riches (or in her richness), who is all his joy; her body is worth a thousand times more than all that is said above. Here ends the Praise of Women. The beauty of women follows.]

physical beauty, and a section explaining the moral strictures that must be placed on women's beauty. The English poem begins with 32 lines of introductory praise in *ottava rima* or Monk's Tale rhyme—not, however, set as stanzas as in the French but printed continuously without line breaks.[26] It seems that the translator tried to create an original prologue with stanzaic versification, but the printer's spacing does not support the rhetoric of the translator's chosen form. Next come 100 lines of description of women's beauty, presented in "threes" just as the final "beauty" section is handled in French. This "threes" section retains much of the French content. The English version is in 25 *abab* quatrains, however. (Were short-line triplets simply impossible in English, or did quatrains provide just enough change in pacing and a clear formal break for the work into three sections, without too much challenge in rhyming?) The third and final section returns to the Monk's Tale stanza to introduce the rejoining of physical and moral worth. Each stanza in this section ends with the refrain "Beaulte sans Bonte ne vault rien," Frenchness fully visible, with the ring of a proverb or commonplace.[27] Each of the three sections reveals the translator's rather more ambivalent take on the question of women's value.

The translation opens by adding what were, for early modern English readers, unassailable examples of female virtue—Mary and her mother Saint Anne:

> The sone of the mayde whome neuer none resembled
> In beaulte nor bounte syth the worlde began
> For both in hyr were perfaytely assembled
> Named is she Marye doughter to saynt Anne
> Guyde myne hande so that the gentylman   5
> That me desyred to reduce thys boke
> From frenshe to englyshe/be content/and than
> I take lytell cure what other there on loke.

These lines are new to the English version; the French simply begins by castigating those who speak ill of women. The translator invokes Jesus as the muse of the work, which he states was a commissioned translation with a French source (ll. 5–10). Jesus the Muse, however, is invoked in terms of his female forbears, Mary and Anne—the ultimate early modern genealogy of female goodness. Next the translator presents himself as a conventionally inexperienced persona cast out

---

[26] The undated Vieillard imprint is also printed without breaks.

[27] "Biaute ne vaut rien sans bonte" is a close match (Isopet, *Fables de Robert*, I.276; thirteenth century), as is "Bauté [sic] sans bonté est comme un esvauté" (Gabr. Mecrier, *Trésor des Sentences*). I have been unable to trace the phrase completely; like the title woodcut, it is obviously foreign but not precisely pinned to a source. Hodnett says the cut is "clearly not native" (p. 54) and reproduces it as Figure 230. See also entry 2057 s.v. Fakes [Faques, Fawkes].

from female presence who has to do the job since more experienced lovers will not take the trouble:

> whereof to treate / I ought well to be blamed
> Consydered that I had neuer the vsage
> Womens beaulte in body nor vysage
> For to regarde / and there vpon good reason
> Syth I am made (as an unpleasant page)   15
> A cast a way from presence at eche season
>
> But what therof shall I leue of to wryte
> Syth no man hauyng more practyse then I
> wyll take the payne to set blacke on the whyte

This writer is not as skillfully disingenuous, however, as Chaucer's servant of the servant of the god of love. Nor is he as skillful as most of his fellow translators at creating a framing literary coherence for the revised composite work.

Next he speaks of the worthiness of the work and says he will follow the "sentence" of the French—which, clearly, if he is using the extant *Louenge et Beaulte* imprints, he does not do. We see his highly charged but ambivalent relationship to female beauty: he intends to glorify beauty, "as ryght requyreth," no matter what the bad consequences of beauty are. And he tells us that its consequences are serious: instead of the French catalogue of exemplary men whose virtues are encompassed and surpassed by female excellences, his catalogue is of legendary men (romance or epic protagonists) harmed or destroyed by women's beauty:

> What caused the wourthy Troylus of Troye   25
> To cast hys loue on Cresyde the s[h]ene
> why set Parys on fayre Helayne hys ioye
> what caused Achylles to loue Polexene
> why loued Trystram la belle Isoude the quene
> Or Arthur of bretayne the fayre Florence   30
> All cam of them beaulte and theyr plesant eyen
> what haue I to do as of the consequence.

The translator has either missed the whole point of that French catalogue or has willfully revised it from praise of women's beauty to condemnation of it.

The poem then breaks out of prologue-style *ottava rima* or Monk's Tale verse and launches the *abab* quatrains prescribing and proscribing what women are to look like and how they are to act. This is where the direct content of the *Louenge et Beaulte* sources becomes most clearly visible. (Here we see why it has been so hard to identify the sources of the translation: the closest likeness is not in the opening or closing lines of a source; rather, it is in this revised and reordered mid-section, some 50 to 100 lines in, in a different form.) Since the full text of the *Beaute* appears in Appendix 1, I shall summarize this long, central body of the work. Beauty requires "symple maner and countenaunce"; otherwise, a woman will empty the room, and "her beaulte tourneth but all to dysplesance" (l. 40). A woman needs natural, simple, pleasant looks; otherwise, "that is the manner of the lyon" (l. 48). Steadfast, discreet, and simple language is also required. Three kinds of simplicity are required of women if they are to be found beautiful. The requirements echo what were praises in the *Louenge*, but these are challenging standards, and the punishments for failing are severe in English.

Next come the "threes" of physical beauty, selectively translated from that final "Beaulte" section of the *Louenge et Beaulte*. Three things should be "hollow," meaning arched or curved: brows, "raynes" (the small of the back[28]), and feet. The translator adds that they should be slenderly arched, not thick like animal feet. Three things should be high: forehead, head, and breasts. Here the translator has suppressed some erotic elements in the French (for example, "Hault front/ Hault poitrine/ Hault enconnee"; Montaiglon 300). He has also moralized (in a small etymological pun): a low forehead in a woman is "the frontelet of evyll." Three things must be low: a low laugh, a low or modest look, and low or quiet sneezing even when sick, "For other wise she leseth her beaute" (104). Three dimpled things, three slender things, and three things wide set: eyes, shoulders, and "reynes," which, as we have seen, must also be curved.

Three reddish things imply the use of cosmetics: nails, lips, and cheeks (after all, who has naturally red nails?). Not only did actual Englishwomen get their cosmetics from France, they seem to have absorbed French norms for beauty and, judging from this poem, some early French discussions or debates about the issue. As Fran Dolan has explained, anticosmetics discourses in England paralleled the art-nature debates in associating female creativity and cosmetics, "repeatedly warn[ing] that women who attempt to remake and relocate themselves achieve only debasement" (229).[29] Dolan's examples are all post-1583, but in them "a woman who paints herself refuses to submit to her passive role as a creature, a being with no legitimate capacity for self-transformation or self-determination,

---

[28] Often translated as "loins," the word is from Fr. reins, kidneys, also thought to have been a seat of the passions.

[29] Dolan, "'Taking the Pencil Out of God's Hand': Art, Nature, and the Face-Painting Debate in Early Modern England," *PMLA* 108.2 (March 1993): 224–39. See also, Crystal Downing's historical objections in "Face Painting in Early Modern England," *PMLA* 109.1 (January 1994): 119–20 and Dolan's reply there. On late medieval and early Renaissance French women as "far in front of the English" in cosmetics and on English women imitating and importing French cosmetics, see Maggie Angeloglou, *A History of Make-Up* (London: Macmillan, 1970), pp. 44, 45, 47; on Elizabethan-era cosmetics, pp. 48–54. William Neville's *Powder and Paint: A History of the Englishwoman's Toilet* (London: Longmans, 1957), also notes the English importation of French cosmetics (pp. 16–17, 22) and the influence of France on English norms of beauty (pp. 31–3), though his examples are all post-1558. Carroll Camden details these norms, and even quotes without attribution this poem; *The Elizabethan Woman* (New York, 1975), p. 25.

and insists on herself as a creator" (229–30). In the *Beaute of Women* translation, the threat of female agency is enclosed in general warnings about moral virtue. No thought is given to the strictures, the "threes," as the root of the real problem—that is, the problem of placing specific demands on the shapes and colors of the female body in a cultural context that prohibits cosmetics. A woman must thus either fail to meet the demands for physical beauty or try to meet them by using cosmetics and participating in that damnable, self-transforming agency. Dolan likewise notes "the contradictory requirements women face: they must meet certain standards of beauty but must appear to do so naturally" (232). This contradiction, like the tension male writers and readers felt or imposed between female beauty and female virtue, persists even today. The *Beaute* translation shows this persistent contradiction coming to English readers from France in a particular form and quite early.

The overall effect of these "threes" is to slice up the female form and to classify its body parts by their desired attributes. This anatomizing differs from the anatomizing and, some say, reifying lyric blazon, best known in Petrarchan poetry but dating from Sappho and Anacreon, with Latin examples as well, and having been popular in France in troubadour lyric. In fact, this poem's corporeal analysis makes the typical Renaissance blazon look positively warm and appreciative, humanizing by comparison. The blazon records a particularized and usually favorable erotic response (when not in a parody or ugly-mistress poem) to particular body parts of a named or specified individual—a singular beloved is the point. This poem instead assumes that all women's parts are alike and can be broken down into categories. Instead of idealizing and praising a single, special woman, this poetic practice insists that all women's body parts must meet certain categorical standards: three small things, three arched things, and so on. Female individuality or particularity, so fetishized in blazons, and the exemplarity of individual women, so often used in the woman's side of gender debates, are in fact erased here. Quite unlike the translations that appropriate a unique "Dydo" or a representative "La Femme" from France, this poem appropriates a view of women *en masse*, composed of pleasing or not pleasing attributes. The translation not only suppresses material that values women as more than objects, but it also expands the proscriptive, admonitory elements of the source.

The final section of the poem begins in a spirit quite contrary to that of the French analogues:

> I haue expressed theyr preemynence
> As well of theyr bodyes as of theyr mayntyen   130
> But speke what ye wyll apert or in scylence
> Beaulte sans bonte ne vault rien.
>
> Beaultyes there be in women infynyte
> But of bontyes there is but lytell speche
> Beaulte is them geuen as thyng requisyte   135
> who wyll haue bonte let hym go [s]eche

This is far from the high praises found in the central sections of the French works. The translator does admit that men have not granted women their due ("of bontyes there is but lytell speche"). Yet the snarling "who wyll haue bonte let hym go seche" implies, as Donne's persona would put it a century later, that women both true and fair are hard to find. The translator could show you one, he says, yet continues to hammer away at the didactic point:

> Thys not wythstandyng I coulde a man teche
> To fynde ryght good of the gendre feminyn
> And fayre also/but what euer we preche
> Beaulte sans bonte ne vault rien.

When the refrains begin in this final section, the poem begins to contrast physical and moral attractiveness; this element of contrast is not in the French text. The English poem poses a dualism and then argues for re-joining physical and moral beauty in one female person. In this section, the poem becomes much more metatextual and self-conscious (lines 129, 137, and 147), as if the translator is aware of turning new ground. Like the translator of Dydo, he addresses women directly here, which raises again the question of early English female readerships for these poems. All estates of women must heed the admonition—which here means women in any marital state; for again, this translator's habit of mind is to categorize women in terms of their use (or pleasure) value for men:

> Mayde / wife / or wydowe / dame/or damoysell
> That haue the raye of beaulte comprysed in your face   150
> Adiouste therto bonte / than shall ye do ryght well

> For beaulte with bonte assembled in a place
> Gyue demonstracion of an especyall grace...

The translator has reordered and selected material from the French, suppressing the erotic but also strongly suppressing the superiority of women found in the opening section. His original ending displays little skill: "As dayly yt is sene / and there a fynall clause."

Women's physical and moral qualities are put in opposition but are inextricably linked in this work. When the cautionary refrain repeats in French, "Beaulte sans bonte ne vaut rien," the translation edges toward a wider philosophical debate about the connections between inner being and surface appearance, between essences and signs, *res et verba*. Yet if the translator's concerns are moral and didactic, the printer seems not to notice or care: The title cut would certainly not lead a buyer to think that this is a moral, didactic work about joining inner and outer beauties. The title woodcut is a functional part of the translation, and it reveals tensions in the work and a gap between how the printer and the translator, respectively, perceive the value of women and women's beauty. Although the translator suppresses erotic elements in the "threes" section, the printer's woodcut highlights the erotic. (The French woodcuts that we know of for analogous imprints are quite sedate.[30]) The translator moralizes heavily about beauty, but the title woodcut, with its devil-jester, lute, and cautionary inscription, poses beauty as primarily enticing, though morally dangerous. This may be an early triumph of publishers' marketing: to advertise a French treatise on women's beauty with a nude pictured on the front and then to suppress erotic content and to create a fully proscriptive, moralizing, "safe" work.

This poem is an odd entry into literary history as well. Early modern debates about women's beauty ranged widely, from the philosophical or neo-Platonist to the bourgeois proscriptive to the satiric. This work is one among many and varied French discourses on women's beauty—from cosmetic advice poems to platonic or humanist poems to poems that verge on the "how to buy a good horse" type to satiric "ugly mistress" poems. English poems on women's beauty are not as varied or as prominent, even toward midcentury, where the contrast with the continent becomes significant and persists. In Italy, for instance, beauty was a more frequent topic than it was in England, even late in the century; for instance, Firenzuola's popular "Dialogho delle bellezze delle donne," while in French translation at least by 1578, has no English counterpart until much later.[31] Nor is the translation treated here like Thomas Sébillet's satiric poem *La Louenge des femmes: Invention extraite de commentaire de Panatgruel, sur l'Androgyne de Platon*.[32] In that popular work, a blazon section begins, "La femme ... n'est rien qu'un sac de malice, de haut en bas" [Woman is nothing but a bag of malice from top to bottom] (10) and proceeds by revealing each body part to be hiding a horror (one thinks of Spenser's Duessa when reading this French poem). The prose preface to Sébillet's work alludes to Juvenal and other writers in the misogynist tradition and doubts that women have reason; an antimarriage tract follows the poem.

The tripartite structure and blazon concept may be the same as those in the French source chosen for the translation treated here, but the content and execution are quite different. The English printer and translator choose as source one of the more profemale poems in the French tradition, with its long, persuasive praise section. Yet they then suppress most of that praise in English, along with the sexy

---

[30] Montaiglon describes an almost allegorical cut with four ladies, two at the right, representing the liberal arts, and two at the left, one a queen with two children at her feet (p. 287, note 1). A *Beaute des femmes* imprint of 1497 held in the Rothschild collection of the BnF has a similarly decorous title cut, an education scene among aristocratically dressed women.

[31] Agnolo Firenzuola, Opere, ed. Adrian Seroni (Firenze: Sansoni, 1971); or in English, On The Beauty of Women, ed. and trans. Konrad Eisenbichler and Jacqueline Murray (Philadelphia: University of Pennsylvania Press, 1992).

[32] Lyons 1551; a digitized version is available at gallica.bnf.fr, côte NUMM-52963; see also a printed edition by Ruth Calder; Wakefield: S. R. Publishers; New York: Johnson Reprint Corp., 1967.

French body parts, which only show up visually in the title cut. We may be able to explain this odd, contradictory content as a rhetorical exercise in *mel-sel-fel* [sweet, salt, and bitter, or praise, satire, and gall] or in the rhetoric of praise and blame. The English imprint may not be best understood strictly in terms of literary history (since so few English poems, relatively speaking, are printed about women's beauty), nor in terms of the history of ideas (since this work does not engage in the pan-European humanist and neo-platonic interest in Beauty, female or other). Instead, we might think first of the practical context of the early marketplace of print: the available French work's composite parts—the idealizing first section and the final proscriptive fragmenting "threes"—were deliberately packaged in ways that the early printers conceived as saleable. The discrete interventions of translator and printer mix the content and formal strategies of several different strands of the wider discourse, but these interventions do not seem to have been driven by any coherent literary or intellectual traditions on the topic. This imprint suggests that in the early marketplace of print, poems about gender, even such an oddly mixed didactic poem, seem to have had a healthy audience—and that title cut has to have helped sales.

Conclusion

These translations—the *Interlocucyon*, the *Letter of Dydo*, and the *Beaute of Women*—provide a sample of the more- and less-formal debates about the nature of women appropriated for early English readers of print. Although these poems deploy various dialectical strategies taken from French, there is only an indirect line from the *querelle des femmes*, even in such a sample chosen to show a broad idea of "debate" and the voicing or silencing of the woman's part. The speaking woman so prominent in the *Interlocucyon* and on its title page, the eloquent, accusatory, doomed Dido, and the completely silenced body parts of the *Beaute of Women* illustrate a range of ways the English printer-translators handled French material about gender. Acutely aware of versification and "literariness," they easily make new material from composite imprints and manuscripts, create new frames that often contradict the implications of their central materials, and are willing to choose a new English verse form and stick with it (gracefully or not). Most of all, by the 1520s, they seem equally aware of visual marketing strategies and the power of images. The results anticipate the later, better known "woman question" debates and pamphlets that became popular from the mid-sixteenth century onward.

A range of poetic debates about women and gender clearly sold well in the new marketplace of print. When these poems cross the channel, the printers' visual and technical interventions are as important as the translators' verbal interventions. Certainly the printers' interventions when appropriating gender discourses are more obvious, more striking than the sometimes-subtle adjustments the translators make (even when the printers and translators may be the same person). The printers, probably for their own commercial purposes, actively reshape and re-present

French gender discourses. Their paratexts are key in whether a readership receives a fully voiced "woman's part," as in the *Interlocucyon*, or not, as in the dissection and reassembly of both the texts and their subject, the woman, in the *Beaute of Women*. Their paratexts, in fact, may contradict the very point of the poems themselves, as in the *Letter of Dydo*. In this foundational phase of English poetry, translation is an agent of change—here, an agent of cross-cultural transmission of gender discourses—that cannot be separated from the technological "translations" of the early printing houses.

Chapter 4
Framing Misogamy:
The Prologue and Prohemye to
The Fyftene Joyes of Maryage (1509)

On 1 June 1599, the Master and Wardens of the Stationers' Company suppressed and had burned certain books unacceptable to London's ecclesiastical authorities, volumes including translations of Ovid, all of the works of Nashe and Harvey, Davies's *Epigrams*, Marlowe's *Elegyes*, and several historical and satirical works (Arber II.829, III.677–8). Among the titles deemed inflammatory was *The xv Joyes of marriage* (London: Adam Islip, n.d.), a translation of the anonymous *Les Quinze Joyes de mariage*. This set of fifteen racy antimarriage stories had been an early bestseller in France, with at least seven printings between 1480 and 1520.[1] English versions seem to have enjoyed a similar popularity, better documented after 1603 than in early print. The irreverent title—an obvious parody of the popular religious works of "fifteen" like the "Fifteen Oes," the "Fifteen Joys of Mary," or the "Quinze Joyes de Nostre Dame"—could well have drawn official disapproval even without its subversive and sexual content.[2]

My focus here, however, is not the rationale for the censorship of the mysterious version of 1599 or the extremes of the work's reception history, but rather the complex effort of an early printed translation to appropriate, and indeed to soften or tame, this potentially subversive, satiric misogamy. The first known English version of this poem, *The Fyftene Joyes of Maryage* (London: De Worde, 1509), was never condemned to ashes. Although this early version of *The Fyftene Joyes* was popular in its time (Łobzowska 18), it is now virtually unknown and has

---

[1] Joan Crow, ed., *Les Quinze joyes de mariage* (Oxford: Blackwell, 1969), xii; Tchemerzine; Fernand Fleuret, "Bibliographie des éditions des *Quinze Joies de Mariage*," *Les Quinze joyes de mariage* (Paris: Garnier), 1936; Krause, *Neue Beitrage zu der Quinze Joyes de mariage* (Wangerin, 1929), 52–62, cited in Joan Crow, "The 'Quinze Joyes de mariage' in France and England," *Modern Language Review* 59 (1964): 71–7. The French was formerly attributed to Antoine de la Sale and is now recognized as anonymous; see Claudio Galderisi, "Stratégie de l'anonymat et saturation mimétique dans *Les Quinze Joies de Mariage*," *Littératures Classiques* 31 (Autumn 1997): 13–26.

[2] Since we know nothing about Islip's burned edition of 1599, its relation to the many other French and English versions is uncertain. Four years later, another version, the *Bachelars Banquet* (London: T. C., 1603), circulated freely and was frequently reprinted and re-edited during the next four centuries; for complete details, see the introductions to F. P. Wilson, ed., *The Batchelars Banquet* (Oxford: Clarendon Press, 1929), and Faith Gildenhuys, ed., *The Bachelor's Banquet* (Binghamton, NY: MRTS, 1993).

never been edited. The only texts that remain are one complete copy of 329 pages (Pierpont Morgan Library), one incomplete copy (Folger Library/UMI microfilm, STC 15258), and one fragment (Bodleian Library, Douce C.10). Here I treat the "Prologue of the Translatour" and "Prohemye of the Auctour," the prefatory poems that first reframed, reshaped, and re-presented the *Fyftene Joyes* for early modern English readers. (Appendix 2 contains my transcription of these prefatory poems, which is, to my knowledge, their first since 1509.) In the Prologue and the Prohemye, the printer and translator set up the particular cultural filtering that this translation performs as it repositions the work for a new readership in an entirely new set of English contexts.

The French work was, in its first contexts, a hip, topical, funny engagement with, and an elaboration of, the thriving misogynist and misogamist line that runs from Theophrastus and Juvenal to the *Miroir de Mariage* and Mathéolus. Each satiric story presents a "joy" of marriage. The first story explains the husband's increasing discomfort and impoverishment as the wife wants to buy more and better clothes. She chooses a bedtime moment to make her desires known, and his desire, by implication, is traded for her desire: sex for a new gown. Here, as in some lovers' complaints and marriage complaints, marriage as a kind of prostitution, or at least as an overtly economic trade of material goods for sex and domestic comfort, is not far below the surface. The next story details the wife's constant attendance at pilgrimages and social events. Pregnancy (with its cravings, mood swings, and the husband's doubts about paternity) and childbirth (with neighbor women, midwives, and friends in voluble attendance) are the topics of several of the "Joyes." In these, the husband is crowded out of his own home, nagged, and forced into incomprehensible expenditures. Mentioned several times is the husband's inability to control the household or even to be welcomed home comfortably after absences:

> Lors toute la famille est contre luy, et ainsi le bon homme ... voit bien quil n'y gaigneroit rien, s'en va sans soupper, sans feu, tout mouille et morfondu...puis sen va coucher, et oyt les enfans crier la nuitee...ainsi passe la nuyt en soussy et tourmens, quil tient a grant joye ... et finira miserablement ses jours ("La Quarte Joye").³

The mother-in-law's visits, the growing children, and daughters' dowries are also common topics in the later stories. Usually some economic component enters the stories: clothing costs a fortune, the pregnant wife craves rare fruit, and the hardworking husband cannot find a morsel of food on his return, although his own work seems to have provisioned the rest of the neighbors, who visit the wife

---

³ [Then all the family is against him, and so the fellow ... sees clearly that he will get nothing out of it, goes without supper, without a fire, all wet and cold/chilled ... then he goes to bed and hears the children crying all night ... and thus spends the night in care and torment, which he holds to be a great joy ... and [thus] he will end his days in wretchedness.]

constantly. Marrying above one's station (which means, here, marrying a spoiled, demanding, expensive wife) is the topic of the fifth joy. The fear of cuckoldry and impotence—and the experience of them—also beset the husband in the sixth, seventh, and later joys. The friends and neighbors, "gossips" who seem to have more power in the household than the husband, and the ever-more malevolent and lying wife figures, feature in several stories. Each story in French ends with some version of "La est le bon homme en la nasse bien enclous, en douleurs ... quil prent...pour joyes ... et finira miserablement ses jours" [There the good man is indeed closed up in the trap, in sorrows that he takes for joys ... and he'll end his days miserably]. This word *miserablement*, meaning both penniless and woeful, illustrates in compressed fashion how marriage is the common site of poverty and unhappiness in so many of the translations about gender.[4]

The French stories' local details—beyond the scope of this chapter—expand the critique of marriage to take aim at religious, military, and social institutions governing early modern life.[5] Their village settings, middle- and working-class perspectives, and colloquial voice[6] also succeed, I think, in slyly attacking "courtly" literature and its mutually reinforcing social ideologies. Moreover, the French stories have literary-historical interest as narratological hybrids. Their discursive style closely resembles that of fifteenth- and sixteenth-century conversation manuals.[7] They blend the modes of the *récit bref*, *nouvelle*, and *roman réaliste* with the dramatic techniques of the *sottie* and farce.[8]

Removing this disruptive hybrid to an English context might seem to position it in a less active branch of the ongoing *querelle*,[9] where it might not be as easily

---

[4] The languages have diverged such that "miserablement" now suits the economic emphasis of the stories better in French than in English, but this may not always have been so. "Misère" now has a double connotation of poverty and unhappiness, but the first such usage is noted at 1611 (*Grand Robert*, s.v. miserablement). In English, "miserable" (*OED* A.2) also had, as early as 1585, the connotation of poverty, a sense now obsolete, and "misery" could mean stinginess as well as unhappiness. In other words, the stories' repeated closural assertion of "misery" would not necessarily yet have suited the stories' economic emphasis, but this treatise might be one place where that sense was developed, in both languages. This detail is one of many to strengthen the connection between marriage and poverty.

[5] Monique Santucci, "Pour une nouvelle interpretation des *Quinze joyes de mariage*," *Le Récit bref au moyen âge*, ed. D. Buschinger (Amiens: Université de Picardie, 1980), pp. 153–73.

[6] Marcel Cressot, *Le Vocabulaire des Quinze joyes de mariage d'après le texte de la seconde édition de la Bibliothèque elzévirienne de 1857* (Paris, 1939).

[7] Jean Rychner ed., *Les XV. Joies de mariage* (Geneva: Droz, 1967), xxvii–xxix.

[8] Rychner, ed., xxv–xxvii and xxx–xxxii; Monique Santucci, ed., *Les Quinze Joies de mariage* (Paris: Stock, 1986), pp. 146–8.

[9] We know of no early English imprints of, for example, the misogamist texts directly part of or indirectly cited in the *querelle* and so widely available in France: Mathéolus, Gerson, Col, Montreuil, *et alii*.

received. Although satires outsold even religious works at this time (Gildenhuys, ed., 13–14), and although the success of the *Quinze Joyes de Mariage* in France made this translation in one sense a safe commercial bet for Wynkyn De Worde, it is in several ways a risky proposition. Its first risk was to bring such a heavily French generic hybrid before English readers. The big literary bestsellers circa 1509 were Hawes's and Brant's allegorical narratives—satires, yes, but in a form quite comfortable for English readers. This translation and others like it may indicate an effort to align the French material with the styles and genres that Hawes and Brant (or his translators, Alexander Barclay and Henry Watson) had made popular. A. S. G. Edwards explains the unusually close collaboration between Wynkyn De Worde and Stephen Hawes.[10] All of Hawes's poems came out in 1509 with De Worde. The printer took great care to connect the woodcuts with the poetry, to reprint the poet's works, and to attend to the poet's reputation. Given this important, ongoing publisher-poet relationship, and given the translation's verbal echoes and similarities to Hawes's work—its rhyme-royal paratexts, its careful pentameter, its interstanza enjambments—it might be tempting to speculate that Hawes could be the translator of the *Fyftene Joyes*. (Wynkyn, too, who translated other works from French, or Robert Copland, translator of the *Complaintes* and printer-author of other verse on gender topics, might have translated this work.) Then, too, Wynkyn printed *The Payne and Sorowe of Euyll maryage* (c. 1530), a translation of a widespread and widely varied thirteenth-century antimatrimonial poem, *De Coniuge non ducenda*.[11] Judging from his publication list, Wynkyn was a purveyor of misogyny and misogamy, as Julia Boffey has more thoroughly explored,[12] so the *Fyftene Joyes's* conjunction of misogamist theme and Hawes-like form would have been right in his line.

---

[10] Edwards, "Poet and Printer in the Sixteenth Century: Stephen Hawes and Wynkyn De Worde," *Gutenberg Jahrbuch* (1980): 82–8.

[11] See A. G. Rigg, ed., *Gawain on Marriage: The Textual Tradition of the* De coniuge non ducenda *with Critical Edition and Translation* (Toronto: Pontifical Institute of Medieval Studies, 1986), for stemmata and extensive details of the textual tradition. In one note, p. 11, he even suggests that Mathéolus's *Lamentationes* is based on this work, not the other way around, although the prologue seems to indicate otherwise; Rigg offers analysis of the clerical tradition and how this work's working-class emphasis stands out from it and from the philosophical line of misogyny and misogamy. The other works treated in the present book also depart from it, although they use and revise the clerical and philosophical misogamist traditions. Formally, the *De coniuge* is written in asclepiads. Like goliardics, this is a meter well suited to and often used for satires of various kinds. French *octosyllabes* can convey that satiric tone well enough; the English pentameter couplets of the *Fyftene Joyes* or the rhyme royals of the *Payne and Sorowe* convey it less well. Rigg gives examples of other goliardic and asclepiadic verses on comical and satiric topics (12).

[12] Boffey, "Wynkyn De Worde and Misogyny in Print," in *Chaucer in Perspective: Middle English Essays in Honour of Norman Blake* (Sheffield: Sheffield Academic Press, 1999), 236–51; see especially 244–5 and 247–8. On Caxton's antifeminism, see Deanne Williams, *French Fetish*, pp.110–12.

Yet some subtle risk for this translation may have lain in its dangerous style, given the English historical context. This work's satire aimed at marriage, the institution that would (or so it was hoped in 1509, the year of Henry VIII's accession) guarantee the Tudor line. Only a generation after the Wars of the Roses, the power of marriage to stabilize a political situation would not have been forgotten. Outside the royal context, marriage is strong cultural glue, and these misogamist works' acidic satire threatens it. As Santucci has demonstrated, *Les Quinze Joyes* targets several early modern institutions in addition to marriage. Beyond this, I would add that the French work does so vividly, colloquially in a raucous bourgeois and sub-bourgeois voice. Some of this broad subversiveness in French derives, in other words, from its style. The first "safe" move of the translation, in fact, is to turn the raucous French prose into very steady iambic pentameter couplets. This elevates, regularizes, formalizes, and slows the pacing of the work. The uniformity of the English verse masks and never finally conveys the narratological hybridity and disruptiveness of the French work. Some of the dialogue and many of the allusions are preserved, but overall the translation quiets the challenging, edgy voice of the French prose. The *Fyftene Joyes* translation seems not to use the resources of print to try to reproduce or equal the work's racy prose style. Instead, the translation naturalizes the work into the milieu of Wynkyn's other imprints and into the conceptual context of a familiar verse form. These changes calm what was at once a commercially prudent choice of material and, potentially anyway, an ideologically, generically, and stylistically risky one.

Beyond this general effect of the more sedately literary "Englished" stories, the most interesting transformative work of the translation takes place in the prefatory material or paratexts of the English version. The paratexts strongly shape and direct this English appropriation of misogamy, misogyny, and institutional satire. The "Prologue of the Translatour," eleven original rhyme-royal stanzas, uses traditional translator's disclaimers and deliberately nostalgic Chaucerian poetic strategies to introduce the material. The "Prohemye of the Auctour" follows, translating the French prose Prologue into 30 introductory stanzas that alter subtly the content and emphasis of the French Prologue. The Prohemye explains the misogamy of the *Joyes* with a provocative, extended meditation on individual liberty and thus connects domestic and political forms of authority and resistance.

"The Prologue of the Translatour"

The translator's Prologue, of course, has no French source since it is the translator's own work. It is a useful space in which to observe this poet unconstrained or not guided by a direct model. The Prologue consists of eleven rhyme-royal stanzas in a post-Chaucerian or perhaps anti-Chaucerian mode:

> Somer passed | and wynter well begone   [A2r]
> The dayes shorte | the darke nyghtes longe

>   Haue taken season | and brynghtnes [sic] of the sonne
>   Is lytell sene | and small byrdes songe
>   Seldon is herde | in feldes or wodes ronge
>   All strength and ventue [sic] | of trees and herbes sote
>   Dyscendynge be | from croppe in to the rote
>
>   And euery creature by course of kynde
>   For socoure draweth to that countre and place
>   Where for a tyme | they may purchace and fynde   10
>   Conforte and rest | abydynge after grace
>   That clere Appolo with bryghtnes of his face
>   Wyll sende | whan lusty ver shall come to towne
>   And gyue the grounde | of grene a goodly gowne
>
>   And Flora goddesse bothe of whyte and grene
>   Her mantell large | ouer all the erthe shall sprede
>   Shewynge her selfe | apparayled lyke a quene
>   As well in feldes | wodes | as in mede
>   Hauynge so ryche a croune upon her hede
>   The whiche of floures | shall be so fayre and bryght   20
>   That all the worlde | shall take therof a lyght

The seasonal opening of these first three stanzas is a common late-medieval introductory topos, but this instance gestures quite specifically to the initial lines of the *General Prologue* of the *Canterbury Tales*. The lines describe a winter dormancy, a dry period of waiting and hope in which "the strength and ve[r]tue of trees and herbes sote / Dyscendynge be from croppe in to the rote," awaiting the drought-piercing April showers. Blended natural and classical references, the use of caesura and enjambment (for example, ll. 3–5, 10–11), focused alliteration (l. 14), and, in the next stanzas, a disingenuously humble narrator further mark a post-Chaucerian method.

Stanzas 4 and 5 connect the inverted seasonal opening to the occasion of writing. In this cold, dry season, the translator says, he was asked to do this work (ll. 22–5). He undertakes the task, although, like the French Prologue writer, he is now older, in his own dormant season, and has no personal experience of marriage (ll. 30–31). This version of the disingenuous Chaucerian narrator is perhaps also a kind of anti-Lover, gesturing to romances in which an inexperienced persona narrates a love story and may or may not himself be struck with Cupid's arrows. This persona agrees to translate, hoping to find some joys to write about but having observed that many men are miserable in marriage. As an observer, then, he may gain in objectivity what he loses in authority about the subjects he will treat. After placing himself against a recognizably Chaucerian tradition and establishing a fairly specific literary horizon of expectation for the work, he establishes his own ethos and position with respect to the subject of marriage. His topic is:

> The Payne | travayle | besynes and hete
> That some men haue after they wedded be
> Because theyr wyves want humylyte. (ll. 40–42)

He spends only three of the Prologue's 77 lines to declare the misogamist theme and its imputed misogynist cause: proud wives. His purpose in the Prologue is clearly not thematic or explanatory but is instead generic, stylistic, literary.

Next the translator wonders aloud about invoking a muse for the project and wittily proposes and discards three possible Muses. In a self-deprecating pseudoinvocation of a muse, the translator tries out Venus, Cupid, and Hymen. These funny, fairly well-written stanzas are some of this translator's best work:

> Who shall I pray | to helpe me to endyte
> Cupyde or Venus | which haue me in dysdayne
> And for my feblenes | in grete dyspyte
> For yeres passed | may not retorne agayne
> Now may I speke | and shewe in wordes playne
> Whan youth is gone | and comen is stoupynge age
> Then worldly Ioyes | must go on pylgrymage
>
> If I sholde praye | unto ymeneus   50
> The god of weddynge | to helpe me in this charge
> Then wyll he bydde me go to Morpheus
> The god of slepe | for he hath wayes large
> Whiche with his rodde of leed dooth stere his barge
> To brynge forthe age | vnto his slepy caue
> Pray hym of rest | and nothynge elles craue

Venus and Cupid are disdainful, for "when youth is gone | and comen is stoupynge age / Then worldly Joyes must go on pylgrymage" (ll. 48–9)—another backwards glance at Chaucer. Next he proposes a more appropriate muse, Hymen, who nevertheless, he says, would only send him to Morpheus (ll. 50–53). The implication that marriage and marriage verse are soporific aims a double dig at his verses and at marriage itself. Or, as Jane Donawerth suggests, the translator is "too old for Hymen, a youthful god," and needs sleep rather than marital activity. But the invocation of Morpheus and Ovid's Cave of Sleep episode may do more. As Colin Burrow writes, Morpheus and the Cave of Sleep are associated with early modern discussions of literary imitation:

> [Morpheus's] ability to make constructive use of his unlikeness to his original is what makes him a great imitator ... a great mutator and reviver of the dead. The episode could be read as a defence of the imitative: mere imitations of reality or other texts may be evidently false or secondary, but they carry as much or greater emotional charge than their originals ... Being a little unlike your original, the

passage intimates, is the best way to affect the emotions of your audience (278–9; emphasis Burrow's).[13]

Burrow does not mention the *Fyftene Joyes*, and he does note that Morpheus in Chaucer is rather less involved with *imitatio* than Morpheus in Statius or Spenser. Our translator is probably not invoking Chaucer's Morpheus directly but may instead be invoking Morpheus in the course of a mild self-deprecation as a fleeting reminder of his own imitative practice: that is, as a reminder of his unlikeness to the French original. This is a tenuous clue (but one of our only ones, despite the long paratexts) to this translator's understanding of his own work in importing such uneasy and un-Chaucerian material as the *Quinze Joyes*.

This playfully self-mocking mock-invocation series also reveals a certain understanding about the work's new audience. While he does not gloss Cupid or Venus, his epithets—"[Y]meneus/The god of weddynge" (ll. 50–51) and "Morpheus / The god of slepe" (ll. 52–3), like the light glosses of Flora and Apollo (lines 12 and 15)—imply his sense that the broadening print audience might need such basic information to get the joke.

Stanza 9 then reverts to a traditional stance of *contemptus mundi*, calling his would-be muses "feigned gods" (l. 59):

I knowe ryght well | it is but vanyte

All worldly Ioye | medled with bytternes
Therfore these fayned goddes I lete them be [A3r]
And me betake to god | whose stedfastnes 60
May neuer fayle | neyther his sothfastnes
Besechynge hym | that for his moders sake
He wyll me teche his lytell boke to make

Given the clearly satiric title and nature of the content to follow, it is hard to read the tone here as entirely serious or Boethian, though the rest of the passage is a standard translator's request for divine guidance (ll. 60–63). Perhaps this is the translator's momentary turn to the serious and conventional, reminding himself and the reader that all worldly joys, including these fifteen "joys," are vanity. This original material is quite unlike the flippant French Prologue translated next, in which the satiric bent is strong and consistent.

At stanza 10, though, one wonders whether the speaker is attempting to convey an immediacy about the act of translation, trying to allow readers to retain a nonsatiric sense of a possible "joy" of marriage, or has even read the French *Joyes* at all: he expresses an apparently sincere wish to gain, by translating, even one of the fifteen joys for himself:

---

[13] "'Full of the Maker's Guile': Ovid on Imitating and On the Imitation of Ovid," *Ovidian Transformations: Essays on the Metamorphoses and Its Reception*, ed. Philip Hardie, Alessandro Barchiesi, and Stephen Hinds (Cambridge: Cambridge UP, 1999), 271–87.

> And with good wyll I shall me soone apply
> This treatyse out of french to translate
> Of .xv. Joyes and yf I myght therby
> Purchace but one my selfe though it be late
> I wolde be gladde for olde paynes I hate
>
> Trustynge to joye now some what in myn aege
> As dooth a byrde that syngeth in a cage. (ll. 64–70)

Here, curiously enough, the translator tropes himself as a captive animal, the same kind of image that is repeated and varied throughout the stories to figure husbands (the fish in the trap, the bear in the pit). The French narrator, so detached and sardonic about his subject, never uses such a self-image. Only in this original part of the English version do we sense that even an old, witty bachelor translator might yet find himself like the spouses in the stories to follow, trapped in the marital state, "though it be late," yet truly glad to be so trapped. This moment records the translator's imaginative engagement with his material, a participation in it so strong that he figures himself in its terms (yet a participation that misses or ignores the central French message against the trap of marriage). In this he brings to mind Chaucer's Geoffrey in the *House of Fame*, where writerly involvement and connection with the material are stronger than "persona" fully conveys.

In a final flurry of standard translators' topoi, he declares he will forge ahead and translate, asks God's help in doing so, and begs in advance the reader's indulgence for his work's lightness or flaws:

> Now to theffecte of this translacyon
> With grete desyre shortly well I procede
> But speke I must | by protestacyon
> Touchynge this mater | or elles gode forbede
> Whome I beseche lowely to be my spede
> Praynge also | eche other maner wyght
> Take no dyspleasure with my wordes lyght
>
> Here endeth the prologue of the translatoure.
> And the prohemye of the auctour begynneth.

Eustache Deschamps famously called Chaucer "graunt translateur"; to evoke Chaucer in a translator's Prologue is to place oneself in a line of productive intertextual relations with France. Yet what is not here is as telling as what is: translators' prologues traditionally establish authority and credibility; claim fidelity to a prior text; promote the work's virtues; announce its origins, purposes, or genre; and deflect the imagined reader's objections in advance, sometimes also seeking or acknowledging patronage. Here, however, there are no standard translator's claims of perfect fidelity to the text, no naming and praises of an original author or source text or patron, and no discussion of method. Apparently all this work—supplying authority, credibility, genealogy, genre, appeals to the reader—can be done by conjuring Chaucer in a rhyme-royal verse form.

Conjuring Chaucer at the start is the more remarkable because the material that follows is distinctly un-Chaucerian. The "Frenchness" of the texts that follow this Prologue is consistently preserved—in the Prohemye and the stories, the frequent allusions to French history, geography, and customs are retained, not anglicized or dropped as in so many translations from this period—but without any of the usual claims to fidelity. The value of Frenchness in England in 1509 was surely not a decided thing given the continuing warfare and marriage negotiations between the two nations, continuing Tudor claims to the French throne, and extensive literary appropriations from the presses during the whole period. Any visible Frenchness in a text of the period falls into this highly contested context and must be dealt with by translators, printers, and readers alike, but the *Fyftene Joyes* offers no guidance on this point, silently allowing all French references to stand, yet without much pro-French advertisement. This translator's work contrasts with the practice of, for instance, Tudor dramatist John Heywood, the topic of Chapter 6, who replaces each French allusion with some English approximation in an effort to suppress the farce's Frenchness. On the other hand, we have seen some translators emphasize in their titles and paratexts the Frenchness of a work, and for them Frenchness seems to be a chief selling point.

In any case, while the visible Frenchness of the original is neither highlighted nor suppressed here, the visible Chaucerianism of the English Prologue is unmistakable. Perhaps one way of addressing the text's French origin is to introduce it with what was at that time England's premier literary ancestor. The translator's main claim to authority is thus literary and unspoken: an imitative poetic that produces a familiar Chaucerian frame for his readers. But what was the value in 1509 of the Chaucerian poetic invoked here? Like the Tudor jousts, was it part of a spectacular nostalgia for a "chivalric" or courtly mode that was already vanishing? Or was it a further part of the printers' revolutionary conservatism to frame potentially subversive material in new technological forms with reassuringly high-status and familiar "old" material? The *Fyftene Joyes* translator certainly aspires to add his work to what was at that time England's central, respected national-vernacular-literary tradition. The translator's prologue places the work within a widespread and continuing pattern of Chaucerian imitation.[14] From a Jaussian standpoint, such

---

[14] See Alice Miskimin, *Renaissance Chaucer* (New Haven: Yale University Press, 1975); Seth Lerer, *Chaucer and His Readers* (Princeton: Princeton University Press, 1993); Theresa Krier, ed., *Refiguring Chaucer in the Renaissance* (Gainesville: University Press of Florida, 1998); Thomas Prendergast and Barbara Kline, eds., *Rewriting Chaucer: Culture, Authority, and the Idea of the Authentic Text 1400–1602* (Columbus, OH: Ohio State University Press, 1999); Paul Ruggiers, ed., *Editing Chaucer: The Great Tradition* (Norman OK: Pilgrim Books, 1984); Jackson Boswell and Sylvia Holton, *Chaucer's Fame in England: STC Chauceriana 1475–1640* (New York: Modern Language Association,

a prologue sets a recognizable (for English readers) horizon of expectation of a series of fictional tales focused on witty social realities. It is an odd introduction, though, for essentially un-Chaucerian material: the translator displays little sense that this literary frame and verse form work against the unruly subversions of the French Prologue and stories to follow.

"The Prohemye of the Auctour"

After the translator's own English-only Chaucerian Prologue has positioned the work in a decidedly English line, the "Prohemye of the Auctour" follows. The Prohemye translates the French prose Prologue into 29 more rhyme-royal stanzas and one oddly appended Monk's Tale stanza (see Appendix 2). That the translator titles this inner frame "Prohemye," or proem, indicates further his literary pretensions for the work and perhaps his self-consciousness about rendering the French prose in verse. The titles of these paratexts also show his care to distinguish himself from his author, a care that extends into the Prohemye itself: "Myn auctour wryteth" (l. 80); "This auctour sayth" (l. 136); "He sheweth eke in maner semblable" (l. 143). This distinction blurs a bit in asides at line 163 ("In whiche dayes I finde it happed so"), line 208 ("I undertake"), and line 261 ("As I say"). Authorial self-consciousness comes together in the Prohemye's final *occupatio* topos:

> Moche more herof myn auctoure dooth declare
> In his prologue or that he wyll begyn
> To shewe these .xv. Joyes but I must spare
> By losse of tyme there is nothynge to wynne
> But pouerte vnthryftynes and synne
> Wherfore in wordes rude to make and ende
> And of these joyes to wryte now I entende

The translator wants to be known as such and wants to foreground his author as well. Overall, the Prohemye omits and reduces some elements in the French Prologue, adds or expands other elements, and thereby shifts the emphasis of the remaining content. A brief review of the French Prologue will highlight the significance of the translator's particular interventions.

In French, the Prologue is a spirited, satiric, and self-conscious prose introduction that breaks down into fairly clear and well-balanced sections.

2004). In "Two English Translations of the XVth Century French Satire 'Les Quinze Joyes de Mariage'," *Kwartalnik Neofilologiczny* 10.1 {1963}: 17–32, Maria Łobzowska mentions Chaucerianism in the prologue and imprint, but without much supporting detail. Thanks to Professor Boswell for suggesting that I write on this prologue, Folger Shakespeare Library, August 2002.

The initial move (ll. 1–17) is an assertion that individual liberty is a natural human state and that only a fool willingly gives it up and places himself in a prison with iron bars. This initial assertion is, historically speaking, rather remarkable, more often associated with eighteenth-century discourses on the individual subject and the polis. Second comes a section of historical proofs of the importance of liberty (ll. 18–54), recalling the long tradition of French liberty from Roman to recent (that is, late-medieval) times. The natural desire for individual liberty is here claimed to be part of the ancient national character as well. Some of the examples are ambiguously and even wittily tied to French national success.[15] Third is a section of natural proofs (ll. 55–84). Here, examples from nature of animals being trapped unwittingly—the fish in the *nasse*, the bear in the pit—are likened to men in marriage. The simile of the fish in the *nasse* gets the most space, and there is a return to the image of marriage as a prison with impenetrable bars.

Then comes a kind of parody of the traditional appeal to clerical or patristic authority. Here the appeal to *auctoritas* takes the form of allusions to the misogynist and misogamist literary tradition already well known in France at that time (ll. 84–101). The narrator places the work in the line of Valerius (Walter Map) and Mathéolus. The author even quotes Valerius's infamous question, probably ultimately derived from Juvenal's sixth satire (VI. 30), to a friend who is about to marry: "Ami, dit-il, naves vous peu trouver une haulte fenestre pour

---

[15] Brent A. Pitts's lively translation (*The Fifteen Joys of Marriage* [New York: P. Lang, 1985]) conveys this aspect of the prologue and captures the tone well: "Since it's human nature to covet liberty and freedom, several great fiefdoms have been forfeit because their lords sought to revoke their subjects' independence; many cities, towns, and other small communities have likewise been undone for their citizens' disobedience and petitions for excessive freedoms, unleashing great wars and slaughters. For this reason the Frankish aristocracy by its great courage won freedom and exemptions from tributes and service due the Roman emperors, for which liberties the Franks fought and carried many a battle. Now it happened that because they were not strong enough to resist the might of an invading emperor, the Franks preferred to abandon and flee their country rather than render service or tribute, and by this act they gave clear proof of their profound nobility. [n.b.: this moment is typical of the satiric technique and tone of the work] ... later, both nobly and by the sword, they liberated their own land, France, and have kept their homeland free to this day, insofar as their own personal benefit is concerned. For this reason all nations of oppressed peoples then longed to be in France in order to be free, so that France was at once the noblest land in all the world, foremost in abundance of wealth, population, settlements, and buildings, and brimming with wisdom, prudence, Christian faith, and all other virtues. Now since the great lords of France are free, it stands to reason that their people should be free as well, and that the lords should give their subjects the same laws that they themselves enjoy, for it's unreasonable to have one law for oneself and another for one's neighbors. Because of this injustice the land is now deserted and depopulated and in the absence of wisdom and several other virtues, sin and vice hold sway" (2-3). Appendix 2 amply demonstrates how little the English version captures the tweaking humor in this mock-historiography, yet how carefully it reproduces the content.

vous laissier trebucher en une grosse ryviere pour vous mectre dedans la teste premiere?" [My friend, he says, couldn't you find a high window over a big river to jump into head first?] The narrator explains Valerius's question in terms of his own focus on individual liberty: "En montrant que on se soit exposer en moult grant peril avant que perdre franchise" [Showing that one ought to face extreme peril before sacrificing one's freedom]. In a drastic move, Mathéolus left the happy state of single cleric to marry a widow and regretted it ever after, writing a treatise, according to our narrator, in order to repent and to comfort himself and for the profit of those who came after him. (Mathéolus is said to have been a bigamist, which makes him a perfect comic *auctoritas* to invoke in an antimarital prologue.) The French Prologue, in other words, places the *XV Joies de mariage* in a typically misogamist, misogynist, deeply rooted, and widely current branch of French letters.[16]

The next section of the French Prologue treats some possible interpretive difficulties the narrator wishes to clarify for the reader. The author explicates his own daring title and makes explicit the analogy between the fifteen so-called "joys" of marriage and fifteen joys of the Virgin Mary widely known from religious works—the annunciation, the nativity, the ascension, and so on (ll. 102–118). In case we missed the sarcasm, he then explains what he means by redefining "joys": " ... celles quinze joyes de mariage sont, a mon advis, les plus grans tourmens, douleurs, tristesses, et quinze les plus grans maleuretez qui soient en terre, esquelles nules autres paines, sans incision de membres, ne sont pareilles a continuer"(ll. 118–23).[17]

Then, in lines 123–47, the tone seems to change rather abruptly. The narrator solemnly says he does not, however, condemn those who marry and really has nothing against marriage. In fact, he says, marriage might be a good thing after all because we are only on this earth to suffer and gain heaven, and—here the sardonic tone returns—what greater suffering and penitence could there be than marriage? A moment of seriousness for the French narrator serves to set up a punch line; the English translator's serious moments are not followed by such zingers. After this, the narrator claims that married people are like donkeys grown so long accustomed to heavy burdens that they think themselves content. Finally, he says, his purpose is to console the married, not to dissuade the unmarried (ll. 143–7). This is clearly satiric in light of what has come before and in light of the closing phrase of the Prologue (ll. 147–8), "Et il finira miserablement ses jours"

---

[16] Karen Pratt demonstrates that Jean Lefèvre's translation of Mathéolus is more misogamous than the original, and cites specific passages. "Translating Misogamy: The Authority of the Intertext in the *Lamentationes Matheoluli* and Its Middle French Translation by Jean LeFèvre," *Forum for Modern Language Studies* 35.4 (October 1999): 421–35.

[17] "These fifteen joys are, in my opinion, the greatest torments, woes, sorrows, and fifteen of the greatest unhappinesses there be on earth, the likes of which no other troubles are as bad to suffer, [not] even being dismembered;" in Pitts's translation that last part is less literal: "with the possible exception of mayhem."

[and he will end his days miserably], which is also the closing phrase of each of the fifteen stories.

The English Prohemye, however, omits much of the French Prologue's content and alters the balance of the rest, thus framing the stories' misogamy differently. First, the omissions: The narrator's allusive literary self-consciousness is lost to the English Prohemye. There is no mention of the fifteen joys of Mary, of the title, of the sardonic revision of the meaning of "joy" for the reader. The English work thus makes no self-referential gesture to the work's parodies of religious-literary conventions, another signal that the translator or printer may have imagined differences in how the new readership would receive the text. This may further signal the translator's choice to tame the material, since similar religious conventions were available in English; it is not that new readers would not catch the religious parodies. Could the printer have thought they would not appreciate such parodies? Nor does the translation place itself openly in a line of misogynist and misogamist literature. The references to Valerius and Mathéolus are suppressed, perhaps because the translator thinks they will have little meaning for his new audience. Although both figures were probably familiar to readers of clerical or university manuscripts, neither writer's work had been printed in England by 1509.[18] The printer's or translator's sense of the new audience's lack of familiarity with Valerius, Theophrastus, and Mathéolus may have meant that these translations were "new" in a way for this readership.

These omissions may suggest the translator's (or the printer's) sense of the widening English audience. The printers were at once creating and feeding readerly demand for misogynist and misogamist literature, but they are doing so with texts deracinated from their original contexts and readerships. In a study of Wynkyn De Worde's many misogynist imprints, Julia Boffey explains his "willingness to experiment with genres and forms which had hitherto apparently been overlooked, if not consciously rejected" and, further, that "De Worde seems to have put some energy into developing a line of short 'mery jests' in which the subcategory of humorous misogynist material played an important role" ("Wynkyn" 248). In addition to beginning to translate and print the old clerical strains of misogamy for their new audiences, the printers may have spied a new market niche: vernacular works about (and for?) common couples of the middling and working sort. No allusions to the long Theophrastan line are needed or desired in such "new" materials. Whatever the reason for the suppression of these framing allusions from French, the translator neither invokes the authority of a long misogynist and misogamist line nor places his translation in that line.

---

[18] In fact, the STC shows no printing of Mathéolus (or Le Fèvre de Ressons) at all; Greek editions of Theophrastus are printed in 1604 and 1628. Walter Mapes' or Map's *Phillis and Flora* is translated in 1598, and a poem translated from French, the *Dysputacyon ... of the Herte [and Eye]*, (Wynkyn De Worde [1516]), may have come from a Latin poem attributed to Mapes.

Next the rapid-fire French catalogue of the superiorities of France is slowed into a brief itemized description in English, to be discussed further below. One of the national virtues, "la foy catholique," is omitted entirely in English. This could not have been the translator's politically motivated suppression, not even an incredibly prescient one, in 1509, Henry VIII's coronation year, when he was yet to be named Defender of the Faith (1520), had yet to write the *Seven Sacraments* (1521), and was a long way from the break with Rome (1534). A big issue in 1509 was instead about a kind of widow-marrying: Henry's marriage to Catherine of Aragon, widow of Prince Arthur, which was in some views at least theoretically incestuous. To read these particular omissions as political, as translation-à-clef, is in my judgment a bit of a stretch. The translator, moreover, omits at least two pieces of French antimarital content, dropping the idea of marriage as penance and the vivid image of married people as habituated donkeys. In general terms, promarriage background pressure may be at work here; the antimarital genres in fact rely on and assume a broadly accepted promarriage attitude for their very existence and humor. Much of the wry humor and verve of the French prose is simply not present in the English Prohemye's rhyme-royal stanzas, which seem, after reading the lively French Prologue, strangely flat. I attribute this more to verbal style than to political context, however. The cheeky statements of purpose are gone, too—the translator, certainly less whimsical than his French source-writer, does not claim that these "joys" will console the woefully married and, in fact, claims no purpose at all for the work.

Furthermore, the important final phrase of the Prologue, "et finiront miserablement leurs jours," has no equivalent here and does not even appear until the end of the first story. In the French work, this closural phrase unifies Prologue and stories: It is to the prose work what a refrain line is to poetic stanzas—or what rhyme is to poetic lines. Such internal devices regulate or punctuate the narrative. When each part of the *Qunize Joyes* ends on the same phrase, the author creates not only internal structures but readerly anticipation: after the Prologue and a story, we are waiting for the punch line. (One can even imagine a sociable audience calling it out in unison or a solitary reader murmuring it.) "Et finira miserablement ses jours" becomes a mock-tragic finale toward which every story—and implicitly every marriage—leads. The English version, however, does not inaugurate that strategy in the Prohemye, nor does every story end with the same words. The French phrase "Et finira miserablement ses jours" is translated in different ways in several of the English stories, changing, it seems, for the sake of rhyme or meter. "And there this poore man shall vse his lyfe / Endynge his dayes in wretchednes & stryfe" (C2r); "There vseth he his lyfe in paynes always / And wretchedly | thus endeth he his dayes" ([C5v]); *et alii*. *Wretched* is the closest thing to a repeating word in the English endings, and it does convey well the dual problem of poverty and unhappiness in "miserablement." Repeating the whole phrase "il finira miserablement ses jours" has much more impact than the English stories manage. The translation thus removes the strong pattern of verbal closure so enjoyable and important in the French version. The Prohemye does not create the expectation of coherent closure for each piece within the frame, as the French Prologue does; in English, death is still the only escape from the miserable trap that is marriage, but it is not every story's punch line. Overall, then, the English Prohemye is less self-conscious, less interested in amusing the reader and in guiding the reader's interpretation, less concerned to indicate its own position, perhaps less satiric in purpose, or at least less witty and more straightforward.

Which is not to say "boring": the English Prohemye adds a few key images and allusions. Beginning at line 90, the translator adds familiar images of the passions, Venus and the bridle. A Boethian addition at lines 99–100 resembles the translator's original work in his own preceding Prologue stanzas (ll. 57–8). There is an allusion to Jesus that has no French equivalent (l. 152). There is a greater specificity in the English rendering of the prison bars and jailor, and that specificity creates a slight but important shift in the basic idea of the problem with marriage. The French passage reads:

> On pourroit dire que ung homme na pas bon sens, qui est en joyes et delices du monde—comme de jeunesse garnie—et de sa franche voulente et de son propre mouvement sans necessite trouve lentree dune estroicte chartre douloureuse, plaine de larmes, de gemissements, d'angoisses, et se boute dedans. Et quant est liens enclos, on lui ferme la porte, qui est de fer, fermant a grosses barres, et est si estroitement tenu que jamais pour nulles prieres ne auoir ne peut saillir ... .[19]

In French, the jail is marriage. In English, it is lust that initially imprisons the young:

> As thus whan men in youth couragyous
> With fre wyll endewed and lustynes
> Of theyr desyre | and mynde outragyous
> Withouten nede | but of theyr folysshenes
> Frome wele to wo | from Ioye to heuynes
> Convey themselfe | from all theyr lyberte
> Nothynge content with theyr felycyte
>
> For whereas they may frely ryde or go
> And at theyr choyse | dysporte them ouer all
> I you ensure these yonge men wyll not so   110
> Whan they leest wene | than sodanly they fall

---

[19] [One could say that a man doesn't have good sense, who is enjoying the delights of the world—such as prosperous youth—and who, of his free will and own initiative, freely enters a narrow, woeful prison, full of tears and cries and suffering, and throws himself into it. And when he's enclosed therein, one closes the door on him—which is of iron, closed with thick bars—and he is so closely guarded that never, not for any prayers or money, could he possibly escape.]

> And unconstrayned make theyr bodyes thrall
> Lyke to a wyght that in to pryson depe
> Without cause | all hastely dooth crepe
>
> So do they oft for lacke of kyndely wytte
> And when they be within this pryson strayte   [A4r]
> The gayler cometh and fast the dore dooth shytte
> Whiche is of yren stronge ...

In this somewhat amplified translation, while the young men may freely play the field (ll. 108–9), when least they know it (l.110), they fall, presumably into love or lust, in which state they "make their bodies thrall," like a man who puts himself in prison (ll. 112–14). Then, "when they are within this narrow prison" (l. 116), the jailor comes and closes the iron door—that is, the iron door of marriage. The lines do not support a perfectly close allegorical reading, but there is some shift and elaboration of the French version. The translator has added an essentially Pauline subtext that rationalizes marriage as a containment system for soul-damning lust. The promarriage argument about the thralldom of the lustful body would normally end in a Christian paradox—that the bond of marriage is therefore liberating of the lust-enslaved soul. Nothing like that exists in the French, which actually begins, "Many have worked to show that man is happier living in freedom." That the translator brings such a Christian subtext to the translation suggests that either his own assumptions are really quite at odds with those underpinning the French version, or he knows that his audience's assumptions will be so at odds, and he adds the promarriage subtext to try to bridge the difference. In either case, the Pauline doctrine beneath these lines sets up a dynamic quite unlike that of the French version. When combined with the suppression of references to the misogamist tradition, and the suppression of parodic allusions to clerical literature, and given the steadier tone and statelier verse forms, this shift makes the treatise still less playful and more serious.

The sentence that follows this passage is greatly expanded in English. The French version reads: "Et par especial doit on bien tenir celui fol et sans nul sens de soy estre ainsi emprisonne sil avait ouy par devant plourer et gemir ou dedens la chartre les prisonniers qui liens estoient" [And one must especially consider crazy and without any sense the person who imprisoned himself like that, if he had heard in advance the prisoners inside the prison cry and wail]. In French, "on" is the only explicit agent of this passage—"on" is we readers, who must think the marrying man crazy to have put himself into the prison. But in English, there is an active and malevolent jailer, and the marital prison is much more specifically imagined in a fully extended two-stanza conceit. It is not quite allegorical, but the personification and detail here recall the method of *Everyman* more than that of Rabelais:

> The gayler cometh and fast the dore dooth shytte
> Whiche is of yren stronge | and in a wayte
> He lyeth oft | for drede that thrugh defayte
> By nyght or day some sholde escape out   120
> Ryght besyly he pryeth all about
>
> He barreth dores | and maketh sure all the lockes
> The stronge boltes | the fettres and the chayne
> He sercheth well | the holes and the stockes
> That wo be they | that lyeth in the payne
> And out therof | they shall not go agayne
> But euer endure | in wepynge care and sorowe
> For good ne prayer | shall them neuer borowe
>
> And specyally men may call hym assoted
> Ferre frome reason | of wysdome desolate   130
> That thus his tyme mysse vsed hath and doted
> Whan he had herde | such prysoners but late
> Wepynge waylynge | and with them selfe debate
> Lyenge in pryson | as he hath passed by
> And put hym selfe therin so folysshely

This expansion and increased specificity were common early modern French-to-English translation habits. Another such common translation habit, that of doubling, is also evident here ("the holes and the stockes," "ferre frome reason, of wysdome desolate," "mysse vsed hath and doted," etc.). The result is a textured, concretely imagined depiction.

Furthermore, there is extra attention to "symylytude," to the analogy between marriage and prison, and to the analogy between between marriage and traps ("lepe" or "nasse"):

> Thus one may say | and therupon conclude
> By such as in to maryage be brought
> And herupon to make a symylytude
> Unto the fysshe whiche hath his pasture sought   230
> And in a lepe | that is of twygges wrought
> Is take | and out can not escape ne twynne
> But euer dwell | and tary styll therinne

The translator points to his literary method of "symylytude" here, as if the reader might miss it.

Finally, in the Monk's Tale stanza that seems tacked on at the end of the Prohemye, the translator explains that men should ignore their wives' misuse of eloquence:

> Some men do call these Ioyes sorowes grete
> But yet they take them well in pacyence
> For of necessyte they must forgete
> The care | trouble | sorowe | payne and offence
> The whiche they suffre at the reuerence
> Of theyr wyues | whiche they may not forsake
> And though they oft | mysse vse theyr eloquence
> Lytell regarde therto a man sholde take   290
> Here endeth the prohemye of the auctour

There is nothing like this in the French. Such an addition engages directly with the problem of the speaking woman. Scholars beginning with Suzanne Hull have shown how early modern conduct literature supported the norm of the "chaste, silent, and obedient" woman and how female speech was suppressed literally and figuratively throughout the early modern period in England. This added stanza would fit in with what we know about prohibitions on women's speech and would also imply that the translator perceived this addition as a necessary one as he is preparing the English reader to encounter the many speaking women in the French text. One translator's addition of such a stanza is not enough evidence from which to generalize, say, that the tolerance for female speech was greater in early modern France than in early modern England. Yet the speech of women in French gender discourses does seem to draw the particular attention of these translators and printers (for example, in the *Interlocucyon*, the *Letter of Dydo*, and the marriage complaints to be discussed in Chapter 5). Here at least it is one more way the translator calms the French work's provocations.

The translator adds certain other elements here and there, like the doubling of antithesis in line 105 or the brief hunting simile about hounds nosing for bones in lines 265–8, that seem particularly English compared with the French prose. The translator's Hawes-like enjambments between stanzas, too, would be an instance of a subtle "Englishness" in the execution of the verse. "Wherby it grewe | somtyme the noblest [stanza break] Realme of the worlde | that knowen were or founde" (ll. 184–5) is a clear example, but other kinds of work across stanza breaks are involved here, too. Similes cross the stanza break at 113–15 and 121–2 and sentences and concepts cross at 17–18, 191–2, 219–20 (see Appendix 2 for these and other instances). We see this translator experimenting with longer units of poetic discourse. This is the kind of work with verse forms that points to the later verse paragraph: attempts to render content using a coherent interlinear and interstanzaic motion, to move not only from the stichic to the strophic but beyond.

Although the translator's techniques—doubling, amplification with a tendency to allegory, enjambments—mark the divergence of the French and English literary systems, the gist of the content is largely the same. The particular arguments against marriage—arguments based on nature and on history—are the same in the French Prologue and English Prohemye, and they appear in the same order.

The Prohemye, like the French Prologue from which it is taken, uses the figures of marriage as prison and marriage as a fish leap or animal trap and specifically attacks men who witness others' marriages but wed anyway:

> And specyally men may call hym assoted
> Fer from reason | of wysdom desolate
> That thus his tyme mysse vsed hath and doted
> Whan he had herde | such prysoners but late
> Wepynge and waylynge | and with them selfe debate
> Lyenge in pryson | as he hath passed by
> And put hym selfe therin so folysshely (129–35).

About 50 lines of the latter part of the Prohemye—nearly one quarter of the whole—expand the idea that "A fole is he | that wyttynge wyll go" into marriage (ll. 213–68). The willing husband is compared to a trapped beast and then, in a familiar extended simile, to a fish in the "lepe," a fish-leap or net-trap (French: *la nasse*). The verse describes a fish swimming past the others caught in the trap; thinking that they are flailing about in pleasure ("Ioye"), the fish tries to join them. "In he gooth gladde and Iocounde / And to the shynynge bayte | he hyeth faste / Wherof anone he taketh his repaste" (245–7). The fish swims in anyway and, to its great dismay, is then stuck forever, "therin to dwell in wo and heuynes" (255), despite all efforts to escape. "Though it so be | that folkes se before / These wedded men | within the lepe enclosed / In poynt to droune & drenche | yet not therefore / Wyll they forbere" (262–5). The poem's elaborate, extended metaphors of marriage as a trap or prison—a scathing indictment of men foolish enough to marry—might have harmonized oddly with the moment's national imperative and chronic concern for the succession. Hanna and Lawler (9–10) point out that the *quaestio* tradition (a rhetorical performance on the question "Should one marry?") had political implications for the Augustan empire; it is not clear how much the Tudor situation was analogous in this respect. Although the *Quinze Joyes* descends from a branch of the rhetorical *quaestio* tradition accompanying the *querelle des femmes*, the *Fyftene Joyes*'s resounding "no" may have sounded more topically subversive in its first English context in 1509; there is no real evidence either way. I would say rather that the printer and translator calculated that their readers would have been more interested in the quotidian and satiric than the national and serious aspects of marriage.

Remarkably, however, in both French and English versions, the Prohemye overtly connects a person's avoiding the domestic entrapment of marriage with the political subject's resistance to various forms of authority. So in a sense, even this satiric and quotidian work keeps the political in view—indeed, frames the satiric quotidian with the political. The initial French assertion that individual liberty is the natural human state is preserved and elaborated in English. Here, as in the French Prologue, the assertion is (as yet) ungendered. For both men and women, marriage is not a civilizing force here—quite the contrary. Figured as an animal trap and as a prison, marriage is unnatural, inhuman: individual liberty is our primary "natural" and necessary state. "By cause mankynde delyteth / Alway to haue fraunchyse and lyberte / Without the whiche nature of man despyteth (136–9). Likewise, to lose personal liberty is to lose reason, and he who does so, "wyllfully dooth cast his grace away" (212). Once lost, the state of grace that is liberty cannot be regained: "[A] man may se the people euery day / Demeane themselfe forsakynge lyberte / And shortely after that repenteth [sic] ... but they ne may ... vnto such grace attayne" (270–75). In this view, "[I]t is great wytte and wysdom more / For euery maner wyght of woman bore / To lyue in fraunchyse at hys liberte" (83–5). (The English translation necessarily loses the Prologue's puns on "Fraunchyse" and "franc.") The next few stanzas are those, as we have seen above, that add Pauline assumptions to the French version, explaining that "lusty folke in theyr adolescence" who marry to satisfy or contain sexual desire are "lyke to a wyght that in to pryson [that is, marriage] depe / Without cause all hastely doth crepe / So do they oft for lack of kyndely wytte" (113–18). Their lack of natural ("kyndely") wit is the trouble; to marry is to enter a prison. In this view, individual liberty is a natural and sensible human state (marriage, by implication, being a prison for the unnatural or the unnaturally witless).

Next, a long historiographic passage argues that individual liberty is essential to the national character (ll. 139–98). However, even in English translation, this means the French national character, and the translator makes no mention of the English nation or its relation to individual liberty. As if to deflect or forestall criticism, or as if unwilling or unable to speak of English history and its relation to individual liberty, the translator uses repeated asides to remind us that he is merely passing on what the French author said about marriage, liberty, and the national history: "This auctour sayeth" (l. 136), "Ryght thus in playne wordes speketh he" (l.139), "He sheweth eke in maner semblable (l. 143); "Moche more herof myn auctoure dooth declare / In his prologue" (ll. 276–7). Yet despite these disclaimers—or thanks to them?—the translator does not shrink from his author's point that the loss of individual liberty has political consequences. In fact, this section expands in the translation to occupy nearly a third of the whole Prohemye, a much larger proportion than it occupies in French. The expanded political consequences of the loss of personal liberty vary, but they are all bad: great lords, for instance, lose their power when they take away the liberty of their subjects (l. 140–42). (On the other hand, great cities are destroyed and wars are fought when subjects claim excessive liberties [ll. 144–56].) A seven-stanza history of France from Roman to (then)-recent times follows, linking French greatness with its preservation of liberty:

> Somtyme the noble realme and men of Fraunce
> Exempte were | and utterly made fre
> By theyr grete | prowes and valyaunce
> Of the emperours of Rome the cyte ...   160
> ...

> Upon a tyme | for cause that they ne were 165
> Of fraunce in puyssaunce | able to withstonde
> The grete army and the myghty powere
> Of an emperour entred in theyr londe
> But for as moche as they ne wolde be bonde
> Than to remayn vnder subgeccyon ... 170

In this version of French history, the nobles refused to pay tribute or to be bound, and:

> ... wente away
> Conquerynge cou[n]trees | suche was theyr worthynes
> And afterward retorned neuertheles 175
> Home to theyr lande | in grete prosperyte
> Whiche they tyll now haue holde in lyberte.

This quintessential freedom of the French nation (both the author and translator explain) accounts for the attempts of enslaved people of other nations to immigrate (ll. 179–83) and accounts for the general superiority of France: "Wherby it grewe | somtyme the noblest / Realme of the world | that knowen were or founde" (ll.184–5). Next is a short list of France's excellences, connected with the subjects' freedom:

> Moost fayre in buyldyng | and inhabyte best
> The whiche in treasure | and scyence dyde habounde
> Then for as moche | as they be fre at leest
> Prudent in fayth | in lyuynge holyest
> They sholde theyr subgets | in fraunchyse kepe and vse. 190

This is slightly reduced from a rather more flamboyant French description:

> ... dont [that is, from the immigration of people wanting to be free] advint que France fut la plus noble terre du monde, la plus riche, la plus peuplee, la plus habitee et la mieulx edifiee, flourissant en richesse, en science, en prudence, en la foy catholicque, et en toutes autres vertuz. Et puis quilz sont francs, raison voulsist quilz eussent leur peuple franc ...[20]

---

[20] [From which (immigrations) it came to pass that France was the noblest land of the world, the richest, the most populous, the most inhabited, and the best built up, flourishing in wealth, in knowledge, in prudence, in the catholic faith, and in all other virtues. And since they are free, it was reasonable that their people be free (*lit.* reason wanted them to have their people free; with a pun on "French").]

The repeated puns in this section in French on "franchise," "franc," and "France" are not exactly irrelevant in translation but are not aimed at an English readership as they had been for a French readership ("Fraunchyse" being the French readers' natural and national state at once). Puns rarely translate well—they mark the point of contact between a word and its multiple meanings in context, so they are reminder of the intractably alien—but here is a rare case where the languages were still close enough for the puns to have worked, more or less. In other words, the translator could have made more of the word play, had he wished, by placing "Fraunce" and "fraunchise" close together in a line or by repetitions—by using ploce to support the pun.

Despite the French national focus that remains in the English translation, a subsequent stanza asserts that it is wrong to hold one law (presumably that of liberty) for oneself and another law (presumably that of enslavement) for one's neighboring land, since "Herof it groweth that lyberte is lost / In people voyde of reason and scyence" (ll. 199–200). So the logic of liberty has to apply to all, even including immigrants and even across boundaries. To all men, that is: this "people" is not an inclusive modern word, but "people" meaning citizenry, political subjects—assumed then to be male—as in the "noble *men* of Fraunce" (l. 157; emphasis mine). The first moment here that the individual subject contemplating marriage is gendered as male comes in the third stanza of the Prologue at line 96 in English; until that point, one contemplating marriage is a "wyght," which could indicate either a male or female person (*OED*) or, if plural, are some "folke" who risk entrapping themselves in marriage. The argument about marriage and liberty shifts from a potential application to both men and women, to application to male political subjects only. By the end, the translator adds that all (men) should love "the comyn wele" (ll. 204–5), which depends on each individual's personal virtue, freedom, and well-being (ll. 206–12). If an individual throws away his precious liberty by marrying, he thus commits an act against the common good, and "who loueth not his wele pertyculerly / Hath but a lytell wytte" (ll. 207–8). Marriage, in short, is a crime against the state, committed by the witless.

After this section, the Prohemye returns to harp on the metaphors of marriage as a prison and marriage as a trap for beasts and fish. Pity the bear that falls in a ditch trap or the fish that swims into a lepe, for a trapped creature is doomed. Antimarriage arguments by analogy to nature, in other words, surround and support the historiographical stanzas. The historiographic section is longer in English than it is in the French analogue and occupies a bit more than one third of the English Prohemye (11 of 29 stanzas), whereas it took up a little less than a quarter of the French Prologue. One could argue that the English audience's unfamiliarity with French history may have led the translator to elaborate or that the requirements of the chosen verse form led to syntactical inversions and *chevilles* that made this section longer. Both explanations are no doubt correct; whether or not the translator deliberately reweighted his content in this way, the result is that French historiography dominates this English Prohemye more than it dominated the French original.

Translating a very selective history of France into an expanded poetic version, the English Prohemye overall frames and inferentially explains the work's misogamy with a provocative, extended meditation on individual liberty (ll. 140–192; ll. 213–75). French liberty, French history, French greatness, all imported to the English context: Are the English to emulate or to avoid the French example? Does the strong French exemplarity in the Prologue distance readers from the question of marriage (marriage is for the witless ones over *there*, the poor frogs; has naught to do with us), or does it lead readers to an unfavorable comparison (we English should not be so keen to marry, like witless serfs, or we might still be holding Guyenne and Normandy)? Can the satiric, shocking connection between political and domestic liberty be translated at all? Or would both the English and French versions of these arguments—the political argument for liberty in service of an argument against marriage—have been seen as equally, comically impossible against such powerful institutions as nation and church? The Prohemye's refusal to anglicize allusions—its retention of and expanded weighting of French historiography—raises but in no way answers those questions. Overall, the translator's introductory poetry at least invites English readers to consider more broadly several institutional checks on individual liberty and to think of marriage as unnatural and unwise. These ideas had been flamboyantly satirical in French, but a calmer style edges the English version closer to something serious.

Woodcuts, the Lost Epilogue, Misogamy, and Misogyny

Beyond the question of the work's double poetic frame, the woodcuts De Worde adds make sense as an effort at sedate or ceremonial framing for the unruly French work. More important, the absence of an epilogue further reshapes this work for English readers and adds misogyny to its misogamy, or at least removes the promise of a hearing for the woman's side.

The woodcuts vary among versions. In French, two of the known versions before 1509 include a large woodcut on the title verso of a man carrying a cradle, surrounded by children, animals, and a wife figure with a distaff. This scene of plainly rendered domestic burdens is quite true to the French text, and in the Trepperel quarto edition of c.1499, it also appears on the last page of the book.[21] At this writing I cannot clearly establish which of the French imprints or manuscripts of the work was De Worde's copytext for his edition of 1509, but he does place

---

[21] Tchemerzine, *s.v.* La Salle, pp. 90–97. Among the other known French imprints are found various woodblock renditions of a couple: one on horseback, one in a courtly interior, and one with the man and woman looking unhappy, back to back, each figure within its own frame, visually depicting the text's verbal theme of the isolating imprisonment of marriage. Martha Driver, *The Image in Print*, (London: British Library, 2004) explains that De Worde's wedding scenes are "based on French picture models" (89) and that they are "derived from print models of the sacraments" in Vérard's imprints (90–91).

large woodcut images on the title page, the title verso, and the final page (after the colophon), just as some French imprints do. His placement of cuts is similar in its framing impulse, but the scenes themselves differ. In De Worde's imprint of 1509, the title cut, also the closing cut in the only complete extant copy, is a wedding scene with all eyes focused on the bride.[22] In the family scene on the title page verso, the well-dressed family, complete with children who have appeared in the blink of an eye (or the turn of a page), welcomes a visitor. This approximates the domestic scene on the Trepperel title page, but without the obvious sense of family burdens depicted there. (However, if the visitor arriving in the English cut is meant to be the husband, this illustration quite contradicts a recurring theme in the stories themselves: that the husband returns to a dark, unkempt house and cold, meager food, with no one to greet him.) These illustrations are decorous, showing personages arrayed in ceremonial order, men on the left, women on the right. The effect of turning the page from one woodcut to the next may also anticipate the effect of the stories themselves: we come to the text as the young couple comes to the marriage ceremony, with desire and hope; but soon enough, our innocence is lost as we turn the pages and learn more about the dreadful nature of domestic life. The closing woodcut, in such a reading, would be a satiric endpoint for the "joys" of marriage, an image that we re-view more knowingly after encountering marriage in the stories.

The ceremonial style of these woodcuts parallels the literary pretensions of the verse form and the Chaucerian frame. The addition of sedate verse forms and sedate scenes may be a coherent translator's (or printer's) tactic, but it is nevertheless fundamentally at odds with the rowdy, unceremonial nature of the French work. Where the French images often show what the stories describe, snapshots of burdensome marriage, the English framing woodcuts reveal a wedding, a rather static and well-arrayed home life, but few domestic burdens. The French version's racy prose, sardonic tone, colloquialisms, grim closural punch lines, and woeful woodcuts all work well with a satiric idea of marital "joy." The formal and presentational strategies in English, however—stories in pentameter couplets, prefatory verses in rhyme royal and Monk's Tale stanzas, and ceremonial tableaux of decorously dressed people—work less well with that basic idea and content. The pictures imply the dignity, not the indignities, of marriage.[23]

---

[22] This is also the title cut for his *Payne and Sorowe of Euyll Marriage*, also 1509, and is found in the *Knyght of the Swanne*, (1512), the pre-1518 *Gesta Romanorum*, and *Olyuer of Castylle* (1518). So the printer found this image at least as useful for courtly romance as for misogamy. See Driver, *The Image in Print*, pp. 90–91. The Pierpont Morgan Library copy is the only complete copy extant; the Folger copy's final quire is missing, and the Bodleian's Douce fragment is of inner pages.

[23] The woodcuts within the work itself introduce each joy. These cuts vary from a quasi-courtly presentation—as in *Joyes* 1, 2, and 3—to images of the domestic sub-bourgeois. The critique of marriage apparently applies to all estates in these images, yet the stories themselves involve only the working and middling classes and do not move

A very important moment of framing in the French, however, is entirely unavailable to English readers. The French versions vary, but some of the *Quinze Joyes* imprints and manuscripts include an epilogue. The epilogue addresses women, claims that the treatise was written at the request of women, and regrets any offense that may have been taken. The full versions of the epilogue contain a verbal riddle promising to reveal this woman-friendly misogamist author's name (a riddle not yet satisfactorily solved). As Claudio Galderisi has argued, however, the strategies of anonymity are integral to the *Quinze Joyes*, and it seems to me that the epilogue's work as apologia or retraction is more important than its *charade d'auteur*.[24] The epilogue states that women have at least as much suffering in marriage as men do and that the author will soon undertake a work about that:

> ... si elles ... vouloient que je preinsse peine a escrire pour elles ... en bonne foy je m'ouffre: car j'ay plus belle matiere de le faire que cette-cy n'est, veu les grans tors, griefs, et oppressions que les hommes font aux femmes en plusieurs lieux, generalement par leur forses et sans raison...[aux femmes] sans lesquelles ils ne sauroient ne pourroient vivre ...[25]

Such paratextual retractions are fairly common in the medieval European misogynist and misogamist traditions,[26] but this one strikes a more sincere, less taunting, and less disingenuous or perfunctory note than many. The author tries here, at least, to separate the stories' misogamy from their misogyny and to retract the latter.

That the English version of 1509 appears without this epilogue means that the text came, first of all, with no authorial clues or claims attached. This is true at least of the one complete copy extant, the Pierpont Morgan Library copy. As so often occurs, interpretations of an early modern work require material evidence, in both senses. In the one copy of the final quire, we can see that the English work's misogamy was not framed with apologetic deflections of anticipated blame from women readers. Where the French text assumes a female readership—and imagines and tries to anticipate that readership's objections—the English texts make no closing gesture to women readers, their objections, their equal sufferings in marriage, or their parallel loss of a "natural" individual liberty. We may assume

---

deliberately from one social estate to the next (another way in which the work is unlike the *Canterbury Tales*).

[24] "Stratégies de l'anonymat," pp. 13–15, 24–6 especially.

[25] [If they (women) wanted me to take the trouble to write for them, in good faith I offer myself: for I have a more beautiful subject than this one, given the great wrongs, injuries, and oppressions that men inflict on women everywhere, indeed generally, by force and without reason, ... (on the women) without whom they (i.e., the men) would not know how to live and would not be able to live...]

[26] Anita Obermeier, *The History of Auctorial Self-Criticism in the European Middle Ages* (Amsterdam: Rodopi, 1999), pp. 45–51, 68–9, 71–2, 113–35, 251–3.

that that liberty was not usually thought to exist for women—recall that the French paratexts' ungendered "on" slips later into an "il," but in English it is "he" as early as the third stanza. Only masculine liberty is assumed from the start in English translation, the "on" and "la liberté humaine" of the French Prologue translated as "his freedom." (Of course, one could argue that "he" was historically a gender-inclusive pronoun that seems gender-exclusive only to moderns, but "on" is and was certainly much more inclusive a pronoun in any era.) Regardless of its pronouns, the epilogue's protofeminist promise of a hearing for an alternative view of marriage is lost in translation. While the jealous, buffoonish, hapless husbands in the stories appear just as stupid and self-defeating in English as in French, the greedy, mendacious wives receive no mitigating final word in English. Also, in the English, there is no promise of attention to the woman's point of view or experiences of marriage. In this work, as so often in studying translations, it pays to attend to what is not there: the elided feminine. Because of this elision, the work's misogamy appears more nakedly misogynistic in English than it does in the French versions containing the epilogue.

Conclusion

Like the political Prohemye, the racy, provocative content of the stories themselves crosses the Channel largely intact. The translator's poetic strategies, however, clearly calm the French text's provocations: First, regular iambic pentameter couplets replace the raucous, satiric French prose in the stories themselves; this elevates, regularizes, and slows the pacing of the stories. Likewise, the framing texts deploy the by-then-traditional formality of rhyme-royal stanzas and, in the Prologue, an obvious Chaucerianism. The woodcuts imply a decorous domesticity utterly belied in the stories themselves. Finally, the epilogue, which voices the woman's side of things and begs women's approval, is absent in English.[27] Even the visible Frenchness of the work, which may have been some kind of selling point, could be considered a "safe" move by the translator and printer since the Prohemye's dangerous analogy between political and domestic subjects' liberty could be written off as foreign, discounted as French. The translator's literary aspirations are evident in the verse forms, in the title "Prohemye" ("proem"), and in the Chaucerian translator's Prologue. But overall the paratexts are an ungraceful, if very interesting, hybrid: the unfiltered Frenchness of the stories and of the Prohemye's expanded historiographical sections is at odds with the anglicized verse forms and the Prologue's efforts at a recognizable Englishness.

Although the translation's opening strategy of clear allusion to Chaucer in the outer frame misses the aesthetic mark—for these stories do not resemble

---

[27] The oddly placed Monk's Tale stanza (ll. 283–90) which cautions men to ignore the speech of wives might matter here; or it may be a printing mistake, since it covers ground already covered and seems appended after a functionally closural stanza.

Chaucer's—this strategy gives the stories a particularly literary horizon of expectation for English readers. The translator introduces the stories as English, as witty, as familiarly Chaucerian, which might have increased their attractiveness and familiarity to the growing reading public. The translator's "Englishing" of the outer frame is not as coherent a strategy as it may seem from a strictly formal viewpoint since, as we have seen, the Prohemye that follows this Prologue retains the original allusions to French history and the praises of France as the best of all nations. If the Chaucerianism that so strongly "Englishes" the outer frame for the *Quinze Joyes* cannot fully naturalize the French-born work, still, it would have preauthorized the work while bearing a nostalgic value for Tudor print readers perhaps something like the nostalgic value found then in jousts, tourneys, and spectacles. The literary Renaissance, after all, made nativizing and naturalizing as well as classicizing moves. Such moves often carried a lingering medievalism and a direct, if uneasy, engagement with French literature. The *Fyftene Joyes* paratexts are a good example of the many efforts in early print to make French content look English or to reserve as French whatever parts of a work cannot readily be naturalized while actually altering a work very little. Paratexts are always useful sites but nowhere more useful than in translations, where they can handle whatever alterity threatens to disrupt a new production.

Finally, as with most literary translations, there are signal absences in the *Fyftene Joyes* of 1509. The text reaches English readers without the French epilogue, which is to say, without its apology to women, without its acknowledgment of women's equally valid viewpoint, without its reminder that women suffer at least as much as men in marriage, and without its promise of a critique of marriage from the woman's perspective.[28] Such a notable closural absence allies this version's misogamy with its misogyny. Whereas a French readership was assumed to have had opposing arguments to consider—and was assumed to include women readers to whom a writer felt the need to answer—the same cannot be said of the early English readership imagined for this imprint, which promises no retraction and implies no need to consider either alternate views or women readers. This early translation records a mixed effort, via *poesis* and paratexts, to naturalize French satiric misogamy into this apparently different English context.

---

[28] Santucci, ed., 137–9, 155–8. On the French manuscripts and imprints with the epilogue, see Rychner's introduction and Arthur Fleig, *Der Treperel-Druck der Quinze Joyes de Mariage* (Greifswald: Julius Abel, 1903).

Chapter 5
Translating Marriage Complaints

Robert Copland, early printer, poet, and translator, plays a considerable role in the history of early English gender discourses. His imprints include the *Seuen Sorrowes That Women Haue When Theyr Husbandes Be Dead*, *Jyl of Braintford's Testament*, and the *Hye Way to the Spittal Hous*, each making a different kind of satiric contribution to the early English literature on women. This chapter explores two other of his contributions: *A Complaynt of them that be to soone maryed* (hereafter, the *Too Soon*) and *The Complaynte of them that ben to late maryed* (hereafter, the *Too Late*), printed by Wynkyn de Worde and translated from French by Copland.[1] This pair of poems shows the printer-translator actively reshaping French poems for an English readership. These poems share, in shorter forms, the themes and images also found in the *Fyftene Joyes*: marriage too soon is prison or animal cruelty; marriage is servitude instead of natural liberty; death or holy vows are better alternatives. Marriage (whether soon or late) brings poverty, everyday and bodily annoyances, and sexual frustrations, as misogamist male narrators typically say. Here, however, both husband and wife say so in a long central section of the *Too Soon*—another female speaker translated from French who offers an alternative viewpoint. The *Too Late* has no such vocal woman but does present unusually specific, erotic depictions of an impotent husband and—a type rare in the misogamous tradition—a chastely sexual, desiring, and desirable wife.

These poems thus raise a number of larger issues: generic (the poems' place in the development of the complaint genre in England and in the history of gendered complaints), formal (the persistence of stanzaic forms in English poetry and their transformation later in the century, particularly with respect to the use of interstanzaic enjambment in the development of the later-Renaissance verse paragraph), feminist (how these early poems compare with later works portraying

---

[1] STC 5728: [The Complaint of them that be too late married], trans. Robert Copland (London: de Worde, c. 1505). STC 5728.5: *Here begynneth the complaynte of them that ben to late maryed* (London: Wynkyn de Worde, c. 1518). Entered in Stationers' Register to W. Copland, 1563–4. STC 5729: *A complaynt of them that ben to soone maryed*, tran. Robert Copland (London: Wynkyn de Worde,1535). Mary C. Erler's edition of Copland's *Poems* is the best guide to Copland's paratexts (Toronto: University of Toronto Press, 1993). Because the *Too Soon* is unedited and the *Too Late* is only available in older, hard-to-find editions, Appendix 3 contains my transcription of them; this chapter provides summaries and basic readings, with discussion of the printer's and translator's efforts to reimagine a very popular strand of French gender poetry.

wifely sexuality and voice), and materialist (how these poems consistently link marriage with domestic physical discomforts, with economic problems, and with issues of labor and class). I find the poems potentially fruitful to pursue in each of these ways, but they are so little known that an introduction seems a better first service to readers. This introductory chapter is therefore divided into three main sections: "Voicing the Woman's Side" provides a basic reading of the *Too Soon* complaint. "Copland's Acrostics, Paratextual Histories, and Printers' Interventions" explains translator Robert Copland's original acrostics to these complaints, gives new evidence for the origins of the texts through reading the paratexts and their sources, and demonstrates the translator's vigorous self-insertions into English gender discourses. The chapter's final section, "'Th' instrument is not in point': sex and the *Too Late Maryed*" is a basic reading of the *Too Late* complaint, with its unusual depiction of the husband's impotence and the wife's positive sexuality.

Like the other translations of French verse on gender treated in this book, these poems involve quite strenuous interventions on the part of the translator and printer. Although the *Too Soon* and *Too Late* were printed separately, and although we have no extant copies of them bound together, the printer and translator, I argue here, seem to have taken separate French imprints, altered them, and recreated them in English as a deliberately literary pair. If what I am proposing in the second section of this chapter is correct, the *Too Soon* and *Too Late* reveal Copland's assertive role in selecting and repackaging the translations as a pair and doing so by changing their verse forms and writing matching, self-naming acrostics for them. The French sources of these particular works, the *Complainct de trop tost marie* and the *Complainte du trop tard marie*, were popular instances of an extremely popular type, much more widespread in France than they ever became in England. The earliest printings of the *Too Soon* complaint, however, may also have been quite popular in England—so popular as to have been "read to shreds": although internal evidence suggests a date around 1505,[2] no extant copy before 1535 remains, and an entry in the Stationers' Register as late as 1563–64 indicates some continuing interest. Whether or not *Too Soon* appeared sooner, these antimarital complaints probably did not have quite the reach or the extraordinary staying power of the long, narrative *The Fyftene Joyes*, which underwent frequent English printing, reprinting, reediting, censorship, and retranslation across several centuries, as explained in Chapter 4. The printer-translators import many of the same themes here, but in a different genre and a different voice—in part, at least, in a woman's voice.

Each complaint poem advocates either a later or an earlier marriage than the woeful speakers have respectively managed. The speakers thus present themselves as antiexemplary, warning others not to follow their dreadful paths of too early or too late marriage. The content of these poems is therefore necessarily negative and specific, as is the content of the *Fyftene Joyes* stories, yet each complaint

---

[2] Copland calls this a "fyrste worke" in the colophon stanzas, which has led scholars to think that this is a reprint of an earlier version.

also implies arguments for and against marriage in general. Although both works assume that readers will marry and the only real question is when, they implicitly raise the question of whether to marry at all. This pair thus forms another literary offshoot of the old *quaestio* tradition and a secularization of the theological position that praises the idea of clerical celibacy as at least equal to or superior to the state of marriage.[3]

In addition to spreading and secularizing that clerical line of argument, these complaints abbreviate and personalize the rather universal narrative types found in the *Fyftene Joyes*. Instead of a parade of any-husbands and any-wives presented by a framing narrator, these first-person complaints focus on marriage from the husband's point of view–and, in the *Too Soon*, from the wife's and the mother-in-law's points of view. Like the *Interlocucyon* and the *Fyftene Joyes*, these complaint poems use framing paratextual verses, but here the frames are shorter and introduce the singular speaker more quickly. Another difference is that these complaints use stanzaic forms not only in the paratexts but for the body of the poetry—rhyme royal in the *Too Soon* and Monk's Tale stanzas in the *Too Late*—instead of the hundreds of roughly pentameter couplets of the *Fyftene Joyes* and the *Letter of Dydo* or the extended dialogic quatrains of the *Interlocucyon*. It is tempting to see these formal and generic changes as edging these complaints closer to marriage lyrics or at least resembling, say, the paired stanzaic lyrics in the early shepherd's calendars, the "Ballade of Woman" and "Ballade of Man" (also translated from French). At the very least, Copland's translations contain some of the same topics and images as the other early poems on gender, but with different results, since they deploy that content as a deliberately dialectical pair in a highly flexible genre: the complaint.

The complaint was a very popular and varied late-medieval and Renaissance genre. Complaints range across topics, treating the political, economic, social, personal, theological, and historical. Complaints tend to feature a first-person speaker recounting ills or losses, attributing causes, lamenting, projecting a future either rosy or disastrous, sometimes including eschatological or prophetic material. Formally, complaints are sometimes brief and epigrammatic, sometimes middle length in stanzaic forms like the canzone or ballade, and sometimes longer narrative verses in rhyme-royal stanzas, quatrains, or even long series of couplets. They may be serious and woeful in tone, or satiric.

In the two complaints treated here, the translator uses the flexible generic elements of complaint to create a distinctive literary pair. In creating a pair with generic and formal similarities, Copland underscores the tonal and substantive contrasts between the two views of marriage. This play of likeness and contrast reveals a dialectical impulse, and while each poem appears to resolve its question one way or the other, taken as the pair I think they were intended to be, they form

---

[3] See *Wykked Wyves and the Woes of Marriage: Misogamous Literature from Juvenal to Chaucer*, Katharina M. Wilson and Elizabeth M. Makowski (New York: SUNY Press, 1990), 8 and 35–60.

an unresolved interrogation of marriage. Furthermore, to use the complaint genre for marriage material is to imply from the start that marriage creates loss, that the married speakers have something justifiable to lament or to satirize, and that a social ill is under scrutiny. The English readership received what amounts to a marriage debate, but in the form of satiric complaints translated from French and strongly repackaged. The poem pair fuses lyric voice and social critique, utters personal resistance against the communal, and answers "auctoritee" on marriage with the expressive, singular "experience" of the poetic speakers.[4]

Voicing the Woman's Side: *A Complaynt of them that be to soone maryed*

Most of the antimarital themes and several of the key metaphors of the 4,206-line *Fyftene Joyes* are also found in this translation, but here they are compressed into 51 Monk's Tale stanzas (transcribed in Appendix 3). *A Complaynt of them that be to soone maryed* (London: Wynkyn de Worde, c. 1535) translates fairly closely the content of the French *Complaincte de trop tost marie*. Several French versions of that title were printed before 1530,[5] and the first English version may have been printed around 1505, although no copy is extant. Certain textual issues and a few changes in phrasing and presentation have wider interpretive consequences; I discuss these below, after providing the basic explanatory readings necessary to acquaint readers with such an unfamiliar poem.

In *A Complaynt,* marriage is portrayed as it is in the *Fyftene Joyes*: an imprisonment and an abridgment of liberty. Here, too, the theme of captivity is expressed in the images of the "nasse" or snare and the caged bird. As in the other misogamous poems, marriage is depicted as an economic burden, with neighbors and friends eating one's food, with the same suspect pilgrimages, and with a meddling mother-in-law. The noisy and expensive children analogous to those in the *Fyftene Joyes* are not yet born to this couple but are fully imagined in the

---

[4] For an excellent review of late medieval complaints, see R. H. Nicholson, "The State of the Nation; Some Complaint Topics in Late Medieval English Literature," *Parergon* 23 (1979): 9–28. Later, Spenser, in selecting specifics and amplifying certain suggestions from the French tradition, gathers parts of this generic variety in his 1591 *Complaintes*, a publication that seems to mark a shift of the genre's position in the English literary system.

[5] Including the following: (1) *La Complainte de trop tost marie* (S.l., s.d.), in 8o; not described by Brunet, currently Réserve YE-3743. (2) *La Complainte de trop tost marie, de nouvel imprime* (Paris: M. Le Noir, 1509). In 4o; Réserve YE-956. (3) *La Complainte de trop tost marie. Nouvellement imprime* (S.l.,s.d.), in 8o. Réserve YE-3011. (4) *Complainte du trop tot et du trop tard marie,* in a volume with *Les Tenebres de mariage* and several other items. (S.l.,s.d.), in 12o. Réserve Y6158 + A (art. 37) <ancienne côte>. (5) *La Complainte de Trop tost marie* (Bordeaux?: Jehan Guyart?, 1530); facs ed. Georges Hubrecht (Bordeaux: Société des Bibliophiles de Guyenne, 1971). This list does not include the several imprints of the related poem, the *Complainte du nouveau marie*.

wife's part of the lament. As in the *Fyftene Joyes*, but with greater compression and force, *Too Soon* contrasts marriage with the preferable alternatives of clerical celibacy and death. However, the usual emphasis of misogamous literature on infidelity or cuckoldry as an inevitable problem of marriage is not present in either French or English versions. This shifts the tone and effect of the poem slightly away from the ribald sexual satire of French misogamy and misogyny that is so well conveyed in works like the *Fyftene Joyes*.

More remarkable than the absence of the theme of cuckoldry is the presence of the woman as a fully voiced complaining speaker. In both English and French versions, the young wife's complaint against marriage occupies the poem's central, most vividly dramatized section. In English, 21 stanzas of the husband's introductory complaint are followed by 11 stanzas of the wife speaking, followed in turn by 15 more stanzas from the husband (and Copland's acrostic finale). In the French version, the wife's complaint occupies only nine stanzas, but the husband's complaint is proportionately shorter as well. The English version, in other words, maintains the basic balance and structure of the original in this respect. In both languages, the spouses' respective complaints are closely but not perfectly parallel, and they deploy the same terms and images. The wife's suffering is portrayed as at least equal to the husband's, and in some ways greater, since she shows herself to be at the mercy of additional systems of patriarchal exchange. She brings up several issues that the man does not mention—her dowry, her lineage, the other beaux she could have chosen. She imagines with dread what their lives will be like in ten years with a house full of children. Her complaint, related to the *mal mariée* tradition, leaps out of the center of this male-voiced poem. The mother-in-law, too, gets a few stanzas of dialogue in the latter husband's section, though she is less sympathetically portrayed than the wife. Jane Donawerth notes that in context, the mother-in-law's arrival gives the wife support in the form of another, more authoritative woman who reminds the husband of the original circumstances of the marriage negotiations (private correspondence).

This central section of the *Too Soon*, ventriloquizing the wife's parallel sufferings in marriage, is remarkable, and I treat it more fully below. The wife's central complaint against marriage, however, is enclosed in multiple layers of male discourse in the English version. That is, the husband's complaint frames and narrates her long outburst, and outside that, the husband's antimarital warnings to other men frame his own story of marital woe. The outermost frame of the work consists of titles and woodcuts in the French version, and in the English translation, of titles, woodcuts, and an original closing acrostic poem written by the translator, Robert Copland.

This multiple framing, as usual in these early translations, is where we find important changes made to the English version. Where the French imprint's presentation emphasizes the voiced woman, the presentation and framing of the English imprint emphasize the poem's man-to-man lines of communication. On the title page of the chief French source for this work, male and female figures are shown in conversation, immediately introducing male-female dialogue as the work's main feature.[6] The speaking woman and listening man illustrate the French poem as a male-female dialogue, foregrounding the argument between husband and wife. In English, however, the two figures on the title page are male, emphasizing that the poem is most centrally a dialogue between men, a man-to-man warning against marriage (Figure 5.1). Furthermore, the closing stanzas and colophon name particular men, Robert Copland the translator and Wynkyn de Worde the printer, closing the imprint with assertive masculine voices that are not present in the original French, which simply ends with "finis." (In fact, the French imprint of 1509 closes with strikingly large female figures bearing a plumed helmet—Michel Le Noir's famous printer's mark, well explored in Martha Driver's *The Image in Print*.) In the English paratexts, however, the male presences are the striking ones. Men converse in the title image, and Copland's elaborate acrostic stanzas on his own name (analyzed further below) claim a kind of authorship of the poem. Here, as in some other paratexts to early translations about gender topics—for instance, as in the woodcut to the *Beaute of Women,* or the absence in English of the epilogue to the *Quinze Joyes*—an imprint that in French had placed women in primary roles as readers, speakers, and judges is translated so that the central addressees, speakers, and agents are men.

French sources and Frenchness in general are invisible here. Nothing in the English imprint gives away the French source—or even that there is a source. No Frenchness has to be repackaged with a Chaucerian frame, as in the *Fyftene Joyes*; no French refrain remains untranslated, as in "Beaute sans bonte ne vaut rien." This complete invisibility of the French sources allows Copland a somewhat untraditional translator's liberty—no promises about fidelity or equivalence have to be made, much less kept, since the poem presents itself as an original, and Copland casts himself as its author.

Copland begins his translation by adding a prefatory rhyme-royal stanza not found in the French. The opening stanza would have been a likely place to explain himself as a translator, but instead Copland adds this uncharacteristically brief *intentio auctoris*:

> For as moche as many folke there be
> That desyre the sacraments of weddynge
> Other wyll kepe them in vyrgyne
> And wyll in chastyte be lyuynge
> Therfore I wyll put now in wrytynge
> In what sorowe these men lede theyr lyues
> That to soone be coupled to cursed wyues

This stanza states the poem's main purpose, to write the sorrows of men in marriage. Since there are two alternatives, he says, marriage and virginity (with a third

---

[6] *La complainte de trop tost marié, de nouvel imprimé.* Paris: Michel le Noir, 1509. 6 fol in 4o. BnF Réserve Ye 956.

Fig. 5.1　Pierre Gringore, tr. R. Copland, *A Complaynt of them that be to soone maryed* (London: de Worde, 1535), Title page.

term, chastity, lumped in oddly with virginity, apparently for the sake of rhyme[7]). Since many choose marriage, he will write about that. This stanza invisibly and immediately "Englishes" the problem and takes the male viewpoint, but it does not at all predict the poem's long central voicing of the woman's own marital sorrows. These lines pose the central problem of marriage as "cursed wyues." As opposed to good wives? Or are all wives cursed? In other words, will misogamy here rely on misogyny, as it largely did in the *Fyftene Joyes* and in much of the long misogamist tradition preceding it? Copland does not pronounce paratextually on this point, but the poem states that even the fully feeling human being we meet in the speaking wife is a curse to be avoided and that "women ben abusement." Yet Copland grants the wife a full hearing in the poem's long central section, without much apparent irony. Even if the qualifiers ("cursed wyues," "proud wyues," "yll wyues") were added merely in *cheville*, as are so many adjectives added to early English translations to fill the longer line, they do imply the alternative possibility of good wives, marriage to whom would, at least in theory, not be so bad. The question of wife quality, however, is not pursued here, but rather is assumed to be low. Misogyny, in other words, here as in the *Fyftene Joyes*, seems an implicit component of misogamy. Yet the wife's lament in the central section challenges that appearance by voicing a woman's own misogamy. Here what makes wives good or bad seems less important than in the *Fyftene Joyes*. Here the male and female speakers' accounts of their respective experiences with the institution—and the flow of line and stanza—matter more. This may in part be an effect of the complaint genre, highlighting as it does the personal voicing of experience.

Another distinction the poem poses, but never resolves openly, is between the problem of marriage "too soon" and marriage, *tout court*. Occasionally, the point is made that one is "to eschewe all unpacyence" [Aii]. Each version supports (but neither version stresses very much) the premise of its title, that the problem is not marriage itself but early marriage. With the exception of the terrible crash depicted just after a three-day honeymoon period, the problems treated here are not related to marriage's timing but are common to all marriage, too early or not. Thus, marriage itself comes to seem to be the problem, and the "too soon" seems a device, a convention for setting up topoi, situation, and speakers—both male and female. As will become clear in the final section of this chapter, this is not true of the "too late" half of the pair, in which the problems are quite specific to late marriage—for example, impotence, fatigue—and are distinguished more clearly from the critique of marriage per se.

Late in the *Too Soon*, in fact, the speaker says "certaynly I wyll not blame / Maryage that god Instituted." This disingenuous disclaimer fuses the poem's misogyny to its disavowed misogamy: "The charge to yll wyues be deled." The French, "Aux femmes la charge ien donne," may be a more sweeping statement—

---

[7] These two distinct states of sexual continence, the never-sexual (virginity) and the sexually-faithful-within-holy-matrimony (chastity), often confused in modern parlance, are here blurred as well, but the rhyme scheme is upheld.

women, not just bad ones, are to blame—where the English adds "yll," a *cheville* opening space for the possibility of good wives [A3v]. It is curious that the male speaker, clearly blaming marriage throughout the treatise, nevertheless voices a fairly convincing speaking wife at the center of the poem. Her stanzas there do not make her seem too much an "yll wyf," and she turns out to express nearly the same position in some of the same language as the complaining speaker-husband. For instance, the wife and husband both use the traditional image of the married person as a bird in a cage. "In lyke wyse I am in maryage / Enclosed nedes I must endure."[8] This appears to resemble the *Quinze Joyes* prologue, with its disingenuous teasers and jokes; this poem unevenly attempts the same kind of wit, and does not succeed as often (and neither English version jokes as well).

The *Too Soon* speaker spends his first 20 or so stanzas in a cautionary lament, warning other men: "I wyll all louers clene discourage / That wolde not [with] there wyll take them adame / And put them selfe in suche domage." The irregular syllabification of these lines is typical of the translation's wavering between tetrameter and pentameter; or, rather, between two and three stresses around an implied caesura; or among 8, 9, 10, or sometimes 11 syllables. The French is tightly octosyllabic, but the English lines contain a typical latitude, allowing occasional doubling or elaboration of the problem. In stanza three, marriage is worse than feral living:

> Better it were to be a man sauage
> Than to be take in that ylke lase
> Gentell galauntes flee that passage
> Besyde that waye loke that ye passe

This third stanza introduces the "lase" (the word translates "la nasse" in the original), a string trap or lacing, a net or noose (*OED* †1[13]). The next few stanzas imitate the French version's anaphoric structure to reiterate warnings to other men, like those in the *Fyftene Joyes*, to flee marriage: "Go ye thense ... Go ye therfor ... Go ye fro ..." The additions made in "Englishing" this passage connect with one another in that they are all associated with seagoing or watercraft. "Go frome that waye to another coste" and "Go ye fro the bonde of welawaye / Which is the arke of all folye." In French, there is no equivalent for "go to another coast." In French, likewise, marriage is the abstractly conceived "comble" or culmination of folly, not the concretely conceived "arke." This image recalls literary ships of fools: as the "ark of all folly," marriage would bear heavy freight indeed. Another watery change is in the next stanza:

> Fle I praye you ...
> Fle this passage that is ryght daungerous

---

[8] This final line connects in chiasmus to the next stanza, which begins, "Endure I must."

> Fle ye frome that peryllous lake
> Of muddy myre so clam[9] and comberous
> Fle that darke place so myrke and tenebrous …

These lines are new to the English, the description seemingly stimulated by the word "lake," which in French is merely "lieu" {place}. Like several other such moments in the text, this one could be born of a mistranscription, misreading, or misunderstanding: *lieu* could look like *lac* in a messy text, if one were working quickly. In any case, the translator has chosen to elaborate the description and water imagery in this passage. It is difficult to say whether this is simply a feature of the descriptive habit of mind of writers and readers in an island nation; Copland also translated a French treatise on coastal navigation, *The Rutter of The Sea*, so he was well familiar with perilous waters and clammy passages, at least on the page if not in real life. A psychoanalytic reading might venture here into an association among the perilous, the watery, and the feminine. At very least we can say that the effect of this set of translation changes is to add descriptiveness and figurative coherence to the passage.

The issue of marriage as antithetical to human freedom——an issue so important to the translator and author of the *Fyftene Joyes*—is raised here as well. Stanza 10 admonishes:

> Thynke thou now what it is of seruyce
> Thynke also what it is of franchyse
> The seruytude of maryage
> Afore all other servage lyse   75
> All wyse men doth it despyse
> Let none take it nor other make
> For it is the moost fole enterpryse
> That ony man maye vndertake

As in the *Fyftene Joyes*, the pun on "franchyse" does not work as well in English. Likewise, the image of marriage as a snare appears repeatedly here. Sex is not worth a permanent loss of liberty, implies the translator, telling men not to be so foolish "that for one dede ne for a crye / Ye cast your selfe in suche a snare" for [you'll] never "come out thereof therfore beware."

One alternative to dreaded marriage, more fully explored here than in the *Fyftene Joyes*, is clerical celibacy:

> Better ye were withouten harme
> For to become a celestyne

---

[9] "Clam" is an interesting word meaning cold, damp, clammy, sticky, glutinous, adhesive-like, wet clay (*OED*), a word witnessed between 1440 and 1887, so a relatively modern word for this translator.

A grey frere[10] Jacopyn or a carme.
An hermyte or a frere Austyne...

Another advantage of the clerical lifestyle over marriage is that one can get out of the former: "These relygyous maundiens / May well an other order take" or even "forsake" it, and "none maye ayenste them noyse make." But in marriage, one is really stuck, tied up ("alyed," fr., liez). The wedding ceremony is echoed here, too:

> It is wel knyte that is so bounde
> That no man can it undo
> In weddynge knote I haue me founde
> That I counde [sic] not from it go [A3v]

Furthermore, as in the *Fyftene Joyes* prefatories, liberty from such bondage is explained as a natural right:

> Man the whiche hathe no tytell
> Nor seruytude by ony sent
> He is in his owne frewyll
> And at his good commaundemente
> Man maketh his auowe and talente
> For all that god hathe hym gyve
> By no maner for to consente
> For to bynde hym in seruytude to lyue

At this point, the argument shifts slightly to a practical one. In the French version, the main line is still an argument about freedom: it is very restricting to have to be responsible for and to govern a wife ("Se tu scavoyes quel charge cest / De femme prendre a gouuerner / Tu ne feroye pas si prest ..."); [If you knew what a burden it is to take a wife to govern, you would not do it so readily]. In English, however, the problem is of "keeping" the wife—implicitly, the expense of it. The English antimarital discourses tend to emphasize the economic even more than did the French, and these are no exception.

Finally, the woeful husband explains that there was actually a delightful honeymoon period of three whole days. In this passage, the speaker uses verbs that suggest the pastoral to explain how he had gamboled and leapt about happily (and so briefly) in the sunshine of love, before all the marital troubles began:

> Whan that I was newely maryed
> I had good tyme aboute thre dayes
> I was not chyddene haryed

---

[10] Greyfriars' French counterparts were Cordeliers.

> I was fulfylled with loue rayes
> I made gambandes/lepes/and playes
> I helde me neyther nere ne ferre
> But soone ynoughe I had assayes
> Of sorowe and care that made me bare
>
> Rynnynge they came me to assayle
> On the other syde ryght asprely
> Full sore they made me to auayle
> Were it slepynge or wakyngly
> Thought always was present me by
> And yet before me made frontere
> With them in theyr companye
> Great charge which bare the baner

This mini-allegory of sorrows assailing the husband, with "Great Charge" or expenses carrying the assault flag, is a nice revision of courtly beseigement metaphors derived from the *Roman de la Rose* tradition.[11] The language and arguments of economics, once again, puncture the sweet pretenses and conventions of love poetry. Here, after only three good days of marriage, personified sorrow, care, and expense will not let the husband sleep. On the eighth day, he makes his move:

> About eight dayes or soone after
> Our maryage the tyme for to passe
> My wyfe I toke and dyd set her
> Upon my knee for to solace
> And began her for to enbrace [sic]
> Sayenge syster go get the tyme loste
> We must thynke to laboure a pace
> To recompence that it hathe us coste

This economic argument inverts the lover's *carpe diem*: time is short, my beloved, so let's get back to work and make up the money we have lost dallying in bed.

The wife does not take this well. She jumps off his lap and launches her 13-stanza complaint. Her complaint is longer in the English version largely because of elaborated and expanded descriptions, but the content is very close to the compressed French version, and the overall proportions are about the same. She first says, "Is this the glose?" meaning, "So is this how you interpret our first week

---

[11] See Thomas M. Greene, *Besieging the Castle of Ladies* (Binghamton, NY: Center for Medieval and Early Renaissance Studies, 1995).

of marriage?" (Fr: "Esse cela?" Is that it?) She calls herself[12] a "caitiff," meaning a poor wretch, but the word also meant, and its original meaning was, "captive" or prisoner:

> Alas pore caytyfe well I se
> That I neuer shall haue quod she
> With you more than payne and turmente
> I am in an euyll degre
> I haue now loste my sacramente

"I have now lost my sacrament" is an interesting and ambiguous line. In French, the wife says, "Jay ia mon dernier sacrement" ["I already have my last sacrament"], meaning that she might as well be dead. The English line could be a simple mistranslation—there are a number of plain mistakes in this text that are clearly not interpretive choices or puns. Or it may be a textual error in some interim copy—"loste" for "last" (dernier). There are turned letters and other minor errors in the English imprint that would be consistent with such confusion. Until recently, translation critics have tended to attribute most differences between source and translation to "mistranslation." But poetic translators frequently alter sources for their own reasons. If we take this admittedly unclear instance as a deliberate translator's choice instead of an error, we might decide that the French wife flippantly jumps to her conclusion, from marriage to extreme unction, and thus equates marriage and death; the English wife, on the other hand, remarks that she has lost or wasted the sacrament of marriage, for what was sacred—cherished—is now reduced to drudgery.[13] Whether or not the intriguing shift of implication in the English phrase comes from a simple error, the effect of the translation for readers is what matters, and this remark is consistent with the work's overall characterization of the English wife.

Responding to the husband's (economic) sense of devouring time at their backs, the wife projects into their future, and it is not pretty:

---

[12] On first reading, it seems she is calling the husband "caitiff"; that works with the imprisonment metaphors above and below this passage, but her own meaning is that she is the one trapped. It is clear in the feminine form of the French adjective:
> Helas chetiue bien ie soy
> Que iamais nauray par ma foy
> Auec vous fors que tourment
> Je suis ployee en poure ploy
> Iay ia mon dernier sacr[e]ment.

[13] See Wilson and Makowski, *Wykked Wyues*, pp. 118–21, on the long-running arguments about marriage as a sacrament and as two implied sacraments. Such clerical arguments form a more meaningful background to the satiric remark of the French, equating marriage and death, than they do to the English wife's remark, error or not.

> Alas I ought well for to thynke
> What we sholde do within ten yere
> Whan we shall haue at our herte brynke [A4v]
>
> Many chyldren on for to thynke
> And crye after vs without fayle
> For theyr meate and theyr drinke
> Than shall it be no mervayle. (B.i)

"For theyr meate and theyr drynke" is added; the English poet portrays the wife responding to the husband's economic argument by imagining specific hungry children. These lines also lose part of the sense of the couple's mutual fate that is in the French: "Se noces en somes desplaisans / Ce nest a nye mervaille" [If we are unhappy in marriage, it's no wonder]. "Somes" is the key word here—the first person plural of couplehood lost to the English version. The English sense is closer to "There will be so many demanding children in this household; and then it won't be so wonderful!"

Just as the husband does in his stanzas, the wife thinks of the preferable clerical alternative to marriage. She curses the hour she did not enter a cloister. She cries, "By god ye speke to sone of werkynge," and then begins a stanza of exaggerated mock submission, calling herself the chambermaid and him the lord of the castle, in sarcastically faux-deferential language:

> But syr sythe it dothe you please
> It pleaseth me as is reason
> Your wyll dothe not me dysplease
> It pleaseth me at eache ceason [sic]
> ye be syr of this mansyon
> And I am your chambere

Next she wishes she were a corpse lying on a bier and restates twice the wish that she were dead. Marriage, cloister, chambermaid service, or death: these were the likeliest options for nonelite women, so the poem's complaints speak directly to the actual conditions of early modern life.

In the following stanzas, the wife speaks of former suitors and how she refused them all for love of him. In doing so—revising another topos of *mal mariée* poems—she adopts the language of economics he introduced while holding her on his lap. "Thoughe they had moche greate rychesse / No man but you was to my paye." In French courtly traditions, love or a lover is frequently figured as the "grant tresor." In the French version, the husband was the only "grant tresor" to the wife; but in English, "my paye" is definitely outside the courtly lexicon. Husband-as-treasure is reduced in English to husband-as-wages. The English version more strongly undermines the courtly. In both versions, this tension between the language of courtly convention and the economic realities of married life persists.

The husband's initial breaking of courtly illusion by suggesting they get to work seems to spark the wife's very uncourtly speech on lineage and inheritance, on the local social scene, and on dowries and rents:

> Am I of suche lygnage comen
> For to haue payne and greate trauayle
> I that was so derely holden
> And neuer loked for none auayle
> No that thynge sholde me prouayle
> I was wonte but to go and playe
> Daunce and synge at eche spousayle
> And ye frome me put all that awaye   240
> Thanked be god ye haue had of me
> Of ryche cheuaunce good and fayre
> Golde and syluer greate plente
> Rentes and herytage you to prepayre
> In all this countre there is none ayre   245
> Be ye neuer so ryche of lynage
> But he myght of that affayre
> Make ryche all his parentage

These last two lines are different in the French version. There, it is the wife's person that is the best in the county ("de ma personne / auoir bien joyeulx") and from which any man could enrich all his family line—not her "affayre" or business holdings. But the English wife sees her own value less in her person or lineage than in the list of specific goods her dowry provided. She feels she has married down for love: "I had my herte rauysshed truly / For greate pleasure and solace."

At this point, the French wife cries some more, but the English wife reacts much more hysterically, fainting, weeping, hand-wringing:

> Whan she had made her complaynt
> Lyke an woman all an angred
> She than seased vnder a faynt
> Full of sorowe and all be weped   260
> The daye and houre there she cursed
> With a tryste herte wryngynge her hande
> That euer she was nourysshed
> For to espouse suche an husbande

Here the poem has pulled back from the bawdy comic-satiric style of the *Fyftene Joyes*, moving the tone of the English version more clearly into pathos or bathos, even melodrama, by expanding and amplifying the wife's weeping.

The husband-speaker's response to the wife-speaker's lament is actually quite touching: he feels himself suddenly terribly inadequate and baffled. It is the "doghouse" in a sad and almost confessional tone:

> Whan that I herde and vnderstode
> That the whiche she me reproched
> I was abasshed and styll stode
> And durst not to her be approched
> Her tonge towarde me was declyned
> I wote not where that she had fysshte   270
> The wordes that she there dysgorged
> That I was fayne to be whysshte
>
> In this sayd dolorous songe
> I dyde me put for to haue pease
> Force it was in to be thronge   275
> Yet wente I not in with myne ease
> But my wyfe me to dysplease
> Abode not longe for to perceyue
> The sorowe that dyde my herte payse
> Where throughe she dyde deceyue   280

The husband's interiority is not expressed in this way in the other misogamous poems, where we do not see this sort of emotional detail. These stanzas are not perfectly clear; in French the sense of it is that he could not understand where she "fished up" those words, so he shut up and hid himself from her.[14] The interesting image of her vomiting up her words, in "dysgorged," is the translator's invention, another element that intensifies the English passage. The husband is in a sad, domestic self-exile—and all because of thinking of the couple as an economic rather than an emotional or personal unit; the wife responds in kind.

    This poem, then, explores the uneasy juncture of sex and economics; after the husband takes the wife on his lap and tells her to get back to work, there is a clear fall from the idealized language and imagery of the courtly and romance traditions. It is a very different kind of gender discourse, drawing on a realism more comfortable in satires or third-person narratives like the *Quinze Joyes*—more comfortable, that is, because easier to laugh off in open satires. Here, expressed in vivid first-person voice, in the genre of complaint, the discussion about marriage insists on loss and the potential for loss. As hard-nosed and realistic as some of this discussion can be, both parties express a sense of having been swindled in the deal that is marriage—and in this genre, that translates to something sadder than most misogamist satire: a sense of genuine regret.

---

[14] In French, the phrase parallel to "this sayd songe" is the "nasse," but the *OED* shows no equivalent usage of "songe."

Suddenly, though, the complaining, rueful comedy returns: in the stanza immediately following this exposition of internal troubles, the mother-in-law arrives. The mother-in-law and husband have a few stanzas of dialogue in which she asks why he has made the wife so sad. He explains, and she counters that the wife has never had to work before but that now "she wyll do well here after." The mother-in-law also thanks God she herself never had a situation quite so bad. The narrating husband, in other words, has now voiced two female speakers who reveal themselves to be strong-minded. This indirect character construction through ventriloquized dialogue, which in some measure resembles dramatic irony or theatrical technique, results in added attention to female speakers reinforcing one another.

After this scene, the poem relies more on the standard topoi and content of early misogamous verse. The cousins, gossips, and neighbors all visit in a never-ending stream, "semblynge lyke a prosession," drinking the husband's wine and enjoying themselves at his expense. "It wyll make a man all threde bare," adds the English version, in the land of the textile trades. There is a pilgrimage ("trottynge," another instance of the *instabilitas loci*) requiring expensive new clothes; the French place names are changed to English ones. One stanza is a comic catalogue of these items in which the general idea—too many gew-gaws—is the same, but the items themselves differ between French and English versions. In French, the husband wishes that "le feu Sainct Anthoine"—as Durling explains, St. Anthony's fire or ergotism—might burn them all. The English husband issues rather a different curse, that "The devyll brenne them on an hepe." The specific legend of St. Anthony and the pigs, and the painful skin disease, are here lost to a more general reference to the devil. Such changes may indicate Copland's sense of the relative cultural availability of a particular reference for his intended readership. But given the widespread iconographic representations of St. Anthony—indeed, the image recurs often in early works on gender and marriage—this change may have more to do with Copland's concern for versification than for readership. Most other differences of detail indicate that the translator was replacing certain elements in the French text with English cultural references: place names, clothing items, seafaring or water-going emphasis, and so on. The translations' French origins, in short, are completely erased. This is an *English* couple's complaint.

The husband, like the wife, calls himself "caytyfe" (B3v) and wishes he were dead. "I wysshe my dethe euery daye" and "desyryng dethe is my resorte / Chowynge my bytte in this maner" (B3v). At this point, he leaves the inset narrative with which he has voiced his dialogues with the two women. He steps back to the frame, turns back to the bachelors to whom the poem is addressed, and asks for their prayers for his martyrdom (B3v/B4r). In a moment recalling the *Fyftene Joyes* Prohemye, the speaker also says that women make men irrational: "For by women men be so varied / Eche leseth his vnderstondynge" (B4r). Women will drive a man crazy: it is an old story. His final word, just as in the French version, is that women are an abuse:

> For suche is my dyffynement
> And wyll proue it before our lorde
> That women ben abusement.
> All aboute in playe/stryfe/and borde
> To soone maryed may mete accorde
> ...
> I leve them here at this sayd worde
> And no more of them wyll I saye.

Copland's Acrostics, (Para)textual Histories, and Printers' Interventions

The speaker's misogynistic declaration ends the poem in French, but in English, Robert Copland adds an authorial acrostic (on "Robertus Coplande," spelling his name this way so as to keep his chosen monk's tale stanza form). The acrostic includes an unusual self-mocking simile about writing as flatulence. Although the middle sections of the complaint have included real interiority and even pathos, Copland ends his translation on this more ribald, original note:

> Ryght dere frendes louely I do you submitte
> Of my fyrst werke into correccyon
> But myne owne wyll can not as yet
> Endewe ony thynge of myne intencyon
> Rather I wyll abyde a lytell season
> Than to put my wytte afore intellygence
> Uentosyte must abyde dygestyon
> So I muste do or I come to eloquence
>
> Cunnynge must I haue fyrste of all   [B4v]
> Or that I come to perseueracyon
> Put forthe I wyll and than somwhat call
> Lernynge with good delyberacyon
> And than I wyll with good intencyon
> Note some werkes of god almyghty
> Desyrynge to come vnto his regyon
> Euer there for to dwell perdurably

Now the poem's address has shifted further outward again, from the initial frame (the husband-speaker cautioning his audience of bachelors and describing his marital troubles, including his voicing of dialogues with the wife and with the mother-in-law) to an outer frame (the translator asking the readers' indulgence of his undigested work). At first, Copland's stanzas look commonplace: "[R]eaders, correct this early work; I'll wait until I know more before writing more." But the analogy he creates is bawdy: "Ventosyte" or flatulence must wait on digestion, just as his eloquence must wait on his own "digestion" of more matter and his incorporation, so to speak, of cunning, learning, deliberation, and the other virtues of stanza two. He thus self-mockingly equates his own eloquence with a windy emission, making it impossible for us to take the work too seriously.[15] Unlike the rest of the imprint, which moves slightly away from the more ribald comic elements in the French, this translator's acrostic poem reminds us of the bodily and bawdy. However, like the rest of the imprint, these stanzas utterly ignore the fact that the *Too Soon* is a translation.

What is Copland up to with the two acrostics to these complaints? What kind of authorial position does he claim, and how does that position guide readers of the texts? Although there is no known French original for this acrostic, it is a first clue to the revealing, complicated textual histories of the *Too Soon* and *Too Late*. Copland also writes an acrostic for the *Too Late*, the idea taken apparently from Pierre Gringore's authorial acrostic to a French version of that poem. Copland's two acrostics—the one imitating Gringore's and the original one quoted above—differ considerably, however. Before exploring the textual history of this pair of poems, it is worth reading the pair of acrostics together to see what Copland's interventions achieve. Gringore's acrostic to the *Complaincte de Trop Tard Marie* is a typical French authorial acrostic: compact, self-referential, with a final flourish. The *rhétoriqueurs* favored acrostics, and Copland surely saw here not only a clever poetic device that might catch on but an opportunity for positive authorial self-representation. Gringore's acrostic is introduced by a paraph and a visual reminder to the reader that the treatise has ended and the author is speaking:

   Lacteur
Gouuerner deuez la maison
Renger vos gens vostre famille
Iouyeusement et par raison
Noyses euiter et castille
Gentement faire vostre estille
Ordonnez voz cas promtement
Rigueur a battre estre habille
Espoir fait viure longuement[16]

---

[15] Copland's bawdy image may be more sophisticated than it seems: there is a long, serious history of metaphors of translation as incorporation and no reason to think Copland was not familiar with it (Erler explores Copland's literary leanings). In terms of the history of metaphor, this figure casts him as a "young" translator whose work is not yet substantial. For the history of translation as incorporation, see Theo Hermans, "Images of Translation: Metaphor and Imagery in the Renaissance Discourse on Translation," in *The Manipulation of Literature: Studies in Literary Translation*, ed. Theo Hermans (New York: St. Martins Press, 1985), 103–35.

[16] [You should govern and order your household, kin, and family joyfully and justly; avoid disputes and quarrels; make your manner gentle; take care of your affairs promptly;

160   *English Printing, Verse Translation, and the Battle of the Sexes, 1476–1557*

This commonplace advice—arrange your household properly and hope for a long life—aims at any household problem, not particularly those exposed in the *Complaincte* poem itself. As an authorial self-representation, the acrostic presents the already well-known public poet Gringore as an authority on domestic matters as well, and it closes the marriage complaint on a serious, admonitory note.

Copland's acrostic to his *Too Late* is as serious and advisory as Gringore's acrostic, though less epigrammatic and compact. Copland doubles the acrostic's length by including his first and last names. This time, to keep rhyme royal, he is "Roberte Copland," his name conveniently flexing to both his chosen forms. Pierre Gringore, prolific chief poet at the court of Louis XII, would not have needed more than his patronymic, but Copland apparently wants either a complete self-identification or the extra stanza space that a first name provides. (He adds a third stanza, too, naming printer Wynkyn de Worde and including details of the printing typical in a colophon.)

        The auctour

Rychenes in youth with good gouernaunce
Often helpeth age when youth is gone his gate
Both yonge and olde must haur theyr sustenaunce
Euer in this worlde soo fekyll and rethrograte
Ryght as an ampte the which all gate
Trusseth and caryeth for his lyues fode
Eny thynge that which hym semeth to be good

Crysten folke ought for to haue
Open hertes vnto god almyght
Puttynge in theyr mynde thyr soule to saue
Lernynge to come vnto the eternall lyght
And kepe well theyr maryage and trouth plyght
Notynge alwaye of theyr last ende
Durynge theyr lyues how they the tyme spende

Here endeth the complaynt of to late maryed
For spendynge of tyme or they a borde
The sayd holy sacramente haue to long taryed
Humayne nature tassemble and it to accorde
Enprynted in Fletestrete by Wynkyn de Worde
Dwellynge in the famous cyte of London
His hous in the fame at the sygne of the Sonne

---

learn how to (probably soften rigor/rigidity); hope makes for a long life.]

Copland expands the verses to be consistent with the rhyme-royal stanzas of his *Too Late* translation, just as he has matched the Monk's Tale stanzas of the *Too Soon* acrostic with the body of the poem. The acrostics, in other words, are matched formally with the poems they each follow. Copland also lengthens the short French line. The English version is thus more expository, specific, and descriptive than the abstract, compressed, epigrammatic French. Unlike the generalized domestic advice of Gringore's acrostic, Copland's first stanza addresses the youth-age issue of the *Too Late* imprint. Copland's second stanza, however, and even his added colophon with details of the printing depart from Gringore's original in blanketing the work with moral sententiousness and a reminder to remember the state of one's soul. Copland thus deliberately crafts the acrostics to suit his translation of the complaints. His work quite exceeds the mere following of a source. Additionally, the general advice of this acrostic would connect the works as a pair, capping the youthful appeal of the earlier work (and its acrostic's comical promise) with the appearance of mature, advisory wisdom.

Taken together in this way, the two English acrostics—this one very much expanded and adapted from Gringore's and the other, original to Copland's *Too Soon* translation but self-deprecating and comical—point to the extent of the English effort to create these complaints as a new literary pair. Copland shows himself willing and able to translate quite freely and generatively. He takes only the idea of a closural acrostic (so popular among the *rhétoriqueurs* but, like other poetic devices, less often used in English until much later), amplifies it in translation so as to adapt it to his own name and then creates an entirely new acrostic so as to make the two complaint poems into a pair. In doing so, he elides the distinction between authorship and translation. Never mentioning Gringore, French, or the act of translating, Copland's acrostics claim his authorship of—and the Englishness of—these anti-idealizing, antimarital works.

Furthermore, the history of the French texts reveals that Copland and de Worde did not find these particular poems as a pair in French but instead probably divided a different pair and replaced the *Too Soon* with a separate poem that they found preferable. There has been much scholarly confusion about which of the dozens of French marriage complaints are the real sources for Copland's translations. While I do not pretend to have solved this puzzle perfectly, the acrostics are a first clue to some new evidence for the following: Copland and/or de Worde probably took a particular French pair of complaints of "too soon" and "too late," uncoupled them, rejected the "too soon" component, translated a different "too soon" in its place, and issued their new pair in separate imprints but with matching authorial acrostics, typeface styles, woodcut styles, and similar verse forms. In other words, Copland kept the French concept of a pair of marriage complaints and expanded and experimented with the idea of an authorial acrostic to them, but he substituted the content of one *Trop Tost* for the content of another with a similar title. Here are my reasons for thinking so.

Mary C. Erler's superb edition of the works of Copland offers a wealth of essential information. However, the note to the *Too Soon* acrostic says that the

Too Soon is a translation of "Dehors nassiez de ceste nasse"; but this is not exactly so (44). The "Dehors," I propose, is more likely to be a fragment or fragmentary version of the whole *Complainte* that Copland translates. Copland's *Too Soon*, which begins, "Now that I am in grete myschefe and sorowe," almost exactly translates the poem that begins "Or suis ie bien en grant souci / Trop tost me suis mis en mesnaige," the *Complainte de trop tost marie* found in BnF Res Ye 956, an imprint of 1509 by Michel le Noir. (There may be earlier versions of this as well; to illustrate the closeness, I transcribe the first several lines of BnF Ye 956 in Appendix 3.) Both imprints, Copland's *Too Soon* and Le Noir's *Trop Tost* of 1509, use similar factotum cuts and layout, which differ from those of the "Dehors nassiez de ceste nasse."[17] That in itself means little, but the "Dehors" seems to have been another, later publication, taken from the larger Le Noir *Complainte*; some of the "Dehors" stanzas replicate the middle section of the Le Noir *Complainte*, the anaphoric part of the poem that corresponds to the English translation beginning about stanza 6 ("Go ye thense my frendes I you praye"). This matters first because when we know this, we can no longer attribute the opening stanzas of the *Too Soon* to Copland since the stanza that begins, "Now that I am in grete myschefe," like several after it, is not original to Copland but is in the actual, heretofore unnoted French source, the Le Noir *Trop Tost*, which begins, "Or ie suis bien en grant souci." Of course, like any such reconstruction, this could be completely wrong—there could be earlier imprints of each that have not survived—but from what survives, it seems most reasonable to assume that Copland (and/or de Worde) worked from a copy of the *Complainte de trop tost marie* (Le Noir 1509), a fragment of which is now called "Dehors nassiez de ceste nasse."

However, the textual plot thickens. Erler correctly notes that Copland's *Too Soon* is not a translation of the *Complainte de Trop Tost Marie* that begins "Ie suis le trop tost marie." That is a completely different poem, found in *La Complainte de trop tost marie. Nouuellement imprime* (s. l., s.d.) now identified as BnF Rés Ye-3011.[18] Although as Erler says, it is not a source for these translations, that work still figures as important background to the question of Copland's and de Worde's actions on French marriage complaints. The octavo volume containing this *Complainte* (Ye-3011) contains other poems, including the "shadows of marriage" and, more important, the *Complainte de Trop Tard marie* by Pierre Gringore. The relation of the *trop tost-trop tard* complaints in this French octavo volume is clearly a paired one: Gringore almost certainly wrote both poems. Brunet points out that they are bound together by using common typefaces. The acrostic ("Gouerner deuez," as in the text cited above, not "debuez" as transcribed by Gringore's modern editors) seems to cover and cap both poems. Furthermore, I think the woodcuts in Ye-3011 provide additional evidence if not for Gringore's

---

[17] The "Dehors" is available in a modern edition as *La Douloureuse complainte du nouveau marie* (Paris: Firmin Didot, 1830).

[18] In-8°, 4 ff. The BnF catalogue says, "non chiffrés, sans sign.," but one page is in fact marked: Aii.

authorship of both, then certainly for the poems' status as a linked pair.[19] If Copland did find these together, his (or De Worde's) action was to keep the idea of a pair but to reject this particular *trop tost*. And what a good call that was, for this *trop tost* is almost entirely a laundry list of the various costs of marriage, a dull catalogue of expensive goods and demanding children's needs. Copland (or De Worde) chooses a poem, instead, that includes the economic material (remember the "gew gaws" passage) but does not consist entirely of it. That alone shows literary sensitivity to an audience: the French poem they choose to use for the new English pair is a much richer and more interesting poem, providing real points of contrast in voice and tone. Whether or not my speculation about these particular imprints is correct, the fact is that Copland and De Worde had access to a considerable stock of French marriage complaints, and they narrowed it carefully, probably selecting one from Gringore and one from another imprint, retaining the idea of a pair, but re-creating a very different and literarily balanced pair.

The suppression of Gringore's authorship in the acrostic also raises the question of Copland's claim of authorship—and of Englishness—for these revised, paired, re-presented poems. Was Copland trying to become the English Gringore? Had the French imprints solved or addressed something that was also at issue in England? What was the relation of each of these imprints to its national context? On both sides of the channel, each nation's paradigmatic household was having to examine different aspects of too-soon and too-late marriage, with extremely high stakes. That Gringore was so close to Louis XII may be important; Louis XII was, after all, an early marrier, a remarrier, a late marrier, and a powerful patron of poetry. Gringore wrote pageants for Louis's last marriage, the one to Mary Tudor, the sister of Henry VIII in 1513–1514,[20] and Louis XII certainly used Gringore to promote his political agendas. That Gringore also wrote marriage debates, satires, and complaints may mean nothing more than that these complaints were conventional, witty things, rather than topical commentary. Certainly, the *Trop tost* and *Trop tard* do not comment on royal marriage, though there would have been plenty on which to comment: Louis XII, like Henry VIII, was plagued by the need for a male heir (all discussion of the *loi salique* aside). His first marriage, to Jeanne de France, was annulled so that he could marry Anne de Bretagne, the widow of Charles VIII of France. They did have two daughters (one of whom, Claude, married the future François I, so the line was finally secured), but Louis's marriage

---

[19] The woodcut that introduces the "trop tost" shows a young man at right holding a long flowering plant in his left hand and a short flowering plant in his right, looking down. A lady is seated on the grass in the background. Two symbols are above and below the lady in inset circles: above her, a ram, and below, a goat. Aries and Capricorn, yes, but also youth and age in the seasons of man, as traditionally found in almanacs, shepherds' calendars, and elsewhere.

[20] "Journey and Ambassadorship in the Marriage Literature for Mary Tudor (1496–1533)," in *Renaissance Tropologies*, ed. Jeanne Shami (Pittsburgh, Pa: Duquesne UP, forthcoming), pp. 166–206.

to Anne was followed by another late effort at heir-bearing, with forestalling war and scheming against the Holy Roman Empire as additional motives: Louis at age 52 married Henry VIII's 18-year-old sister, Mary Tudor. In England, Henry VIII's marriage to Catherine of Aragon was more vexed by the question of incest and widowhood (because of her previous marriage to his brother Arthur), a topic these translated works do not raise even obliquely. Henry's divorce and subsequent remarriages occur well after the original translations. Copland or de Worde would have issued these complaints around the time of Arthur's marriage to Catherine of Aragon, if we assume the earliest possible date for them, or right after Catherine's marriage to Henry VIII if we accept c.1509 (that is, if we see the Michel le Noir imprint of 1509 as having been influential); the imprint of 1535 would have just followed Henry's divorce and remarriage to Anne Boleyn, topics not mentioned here either.

Thus, the topical reading is not, finally, as persuasive as the reading from the printer's shop. Widow-marrying (in some eyes, bigamy or incest), remarriage, lineages, and heirs were pressing concerns on both sides of the channel at the time of these publications. However, as concerned as the royal households were with these questions, these poems aim at the common reader's common experience. (The *Too Soon*, furthermore, aims dissuasion at that reader, dissuasion that if taken seriously would oppose the main promarriage position of the royal households or at least would highlight the distance between that position and the common reader's experience.) The deliberately anticourtly discourses herein show us a view of marriage quite distinct from the royal or court-based one. Compare, for instance, the marriage complaints with the pageants Gringore wrote for the marriage of Mary Tudor and Louis XII: utterly abstract, in the allegorical and romance traditions of poetry, with specific heraldic blasons and literary devices, epithalamic in tone, deictic and epideictic in stance. Moreover, although the printers and authors on each side of the channel did have royal connections, they were not parallel connections. De Worde and Copland were certainly known to the Tudors but were not "court printers" or court writers in anything like the direct, close, well-supported relation to the throne that Gringore enjoyed. In fact, these poems reveal how different were the focal points of concern, and how very different the expressions of them, for the new reader of print. These imprints suggest that the attention of the new readers of print might not have been as obsessively court directed as, say, our literary criticism and historiography have been until recently. As the present book demonstrates, English and French gender discourses had different histories and were in different states. The archetype for the woes of remarriage is the widow-marrier Mathéolus, a chief misogamous voice and example in the long tradition against whom Christine takes up the *querelle*, but his work, widely known in France, was not even printed in early modern England. Given these uneven contexts, the marriage poems treated here, plus the Latin-based poems treated in Utley, form a kind of secondary or alternative discourse. In short, a topical-historicist view of these poems will only take us so far. At least we can say that marriage is a topic of perennial interest, the literary expressions of which work out differently on each side of the channel and not necessarily in direct topical relation to events at court(s).

"Th' instrument is not in point": Impotence, Wifely Sexuality, and Late Marriage

The antiexemplary speaker of the cautionary *Too Late* complaint is an older man who waited too long to marry. Fifty rhyme-royal stanzas are followed by three colophon stanzas, also in rhyme royal, titled "The auctour," again with no indication of a French source. After a few stanzas of promarriage platitudes (for example, "There is no greater pleasure than for to haue / A wyfe that is full of prudence and wysdome"), the first third of the poem is devoted to an account of the speaker's misspent youth: drinking, staying out late, and, most of all, promiscuity. When the speaker finally does marry, he tells us that he regrets not marrying sooner since many of the joys of marriage are no longer available to him. He gives a vivid account of his wife's beauty and sexuality and of his frustrating impotence. The usual French *senex* poem focuses at this point on fears of cuckoldry, often railing against the wife's affairs with various younger men. Instead of blaming the wife's desires, this poem de-emphasizes the fear of the wife's promiscuity and devotes much more space to potentially happy marital sexuality that has been thwarted by the aging husband's impotence. Nor will the speaker live long enough to see his children grow up to become prosperous merchants. Finally, the speaker fears his soul may be in jeopardy from all that catting around in youth. The poem repeats the Pauline notion about marriage as a spiritually safe outlet for lust; here marriage is a cleansing or atonement system as well. While parts of this poem are bawdy and comical, its overall message is serious and regretful. The speaker is sympathetic and wistful rather than ridiculous. Marriage in this poem is potentially a very good thing, clearly much better than youthful promiscuity, which leads to disease, poverty, betrayals, and mistrust. However, we do not hear from the young wife herself in this complaint, as we do in the *Too Soon*. Here the wife is a pleasant, compliant creature, and one who takes sexual initiative in bed but is, finally, an object of frustrated male desire (and a very un-Petrarchan object at that).

As usual in these early printed translations, the printer-translator's interventions make real interpretive differences. Several changes signal Copland's concept for the piece. The first four stanzas are mostly new to the English version. Copland has kept the first line of the piece ("Apres esbatz ioyeusestes soulas" becomes "After playes sportes and daunces of solace"), but he omits a truly clever, 18-line prologue section in the French that features homonymic and nearly-homonymic feminine rhymes.[21] Copland may have been using good translator's judgment to

---

[21] Apres esbatz ouyeusetes soulas
On se treuue [soeu] foys soubz las
On est prins comme grief a fille
Car beau parler eloquent effille

omit the passage, whose playful phonetic punning would be impossible to recreate in English. This decision, however, has a number of effects on the English version. In French, the separation between the 18-line prologue or frame and the main body of the poem is clear, marked by a change in verse form and tone from light, quick couplets to a more decorous rhyme-royal stanza. In English, however, Copland's steady rhyme-royal stanzas blur the line between the frame and the body of the piece. Until the poem's final three stanzas, which are Copland's added authorial acrostic and colophon, nothing in Copland's poem demands interpretation as a frame.

Furthermore, in the opening stanzas and then scattered throughout, Copland adds religious references. For instance, the English speaker adds, "We must thynke to come to prosperyte / After that God of his hanoundante grace / Wyll prouyde how that I may gouerne me" (stanza 1). The poem ends by adding, "So wyll I lyue in maryage clene and pure / To Goddes be houe and increasinge of nature." Likewise added in stanza three are these lines: "For saynt Iohn sayth that he is sage / That ayenst his wyll doth him gouerne / And our Lordes preceptes hym selfe for to lerne."[22] While not making any major theological gestures, these allusions do render the speaker pious, almost confessional, and the tone more serious than that of its counterpart. This suggests that Copland found such generalized religious insertions one way to enhance the contrast between the tones of his paired poems or perhaps, as Jane Donawerth notes in private correspondence, signals Copland's awareness of "an increasing lay interest in private devotions":

Copland's third original stanza is worth special note:

There is no greater pleasure than for to haue
A wyfe that is full of prudence and wysdome
Alas for loue nygh I am in poynte to raue
These cursed olde men haue an yll custome

  Jeunes amans regit maine [&] co[n]duyt
  Le quel ne peult a peine estre escondit
  Et sy auant en la grace des dames
  Le fait mettre que de cueur [&] q~dames
  Prennent plaisir achanger damourettes
  Et se entre vo[us] q[] dmour charge estes
  Voulles nyer q[ue] trop tost onn pre[n]t femme
  Je dy que non car le regnon ou fame
  De lhomme en croist dont sa perte parie
  Se auec femme dheure ne se aparie
  Et me repens quant iay par tout regard
  Que iay consenti moy marie si tard
  Par quoy iestais ceste complainte briefue
  Tard marie son corps et ame grefue

[22] Copland's stanza 6 does rely on Gringore's stanza 2, explaining marriage as a holy sacrament intended for procreation.

> Women for to blame both all and some
> For that they can not theyr mindes full fyll
> Therfore they speke of them but all yll

Thus Copland adds to the beginning of his version a direct argument against the misogynist writers, the "cursed old men" who blame all women mindlessly. This passage is one of the few in which Copland openly counters the traditional discourses of misogyny and misogamy. We can see immediately the pro-marriage, pro-woman (or at least, less misogynist) stance the poem will take. Yet even though this stance was part of an anti-misogynist hermeneutic in the *querelle* and associated poems in France, Copland does not take up the wider suggestions of that part of the French tradition, and instead works locally to create contrast within the complaint pair, on the specific topic of marriage.

The stanzaic portion of the French poem begins, "Or ayge tout mon temps use/ A suyure mes folles plaisances ... " [Since I have spent all my time in following my foolish pleasures] (ll. 19–20). At this point Copland begins staying closer to the French text: "Now syth that I haue my tyme vsed/ For to folowe my folyshe pleasaunces ... ." At the end of this stanza, Copland also adds a line that leads well into the first main section of the poem, the very descriptive section about the speaker's promiscuous youth.

> He is a fole that elles where [i.e. outside of marriage] doth nature spylle.
> I haue done as the labourer doth
> That somtyme is payned with trobyll grete
> For he leseth his payne for certanye soth
> That in the hye waye soweth his whete
> Well I perceyue that I dyde me forgete
> Or that I put me in to housholde
> I haue lost my seed my worke is but colde

"Seed" and "soweth his whete" lose the sound-play in French between "semence" and "semen," but the metaphor is apt enough. Having sown his seed on the busy sexual highway, and regretting the waste of having it always trampled by the crowd, he spends twelve lurid stanzas describing his earlier promiscuity. During those years "Women and maydens both good and yll / With me I helde myself for to please" (ll. 50–51). Drinking, wild companions who also slept with his lovers, the pain of his paramours' unfaithfulness, and even venereal disease were part of the speaker's pre-marital experience. "But in the stede [of] chyldren to conceyue/ Botches pockes and goutes they [the promiscuous] engendre/ In hedes and in legges and in euery membre" (ll. 125–6). The speaker advises, "Hast you to be wedded thus I you rede/ Vnto the ende that ye be not cappable/ Of this grete daunger deedly and vncurable" (ll. 131–3). Animal imagery here figures unhealthy pre-marital wildness.

> Lyke vnto a best, an hors, or an asse
> That careth not for to tomble in the fen
> ...
> Mo gallantes a man sholde se that ren
> After a wentche and lepe and hytche
> Than dogges do about a farowenge bytche (ll. 113-9).

Contrast this with the *Too Soon*, the *Fyftene Joyes*, and other anti-marital works, in which animal imagery figures the imprisonments of marriage that deprive people of their freedom and humanity (the bear in the pit, the fish in the lepe, the caged bird). In those works, marriage dehumanizes; here, promiscuity dehumanizes, but marriage rehumanizes.

By stanza 20, the speaker turns to describe his happy marital state (although we will soon see that it is not perfect, and we never hear directly from the wife he "commands," "both late and early").

> Out am I now of thought dole and mone
> Lyuynge euer more ryght amorously
> For I haue a wyfe by my selfe alone
> At my commaundement both late and erely
> And yf it happen that I loke heuely
> My wyfe me kysseth and than she me colleth
> And ryght woman there she me consolleth
>
> To that I wyll haue done she is redy
> Neuer wyll she ageynst my wyll saye
> She doth to me the best that she can truely
> Nothing of my volenty she doth me naye
> Yf I be angered or trobled ony waye
> Redy she is to chaunge my purpose
> Vnto the ende that I may haue all my repose (ll. 141–54)

These stanzas emphasize the emotional comfort the wife consistently gives the husband as well as the complete submission of her will to his. These sweeter depictions directly contrast with the argumentative couples and willful, insubordinate wives deplored in the antimarital and misogynist tradition. Showing the "good" wife, they simply work out the opposite side of the same general assumptions about what constitutes "good" and "bad" wives.

Nevertheless, despite his "good" wife (as then defined), this speaker has a problem, one due to his age: "I haue me all to long refrayned/ Furnysshe I can not to all her pleasyre." This is followed by fairly specific, voyeuristic passages in which the wife is depicted as asking in various ways for sex. The speaker-husband despairs over his impotence. "She appetyteth it moche and doth me enspyre /

Gorgyously shewynge her fayre corsage/ But I am all caduc and wery for age" (stanza 23).²³ The following soft-core verses need no comment:

> My wyfe shewed me her proper dugge
> On the mornynge her delyte for to make
> And to haue me for to play nugge a nugge
> Alas!
> ...
> Whan I se her lye in shetes fayre and whyte
> As rede as the button of the rose
> With good wyll wolde I take then delyte
> Nuertheles I lete her haue her repose
> For it is force that I cast agayne on the close
> And to make a pawse than I am conioynt
> For thynstrument is not yet well in poynt
>
> But yet somtyme I me constrayne
> To take nature solace thus thynke I
> But all sodeynly I me refrayne
> For I do fere to be to soone wery
> ...
> Often ynough...
> She me assayeth and toueneth by kynde
> Castynge vnto me her beggynge legge
> But I do slepe: I care not for such a begge.
>
> With her eyen pleasaunte castynge a regarde
> In chasynge a laughter amerous
> Than wyth a praty smyle she doth me larde
> And that maketh me somwhat joyous
> But comynge to a bed delycyous
> For to hold the spere in a full hande
> It plyeth and fayleth for will not stand
> ...
> I do me wyshe for to be in to the age
> Of eyghten neyntene or foure and twenty
> Such assautes than gyue wolde I
> > That for it sholde haue no nede to craue
> > Of the grete pleasure that she sholde haue (ll. 169–209)

---

²³ "Caduc" is a cognate, the more common English spelling of which is "caduke," meaning infirm or feeble; another meaning, fallen or liable to fall, creates a possible sexual pun here. The word was in current use throughout the period (*OED*).

Such an extended consideration of impotence is usually followed in misogamous literature by an equally vivid expression of fears of cuckoldry or its actualization. This speaker admits, "Constrayned I am to be full of Ialousy / Seynge that I can not content her mynde / Touchynge the playe of loue" (ll.191–3), but the wife's excellence deflects all such fears and recovers this poem for the promarital forces. "If she go to banckettes and daunces / She doth none offence therein certayne" (ll. 210–11). He continues that the two of them should have spent their youth together and that their children would have grown into prosperity by now (stanza 34). In a stanza not found in the French, the speaker says, "I be wyall the tyme that is so spent / That I ne me hasted for to wedde" but vows to see it through anyway: "But syth that our Lorde hath ordeyned / That I this sacrament take me vpon / I wyll kepe it trewely at all season" (stanza 35).

At this point, the poem turns away from the speaker's personal situation and begins a series of arguments against various antimarital authorities. Again, the poem echoes in part the *querelle des femmes*, at least in abbreviated and general form:

> Theophrastus vs sheweth in his prose
> That in maryage all is out of tune
> So doth also the romaunte of the rose
> Compoased by mayster Iohan de mehune
> Yet neuertheles it is all comune
> That they neuer were in bonde of maryage
> Wherfore at all auentures is theyr langage (ll. 245–51)

This stanza uses one of the arguments, citing the same names, from Christine's side of the *querelle*: those old misogynists have no experience of marriage, so their authority on the subject is not reliable. The poem continues:

> Matheolus that was holden so wyse
> For to blame women was all his ebate
> Suppose that he was maryed twyse
> For he was so olde that balde was his pate
> For he came the last tyme so very late
> That in hym there was no puyssaunce
> Amyte solace joye ne pleasure (ll. 252–8)

Known as a bigamist because he married a widow, and known as an antifeminist, here Mathéolus is also accused of impotence. Unmarried, inappropriately married, or late-marrying authorities, in this speaker's view, are no authorities at all. This section is a departure from the topoi of practical economics and bodily elements that characterize most early English printed marriage poetry, and it brings the more academic strand of the long debates to popular readers. Its satire, gentle as it is, is more against old husbands than bad wives. Although the husband self-deprecates, the English version manages more sympathy for him, departing from the scornful *senex* tradition of the French. Thanks also to its longer lines, the English version feels more treatise-like than the epigrammatic French, especially in these stanzas that cite authorities in the *querelle*.

Conclusion

Overall, Copland's translation is a particular, flexible appropriation of a representative marriage complaint that maintains chosen elements of the debate about marriage. Where the French complaints, not actually a pair, were variants of the same satiric misogamous type, here Copland and De Worde create a contrasting pair that debates marriage with somewhat more ambiguity: the *Too Soon* is an antimarital satire, but one that includes alongside its traditional misogyny the woman's voice and experience; and the *Too Late* is a more serious promarriage argument that nevertheless retains elements of the French antimarital genres. The English woodcuts, however, show that this is a discussion among men, not among men and women, as the French woodcuts show. Additionally, the acrostic stanzas Copland adds make the French sources invisible and assume—create—an English "authorship" and origin for the poems. Taken together, the acrostics shift the pair toward the promarriage side: the *Too Soon*'s acrostic casts it as a first work that needs emendation. Then comes the *Too Late*'s sententious, admonitory, acrostic, from an older, wiser speaker-author, whose argument is, although still misogynist from our perspective, ultimately in favor of marriage.

Where the *Fyftene Joyes* stands in the direct line on one side of the *querelle* (that of Mathéolus's *Lamentations,* telling a series of framed stories against women and marriage), the *Complaintes* present as a pair the specific marital experiences of two male antitypes—one too soon married and one married too late. The printer-translators, De Worde and Copland, select from a very broad French tradition of satiric marriage complaint and keep many of the topoi and images, the idea of pairing early and late marriage complaints, and the idea of creating authorial acrostics. The English idea of adding frames to shorter imprints, related visually and logically to each other, promised good commercial viability. The result is anticourtly, anti-idealizing, and popular, raising down-to-earth questions about the pros and cons of marriage, early and late. The nearly satiric, woman-voicing *Too Soon*, with its young, bawdy "author" acrostic, is followed by the nearly woeful sexual and personal longings of the *Too Late*, with its graver, wiser, "authorial" acrostic. Thus, the complaints pair the two main tones of the complaint genre itself, satiric and lamentational. The English *Complaintes*, furthermore, feature a dialectical motion not only between the two poems, but within each. The *Too Late* contrasts premarital and postmarital states, and the *Too Soon* gives the woman a prominent antimarital voice. Although the English paratexts suppress and quiet the woman's voice, framing it with male-to-male discourse, that insistent voice, like the dialectical habits of French gender debates, is here to stay.

Chapter 6
Misogamy and Translation at Henry VIII's Court: Heywood's *A Mery Play*

Sometimes called the first Tudor drama, *A mery play betwene Johan Johan the husbande, Tyb his wyfe, and Syr Johan the preest* (London: Rastell, 1533) is a verse play John Heywood translated from a late-fifteenth-century French farce, *La Farce du Pasté*.[1] The French play was one of hundreds of such farces, but the translation is in most respects unusual in its English context. Heywood's singular, skillful handling of the play's common themes actually heightens the misogamist and misogynist content. His transformations of French poetic forms and conventions, his changes to the names in the play, and his changes to the play's ending all intensify the play's central problems: the absent woman and the fear of cuckoldry.

The play shares its main ideas and overall effect with the other antimarital and misogynist works discussed in this book, as a quick plot summary will demonstrate. The wife is a sexually ungovernable shrew, and the cruel, stupid, and cowardly husband is her dupe. In French and English, the basic plot of this farce is the same. A husband who fears his wife is having sex with the local priest rants angrily about her in an opening monologue. He threatens at length to beat the errant, absent wife, but the moment the wife enters, he becomes docile and subservient. The wife makes the husband invite the priest to their home under the pretext of sharing a pie. The husband visits the priest, tests his suspicions, and invites him to supper. Back at home, the wife orders him to do domestic chores: set the table, wash cups, fetch water. During supper, as she and the priest eat the pie, she makes the husband stand by and "chafe the wax" (that is, he is supposed to warm and reshape a wax plug so as to fill a hole in the water bucket). Meanwhile, the priest recounts several marital "miracles"—for instance, the miraculous birth of a child to a woman after only a short marriage and the miraculous birth of many

---

[1] English passages are cited from the edition of Richard Axton and Peter Happé in *The Plays of John Heywood* (Cambridge: D. S. Brewer, 1991); this edition works from the Pepys copy of the play. French passages are cited from Gustave Cohen, ed., *Recueil de farces françaises inédites du XVe siècle...* (Cambridge, Mass: Medieval Academy of America, 1949), entry XIX, pp. 145–58. *The BBC Production of the First Stage, Part 3* (New York: Spoken Word, 1991) contains a recent sound recording of the play. Thanks to Kent Cartwright for thoughtful discussion of Humanist drama in the More circle (Folger Shakespeare Library, June 2002) and to Melanie Parker for research assistance.

children to an absent father. Finally, when the wife and priest have eaten all the food and pretend to be surprised that the wax-chafing husband has had none, the husband erupts in anger and the play ends in a brawl among the three, resolved differently in the two versions.

This play, then, has a common French farce plot, that of a husband cuckolded by a priest. As the play's editors explain, "At a stroke Heywood imported into English drama the strongly marked sexual stereotypes of late medieval anticlerical farce— the lustful shrew, the henpecked husband, the rapacious priest—compelling them with unflinching satire …." (Axton and Happé xi–xii). But Heywood's translation is invisible as such, never declaring its French origins and indeed having no printed paratexts in which to do so. Heywood's strategy is thus quite unlike that of the *Fyftene Joyes* translator, who retains elaborate French historiographic details, and quite unlike that of the other translators studied here whose titles announce "translated from French" or who repeat particular words, phrases, or rhymes from French works. Heywood instead replaces all French allusions with English equivalents (Notre Dame cathedral, for example, becomes "the churche of Poules"). Nevertheless, Heywood conveys many of the French source's more fundamental literary characteristics rather better than did the translators who claim close kinship to their French sources. In addition to the farce plot and stereotypes Axton and Happé note, Heywood captures the spirit of French farce. The play's colloquial diction and frequent oaths, its urban working-class characters and setting, and its short tetrameter lines all work together as bawdy antimarital satire better than do the pentameters, rhyme-royal Prologue and Prohemye, and colophons of some of the other translations made in the early decades of printing. In other words, Heywood conveys the general tone, form, and concept of the French misogamist verse farce fairly well; but he steadily refuses to capitalize openly on whatever cultural value the original Frenchness of the work might have offered.

The Contexts

The invisibility of this translation as such is especially curious because this sort of verse would seem to have had considerable value at the "heavily Frenchified" court of Henry VIII (Axton and Happé xii). The French ambassador, Jean Du Bellay, wrote that Wolsey had insisted on French farces being played in French in 1527.[2] Roberta Mullini notes that for the arrival of the French ambassador at

---

[2] Roberta Mullini, p. 229, quotes the letter from Du Bellay to Montmorency, 1 June 1529: "Tout ce temps de festes s'en est allé en festiements du cardinal Campège, tant par le roy que par monseigneur le légat [il cardinale Wolsey], esquelx me suys quelquefoix trouvé pour tesmoing. Et croy que mondict segneur le légat ne seroyt content s'il sçavoit qu'eusse failly de vous faire la feste qu'il a faict jouer des farces en françoys au grant appareil, disant au partir qu'il ne veult estre rien par dezça qui ne soyt en faict et en parolle françoys" (Bourilly et Vassière, eds 1905: 521). The French-style spectacles in and around Henry VIII's court, not to mention the rival displays at the Field of the Cloth of Gold, have been

Greenwich, John Rastell "approntò un 'pageant of the Father of Hevin' (Anglo 1964, 1969, Spectacle pp. 218–19, Lancashire 1984: 721)." Mullini explains that young Heywood was there and was so impressed and influenced by the pageants that he incorporated their styles into his later drama (228–9). Richard Axton even shows that some of Heywood's staging can be seen as an imitation of the court of François I, especially of his *lit de justice*.[3] Heywood was well placed to bring French or French-style music and spectacle, including farce, to the court. A Catholic family member of the More circle, Heywood enjoyed a long and successful career as an entertainer (musical and dramatic) in the courts of Henry VIII, Edward VI, Mary I, and even Elizabeth I.[4] Rastell, his printer and brother-in-law, was the first printer of plays in England, and the whole More circle was at the center of intellectual and cultural life at court. Heywood may have aspired to the place of an earlier court dramatist, William Cornyshe, or perhaps to be to England what Pierre Gringore had been to France: the major royal writer of spectacles and plays, with political clout and opinion-making power. Some of Heywood's plays contain topical and political content, as several scholars have recently demonstrated.[5] Was *Johan Johan*, his first play, somehow a "safe" work since it was not overtly political? We have no record of the reaction to *Johan Johan*, though it is possible to see how its topics—adultery and anticlericalism—could have hit close to home, though without any link to specific current events: a farce about a man deceived

---

often studied. See, for instance, Sydney Anglo; Coldiron, "Journey"; Mary Hill Cole; Roy Strong.

[3] "Royal Throne, Royal Bed: John Heywood and Spectacle," *Medieval English Theatre* 16 (1994): 66–76.

[4] Greg Walker notes that Heywood was "profoundly out of sympathy with the religious reforms of the 1530s and 1540s. Indeed, he came perilously close to dying for his beliefs in 1543, when he was condemned for denying the Royal Supremacy in the aftermath of the Prebendaries Plot"; *The Politics of Performance in Early Renaissance Drama* (Cambridge: Cambridge UP, 1998), p. 76. But earlier, in 1533, the year of this play's publication, Henry VIII's New Year's gift to Heywood, a gold cup, was "a clear indication that Heywood managed to retain favor at a time when other religious conservatives were beginning to feel Henry's wrath," p. 77. In 1553 Heywood wrote a Latin oration on Queen Mary's coronation. Heywood later chose to leave England for France in 1564, under Elizabeth, but had already done an entertainment for her. He was son-in-law of John Rastell and brother-in-law of William Rastell (and thus related by marriage to Thomas More); he was also grandfather of John Donne the poet.

[5] For instance, Greg Walker, *The Politics of Performance*, especially pp. 19, 21, 59, 76–8; pp. 112–13 on the subtle political significances of Rastell's title-page habits and p. 234; Candace Lines, "'To take on them judgements': absolutism and debate in John Heywood's plays" *Studies in Philology* 97.4 (Fall 2000): 401–32; Judith Henderson, "John Heywood's *The Spider and the Flie*: educating queen and country" *Studies in Philology* 96.3 (Summer 1999): 241–74; Peter Happé, "Dramatic Images of Kingship in Heywood and Bale," *SEL 1500–1900* 39.2 (Spring 1999): 239–53; David Bevington, "Is Heywood's *Play of the Wether* Really about the Weather?" *Renaissance Drama* 7 (1964): 11–19.

by a woman and a priest, printed (by Catholic Rastell) in the year before the break with Rome; Anne Boleyn's pregnancy, marriage, and coronation took place within months of this play's publication. Heywood was a "strongly committed Catholic" who was "far from indifferent to religious disputes" (Walker 78). Anticlerical, misogamist satire probably does not qualify either as religious dispute or as indifference to it, but this play at least shows him able to satirize via translation the very structures of church and patriarchy to which his fellow conservatives were committed. In any case, after *Johan Johan*, he turned to other modes of drama and did not translate other farces.[6]

In fact, in the main recent study focusing on the play as a translation, Howard Norland reminds us that most critics see *Johan Johan* as "vastly different in form and style from Heywood's known plays or those of his contemporaries."[7] This distinctiveness leads some critics even to doubt Heywood's authorship.[8] It is the only one of Heywood's plays to have an actual plot: his other plays are built dialectically, so that "the essence of dramatic action is a dispute for preeminence …. Conflict develops dynamically through the process of dialogue and mutual judgment, so that the audience's judgment is awakened; argument and view point are critically manipulated towards resolution" (Axton and Happé 11). The differences between *Johan Johan* and its literary milieu are real and substantive. Yet "all the plays are comic, working satirically through exaggeration and ridicule" (Axton and Happé 11). *Johan Johan* shares a "strong symmetry" (consisting of

---

[6] Heywood's other works—especially scattered epigrams on women and wives in the *Epigrammes* and the *Dialogue conteynyng the number of effectuall prouerbes in the Englishe tounge, compact in a matter concernynge two maner of maryages* (London: Berthelet, 1546)—contain some low-level misogyny and misogamy, sufficient anyway that this kind of material would have been familiar to him. Other editions of the *Dialogue* in 1549, 1556, and 1561 and editions of his works, including the marriage dialogues in 1562, 1566, 1576, 1587, 1598, demonstrate the continuing popularity of Heywood's nondramatic verse. Burton A. Milligan, ed., *Heywood's Works and Miscellaneous Short Poems* (Urbana: University of Illinois Press, 1956).

[7] "Formalizing English Farce: *Johan Johan* and Its French Connection," *Comparative Drama* 17 (1983): 141–52 (p. 141); reprinted in *Drama in the Middle Ages: Comparative and Critical Essays*, eds Clifford Davidson and John Stroupe (New York: AMS, 1990), pp. 356–67. Earlier critics who have treated the play include Robert C. Johnson, *John Heywood* (New York: Twayne, 1970; Ian Maxwell, *French Farce and John Heywood* (Melbourne: University of Melbourne Press, 1946); discussion of *Johan Johan* in Maxwell is overturned by new evidence from T. W. Craik, "The True Source of John Heywood's *Johan Johan*," *MLR* 45 (1950): 289–95; and extended in Stanley Sultan's "*Johan Johan* and Its Debt to French Farce" *JEGP* (1954): 23–27 *et alii*.

[8] C. W. Wallace proposes Henrician court dramatist William Cornyshe as its author in *The Evolution of the English Drama up to Shakespeare* (Berlin: Georg Reimer, 1912), pp. 51–2. A. W. Reed disagrees but speculates on the role or influence, if not the outright authorship, of Thomas More; *Early Tudor Drama, Medwall, the Rastells, and the More Circle* (London: Methuen, 1926), pp. 144 and 146–7.

a prologue, three "scenes," and an epilogue) with his other plays, among other features.⁹ But *Johan* is Heywood's first play, and given the different direction Heywood took later, it may represent an early experiment in short comic or satiric drama. It also imports a fairly extreme form of satiric misogamy and misogyny.

Misogamy and the Translation

Heywood's *Johan Johan* is the only French farce to enter the early English tradition. As such a singular representative of a truly vast body of early French drama, it holds a greater interest for literary historians than it might otherwise have. This translation provokes questions outside my scope here—why, for instance, translate this farce but no others? What in the English temper or context did not easily accept that large body of French drama, when this play testifies to a Tudor awareness of French farce? How does this play stand amid other, more general Henrician imitations of French culture? In this study, the translation's particularities warrant closer attention in terms of literary polysystems and translation studies.

The play has not been read in terms of gender and as part of a body of French-born poetry about gender; such an approach yields an analysis that differs from some recent readings of the play. For example, Howard Norland enumerates many contrasts between the versions, including the presence or absence of gallicisms, the substitution of English for French place names, the addition of common English oaths, and the overall expansion of details in the English (142–43). An interest in characterization and an increased number of asides add up to a better play for Norland (144–51), who concludes that "in almost every respect the English version is more artistically sophisticated and more dramatic than the French text" (151). He decides that "*Johan Johan* extends the relationship between actor and audience … in addition to developing the characters, adapting the clerical satire, and refining the conclusion of the original" (151). These are reasonable and fair conclusions. For our purposes, though, these changes (and others Norland does not mention) add up to something else when examined in terms of the work's misogamy and misogyny.

The opening of the play differs considerably in the two versions, with implications for gender that Norland does not pursue. The English play opens with Johan in a 110-line soliloquy addressing a male audience, or at least the male members of a mixed audience. His first lines ask them about his wife's whereabouts:

---

⁹ Axton and Happé, p. 15. There are also structural similarities between *Pardoner and Frere* and *Johan Johan* (they both imply a circularity or the restarting of a cycle), metrical and rhyme-scheme similarities between *Johan* and *Witty and Witless* (*abab* quatrains interspersed in a play that is mostly made of tetrameter couplets; see also Axton and Happé, p. 12, note 1), and a few verbal echoes, for instance, the same stage direction, "they fyght by the erys," in *Pardoner and Frere* and *Johan*.

> God speed you masters, every one,
> Wot ye not whither my wife has gone?
> I pray God the devil take her
> For all that I do I can not make her
> But she will go gadding very much
> Like an Anthony pig with an old witch … (1–6)

In French, however, the play begins with a *demande d'amour*: an inset lyric passage that traditionally opens love literature and indicates a courtly setting. The *demande d'amour* was also a familiar and elegant social and courtship game and, in the hands of a writer like Alain Chartier, a minor literary genre.[10] The *demande d'amour* was both a popular and a courtly genre, and it seems to me to be a site of critique of the courtly; but this is not an aspect Heywood particularly exploits. The French *demande* passage that Heywood omits in order to open with Johan's rant is this:

> Or devinez que je demande
> Et je vous diray que je quiers
> Sans que nully le vous commande
> Or devinez que je demande.
> Puis que ma cervelle m'y mande
> Pour mieulx scavoir de quoy m'enquiers,
> Or devinez que je demande
> Et je vous diray que je quiers.
> C'est ma femme que je requiers
>
> A Dieu que le deable lemporte
> Elle sen va de porte en porte … (1–11).[11]

---

[10] See Margaret Felberg-Levitt, *The Demande d'Amour* (Montreal: CERES, 1995), and "Jouer aux demandes d'amour," *Moyen Français* 38 (1996): 93-124; also Leslie C. Brook, "The demandes d'amour in the Chantilly and Wolfenbuttel Manuscripts," *Fifteenth Century Studies* (1997): 222–35. William Dunbar's *Ane Tretis of Twa Mariit Wemmen and a Wedo*, dated c. 1507, may provide a parallel example of the use of the *demande d'amour* to frame a satiric treatment of gender issues, in this case, *mal mariée* verse; see *The Poems of William Dunbar*, ed. Priscilla Bawcutt (2 vols, Glasgow: Association for Scottish Literary Studies, 1998), poem 3. Alain Chartier's *Les Demandes damour* was very popular in France but was not translated into English print, though some of his other works were; the *Delectable Demaundes* of 1566 often called a translation of Chartier is in fact a translation of *Les Questions diverses* (Lyons 1558).

[11] [So guess what I'm asking, and I'll tell you what I want, without anyone ordering you; So guess what I'm asking, since my brain orders me about this [lit., so mandates], in order to know better what I'm seeking; So guess what I'm asking, and I'll tell you what I'm seeking. It's my wife I pray/ask God to have the devil carry off! She goes around from door to door …]

The French play's *demande d'amour* is revealed as ironic and decidedly uncourtly as soon as the husband begins his violent soliloquy, really at line 10, "…que le deable lemporte." This *demande d'amour* is in the form of a rondeau, and there are two other rondeaux or near-rondeaux in the play (lines 463–70 and 694–701), suggesting perhaps moments of song or dance or at least brief inset poems punctuating the plainer couplet-verse narration of the drama. Axton and Happé point out that "the use of rondeaux in the *Pasté* may indicate that song and mime were an integral feature of original performance" (310). I am not aware of any full argument or evidence for these lines as having been sung or danced, but the French verse would lend itself very well to such. The rondeaux present a situation and are followed by stichomythic comic lines divided among the characters that would move very fast as repartee or would also work well as lines sung across one another. Heywood's translation conveys the fast-paced repartee but loses the songlike short crossing lines of the French form. Although we have no performance records to indicate how Heywood's translation was staged, the opening *demande d'amour* could easily have been sung, as some dramatic prologues were sung, to capture the attention of the audience. In any case, the other two rondeaux emphasize key answers to the opening *demande* itself, which is an inquiry after the wife. The second rondeau answers this initial inquiry with a "hole in the bucket" section (a sort of answer, given the wordplay in the passage, that the wife is sexually insatiable). The third rondeau occurs where the husband chafes the wax while the lovers eat the pie (another kind of answer to the husband's initial question). These rondeaux can be seen as structural moments of response in the play in which plot elements are showcased in the same lyric form as the initial *demande*.

Heywood, however, does not render these heightened moments with any special verseform or any indication that they would alter the momentum or presentation of the play. The very fast-moving second rondeau he renders in a couplet (ll. 449–50), and the third he renders in a series of couplets (ll. 615–22), for an effect overall less punctuated, more fluid, and drawing less attention to these key moments. Yet Axton and Happé note that while Heywood's other plays use rhyme royal:

> His most frequent verse form, the couplet, is used with great variety, especially in argument where rhymes are made to pick up keywords, or where the pace is varied as the speakers exploit opportunities for making points in debate. These characteristics are enhanced by Heywood's skillful use of "leashes" where a word may be turned inside out by frequent repetition, so that its meaning is destabilized. Many examples of this "French" technique occur in *Witty and Witless* and in *A Play of Love*.[12]

---

[12] P. 12. The plays using rhyme royal are *Witty and Witless*, *The Foure PP*, *Play of Love* (in which rhyme royal is a frame), and *Play of the Wether* (in which Jupiter speaks in rhyme royal). Although he does not discuss *Johan Johan*, Hiroshi Ozawa argues that the More circle's innovations in dramatic form included "pseudo-stichomythia" and the inversion of denotative and connotative meanings to get the audience to experience satiric

I would agree that Heywood does convey the pacing and bawdiness of the original *Farce du Pasté* with these French-born verbal techniques (techniques that in some ways anticipate the English euphuistic style and that certainly anticipate Shakespearean comic stichomythia). But when he suppresses the rondeaux and the *demande d'amour*, he omits the French version's popular mockery of traditional love-literature genres and of "courtly" love play. For example, the French version plays wittily on a familiar love lyric refrain, having the unfaithful wife repeat, "A vrayment je vous ayme bien" (ll. 205–8) [literally, "Ah truly I love you well"]. Heywood entirely skips the half-rondeau containing this jab at courtly lyric. It is a choice, then, not to use certain literary-historical and social elements that were important to the satiric method of the French. Perhaps Heywood understands that some aspects of the farce will not be as easily recognizable to an English audience at Henry's court, who after all do not bring to their experience of the play any similar tradition of public farce (nor as strongly marked and familiar a convention of *demande d'amour*).

While the English opening omits the formal and generic implications of the French *demande d'amour* rondeau, its expanded content immediately poses the central problem of the piece as an absent female. Johan's domestic trouble is an ungovernable woman who has left the house. The solution, in this view, is to be found among men, whom Johan asks for advice and whom he asks not to intervene when he vows to beat the errant wife. (The larger idea of the play nevertheless strongly challenges this implied solution of containing the unruly wife by means of masculine collaboration.) The central problem in the courtly and especially in the Petrarchan traditions, of course, is the absent female who provokes masculine desire—in fact, that absence and provocation could be said to fuel the Petrarchan tradition and to energize courtly traditions. But in this marriage satire, the woman's absence provokes a different kind of frustration. Here the signal female absence leads not to lyric idealizations of the woman or to the lover's vows of service and fidelity but instead leads to Johan's invective against the woman, to vows of violence, and finally to actual violence.

After the initial lines, Johan spends 84 lines of soliloquy swearing to beat his wife as soon as she returns. The actual beating he delays until the end of the play, but he threatens it in the opening monologue. He engages in imagined debate with the audience and with imagined neighbors about the risks and benefits of beating her. The tone and implications of this passage are better read than described:

> Beat her, quotha? Yea that she shall stink
> And at every stroke lay her on the ground,
> And train her by the hair about the house round
> I am even mad that I beat her not now
> But I shall reward her, hardely well ynowe

---

effects. "The Structural Innovations of the More Circle Dramatists," *Shakespeare Studies* 19 (1980–81): 1–23.

There is never a wife between heaven and hell
Which was ever beaten half so well.
Beaten quotha? Yea, but what and she thereof die?
Then I may be chance to be hanged shortly,
And when I have beaten her till she smoke,
And given her many a c. stroke,
Think ye that she will amend yet?
Nay by our lady the devil speed whit
Therefor I will not beat her at all
And shall I not beat her? No shall?
When she offendeth and doth amiss,
And keepeth not her house, as her duty is?
Shall I not beat her if she do so?
Yes by Cock's blood, that I shall do;
I shall beat her and thwack her I trow
That she shall beshit the house for very woe.
But yet I think what my neighbor will say then
He will say thus, Whom chidest thou, John John?
Marry, I will say, I chide my curst wife,
The veriest drab that ever bare life
Which doth nothing but go and come
And I can not make her keep her at home. (12–38)

It is a clear, if colloquial and coarse, statement of early modern marital expectations: the wife is to be at home and keep the house clean, and the husband has the right to beat her until she loses control of her bodily functions if she does not. Yet that right is not absolute. He could be hanged for it if she were to die (ll. 19–20), and a beating might not work to improve her anyway (ll. 21–23). The community, especially the neighboring male community, must be consulted. Johan voices hypothetical discussions with a neighbor or neighbors, which perhaps has the effect of engaging the audience's judgment on this matter. Johan imagines the support of the neighbor, who might suggest he "walke her cote, Johan Johan, and bete her hardely" (40). The idiomatic expression "walking the coat" typifies Heywood's method of lexical naturalization; he adds this wool-industry slang about beating or pressing wool cloth during the felting process (*OED* s.v. walk v.2). Heywood's choice of diction throughout the play locates the characters as part of an English, more or less urban working class, just as other, nonequivalent French slang has located its characters.[13] In other words, Heywood does not try to translate

---

[13] The French play locates its characters somewhere in Picardy, or Normandy-Picardy, according to Halina Lewicka. Unlike so many farces, the setting is not at all certain to be Paris since the named churches exist in several regions and towns. One of the play's oaths is Norman in origin and occurs in other Normandy plays but not, as far as Lewicka knows, in Parisian literature of the period (109–10). The pronunciation of certain rhyming pairs

the French colloquialisms directly but instead finds English colloquialisms to accomplish similar results.

Johan imagines himself to answer, "The more I beat her the worse is she / And worse and worse make her I shall" (ll. 42–3). The neighbor in Johan's imagined discussion might then suggest that he not beat her at all, but Johan answers, "And why, shall I say, this would be wist, / Is she not mine to chastise as I list?" (ll. 45–6) Johan then explains that the worst problem is being mocked for fighting with her and decides that if it succeeds in keeping her at home, "By Saint Mary / That is the point of an honest man / For to beat his wife well now and then" (ll. 52–4). The next 30 lines form a catalogue, more than an antiblazon, of how soundly and painfully he vows to beat her in every body part, and he asks the male audience not to intervene on her behalf when it happens (ll. 65–7). Johan also complains:

> She will stink without a beating
> For every night she giveth me such an heating
> From her issueth such a stinking smoke
> That the savour thereof almost doth me choke. (75–8)

In another of the play's inversions of the courtly tradition, he recalls not the sweet odors of the absent beloved's breath or body, but the gaseous stench that body emits.[14]

After this, Johan reflects on where she might be. In English, the passage names the wife's suspected lover as only "Sir John" (86). In the French play, there is no such suggestion of *pastourelle* (or *anti-pastourelle*); we learn immediately that Jehan suspects that his wife is with the priest. "Mais ou grant diable peut-elle estre? / Je gaige qu'elle est chés le prestre" (ll. 86–7; but great devil, where is she? I bet she's at the priest's ...). The French version builds some minor suspense

---

seems to her to rule out Paris, too: "on relève dans la pièce plusieurs rimes qui font penser à une region picarde ou normanno-picarde" (she then gives several examples). *Études sur l'ancienne farce française* (Paris: Éditions Klencksieck, 1974), p. 110; see also pp. 105–110.

[14] In France, marital bodily odors could be seen as actionable: "In April 1502, a young woman named Nicole asked the court to release her from her pledge to marry Jean Defer because of his atrocious bad breath. Nicole claimed this defect had been unknown to her at the time of betrothal and called a neighbor of Jean Defer to support her case. The witness testified to the veracity of Nicole's claim: '... il puait, soit de la bouche ou du nez, tant que personne ne pouvait faire société ou conversation avec lui' [... he stank, either from the nose or the mouth, so badly that no one could be around him or talk with him]," M. H. D'Arbois de Jubainville and M. Francisque André, eds. (Aube: Archives ecclésiastiques, série G. vol 2 of *Inventaire Sommaire des Archives Départementales antérieures B 1790*. Paris: Alphonse Picard et Fils, 1896; 319), cited in Collingwood 137. See also Collingwood 133–8 on other reasons for the breaking of marriage bargains. I know of no parallel in England; was it the land of fragrant husbands, or were such odors considered normal, beneath the notice of law and satire? On the other hand, as Donawerth reminds me, later Tudor plays made frequent references to women's breath.

since we do not learn the priest's name, Guillaume, until line 168. In English the suspected lover's name comes first, and we do not learn until line 140 or so that Sir John is no courtly seducer but rather is the scurrilous parish priest.

Heywood's use of names merits further consideration. The name *Jehan* or *Jehannin* in the French tradition was long associated in farces, *sotties*, and other comic literary forms with hapless male dupes, most particularly cuckolds.[15] The English husband's name necessarily loses the full force of that cultural accretion. However, the doubling of the names of the two men, Johan and Sir Johan, also seems more significant than many critics would allow. Naming the priest Sir Johan (instead of Guillaume) does more than "emphasize the priest's assumption of the husband's role" (Norland 144). I suggest that it serves the misogyny and misogamy of the play, stressing the "anyman" nature of the woman's sexuality: any John will do—and does. The class marker "Syr" tagged to the priest's name may add a slight critique of privilege or clerical pseudoprivilege to the mixture, supporting the play's anticourtliness. In addition, there may have been some minor in-joke at court involved in Heywood's choice of naming.[16] On characters and naming in the play more generally, Norland sees the addition of characters' names to the English title and the English naming of what Norland says is an unnamed French wife as a sign of Heywood's superior skill.[17] The addition of names to the title is certainly a personalization of the more generalized French types. I would add that the French title retains the metaphoric subject of the farce better: *La Farce du Pasté* announces its central subject as the division (or misdivision) of the domestic pie and the satisfaction (or lack of satisfaction) of appetites. The English names added to the title shift slightly away from that emphasis. The full title of the French, furthermore, keeps the anticlerical stereotyping in view: *Farce nouvelle très bonne et fort joyeuse du Pasté, et est à trois personnages: c'est assavoir l'homme, la femme, le curé*. The changes Heywood made to the title may also indicate his sense of his audience's unfamiliarity with the genre: to specify names and roles not only helps keep the now-doubled Johans straight but also informs the English audience about who's who in the standard farce trio (which was not, after all, standard in England). A final point about Heywood's naming is that the name he gives to the wife, Tyb, "becomes [a] typical name for a woman of lower class and

---

[15] For an excellent compact history of these connotations, see Bernadette Rey-Flaud, *La Farce ou la machine à rire: théorie d'un genre dramatique 1450–1550* (Geneva: Droz, 1984), pp. 183–4. See also, Halina Lewicka, "Un Prénom spécialisé," *Études sur l'ancienne farce française*. (Paris: Éditions Klencksieck, 1974), pp. 78–84.

[16] "One of Heywood's fellow servants of the King had a strikingly similar name. The Treasurer of the Chamber's accounts from 1 October 1529 record payments of 50 shillings to Heywood and also to 'John de John, priest, organ maker' [L&P V 306]" (Axton and Happé, 230).

[17] "The wife in the French version is never named" (144), and it is true that her speech prefixes are "La Femme," but in line 83 the husband refers to her as Marion, a traditional wife's name in early French popular literature.

a strumpet" and can also be a cat's name (Axton and Happé 232, note J111). Tyb is associated throughout the play with cats and a randy, prowling promiscuity (ll. 73, 110ff, 129, 588–9; the editorial notes to these lines provide full cultural context). The altered English characterizations signaled by the changed names may slightly enhance the translation's misogyny and misogamy.

At the end of this long opening monologue, the husband's vehement vows to beat the wife evaporate the moment she returns:

[Johan]...
But she shall have her payment styk by her syde
For I shall order her for all her brawlyng
That she shall repent to go a catter wawlyng
[Enter Tyb.]
Tyb.   Why whom wilt thou beat, I say, thou knave?
Johan.   Who, I, Tyb? None, so God me save.
Tyb.   Yes, I heard thee say thou wouldst one beat.
Johan.   Marry wife, it was stockfish in Thames Street,
Which will be good meat against Lent.
Why Tyb, what hadst thou thought I meant? (108–16)

The analogous French moment consists of a simpler and briefer exchange: The wife enters while Jehan is muttering that he will pay her back, and she asks what he is muttering about. He says, "Nothing." Heywood's translation amplifies the comedic contrast between the husband's bluster and his obedience to Tyb and adds sexually charged wordplay.[18] The husband's angry ranting is fully undercut and rendered impotent and comical.

The rest of the plot maintains this dynamic, with Tyb manipulating Johan into inviting the priest-lover to dine with them. When Sir Johan arrives, he and Tyb share the pie that Johan's household money has paid for while they persuade Johan first to fetch water, then to try to repair a hole in the water bucket. To do this, he must stand by the fire warming wax between his fingers by rubbing it. Sexual innuendo abounds, and the repeated phrase "chafing the wax" to "stop the clift" in the bucket takes on sexual meaning. The trio's appetites for dinner, the husband's continuing hunger and the lovers' satisfactions, the gaping hole of the household bucket, the cuckolded husband's inability to fill that gap, though he rubs and rubs:

---

[18]   Here, on "payment stick" and "stockfish." Axton and Happé point out Heywood's frequent bawdy puns (lines 73, 80, 104, 108, 110, 114, 129, 164, 222, 350, 361, 447, 457–8, 492, 536, etc.). Again, these are usually not exact equivalents to the French puns—Heywood generally drops French puns and creates his own in other places—but his wordplay achieves the same bawdy effect. Likewise, Heywood's frequently added oaths and epithets like "Cockes blood" and "whoreson" carry sexual implications. Stockfish and woman-beating are also associated in *The Seyenges of Salomon and Marcolphus* (1529).

all are fairly obvious figures for the sexual content. Johan stands aside chafing the wax, unable to fill the hole in the bucket, while Tyb and Sir John consume the pie.

The antimarital satire is also anticlerical, but it is so in somewhat different measures in the French and English versions. Not only is the priest also lightly associated with lower nobility in English (Sir John), he blatantly calls the husband "cuckold" (ll. 656–7) and admits to fathering children, as Norland notes. The French priest is sneakier: when the husband arrives to invite him to supper, Guillaume refuses, implying there is some dispute between himself and the wife or that she speaks ill of him, but he admits in mock-wounded forgiveness that she is, after all, a good woman and parishioner. In fact, says the priest, "Qu'elle ne soit nette devant vous / Et de son corps femme de bien,/ Si est" (ll. 367–9) [Although she may not seem clean or pure to you, she is a worthy woman in body]. The husband caps this line with:

> Je nay doubte de rien
> Dieu mercy et vostre doctrine.
> Pourroye savoir la racine
> Du debat entre vous et elle? (369–72)[19]

The husband is completely duped by Guillaume's pretenses and soon chides himself in an aside:

> Mais suys-je bien fils de putain?
> Je cuidoye a pur et a plain
> Qu'il l'aymast pour la decepvoir
> Et il s'acquite et fait devoir
> Comme bon patron et loyal. (384–8)[20]

The wily French priest uses double entendre that the husband does not understand; the understanding audience wonders whether the husband might at some point catch on but then feels superior to the husband and somehow complicit with the lovers. In English the scene is much less subtle, losing that dramatic irony. The priest admits he has lain on top of her repeatedly:

> Sir Johan   Yet thou thynkyst amys peraventure
> That of her body she shuld not be a good woman,
> But I shall tell thee what I have done, Johan
> For that matter: she and I be sometyme aloft
> And I do lye upon her, many a tyme and oft

---

[19] [I never doubted anything; thank God and your learning. Might I know the root of the dispute between you two?]

[20] [But am I really such a whore's son? I thought for sure he loved her to deceive her, and here he is acquitting himself and doing his duty like a good and loyal benefactor.]

> To prove her, yet I could never espy
> That ever any dyd wors with her than I.
> Johan Syr that is the lest care I have of nyne
> Thankyd be God and your doctrine ... (346–54)

We cannot feel suspense after the priest's admission, and contempt for the husband competes with sympathy. Tyb, too, has called the husband "cuckold" (505–6), and the English play makes this masculine fear more explicit by the repetition of the word, even while it much more clearly specifies a male audience.[21]

Back at the house, Johan keeps ineffectually chafing the wax to fill the hole in the bucket while Tyb and Sir Johan share the pie. Sir Johan entertains them by telling three stories of supposedly religious miracles. First is the story of a man who went to sea for seven years, and when he returned, his wife miraculously had had seven children. The priest admits, or brags, "Yet had she not had so many by thre / Yf she had not had the help of me" (ll. 547–8). The next miracle is of a long-married, barren woman, who then went on a pilgrimage and a month later gave birth. The third miracle is that of a woman who gave birth to a full-term child after only five months of marriage.[22] The husband's response to the three miracles in French is a heavily ironic and aphoristic "C'est grant faict que de marriage / A jamais homme n'en desbate" (ll. 660–61) [What a great thing marriage is; no man can ever dispute that]. Johan, apparently lacking his French counterpart's knowledge and thus incapable of that sarcasm or double-entendre, simply says:

> A wondrous myracle so God me mende!
> I wolde eche wyfe that is bounde in maryage
> And that is wedded here within this place
> Myght have as quicke spede in every suche case. (583–6)

Omitted from the English translation is a similar aphoristic comment on marriage in French: "But must we all be marrying? What a blessing marriage is!" (ll. 84–5).

---

[21] There is one ambiguous reference at the end of the French play to "Messigneurs." But the English play opens "god spede you, maysters, everychone" (1); Johan addresses the audience as "maysters" (65) and in closing, as "syrs" (665).

[22] Heywood has altered these stories a bit; in French, the priest calls them the miracles of Saint Arnoul (l. 590), in some folklore the patron saint of cuckolds (though I have not been able to verify this). In the first French story, the man goes away into the brotherhood of St. Arnoul, and his wife bears 14 children. The second French story is an incoherent account of what sounds like an incestuous relationship between the priest and his stepsister (ll. 617–37). In the last French story, a bride vows on her wedding night to join the sisterhood of St. Arnoul (apparently a celibate order), and seven months later, she gives birth to a full-term child. Heywood suppresses the references to St. Arnoul that frame the French stories, probably a gesture to his audience, who presumably would be more familiar with Saint Modwyn, the Irish virgin saint whose red staff was said to assist women in childbirth (Axton and Happé, 234 note J561).

Such asides would have seemed ideal taglines—a real opportunity for an epigram writer like Heywood—but he suppresses these sardonic moments, working perhaps more bluntly with character and event.

The changed ending, too, alters the tone and character of the English work. In French the ending seems deliberately ambiguous, and speech prefixes are lacking in the original, though some editors supply their best guesses. The husband in the French version chases the priest out of the house. The wife encourages the priest, who apparently beats the husband. The husband decides to leave then, and the wife asks the priest which way the husband went. The priest says, "Let's follow him." The stage direction then says, "The man comes from behind them with a bag full of bread." Someone, presumably the husband, then says these very unclear words:

Apres cure apres apres
A vous me gastes le paste
Apres cure apres cure
A ly A ly A ly A ly
Or Messigneurs, adieu vous dy![23]
Explicit   (761–7)

If the husband speaks the words "Run after him!" and "You're ruining my pie," then the implied stage business is that the husband is chasing the priest from the stage while pummeling him with the bread sack. In that case, one way to read the last lines is that the priest then cries, "A ly a ly," and the wife tells the men goodbye. Or the husband cries "after him," the wife cries "you've ruined my pie," the husband continues shouting "after him" as the priest yells "A ly A ly," and someone—everyone?—calls "goodbye, sirs." The scene seems too action-filled for the last line to be a decorous epilogue-type farewell to "Messigneurs" of the audience. (Such a decorous ending, however, is just what Heywood creates from this rather chaotic, potentially slapstick moment in the French.) But unless they all exit in a tumble, each delivering one of the last three lines, but more or less simultaneously, the lines do not really make sense. Thus Norland is right to say that "the French farce unquestionably ends with the dispute unresolved" (147).

The English version, though, resolves the dispute very clearly, and it leaves the husband in a melancholy version of his original predicament. As Kent Cartwright points out, "Heywood increases the poignancy of this ending over its French original" (46). The English version slows its pace and creates a framing epilogue addressed to the (male) audience. The play's new closing verses are very like the opening ones in which the husband rants about his absent wife, wondering aloud

---

[23] Nancy Vine Durling's translation: "After run after, after; Ah, you're ruining my pie; after run after run; ah li ah li ah li ah li; well, sirs, I tell you goodbye! The end." However, if "cure" were taken not to be a form of the verb courir, to run, but rather an unaccented form of le curé, curate, the cry might mean "after, priest, after him!"

whether he should beat her savagely. In the end, his suspicions are confirmed and he has beaten the wife and priest enough to drive them from the house:

> I have payd some of them even as I lyst
> They have borne many a blow with my fyst.
> I thank God I have walkyd them well
> And dryven them hens. (665–8)

His final question to the assembled men of the audience breaks the fourth wall, recalls his opening question, and expresses the same sexual fear, with perhaps an added note of desperation:

> ... But yet can ye tell
> Whether they be go? For by God I fere me
> That they be gon together, he and she
> Unto his chamber, and perhappys she wyll
> Spyte of my hert tery there styll,
> And peradventure there he and she
> Wyll make me a cockold, evyn to anger me ... (668–74).

The English version, unlike the French version, sets up the reason for his exit by repeating the initial questions and assumptions (that is, where is the absent wife, and isn't an absent wife an adulterous wife?). The husband drives the wife and priest away with physical violence and the threat of it but ends as he began, wondering where the wife is and whether she and the priest are lovers. "Therfore by God I wyll hye me thyder / To se yf they do me any vylany: / And thus fare well this noble company" (676–8). Where the French version ends ambiguously in a brawl-à-trois, in this ménage, the English husband ends where he begins, alone, in jealous suspicion, but on the other side of the threshold of violence. The translation's changes, however, have completely justified that suspicion: instead of wordplay and innuendo as in the French, the English version allows full open admissions of cuckoldry, adultery, and bastard children and has the wife and priest leave the stage together, confirming the husband's misogyny (and perhaps, for that culture, his right to do violence) and the audience's potential misogamy.

Johan and Literary History

Critics of the French farce usually note that while the women are portrayed as lascivious, stubborn, and loud, the men are cruel, much stupider, and uniformly duped and punished. For this modern reader, the play feels too cruelly misogynist and misanthropic to be funny. Bernard Faivre captures this sense of the play: "Cette farce est peut-être la plus féroce qui existe ... [S]e faire l'entremetteur de son propre cocuage, la chose est dure ..." (321); "Pour rire au bon coeur au *Pâté*, il faut trouver très amusant d'arracher une à une les pattes d'une mouche" (322). [This is perhaps the most savage farce extant ...; to make oneself the go-between of one's own cuckoldry, that's a hard thing ... Anyone who laughs heartily at the *Pasté* must find it very amusing to pull off the legs of a fly one by one]. The changes Heywood made in translating this play somehow enhance this painful effect.

In literary-historical terms, *Johan Johan* is anomalous on several levels, a sort of bolt from the blue without obvious connections in English either to literary or to biographical and political contexts. From the broadest polysystem view, *Johan Johan* is a missed opportunity for English drama. Comic secular drama was a major, thriving concern in fifteenth- and early sixteenth-century France, with about 150 farces surviving and probably more lost, not to mention the hundreds of *sotties* and secular *moralités*, with conventions quite distinct from English morality plays of the same period. French farces were performed either by the *Basoches*, with legal settings, players, and themes, or more widely, as this farce probably was, in public marketplaces and halls by semiprofessional troupes of four or five players, usually men. They were plainly staged on planks atop barrels and were short, usually around 500 lines. Audiences were of course popular and broad but sometimes included nobles or even royals.[24] We should wonder why this staple of early French literature, the priest-wife-cuckolded husband plot, in which the Church steals what rightfully belongs to the common householder, did not make it big in early modern England. The social background of clerical corruption and misogyny and the literary background of anticlerical satire did surely exist in England as well as in France, but I know of almost nothing like this play in early English drama.[25]

To understand this apparent gap in cross-cultural literary history, we might recall that early French drama and Tudor drama developed along different lines, Tudor drama having been dominated by the Humanist interludes and household productions analyzed by Suzanne Westfall or Kent Cartwright.[26] Cartwright, in

---

[24] See *The New Oxford Companion to French Literature*, s.v. *farce*. We know that a *Farce du Pasté* was played at Saint-Omer; Justin de Pas, *Mystères et Jeux Scéniques à Saint-Omer au XVème siècle*, p. 28; cited in Cohen, p. xiv, n11.

[25] Yet Heywood's other work, especially T*he Pardoner and the Frere*, has long been seen as "medieval": George Lyman Kittredge, "John Heywood and Chaucer," *American Journal of Philology* 9.4 (1888): 473–4, who points out passages in *PF* and in the *Dialogue of Proverbes...[on marriage]* that connect to passages in Chaucer's *Canterbury Tales* and *Troilus*. Richard A. Long, "Heywood, Chaucer, and Lydgate," *Modern Language Notes* 64.1 (1949): 55–6, shows that Heywood read not only Chaucer but more likely Lydgate's *Siege of Thebes* and connects passages in it to *PF*. More recently, see Allan B. Fox, "Chaucer's Prosody and the Non-Pentameter Line in John Heywood's Comic Debates" *Language and Style: An International Journal* 10 (1977): 23–41.

[26] Westfall, Patrons and Performance: *Early Tudor Household Revels* (Oxford: Clarendon, 1990), *passim* but especially pp.108–22 on the playwrights. Cartwright, *Theatre and Humanism: English Drama in the Sixteenth Century* (Cambridge: Cambridge UP,

arguing persuasively against a "two-tradition" paradigm of moralities versus humanist drama, also demonstrates that early plays must be understood first in theatrical terms (46). Such an understanding would factor in the two nations' divergent histories of staging and performance; such an understanding thus widens the gaps that must be bridged in translation beyond the literary-historical and linguistic. The interior physical spaces, semiprivate court contexts, and consistently noble, court-based audiences of Heywood's England form a very different set of theatrical contexts for the play than do the open public staging of the rowdy French farces. While these differences do not fully explain Heywood's changes—particularly the suppression of the poetic forms and the changes to the *demande d'amour*—theatrical factors do seem to make excellent sense of Heywood's revised and more melancholic ending. Cartwright further notes that "Tudor humanists introduced attitudes toward women sharply opposed to popular misogyny" while "[acknowledging] the complexities, limitations, and differences among humanist approaches to women" (136). Certainly, the misogyny and misogamy of this play—its character of Tyb alone—would oppose a humanist defense of women's virtue or dignity. Inasmuch as the play was out of synch with humanist interests in the education and elevation of women, then, it would not have come before as friendly an audience as it did in the *places publiques* of France. Westfall, along similar lines, notes that:

> Virtually all Tudor interludes address themes of vital interest to the aristocracy in language and through structures that reflected life in the great households. The playwrights were careful writers, who aspired to call attention to abuses, to reform degenerate behavior, and to advise those in power without offending their audiences or their noble patrons. Early Tudor plays continually demonstrate that their authors had detailed and complex knowledge of the social class about which they were writing .... The early Tudor interlude, therefore, reaffirmed the existing social structure to all classes at the same time as it subtly manipulated audience response to accept the more specific political persuasions of the authors and their patrons. (198)

Clearly, *Johan* stands apart from other early Tudor drama; had it been understood to accuse or reform Henrician sexual triads, Heywood might have been in some jeopardy. The play and the context are more complex than that, however. The patronage of a noble household is a support and a context for satire very different from the open, public, professional troupes who played the hundreds of French farces and *sotties* for majority urban audiences ranging in class from pauper to monarch. The translation from what Bernadette Rey-Flaud calls the "machine à rire" to a very different, more serious, more didactic, more private Tudor "machine" may help explain why other English dramatists did not take up the misogamist-satiric French farce except in bits here and there, or why Heywood himself tried

---

1999), *passim*, especially pp. 45–6 on this play and pp. 135–66 on portrayals of women in the drama.

it once and moved on. Context is all, and without the support of an equal literary tradition and an appropriate audience, Heywood's rather skillful translation of this play stands apart and is not followed by a parallel, thriving English tradition. Since "the play is unlike anything before or since in English drama" (Axton and Happé 36), it shows that even if a translation succeeds aesthetically and is familiar ideologically—for, as we have seen, this kind of misogamy and misogyny was surely available in England in 1533—it still may need the support of "high-culture" ideology (for the Tudors, "humanist" support) and certainly will need the right venue and the practical and financial support of audiences. A translation's entry into English literary systems, in other words, is here complicated by mixed ideological and theatrical contexts.

Overall, Heywood adapts and alters the French material so as to naturalize it for the English context and to render the Frenchness of the text invisible. Unlike the other translations treated in this book, this one has no paratexts to show us his thinking on the topic: there are no prologues, epilogues, illustrations, colophon verses, or other metatextual clues about what the translator and printer were aiming for in appropriating this text. Its misogamy and its misogyny are bicultural enough to allow Heywood a fairly close imitation with some tweaking of details, but the French play's farcical critique of marriage finds no parallel English dramatic tradition and apparently no venue in which to take root and flourish. That the antimarital verse and misogamous farces so popular in France missed a full English appropriation reveals another of the curiously selective filters operating between the two cultures and literary systems on gender discourses in early Tudor England.

Appendix 1
The "Letter of Dydo to Eneas"; The Beaute of Women

A. The *Letter of Dydo to Eneas* (in *The Boke of Fame*, London: Pynson, 1526)
B. The *Beaulte of Women* (London: R. Fawkes, 1525).

A. The *Letter of Dydo to Eneas*
    [¶] Thus endeth the co[m]plant of Mary ma
    gdeleyn / and herafter foloweth the
    letter of Dydo to Eneas: and
    fyrst the prologue of the translatour.

Folke disc[om]forted / bere heuy cou[n]tenau[n]ce
As ye haue cause / so order your chere
But yet some folke / whiche vse disse[m]blaunce
Wolde say / other meanes moche better were
That is to say / good cou[n]tenau[n]ce to bere   5
Wha[n] ye haue cause/ of thought or heuynesse
That folke [per]ceyue nat your grefe [&] distres

But as for me / me thynke playnnesse is best
After your chere / to shewe your wo
Shewe outwarde / what ye bere w[ith]in your brest   10
Sithe ye of force / must chuse one of the two
Eyther among the dissemblers to go
Or els be playne / chose after your lust
But playnnesse is the waye of parfyte trust

To purpose lo/ thus wyse it is ment   15
Bycause that I haue loued very long
And haue no ioye/vnto this day present
Co[n]strayned me.to write this rufull songe
Of poore Dydo / forsaken by great wronge
Of false Ene / who causeth my ha[n]d to shak   20
For great furye / that I ayenst hym take

Ah false vntrouth/unki[n]de delyng [&] double
My ha[n]de quaketh / whan I write thy name

Thou hast brought all true louers i[n] trouble
By thy vntrouthe / wherfore o lady Fame 25
Blowe up they tru[m]pe of sclau[n]der [&] of shame
Forthwith to shewe / of Ene his false delyte
Make me your clerke / Si[m]ply as I can write

Shall I go to the well of Helycon
To the muses/for to pray them of ayde 30
Nay nay alas / for they wepe euerychone
For pore Dydo / thus pytously arayde
And now Iuno / acco[m]pteth her dismayde
For the knot the she trusted shulde last
Is nowe become/bothe lose and vnstedfast 35

What remedy / where shulde I seke socour
Of Niobe / of Myrra / or of Byblis
Of Medea or Lucrece / the romayne flour
None of the[m] all / may grau[n]t me helpe in this
Nor yet Venus / that goddes of loue is 40
She is parciall / she loueth Enee so
Wherfore helpe me / ye cruell Celeno

For lyke as I / barreyne of eloquence
Presume to translate / nat worthy to bere
The ynkehorn of the[m]/y[t] write i[n] good sente[n]ce 45
For lernyng lacketh / and reason is nat clere
Afore poetes / my workes dare nat appere
Whiche causeth me helpe to requyre
Of Celeno / full of enuyous yre

Prayeng all them / that shall this rede or s[e] 50
To be content / at this my poore request
In this translacion / to pardon me
And of my mynde / to reporte the best
To translate frenche / I am nat redyest
No marueyle is / sithe I was neuer yet   \ 55
In those [par]ties / where I might la[n]gage gete

Fro[m] Troy distroyed full of passed yeres seuyn
Thus Eneas / arryued at Carthage
And at the last / by influence of heuyn
Mette with his folks / tossed in y[e] sees rage 60
Venus and Iuno / entended maryage
Bitwene him and Dido/but this vntrue man

Brake y[e] [pro]myse / wherfore thus she began.
[¶] Thus endeth the prologe.
[page break]
[woodcut of Dido committing suicide]
Right (as y[e] swan) whan her dethe is nye
Swetely dothe syng / her fatall desteny
Lykewise / I Dido / for all my true loue
Whiche by no prayer / can you remoue
Nor hath in you / no more hope of lyfe   5
Write vnto you / my sorowes most pe[n]syfe
For well knowe I / my chaunces be so yll
That they shalbe y[e] troublers of my wyll
But sithe that I haue lost all my renowne
Whiche y[e] through the worlde dyd sowne   10
But a small losse is / of the surplusage
As for to lose words / writyng / or message
Enee/ye take a great iourney in hande
To forsake poore Dido / [&] all her lande
So by one wynde shalbe forthe past   15
your faithe / [pro]mise / your sayle [&] eke your mast
Nowe ye delyte to dresse your passage
In hope therby / to haue auauntage
And for to seche Italyens groundes
Whiche be nat yet within your boundes   20
Pleaseth nat you / this cyte of Cartage
Nor the cou[n]tre nor la[n]de good for tyllage
The thynges well done and sure / ye dispice
Thyngs vncertayne / ye sertche [&] en[ter]prise
But what be they at your aduyse Enee   25
By whom their lande gouerned shalbe
And submyt the[m] to you a poore stra[n]ger
Wyll they to your lawes / put the[m] selfe in da[n]ger
Certe[n]ly/as by your dedes I [per]ceyue
Other louers / in recompence ye haue   30

And if ye haue faithe of another lady
She shalbe disceyued / as well as I
But whan tyme shall co[m]e / the day [&] hour
That ye shall bylde a mighty stro[n]g tour
And a cyte / Cartage to resemble   35
To the whiche people shall assemble
That your renowne may be spred ouer all
Holdyng your ceptre / in your chere ryall
Nowe put the case / suche be your desteny

That ye may happe / gouerne all Italy 40
yet shall ye neuer haue spouse nor wyfe
Kynder than me / I loue you as my lyfe
I bren as hote / sithe loue made my hert ta[m]e
As bri[m]stone / whiche in y[e] fyre dothe flame
Knowe ye for trouth / whan ye saile in y[e] sees 45
I shall haue you alway before myn eyes
yet alway feirs and forgetfull ye be
Of others welthe / ye haue enuy I se
Well ought I than / were I a symple wight
Hat his swete words / [&] flye fro his sight 50
But though that he wyll flye fro me
I can nat forgete / nor hate my swete Ene
I playne ynough / of his dealyng vntrue
But so moch more / loue doth my hert subdue
[O] Cupido / [&] ye Ven[us] his moder dere 55
Haue some pyte / of my soroufull chere
And lyke as ye / with your peersyng darte
With loue of false Ene / stroke me to y[e] hert
To thende that he / in whom I put my trust
Pyte my wepyng / and be nat vniust 60
Alas/howe moche hath it be my domage
That I trusted to his plesa[n]t visage
And to moch for trouth / deceyued was I y[e] hour
Whan his beaute wan me w[ith]out socour
Certes in maners / in swetenesse / [&] in grace 65
To his mother / vnlyke in euery place
For she is swete / and he is vnkynde
A droppe of trouthe / in hi[m] I can nat finde
I beleue than / [&] thynke it without blame
ye were neuer borne / of so swete a dame 70
But borne i[n] rock[s] / i[n] thornes / or amo[n]g breers
Among tygres [&] wolues / cruell and feers
There were ye borne / [&] lyued w[ith]out norture
For without mercy / y[e] arte of thy nature
Or I may saye surely without dout 75
In the see / thy byrth was brought about
And in y[e] same / where y[e] haddest thy spri[n]ging
Thou folowest in nature thy begynning
        But

But wheder flyest thou / thou false Enee 80
In what perill is thy lyfe ordayned to be
What/seest nat y[e] vntrue and frowarde

The gret troubles / y[e] cou[n]tre colde [&] harde
And of the see / the water whiche dothe swell
Whiche for to passe / be right depe [&] cruell   85
Seest y[e] nat also / howe force of y[e] wynde
Is ayenst y[e] / print these thi[n]gs in thy mi[n]de
Certainly / the tempest and the rage
Is more stedfast / than is thy false corage
And more there is / of surete in the see   90
Than i[n] thy will / which maketh me to blame the
Alas / I haue nat at y[e] somuch enuy
To wisshe y[e] hurt / though y[e] thi[n]ke co[n]trary
Nor to desyre / for to reuenge myne angre
To put your lyfe in so pytous daunger   95
But ayenst me / great hate ye haue co[n]ceyued
And moche desyre / y[e] I shulde be deceyued
Sithe that ye wyll / suche dau[n]ger vndertake
But to thentent / y[t] ye may me forsake
It appereth well / ye care nat for to dye   100
Sithe ye so sone / put your lyfe in ieo[par]dy
Tary a space / if that it may you please
Tyll that the see be more calme [&] at ease
To thende that ye / for enuy or for stryfe
Of your goyng / ye do nat lese your lyfe   105
Haue ye nat knowen / the troublous tempest
Whiche in y[e] see doeth ryse / fro[m] Est to West
Thousa[n]de da[n]gers hourly there doth encrese
Ought ye nat than of your iorney to cese
But sithe ye haue dayly great busynesse   110
Wherof co[m]meth your froward wylfulnesse
That ye wolde sayle / [&] in payne be moued
Marueyle nat than / though ye be re[pro]ued
For certainly / they be neuer well assured
Whiche vnto ladyes / so ofte be periured   115
But tosse [&] sayle / after their faithe is gone
Whan they haue lef[t]e their ladyes alone
Of trouthe y[e] see dothe ofte drowne [&] receyue
Win his wawes / folk which lust deceyue
Chefely on false louers / that dothe befall   120
And the reason is this / for fyrst of all
Venus y[e] goddes / whose seruau[n]t louers be
Was engendred of the fome of the see
Alas / what feare my hert distroyeth
Why doute I to anoy hym y[t] me anoyeth   125

Better were to lyue and contynue brethe
I loue moch more / yo[r] lyfe than yo[r] dethe

And rather desyre / to dye with a good wyll
Than ye shulde / sayle [&] be in great peryll
I pray you nowe / set your hert at rest 130
Se howe the sees are troublus / w[ith] te[m]pest
In you sayling / is many a quicke sande
Whan ye departe fro me / and fro my la[n]de
And if it chau[n]ce / ye be drowned at a clappe
But I pray god kepe you / fro suche mys-hap 135
Whan ye [&] your ship be lyke to perishe
That ye were here / than wyll often wyshe
Than Enee / your false forsweryng
First shall come / to your vndersta[n]dyng
Than in your mynde / Dydo ye shall espy 140
Whom by disceit / ye haue caused to dye
Than shall ye se / to make your hert pe[n]syfe
The colde ymage / of your disceyued wife
Heuy / thoughtfull / w[ith] heres pulde fro her hed
Spotted w[ith] blode / wou[n]ded/ nat fully ded 145
Whan yo[r] lyfe fayleth/tha[n] shall ye sigh [s]ore
And say / I haue deserued this [&] more
Ha my dere frende / gyue a lytell space
To y[e] sees rage / which doth you manace
Tary a whyle / soiourne a space ye may 150
Tyll that there come / a more goodly day
And it may be / that all these wawes great
Shall well apese / [&] no more y[e] rock[s] bete
And if ye haue banysshed fro me [pery]
Haue ye regarde / to your sonne Ascany 155
Shall your sonne se my sorowfull trespace
Who[m] ye haue kept / i[n] many a diuers place
Saued ye your folke fro fyre of Troy town
To the[n]de / y[t] the gret see shulde the[m] drown
I am nat the fyrst / I knowe for certayne 160
Whom your langage / hath caused to co[m]-playne
But ye y[t] were / well lerned for to lye
Haue abused me alas / through my folly
your pitous words / wha[n] I herd w[ith] myn eres
My eyes were moued to sta[n]de ful of teres 165
After / my hert moche enclyned to pyte
Was holly moued / to haue your amyte
That redy wyll / and my defaut sodayne

Shall nowe be cause / of my later payne
I thynke for trouth / that god for your vice 170
In eche place / shal you punishe [&] chastice
Seuyn yeres w[ith]out rest / by lande [&] by see
Ye were in watres / and great aduersyte
At the last / weder driuen ye were hyder
I was content / y[t] we shulde lyue togyder 175
     And

And by payne had / of your name knowledge
My body [&] landes / to you I dyd pledge
Wolde to god that the fame [&] yll renowne
On my synne / were vtterly layde downe 180
I was to blame / to enclyne and reioyce
In the swete words of your pitous voice
Trustyng your true spouse to be
But the fayntesse of loue disceyued me
Pardon ye me / of that I was so swyfte 185
I dyde it nat for golde / nor for no gyfte
One that semed kynde / louyng and honest
Ouercame me / to folowe his request
His noble blode / and hir swete cou[n]tenaunce
Gaue me good hope / [&] of mynde assurau[n][c]e 190
I knowe no woma[n] / so good nor so wyse
That wolde the loue of suche one dispice
For in hym is no defaut but one
He lacketh pyte / whiche causeth me to mone
yf goddes wyll be / that ye shall nedes hens 195
I wolde he had forbode you my prese[n]s
Alas / ye se and knowe this without fayle
That your people be wery of traueyle
And to haue rest / they wolde be very fayne
Tyll that they may be esed of their payne 200
Also your shippes be nat fully prest
your sayles broken / you gables yet vnfest
yf I of you haue ought deserued
By any thyng / wherin I haue you [preser]ued
And euer wyll serue you / in my best wyse 205
For recompence at lest of that seruyce
I pray you hertely / let this be done
Purpose your mynde / nat to go so sone
Tyll the tyme that the see and the rage
Be well apesed / [&] of his wawes as wage 210
And tyll that I may suffre with good hert

your de[par]ture / sithe ye wyll nedes depart
And more easely / suffre and endure
Thought / traueyle / payne / [&] displeasure
For in goodfaithe / I trust of very trothe   215
That aye[n]st me ye can nat long be wroth
yet I pray you / come regarde the ymage
Of her that wrote to you this langage
Alas I write / and to encrease my sorowe
There sta[n]deth y[e] swerde / y[t] shall kyll me tomorowe   220
w[ith] my teres / this swerd is spotted
Whiche in my brest / in hast shalbe blotted
And all shalbe in stede of teres on y[e] sworde
Spotted with blode / trust me at a worde

Ha/the swerde ye lefte me whan ye went   225
To my desteny is conuenyent
Of an vnhappy offryng [&] gyfte but small
My sepulture is made great therwithall
This shall nat be the fyrst glayue or darte
That hath peersed me to the herte   230
For afore this/loue y[t] setteth folke to scole
Wounded me sore / I se I was more fole
O suster Anne / ye knewe my hert dyd blede
Or I co[n]sented vnto this dede
Whan I am deed / and brent to asshes colde   235
Than shall ye serch / [&] w[ith] yo[r] ha[n]ds vnfolde
The pouder of my bones/and surely kepe
In your chamber / there as ye vse to slepe
Fro I be deed / folkes wyll no more call me
Chast Dido / somtyme wyfe to Sechee   240
On the marble shall stande this scripture
As an Epitaphe / vpon my sepulture
Here lyeth Dido/to whom Enee vntrewe
Gaue cause of deth/[&] y[e] swerd y[t] her slewe.

[¶]Lenuoy of the translatour.   245

ye good ladyes/whiche be of tender age
Beware of loue/sithe men be full of crafte
Though some of the[m] wyll [pro]myse mariage
Their lust fulfylde / suche [pro]mise wylbe last
For many of them / can wagge a false shaft   250
As dyd Enee / cause of quene Dydose dethe
Whose ded[s] I hate [&] shall duri[n]g my brethe

And if that ye wyll you to loue subdue
As thus I meane/vnto a good entent
Se that he be secrete / stedfast and true   255
Or that ye set your mynde on hym feruent
This is myn aduyse / that ye neuer consent
To do y[e] thing / whiche folkes may reproue
You in any thyng/y[t] ye haue done for loue.

[¶] Thus endeth y[e] letter of Dydo to Eneas
and here foloweth a lytell exorta
cion/howe folke shulde be-
haue them selfe
in all co[m]pa
nyes.

B. *Here foloweth a lytell treatyse of the Beaulte of Women.* London: R. Fawkes, 1525.
The sone of the mayde whome neuer none resembled
In beaulte nor bounte syth the worlde began
For both in hyr were perfaytely assembled
Named is she Marye doughter to saynt Anne
Guyde myne hande so that the gentylman   5
That me desyred to reduce thys boke
From frenshe to englyshe / be content / and than
I take lytell cure what other there on loke.
[¶] In frenshe (la beaute de femmes) is yt named
The beaulte of women / in our Englyshe languag[e]   10
whereof to treate / I ought well to be blamed
Consydered that I had neuer the vsage
Womens beaulte in body nor vysage
For to regarde / and there vpon good reason
Syth I am made (as an unpleasant page)   15
A cast a way from presence at eche season
[¶] But what therof shall I leue of to wryte
Syth no man hauyng more practyse then I
wyll take the payne to set blacke on the whyte
And yt a thynge so [d]ygne of memory   20
May trust me playne I shall my selffe applye
Of the frenshe boke to folow the sentence
Beaulte (as ryght requireth) to gloryfye
What euer foloweth of the consequence
[¶] What caused the wourthy Troylus of Troye   25
To cast hys loue on Cresyde the s[h]ene
why set Parys on fayre Helayne hys ioye
what caused Achylles to loue Polexene

why loued Trystram la belle Isoude the quene
Or Arthur of bretayne the fayre Florence 30
All cam of them beaulte and theyr plesant eyen
what haue I to do as of the consequence.

[¶] Beaulte as for the fyrste require wolde
That the womam [sic] (how euer stande the case)
Symple manyer and countenaunce sholde holde 35
For other wyse she wyll avoyde the place
[¶] womans beaulte eche person reproueth
Yf so be that she bayre the countenaunce
More eleuate or hygh than yt behoueth
Hyr beaulte tourneth but all to dysplesance 40
[¶] Beaulte requireth as for the seconde parte
That woman bayre euer naturally
Symple regade [sic] and not ouerthwarte
wyth playsante and symple castyng of the eye
[¶] Beaulte is lost in woman [outrely] 45
yf she haue thys of very condycyon
As to regarde or loke dyspyteously
For that is the manner of the lyon
[¶] womans beaulte requireth thyrdely
That stedfastly with out oultrage 50
She kepe as dyscrete cotynually
Symple answer euer in her language
[¶] Womans beaulte that sholde be magnyfyed
Lyetly compassed in these thre poyntes onely
what beaulte so euer is to her applyed 55
The woman ought to lede hyr lyffe symply
[¶] Beaulte of [s]uerty doeth that woman folowe
That hath the browes and raynes of the backe
And there withall the fete lyght and holowe
yf these thre be holowe there is no lacke. 60
[¶] Beaulte in woman is nothyng pleasant
That glometh with her eyen with frowarde chere
And is of hyr raynes to heuy and pesant
And of hyr fete as yf a beest yt were

[¶] womans beaulte shall ye fynde doubtlesse 65
In thre hygh poyntes that on hyr body gent
Ought for to be / [&] them I shall expresse
Here after / yf my remembraunce assent
[¶] Beaulte sayeth / the fyrst poynt to knowe
The woman sholde haue the forhed hygh [&] fayre 70

For whan she hath the forhed ouer lowe
Euyll hyr besemeth a frontelet to bayre
[¶] womans beaulte requyreth secondly
Of beaulte a ryght who that enquire wolde
That woman ought to haue the hed high   75
The better ther wyth hyr hat she doeth upholde
[¶] Beaulte in woman playnly doeth habounde
yf she ne fayle as for the thyrde parte
To haue the brestes hygh fayre and rounde
wyth fyne gorgias well and fayre couert   80
[¶] womans beaulte as in preemynence
Requireth these thre poyntes pryncypall
For to be founde upon hyr corpulence
And well on hyght they ought [f]or to be all
[¶] womans beaulte expresly for to showe   85
As to the regarde of hyr countenaunce
Requireth ouer thys to haue thre poyntes lowe
whych all women ought to haue in remembraunce
[¶] womans beaulte that pourcha[s]e wyll praysyng
woll that the woman set her besy cure   90
To maynteyne in hyr selfe a low laughyng
To laugh ouer hygh besemeth no creature
[¶] Beaulte yet co[m]maundeth afterwarde
Unto all women thys poynt secondely
To haue alwayes a lowely regarde   95
Not ouer moche but moderately

[¶] That woman hath the ben[t] of beaultyes bowe
That can regarde in helth and in dysease
Whan she shall neese [sic] to make the sounde but lowe
To do otherwyse ye may no person please   100
[¶] womans beaulte wyll in conclusyon
Of these lowe poyntes without dessoyaulte
That women bere euer a lowly condycyon
For other wyse she leseth her beaute.
[¶] Beaulte demaundeth these poyntes to haue sene   105
In women that be fayre and fayte at all
To haue [trayteys] the browes / and [trayts] eyen
And lytell the handes/[traytys] slendre and small
[¶] Beaulte hath she that hath the chyn dympled
The ioyntes of the handes sholde be in lyke manere   110
The chekes also be they bare or wympled
Especyally whan she smyleth with hyr che[r]e.
[¶] Beaulte requireth large to haue these thre

The fyrste is the space goyng from eye to eye
Betwyxt the sholdres sholde the seconde be 115
The thyrde betwyxt the raynes ye shall espye.
[¶] Perfayt beaulte ye may well determyne
In woman/so that these thre in hyr repayre
The na[y]les and the lyppes co[m]plexyon sanguyne
And ruddy the chekes well vermayled and fayre 120
[¶] womans beaulte thou doest well expose
Or mayst expose wythout taryeng
yf thou retayne in thy mynde close
All that is set before in this wrytyng.
[¶] Of beaulte yf there be any woman 125
More purely sped than is co[m]prysed in this
was neuer woman syth the worlde began
So perfaytly sped of beaulte as she is

[¶] I haue expressed theyr preemynence
As well of theyr bodyes as of theyr mayntyen 130
But speke what ye wyll apert or in scylence
Beaulte sans bonte ne vault rien.
[¶] Beaultyes there be in women infynyte
But of bontyes there is but lytell speche
Beaulte is them geuen as thyng requisyte 135
who wyll haue bonte let hym go [s]eche
Thys not wythstandyng I coulde a man teche
To fynde ryght good of the gendre feminyn
And fayre also/but what euer we preche
Beaulte sans bonte ne vault rien. 140
[¶] Beaulte ennobleth the person doubtlesse
And playnly she is of the more valeure
But wyth beaulte is requisyte goodnesse
To speke a ryght who so wyll sett hys cure
Bonte wyll not be vnder coverture 145
Where euer she be/hyr purete is so fyne
Wherfore I set agayne in thys scrypture
Beaulte sans bonte ne vault rien.
[¶] Mayde / wife / or wydowe / dame / or damoysell
That haue the raye of beaulte comprysed in your face 150
Adiouste therto bonte/ than shall ye do ryght well
For beaulte with bonte assembled in a place
Gyue demonstrance of an especyall grace
Geuen to the person/ [&] as I take the cause
At [eyse] smyleth bonte/where beaulte laugheth at a[c]e 155
As dayly yt is sene/and there a fynall clause.

FINIS
[¶] Thus endeth the Beaulte of women neuly Imprynted
By Rycharde Fawkes dwellyng in duram [k]ent

Appendix 2
The Paratexts to the
Fyftene Joyes of maryage

The "Prologue" and "Prohemye" to the *Fyftene Joyes of maryage* (London: De Worde: 1509)

Somer passed	and wynter well begone	[A2r] 1
The dayes shorte	the darke nyghtes longe	
Haue taken season	and brynghtnes [sic] of the sonne	
Is lytell sene	and small byrdes songe	
Seldon is herde	in feldes or wodes ronge	
All strength and ventue [sic]	of trees and herbes sote	
Dyscendynge be	from croppe in to the rote	

And euery creature by course of kynde
For socoure draweth to that countre and place
Where for a tyme | they may purchace and fynde   10
Conforte and rest | abydynge after grace
That clere Appolo with bryghtnes of his face
Wyll sende | whan lusty ver shall come to towne
And gyue the grounde | of grene a goodly gowne

And Flora goddesse bothe of whyte and grene
Her mantell large | ouer all the erthe shall sprede
Shewynge her selfe | apparayled lyke a quene
As well in feldes | wodes | as in mede
Hauynge so ryche a croune upon her hede
The whiche of floures | shall be so fayre and bryght   20
That all the worlde | shall take therof a lyght

So now it is | of late I was desyred
Out of the frenche to drawe a lytell boke
Of .xv. Ioyes | of which though I were hyred
I can not tell | and yet I undertoke
This entrepryse | with a full pyteous loke
Remembrynge well | the case that stode in
Lyuynge in hope | this wynter to begyn
Some Ioyes to fynde that be in maryage

For in my youth | yet neuer acquayntaunce [A2v] 30
Had of them but now in myn olde aege
I trust my selfe | to forther and auaunce
If that in me | there lacke no suffysaunce
Whiche may dyspleasyr | clerely set a parte
I wante but all | that longeth to that arte

yet wyll I speke | though I may do no more
Fully purposynge | in all these Ioyes to trete
Accordynge to my purpose made tofore
All be it so | I can not well forgete
The payne | trauayle | besynes and hete 40
That some men haue after they wedded be
Because theyr wyues | want humylyte

Who [sic] shall I pray | to helpe me to endyte
Cupyde or Venus | which haue me in dysdayne
And for my feblenes | in grete dyspyte
For yeres passed | may not retorne agayne
Now may I speke | and shewe in wordes playne
Whan youth is gone | and comen is stoupynge age
Then worldly Ioyes | must go on pylgrymage

If I sholde praye | unto ymeneus 50
The god of weddynge | to helpe me in this charge
Then wyll he bydde me go to Morpheus
The god of slepe | for he hath wayes large
Whiche with his rodde of leed dooth stere his barge
To brynge forthe age | vnto his slepy caue
Pray hym of rest | and nothynge elles craue

I knowe ryght well | it is but vanyte
All worldly Ioye | medled with bytternes
Therfore these fayned goddes I lete them be [A3r]
And me betake to god | whose stedfastnes 60
May neuer fayle | neyther his sothfastnes
Besechynge hym | that for his moders sake
He wyll me teche his [sic] lytell boke to make

And with good wyll I shall me soone apply
This treatyse out of frenche to translate
Of .xv. Ioyes | and yf I myght therby
Purchace but one | my selfe though it be late
I wolde be gladde | for olde paynes I hate

Trust[]nge to Ioye | now som what in myn aege
As dooth a byrde that syngeth in a cage 70

Now to theffecte of this translacyon
With grete desyre shortly well I procede
But speke I must | by protestacyon
Touchynge this mater | or elles gode forbede
Whome I beseche lowely to be my spede
Praynge also | eche other maner wyght
Take no dyspleasure with my wordes lyght

   Here endeth the prologue of the translatoure.

   And the prohemye of the auctour begynneth.

Myn auctour wryteth in this prohemye 80
That many men | haue trauayled here tofore
To shewe by reason and auctoryte
That it is grete wytte | and wysdome more
For euery maner wyght | of woman bore
To lyue in fraunchyse | at hys lyberte
Than seruaunt to hym selfe | and thrall to be

Without constraynt | but of his neclygence   [A3v]
His wyll to folowe | and his unclene delyte
As lusty folke in theyr adolescence
Haue suche desyre | and so grete appetyte 90
On Venus brydle | for to champe and byte
Tyll they with loue be stryken to the herte
Wherby full | oft they suffre paynes smerte

Unto whose reason | and opynyon
It may be sayd | and answered thus agayne
Man hath no good wytte ne entencyou [sic]
In his yonge tyme | whan nature dooth constrayne
Sauynge in Ioyes | and delytes vayne
Of this frayle worlde vnsure and transytory
None other thynge is in his memory 100

As thus whan men in youth couragyous
With fre wyll endewed and lustynes
Of theyr desyre | and mynde outragyous
Withouten nede | but of theyr folysshenes
Frome wele to wo | from Ioye to heuynes

Convey themselfe | from all theyr lyberte
Nothynge content with theyr felycyte

For whereas they may frely ryde or go
And at theyr choyse | dysporte them ouer all
I you ensure these yonge men wyll not so   110
Whan they leest wene | than sodanly they fall
And unconstrayned make theyr bodyes thrall
Lyke to a wyght that in to pryson depe
Without cause | all hastely dooth crepe

So do they oft for lacke of kyndely wytte
And when they be within this pryson strayte   [A4r]
The gayler cometh and fast the dore dooth shytte
Whiche is of yren stronge | and in a wayte
He lyeth oft | for drede that thrugh defayte
By nyght or day some sholde escape out   120
Ryght besyly he pryeth all about

He barreth dores | and maketh sure all the lockes
The stronge boltes | the fettres and the chayne
He sercheth well | the holes and the stockes
That wo be they | that lyeth in the payne
And out therof | they shall not go agayne
But euer endure | in wepynge care and sorowe
For good ne prayer | shall them neuer borowe

And specyally men may call hym assoted
Ferre frome reason | of wysdome desolate   130
That thus his tyme mysse vsed hath and doted
Whan he had herde | such prysoners but late
Wepynge waylynge | and with them selfe debate
Lyenge in pryson | as he hath passed by
And put hym selfe therin so folysshely

This auctour sayth | by cause mankynde delyteth
Alway to haue fraunchyse and lyberte
Without the whiche | nature of man dyspyteth
Ryght thus in playne wordes speketh he
That many lordes grete | the whiche haue be   140
And lordshyppes haue be loste and ouerthrowe
For takynge fredomes frome theyr subgets lowe
He sheweth eke in maner semblable
That grete cytees | with many an other toune

And comyn people of mynde unreasonable
Haue ben dystroyed and sodaynly cast doune   [A4v]
Agaynst theyr prynces | takyng opynyon
Desyrynge fredomes | mo than here to fore
Theyr elders had | and thus they haue be lore

By reason wherof | batayles grete and werre   150
Haue ben | and many folkes also slay[n]e
Syth Ihesus deyed | was neuer thynge bought derre
Whan poore subgettes on foly wyll pretayne
Agaynst theyr prynce | or elles theyr souerayne
To moue maters | not beynge obedynge
Suche by the lawe ben execute and shent

Somtyme the noble realme and men of Fraunce
Exempte were | and utterly made fre
By theyr grete | prowes and valyaunce
Of the emperours | of Rome the cyte   160
As of trybutes | for whiche batayles haue be
Betwene them | and the Romayns longe ago
In whiche dayes I finde it happed so

Upon a tyme | for cause that they ne were
Of fraunce in puyssaunce | able to withstonde
The grete army and the myghty powere
Of an emperour entred in theyr londe
But for as moche | as they ne wolde be bonde
Them were leuer go from that regyon
Than to remayne vnder subgeccyon   170

Servynge this emperour | and trybute pay
So of hygh courage | and theyr grete nobles
All sodaynly | these nobles wente away
Conquerynge co[n]trees | suche was theyr worthynes
And afterwarde retorned neuertheles   [A5r]
Home to theyr lande | in grete prosperyte
Whiche they tyll now haue holde in lyberte

Unto theyr owne vse | prouffyte and auayle
Wherfore folkes of many a nacyon
Lyvynge in seruage | constreyned with trauayle   180
Desyred to haue theyr habytacyon
In fraunce | and there vnder domynacyon

To lyue in wele | lyberte | and rest
Wherby it grewe | somtyme the noblest

Realme of the worlde | that knowen were or founde.
Moost fayre in buyldynge | and inhabyte best
The whiche in treasure | and scyence dyde habounde
Then for asmoche | as they be fre at leest
Prudent in fayth | in lyuynge holyest
They sholde theyr subgets | in fra[n]chyse kepe & vse   190
After theyr lawe | and neuer to refuse

Ageynst all trouthe | and inconuenyent
It is certayne | and nothynge charytable
God knoweth well | the lorde omnypotent
A man to haue | a custome reasonable
Onely for hym selfe | ryght prouffytable
And for his neighboure | vse it other wyse
Such vsage sholde | all well dysposed me dyspyse

Herof it groweth that lyberte is lost
In people voyde | of reason and scyence   200
And thus vyces and synnes reygneth most
Some gyue to vertues lytell reuerence
Wherin to god | do they ryght grete offence
The comyn wele | in generalyte   [A5v]
All men sholde loue of perfyte charyte

Why it is thus | a man may reason make
Who loueth not his wele pertyculerly
Hath but a lytell wytte I undertake
Whan he may haue a proufftye syngulerly
Hurtynge none other creature therby   210
And wyll not helpe hym selfe whan he so may
But wyllfully dooth cast his grace away

A fole is he | that wyttynge wyll go
Into a caue | a dyche | or elles a pytte
Which is aboue | both narowe and strayte also
And all within | full wyde and depe is it
So that whan he therin | is fall and shytte
Out may he not | for there he must abyde
As wylde bestes to in forestes syde

Trapped and taken | ryght so this crature   220

In lyke wyse | thrugh his owne neclygence
Is in the dyche | whereas he must endure
Lyke as these bestes | whiche gladly wolde | go thens
Sekynge the wayes with all theyr delygence
Out to auoyde | but so it wyll not be
Tyme is not then | forth of the dyche to fle

Thus one may say | and therupon conclude
By such as in to maryage be brought
And herupon to make a symylytude
Unto the fysshe whiche hath his pasture sought   230
And in a lepe | that is of twygges wrought
Is take | and out can not escape ne twynne
But euer dwell | and tary styll therinne   [A6r]

The fysshe that swymmeth in the ryuer clere
As it shall fall hym ofte by aduenture
To rayle aboute | in places here and there
Fyndeth this lepe | the whiche withoute mesure
Beholdeth he with all his besy cure
And he therin | the fysshes and the bayte
Dooth se | supposynge well in his consayte   240

They be in Ioye and pleasure at theyr lust
And all aboute the lepe he gooth rounde
With grete desyre | hauynge a veray trust
To come to them | and whan that he hath founde
The entre | in he gooth gladde and Iocounde
And to the shynynge bayte | he hyeth faste
Wherof anone | he taketh his repaste

To go agayne | he thynketh but a Iape
Forthe of the lepe | assaynge besyly
A way to fynde | how he therout may scape   250
And thens departe | to other company
He boreth with his byll all hastely
His besynes | and laboure is in waste
Abyde a whyle | he shall for all his haste

Therin to dwell in wo and heuynes
And where as he hath demed certaynly
Afore to haue had Ioye | and lustynes
There shall he passe his tyme ryght heuely
By men it falleth thus moost comenly

That put them into maryage all day 260
Experyence wyll wytnesse as I say
Though it so be | that folkes se before [A6v]
These wedded men | within the lepe enclosed
In poynt to droune & drenche | yet not therfore
Wyll they forbere | ne tyll they be innosed
As houndes be of bones | it is supposed
There is not one | by other can be ware
Tyll they be take | and holden in the snare

Thus what by foly | fortune or destene
A man may se the people euery day 270
Demeane themselfe | forsakynge lyberte
And shortely after that | repenteth they
Desyrynge it to haue | but they ne may
At ony tyme | vnto suche grace attayne
And all to late | for them is to complayne

Moche more herof | myn auctoure dooth declare
In his prologue | or that he wyll begyn
To shewe these .xv. Ioyes | but I must spare
By losse of tyme | there is nothynge to wynne
But pouerte | vnthryftynes | and synne 280
Wherfore in wordes rude to make an ende
And of these Ioyes to wryte now I entende

Some men do call these Ioyes sorowes grete
But yet they take them well in pacyence
For of necessyte they must forgete
The care | trouble | sorowe | payne and offence
The whiche they suffre at the reuerence
Of theyr wyues | whiche they may not forsake
And though they oft | mysse vse theyr eloquence
Lytell regarde therto a man sholde take 290

 Here endeth the prohemye of the auctour. [A7r]

And here begynneth the fyrst Ioye of maryage

Appendix 3
The Marriage Complaints

A. *A Complaynt of them that be to soone maryed* (London: Wynkyn de Worde, 1535).

Woodcut [A1r], two men speaking. Text begins on [A1v].

For as moche as many folke there be
That desyre the sacramente of weddynge
Other wyll kepe them in vyrgynye
And wyll in chastyte be lyuynge
Therfore I wyll put now in wrytynge   5
In what sorowe these men lede theyr lyues
That to soone be coupled to cursed wyues

Now am I in grete myschefe and sorowe[1]
To soone I put my body in gage
I lyue in care/ nyght / euen / and morowe   10
Lytell lacketh that I ne enrage
To be to soone maryed I layde my gage
Cursed be the tyme that I neuer knewe
The deuyll haue his parte of maryage
And of hym that me fyrste therto drewe   15

My herte ryght yll dyd me counsell
To a yonge woman me for to same
To soone wedde there they dyd me compell
Wherfore I holde my selfe in fame

---

[1] This stanza is not, as has been previously thought, original to Copland. It translates a French imprint which begins:

Or suis ie bien en grant soucy
Trop tost me suis mis en mesnaige
Bien peu fault que ie nenraige
Trop tost marie cest mon gaige
Maudit soit qui men parla
Le diable ayt part au mariage
Et celluy qui lame bailla
Mon cueur bien mal me conseilla
De prendre si tost ieune femme...

By god I swere and by his name 20
I wyll all louers clene dyscourage
That wolde not [wth] there wyll take them adame
And put them selfe in suche domage

Better it were to be a man sauage
Than to be take in that ylke lase 25
Gentell galauntes flee that passage
Besyde that waye loke that ye passe
Go out of that waye that wyll the chase [Aiir]
Go out of that waye or ye be loste
Go ye therfro / tourne ye your face 30
Go frome that waye to another coste

Go ye thense my frendes I you praye[2]
Go ye therfro I you do praye
Go ye frome that hote flambe of fyre
Go ye therfro as I you saye 35
Or ye wyll repente an other daye
Go ye therfro full loude I crye
Go ye fro the bonde of welawaye
Whiche is the arke of all folye

Fle I praye you for goddes sake 40
Fle this passage that is ryght daungerous
Fle ye frome that perryllous lake
Of muddy myre so clam and comberous
Fle that darke place so myrke and tenebrous
Fle fro that ylke cursed temptacyn [sic] 45
I fynde it nothynge auauntagyous
But it all tourneth into perdycyon

Alas my bretherne ye crysten men
For goo take ye in pacyence
To heare the sorowe that I in [ren] 50
For to acquyte my con[s]yence
I requyre you in the reuerence
Of the swete vyrgyn mary
For to eschewe all unpacyence
Loke to soone that ye not mary 55
The wyse man vs ensygneth and saythe [A2v]

---

[2] In the margin of the filmed copy "praye" is underlined, and beside it is handwritten and underlined "<u>desire</u>"; clearly, "praye" is an error, but we don't know who the correcting reader was.

That none shulde other repreue
Of any vyce / hurte / yll / or scathe
That they se of hym morne or eue
I saye it for I dyd my selfe meue   60
To lerne to make playes Ioyous
Kepe hym that wyll and me byleue
For there maye be many enuyous

Outragyous alas I dyde not thynke
Thre tymes of that that I wolde do   65
But hastely I dyde me clynke
Unto my wyll and wente therto
Symple I was and humble also
Euyll thought was not myne entent
Now haue I for my laboure lo   70
Anoye / thought / payne / and torment

Thynke thou now what it is of seruyce
Thynke also what it is of franchyse
The seruytude of maryage
Afore all other servage lyse   75
All wyse men doth it despyse
Let none take it nor other make
For it is the moost fole enterpryse
That ony man maye vndertake

Take ye hede where that ye go   80
Poore whystelers folysshe and sturdy
Be not assoted nor [peu]ysshe also
So outragyus nor so hardy
That for one dede ne for a crye   [Aiiir]
Ye ca[s]te your selfe in suche a snare   85
For ye shall not bewrynge nor wrye
Come out therof therfore beware

Better ye were withouten harme
Forto become a celestyne
A grey frere Iacopyn or a carme   90
An hermyte or a frere Austyne
Fle ye therto/ye seke your fyne
And the abregment of your dayes
Wherfore do not your selfe enclyne
To entre with ryght and other wayes   95
Man the wiche hathe no tytell

Nor seruytude by ony sent
He is in his owne frewyll
And at his good commaundemente
Man maketh his auowe and talente 100
For all that god hathe hym gyue
By no maner for to consente
For to bynde hym in seruytude to lyue

Yf thou knowe what charge it is 105
To take a wyfe and her to kepe
So preest thou wolde no be ywys
At suche a snare in for to crepe
Nor let thy selfe so to be yclepe
To be engloted in suche a clyfte 110
Out of whiche thou mayste not pepe
Tyll that she³ be broke and ryfte

These relygyous maundiens   [A3v]
May well an other order take
So many chanons and dekenes 115
Offycers theyr offyces maye forsake
None maye ayenste them noyse make
But we the whiche ben maryed
May nether mount nor yet downe [sl]ake
So ben we in this poynt alyed 120

It is well knyte that is so bounde
That no man can it vndo
In weddynge knote I haue me founde
That I counde not from it go
Yf I were lous no more ther to 125
Woulde I retourne for sothe certayne
I rede them that hathe ben so
Beware and go not to it agayne

Certaynly I wyll not blame
Maryage that god Instytued 130
But honour it withouten grame [sic]
For the order sholde be worshypped
And I haue me auaunced
Than I ought for to speke more

---

³   In French, *elle*, with *la nasse* as antecedent.

The charge to yll wyves be deled 135
For I se euer eche daye wherfore

And for to gyue you for to wyt
The pouerte that therin is founde
I ought well to dysprayse it
For there I haue be bounde 140
Alas my werke dyde lytell rebounde [A4r]
And lytell befell to me than
Than to [l]erne I dyd recounde
By my selfe or by some good man

I nought I wende that I had lerned 145
I thought that I was full sage
But for all that I was clyked
As a byrde is in a cage
That hath nothynge auauntage
But as lone as the cage maye dure 150
In lyke wyse I am in maryage
Enclosed nedes I must endure

Endure I must who that nay saythe
For to endure I and constraynt
For I swere to you on my faythe 155
The Ioye that I make it is but faynte
I am so holden in fere and in craynt
That I am worse than dyseased
I am not come to that attaynt
That I thought in tyme passed 160

Whan that I was newely maryed
I had good tyme aboute thre dayes
I was not chyddene haryed
I was fulfylled with loue rayes
I made gambandes / lepes / and playes 165
I helde me neyther nere ne ferre
But soone ynoughe I had assayes
Of sorowe and care that made me bare

Rynnynge they came me to assayle [A4v]
On the other syde ryght asprely 170
Full sore they made me to auayle
Were it slepynge or wakyngly
Thought alwaye was present me by

And yet before me made frontere
With them in theyr companye   175
Greate charge which bare the baner

About eyght dayes or soone after
Our maryage the tyme for to passe
My wyfe I toke and dyd set her
Upon my knee for to solace   180
And began her for to enbrace [sic]
Sayenge syster go get the tyme loste
We must thynke to laboure a pace
To recompence that it hathe vs coste

Than for despyte she vp arose   185
And drewe her faste behynde me
To me sayenge is this the glo[s]e
Alas pore caytyfe well I se
That I neuer shall haue quod she
With you more than payne and turmente   190
I am in an euyll degre
I haue now loste my sacramente

For me be to longe with you here
Alas I ought well for to thynke
What we sholde do within ten yere   195
Whan we shall haue at our herte brynke
Many chyldren on for to thynke   [Bi]
And crye after vs without fayle
For theyr meate and theyr drynke
Than shall it be no meruayle   200

Cursed be the houre that I ne was
Made a none in some cloyster
Neuer there for to passe
Or had be made some syster
In seruage with a clousterer   205
It is not eyght dayes sythe oure weddynge
That we two togyther were
By god ye speke to sone of werkynge

But syr sythe it dothe you please
It pleaseth me as is reason   210
Your wyll dothe not me dysplease
It pleaseth me at eche ceason

ye [sic] be [s]yr of this mansyon
And I am your chambere
I wolde fayne fynde some enchesom 215
That lyenge deed I were on bere

Wolde to god that I were deed
Than [w]olde ye be quyte of me
In lytell whyle knowe you I dyde
And neyther I perceyue nor se 220
Ne knowe how that reason sholde be
That to me ye speke of that wyrke
By my soule I se at the eye
That of you I shall haue but yrke[4]

For god syr aduyse you wel[l] [B1v] 225
That I dyde neuer besynesse
In the house there as I dyde dwell
Many there were that put them in prese
Me for to loue aboue excesse
And yet I put them all awaye 230
Thoughe they had moche greate rychesse
No man but you was to my paye

Am I of suche lygnage comen
For to haue payne and greate trauayle
I that was so derely holden 235
And neuer loked for none auayle
No that thynge sholde me prouayle
I was wonte but to go and playe
Daunce and synge at eche spousayle
And ye frome me put all that awaye 240

Thanked be god ye haue had of me
Of ryche cheuaunce good and fayre
Golde and syluer greate plente
Rentes and herytage you to prepayre
In all this countre there is none ayre 245
Be ye neuer so ryche of lynage
But he myght of that affayre
Make ryche all his parentage

---

[4] *Yrke* is a nice change from the French *besogne*.

I do not saye that ye were dygne
To haue one ten tymes better than I　　　　　　　250
Alas ye shewed vnto me sygne
Of greate grace welth and curteysy
That whan I herde ony company　　　　　　　　[Bii]
That spake of you in ony place
I had my herte rauysshed truely　　　　　　　　　255
For greate pleasure and solace

Whan she had made her complaynt
Lyke an woman all an angred
She than seased vnder a faynt
Full of sorowe and all be weped　　　　　　　　　260
The daye and houre there she cursed
With a tryste herte wryngynge her hande
That euer she was nourysshed
For to espouse suche an husbande

Whan that I herde and vnderstode　　　　　　　　265
That the whiche she me reproched
I was abasshed and styll stode
And durst not to her be approched
Her tonge towarde me was declyned
I wote not where that she had fysshte　　　　　　　270
The wordes that she there dysgorged
That I was fayne to be [whysshte]

In this sayd dolorous songe
I dyde me put for to haue pease
Force it was in to be thro[n]ge　　　　　　　　　　275
Yet wente I not in with myne ease
But my wyfe me to dysplease
Abode not longe for to perceyue
The sorowe that dyde my herte [peyse]
Where throughe she dyde deceyue⁵　　　　　　　280

Than came her mother to hous　　　　　　　　　[B2v]
That founde her how she was wepynge
And soone she sayd myn owne sone dous
Why maketh she that waymentynge [sic]
And sayd it was not her lernynge　　　　　　　　　285
To have her doughter so to be chydde

---

⁵ This stanza is unclear in the French copy I saw.

And that she had a perceyuynge
That I had her so an angred

By my faythe sayd I good mother
Nought haue I done nor her myssayde   290
Serue her I wyll as my syster
With good herte and wyll puruayed
For ayenst her I nothynge sayd
But that wayes we muste fynde
Us for to store and she me nayed   295
I wys she hath to fyrse a mynde

By god my fayre sone you ne ought
So alwaye for to threten her
For ywys she was neuer taught
For to werke therefore [dele softer]   300
But she wyll do well here after
Wherfore speke no more I you praye
Neuer was I in suche daungere
Wherfore I thanke god nyght and daye

Than cometh her cosyns also   305
For to complysshe my passyon
Her gosseps and her neyghboures to
Semblynge lyke a prosessyon
God knewe what desstruccyon   [Biii]
Drynkynge my wyne all at theyr ease   310
All thynge goeth to perdycyon
Neuertheles I muste holde my pease

To a feest they brought me on a daye
Aboute two or thre myle hense
God knoweth what great Ioye led they   315
Takynge lytell intellygence
Her frendes lede her at myne expence
How that the game goeth they ne care
I saye that by experyence
It wyll make a man all threde bare   320

Now muste they make a pylgrymage
To saynt Lenarde or Saynt Laurence
For good they be for the grete rage
That they haue / as I maye purpence
Who maye than have ony pacyence   325

For to se suche derysyon
Trottynge always without resystence
God not kypynge theyr mansion
Than must they have newe habytes
Gownes and other abyllementes 330
Rynges of of [sic] golde perles and cresolytes
Bedes and gyrdelles with longe pendentes
I haue nether hous ne rentes
Wheron that I maye lyue
A man with many suche paymentes 335
Maye lyue longe or euer he may thryue

Wene ye that they take ony kepe [B3v]
How that syluer is spente anone
The deuyll brenne them on an hepe
Them and all theyr opynyon 340
We gyue to them suche abandon
Be they fayre or be they foule
That we haue therfore suche guerdon
That we be caytyfes be my soule

Almyghty god gyue me suffraunce 345
For I am sore passyoned
With payne / sorowe / and dystourbaunce
As moche as ony man hath suffred
But sythe I am therto condempned
I thanke our lorde of paradyse 350
For therto I am ordeyned
I se it is none otherwyse

Confyderynge that I ne maye
Hyte / nor ho auaunte / ne arere
I wysshe my dethe euery daye 355
Hyde me I muste neuer to appere
In donge stynkynge neuer to come here
Desyryuge dethe is my resorte
Chowynge my bytte in this maner
Without bydynge ony comforte 360

you [sic] the whiche are clene acquyted
Praye ye for that pore caytyfe
The whiche is all dysheryted
And hathe yspended by his wife

His good that neuer in his lyfe [B4r] 365
Shall be rendered to hym agayne
Wherfore I maye with herte pensyfe
Crye out alas and thus complayne

I make an ende I lyue in greate martyre
So do they that be to soone maryed 370
The thynge that moost of all I desire
Is that they be ryght well haryed
For by women men be so varyed
Eche leseth his vnderstondynge
Wherfore I wyll that they be for prayed 375
That god gyue them sorowe euerlastynge

For suche is my dyffynement
And wyll prove it before our lorde
That women ben abusement
All aboute in playe / stryfe / and borde 380
To soone maryed maye mete accorde
Unto them wolde I or naye
I leve them here at this sayd worde
And no more of them wyll I saye

Ryght dere frendes louely I do you submite 385
Of my first werke into correccyon
But myne owne wyll can not as yet
Endewe ony thynge of myne intencyon
Rather I wyll abyde a lytell season
Than to put my wytte afore intellygence 390
Uentosyte must abyde dygestyon
So I muste do or I come to eloquence

Cunnynge must I haue fyrste of all [B4v]
Or that I come to perseueracyon
Put forthe I wyll and than somwhat call 395
Lernynge with good delyberacyon
And than I wyll with good intencyon
Note some werkes of god almyghty
Desyrynge to come vnto his regyon
Euer there for to dwell perdurably 400

 Here endeth a full dolefull complaynte
Of many a man there one concorde
Lokynge with face pale wanne and faynte

Cursynge the tyme of theyr accorde
Fynysshed and done the yere of our lorde 405
A thousande.CCCCC.and.xxxv. at London
Enprynted also by Wynkyn de Worde
In fletestrete at the synge of the son
[woodcut; small printer's mark]

B. Here begynneth the complaynte of them that ben to late maryed[6].

AFTER playes sportes and daunces of solace
We must thynke to come to prosperyte
After that God of his haboundaunte grace
Wyll prouyde how that I may gouerne me
In mynde I purpose wedded to be 5
In a better lyfe may no man lyue in
Than to be maryed and lyfe out of synne

All yonge louers sholde them so affyle
That they loue trewely and so for to lyue
With ardaunte wytte and perfyte style 10
All vnto goodnesse themselfe for to gyue
Than may they be sure that they shall thryue
So wyll I lyue in maryage clene and pure
To Goddes be houe and increasinge of nature

To longe haue I lyued without ony make 15
All to longe haue I vfed my yonge age
I wyll all for go and a wife to me take
For to increase both our twoos lynage
For saynt Iohn sayth that he is sage
That ayenst his wyll doth him gouerne 20
And our Lordes preceptes hym selfe for to learne

There is no greter pleasure than for to haue
A wyfe that is full of prudence and wysdome
Alas for loue nygh I am in poynte to raue
These cursed olde men haue an yll custome 25
Women for to blame both all and some
For that they can not theyr myndes full fyll

---

[6] Transcribed from *Illustrations of Early English Popular Literature*, ed. J. Payne Collier. Vol I, Section 8, pp. 1–19 (London: n.p., 1863). I have removed Collier's punctuation, as the fragment filmed in the Early English Books series is unpunctuated.

Therfore they speke of them but all yll

Now syth that I haue my tyme vsed
For to folowe my folyshe pleaaunces 30
And haue my selfe oftentymes sore abused
At plaies and sportes pompes and daunces
Spendynge golde and syluer and grete fynaunces
For faut of a wyfe the cause is all
To late maryed men may me call 35

The holy sacramente of maryage
Before holy chyrche was ordeyned
For to increse humayne lynage
He that doth other wyse is not receyued
Before God thus was man guerdoned 40
With woman for to lyue at his owene wyll
He is a fole that elles where doth nature spyll

I haue done as the labourer doth
That somtyme is payned with trobyll grete
For he leseth his payne for certayne soth 45
That in the hye waye soweth his whete
Well I perceyue that I dyde me forgete
Or that I put me in to housholde
I haue lost my feed my worke is but colde

Women and maydens both good and yll 50
With me I helde my selfe for to please
The one dyde rebell the other abode styll
Other made me well at myn ease
Cupydo than came me for to cease
Venus lyghted her bronde of fyre 55
For such seryuce suche guerdon and hyre

Thus rauysshed in this sayd abusion
I was taken with a ca[u]telous wyle
That me thought to make conclusyon
Of my weddynge within a whyle 60
But yet dyde they me begyle
They caused me for to make grete dyspence
For I was no soner wed through my neglygence

I wolde do make comune I wys
My proper goodes so was I lyght 65

Of wytte and was all wayes redy as is
A man of armes in poynt to fyght
Other whyles I went me ryght
In to places my selfe solysytynge
But nother frequented that beynge   70
Yf I withhelde ony praty one
Swetely ynough she made me chere
Sayenge that she loued no persone
But me and therto she dyde swere
But whan I wente fro that place there   75
Vnto another she dyde as moche
For they loue none but for theyr poche

I had fyue or sixe companyons
That haunted with me euery houre
But I haue knowen to such garsons   80
In secrete they haue done socoure
Yf that they enioyed my paramoure
With grete payne durste I it to them saye
Force me was to kepe counseyll alwaye

I wote well that I haue ryght sore varyed   85
For to haue wylled for to lyue alone
For to haue ben to late maryed
For that I haue herde so longe a gone
For she that abandoneth to more then one
I dare wyll swere and ther with it sustayne   90
That she abandoneth vnto a dosayne

Folysshe regardes full of vanyte
I ke[s]t ouer twarte and eke contrauers
To daye I had peas rest and vnyte
To morowe I had plete and processe dyuers   95
Breke I dyde dores and fenesters
Sargeauntes met me by the waye
And enprysoned both me and my praye

Subiecte I was to meyny of bawdes
And vnto a grete company of brothelles   100
Whiche to me brought an hepe of rybaudes
Dronkardes that loued well good morselles
Knaues and theues that wolde pyke quarelles
I gaue them clothes I knewe not theyr vse
There is none so subtyll but loue doth hym abuse   105

Alas I haue all my tyme spent and lost
Whiche for to recouer is impossyble
Spent haue I nature at grete expens and cost
Agenst the ryght canon and of the holy byble
Offens done to God neuer ceasyble 110
In daunger for to forfayte bothe soule and lyfe
By defaute for to haue taken vnto me a wyfe

Lyke vnto a best an hors or an asse
That careth not for to tomble in the fen
Yf that ony with me playenge there was 115
An other to helpe I wolde go then
Mo gallantes a man sholde se than ren
After a wentche and lepe and hytche
Than dogges do about a farowenge bytche

She wolde to no maner a man escondyte 120
Eche one she appetyted for to receyue
Takynge therein pleasure and delyte
To the ende theyr syluer for to haue
But in the stede chyldren to conceyue
Botches pockes and goutes they engender 125
In hedes and in legges and in euery membre

In this maner of sykenesse many ther be
That ben Impotentes hanged and dede
But lytell semblaunce they make on to se
Taken as they ben not beggynge theyr brede 130
Hast you to be wedded thus I you rede
Vnto the ende that ye be not cappable
Of this grete daunger deedly and vncurable

Now I am out of this daunger so alenge
Wherfore I am gladde it for to perseuer 135
Longe about haue I ben me for to renge
But it is better to late than to be neuer
Certes I was not in my lyfe tyll hyther
So full of ioye that doth in my herte inspyre
Wedded folke haue tyme at theyr desyre 140

Out am I now of thought dole and mone
Lyuynge euer more ryght amorously
For I haue a wyfe by my selfe alone
At my commaundement both late and erely

And yf it happen that I loke heuely 145
My wyfe me kysseth and than she me colleth
And ryght woman there she me consolleth

To that I wyll haue done she is redy
Neuer wyll she ayenst my wyll saye
She doth to me the best that she can truly 150
Nothing of my volenty she doth me naye
Yf I be angred or trobled ony waye
Redy she is to chaunge my purpose
Vnto the ende that I may haue all my repose

I haue me all to longe refrayned 155
Furnysshe I can not to all her pleasyre
And for to promyse her I am constrayned
More than I can do to her desyre
She appetyteth it moche and doth me enspyre
Gorgyously shewynge her fayre corsage 160
But I am all caduc and wery for age

I ought to haue by this many chyldren
Some sporte and playe & some at fyre syttynge
Other in the felde to shote lepe and ren
And some hardy some mery and tryumphynge 165
In whom I sholde haue all my delytynge
But to late maryd withouten dout
May neuer se his chyldren ren out

My wyfe shewed to me her proper dugge
On the mornynge her delyte for to make 170
And to haue me for to playe nugge a nugge
Alas I wolde it full fayne forsake
But force it is suche lessons to take
And to ryse vp erly as I thynke best
In the mornynge and go vnto my rest 175

Whan I se her lye in shetes fayre and whyte
As rede as the button of the rose
With good wyll wolde I take than delyte
Neuertheles I lete her haue her repose 180
For it is force that I cast agayne on the close
And to make a pawse than I am conioynt
For thynstrument is not yet well in poynt

But yet somtyme I me constrayne
To take nature solace thus thynke I 185
But all sodeynly I me refrayne
For I do fere to be to soone wery
And than I slepe with courage all drery
And yet am I I can not passe
Vpon women more than euer I was 190

Constrayned I am to be full of Ialousy
Seynge that I can not content her mynde
Touchynge the playe of loue all softely
Often ynough the experyence to fynde
She me assayeth and tourneth by kynde
Castynge vnto me her beggynge legge
But I do slepe I care not for such a begge 195

With her eyen pleasaunte castynge a regarde
In chastynge a laughter amerous
Than with a praty smyle she doth me larde
And that maketh me somewhat joyous
But comynge to a bed delycyous 200
For to holde the spere in a full hande
It plyeth and fayleth for wyll not stonde

Whan I herde her bable and langage
Her gentyll termes spoken so properly
I do me wyshe for to be in to the age 205
Of eyghten neyntene or foure and twenty
Such assautes than gyue wolde I
That for it sholde haue no nede to craue
Of the grete pleasure that she sholde haue

If that she go to banckettes and daunces 210
She doth none offence therin certayne
Nedes she must haue her pleasaunces
In some place to make her glade and sayne
Wherfore I dare well say and susteyne
That after with me I wolde haue her ledde 215
If ony soner I had ben to her wedde

We twayne sholde haue all our yongenesse
After maryage custome and ryght
Passed in joye solace and gladnesse
And is wherfore I haue me pyght 220

Force it is to me that the fyre be night
That it a nede I can not haue quenched
To late maryed is for to be complayned

It is sayd that a man in seruytude
Hym putteth whan he doth to woman bende 225
He ne hath but only habytude
Vnto her the whiche well doth hym tende
Who wyll to householde comprehende
And there a bout studyeth in youth alwayes
He shall haue honoure in his olde dayes 230

Some chyldren vnto the courtes hauntes
And ben puruayed of benefyces
Some haunteth markettes and be marchauntes
Byenge and sellynge theyr marchaundyses
Or elles constytuted in offyces 235
Theyr faders and moders haue grete solace
That to late maryed by no waye hase

I be wayll the tyme that is so spent
That I ne me hasted for to wedde
For I shall haue herytage and rente 240
Both golde and syluer and kynred
But syth that our Lorde hath ordeyned
That I this sacrament take me vpon
I wyll kepe it trewely at all season

Theophrastus vs sheweth in his prose 245
That in maryage all is out of tune
So doth also the romanute of the rose
Composed by mayster Iohan de mehune
Yet neuertheles it is all comune
That they neuer were in bonde of maryage 250
Wherfore at all auentures is theyr langage

Matheolus that was holden so wyse
For to blame women was all his ebate
Suppose that he was maryed twyse
For he was so olde that balde was his pate 255
For he came the last tyme so very late
Than in hym there was no puyssaunce
Amyte solace joye ne pleasure

But whan that a man may do no more
He blame that that he can not do   260
To late wedded the surplus therfore
May not furnysshe as other may do
For whan he wened to satysfye lo
Nature at nede wyll not hym preuayle
Suche wenes do to well that other whyle falyle   265

Yf that there be ony tryfelers
That haue wylled for to blame maryage
I dare well saye that they ben but lyers
Or elles God fayled in the fyrste age
Adam bereth wytnesse and tesmonage   270
Maryed he was and comen we ben
God dyde choyse maryage vnto all men

Now sith it is thus befall
Why that ought we it to blame
Vs for to put we ben holden all   275
So sholde we alwayes holde with the same
Or elles holy scrypture sayeth it is shame
And that alleggeth all predycatours
Our Lorde God hateth all fornycatours

I am now sory that I haue no rathe   280
Put my selfe into maryages rout
For many a folyshe loke it hathe
It hath me cost here and there about
But yet my soule is in grete doute
For God fornycatures punyssheth   285
And out of this realme he them banyssheth

There is no man lyuynge that can commyt
Without outen [sic] the worke of nature
But he in maryage doth commy[t]e it
As vs telleth the holy Scripture   290
It is than foly to ony creature
Thus for to blame his creason
For ony maner of folysshe opynyon

All they that by theyr subtyll artes
Hath wylled for to blame maryage   295
I wyll susteyne that they be bastardes
Or at least way an euyll courage

For to saye that therin is seruage
In maryage but it [d]eny
For therin is but humayne company   300

Yf ther be yll women and rebell
Shrewed dispytous and eke felonyous
There be other fayre and do full well
Propre gentyll lusty and joyous
That ben full of grace and vertuous   305
They ben not all born vnder a sygnet
Happy is he that a good one can get

To late maryed now helpe than me
To make my sorowes and complayntes
For by my fayth I swere to the   310
I haue suffred many dolours and crayntes
And haue sustayned mo attayntes
Than euer dede Wat after the hounde
At dyspence I lyued and that haue I founde

Galantes playne ye the tyme that yet haue lost   315
Marry you be tyme as the wyse man sayth
Tossed I haue ben fro pyler to post
In commyssynge natures werke alwayes
I haue passed full many quasy dayes
That now vnto good I can not mate   320
For mary I dyde my selfe to late

Rychely in a raye ought for to go
These women that be obedyent
Better than these cursed wyues do
That ben not to theyr husbandes pacyent   325
To take a wyfe was myn intent
Goddes lawes to kepe and them to obserue
Sauynge of nature and heuen to preserue

Afore that euer I was maryed
Bordeles I haunted and places of infame   330
But I am now vnto a wyfe alayed
The worde to holde and honoure Goddes name
That wycked man I holde to blame
That foloweth eyyll ruell and wyll not amende
Vnto his soulles helth and honoure to pretende   335

Whan a man to olde age is faden and fall
Lerne this lesson herken my sentence
Few frendes meteth he with all
That wyll to his pouerte take ony intellygence
Wo worthe than crye they of the expence   340
That they haue spent vnto youthes lust
And now they must dye for hunger and thurst

Better it is in youth a wyfe for to take
And lyue with her to Goddes pleasuance
Than to go in age for Goddes sake   345
In wor[l]dely sorowe and perturbaunce
For youthes loue and vtterance
And than to dye at the last ende
And be dampned in hell with the foule fende

The auctour

Rycheness in youth with good gouernaunce   1
Often helpeth age whan youth is gone his gate
Both yonge and olde must haue theyr sustenaunce
Euer in this worlde soo fekyll and rethrograte
Ryght as an ampte the whiche all gate   5
Trusseth and caryeth for his lyues fode
Eny thynge that whiche hym semeth to be good

Crysten folke ought for to haue
Open hertes vnto God almyght
Puttynge in theyr mynde theyr soule to saue   10
Lernynge to come vnto the eternall lyght
And kepe well theyr maryage and trouth plyght
Nothynge alwaye of theyr last ende
Durynge theyr lyues how they the tyme spende

Here endeth the complaynt of to late maryed   15
For spendynge of tyme or they a borde
The sayd holy sacramente haue to long taryed
Humayne nature tassemble and it to accorde
Emprynted in Fletestrete by Wynkyn de Worde
Dwellynge in the famous cyte of London   20
His hous in the same at the sygne of the Sonne

Bibliography

Aers, David, ed. *Culture and History, 1350–1600: Essays on English Communities, Identities, and Writing*. Detroit: Wayne State University Press, 1992.

Alexis, Guillaume. *He [Sic] Begynneth an Interlocucyon, with an Argument, Betwyxt Man and Woman & Whiche of Them Could Proue to Be Most Excelle[n]t*. London: Wynkyn de Worde, 1525.

———. *Le debat de lome et de la fe[m]me*. Lyon: Pierre Mareschal s.d. [v.1490].

———. *Le debat de lhomme et de la femme*. Paris: Trepperel 1493.

———. *Sensuyt le debat de lomme et de la femme*. Paris: Jehan Trepperel, s.d. [c. 1500].

———. *Le debat* … Paris: Guillaume Nyverd, s.d. [v. 1520].

———. *Le debat* … Paris: s.n., s.d. but c. 1520; another (Paris: s.n. s.d., c. 1525).

———. *Oeuvres Poétiques de Guillaume Alexis, Prieur de Bucy*. Ed. Arthur Piaget and Émile Picot, vol. I, pp. 121–44. Paris: Firmin Didot, 1896–1908; rpt SATF 1968.

Angeloglou, Maggie. *A History of Make-Up*. London: Macmillan, 1970.

Anglo, Sydney. *Spectacle, Pageantry, and Early Tudor Poetry*, 2nd ed. New York: Oxford University Press, 1997.

Anon. *La complainte de trop tard marie*. See Gringore.

———. *The Beaute of women* (R Fawkes, c. 1525); *The beaulte of women* (R. Wyer, c. 1540).

———. *La complainte de trop tost marié, de nouvel imprimé*. Paris: Michel le Noir, 1509. Bordeaux: Jehan Guyart, c. 1530. Facs. Ed. Georges Hubrecht. Bordeaux: Société des Bibliophiles de Guyenne, 1971.

———. *La Conusaunce Damours*. London: Pynson, 1528.

———. *The Fifteen Joys of Marriage*. Ed. Brent A. Pitts. New York: P. Lang, 1985.

———. *Gesta Romanorum*. London: [de Worde], 1510.

———. *A glasse for housholders wherin thei maye se, bothe howe to rule theim selfes [and] ordre their housholde verye godly and fruytfull*. London: Richard Grafton, 1542.

———. *Here beginneht [sic] a merye iest of a man that was called Howleglas*. [London: William Copland], [1560].

———. *Here begynneth the calendar of shephardes*. [J. Notary, 1518?] and subsequent editions.

———. "Letter of Dydo to Eneas." In *The Boke of Fame*. London: Pynson, 1526.

———. *[Les Quinze Joyes de Mariage]*. Ed. Jean Rychner. Geneva: Droz, 1967.

———. *Les Quinze Joies de mariage*. Ed. Monique Santucci. Paris: Stock, 1986.

———. *The Sayinges or Prouerbes of King Salomon, with the Answers of Marcolphus, Tra[ns]lated Out of Frenche in to Englysshe*. London: Pynson, 1529.

———. *Sensuyt la louenge et beaute des Dames*. Toulouse: Nicolas Vieillard, n.d.

Arber, Edward. *A Transcript of the Register of the Company of Stationers of London 1554–1640 AD*. 5 vols. London: privately printed, 1875; rpt. New York: Peter Smith, 1950.

Archibald, Elizabeth. *Appolonius of Tyre: Medieval and Renaissance Themes and Variations: Including the Text of the Historia Apollonii Regis Tyri with an English Translation*. Cambridge: D. S. Brewer, 1991.

Aristotle. *Sensuyt le Secret des secretz de [sic] Aristote, pour congnoistre les conditions des ho[m]mes, & des femmes*. Toulouse: Nicolas Vieillard, 1538.

Aurner, Nellie S. *Caxton: Mirrour of Fifteenth-Century Letters: a study of the literature of the first English press*. London: Allen, 1926; rpt. NY: Russell and Russell, 1965.

Axton, Richard. "Royal Throne, Royal Bed: John Heywood and Spectacle." *Medieval English Theatre* 16 (1994): 66–76.

Baird, Joseph, and John R. Kane, eds. *La Querelle de la Rose: Letters and Documents*. Chapel Hill: University of North Carolina Press, 1978.

Baldwin, William. *A treatise of Morall Phylosophie, contaynyng the sayinges of the wyse, gathered and Englyshed*. London: [E. Whitchurche: 1547].

Barclay, Alexander, trans. See Brant.

Bawcutt, Priscilla. "An Early Scottish Debate Poem on Women." *Scottish Literary Journal* 23.2 (Nov 1996): 35–42.

Benjamin, Walter. "Das Kunstwerk im Zeitalter seiner technischer Reproduzierbarkeit," In *Illuminations*. 1935. Ed. by Hannah Arendt, trans. by H. Zohn. New York: Schocken Books, 1969.

Benson, Pamela Joseph. *The Invention of the Renaissance Woman*. University Park, PA: Pennsylvania State University Press, 1992.

Berlant, Lauren. "The Female Complaint." *Social Text* 7 (Fall 1988): 237–59.

Berners, Juliana. *Here in thys boke afore ar contenyt the bokys of haukyng and hunting*. [St. Albans: S.n, 1486].

BBC. *The BBC Production of the First Stage, Part 3*. New York: Spoken Word, 1991.

Bevington, David. "Is Heywood's *Play of the Wether* Really about the Weather?" *Renaissance Drama* 7 (1964): 11–19.

Blake, Norman F. *Caxton's Own Prose*. London: Deutsch, 1973.

———. *William Caxton and English Literary Culture*. London: Hambledon, 1991.

Blamires, Alcuin, ed. *Woman Defamed, Woman Defended: An Anthology of Medieval Texts*. New York: Oxford University Press, 1992.

Bloch, R. Howard. *Medieval Misogyny and the Invention of Western Romantic Love.* Chicago: University of Chicago Press, 1991.

Blumenfeld-Kosinski, Renate. "Christine de Pizan and the Political Life in Late-Medieval France." In *Christine de Pizan: A Casebook.* Ed. Barbara Altmann and Deborah McGrady. New York: Routledge, 2003.

———. "Christine de Pisan and the Misogynistic Tradition." In *Selected Writings of Christine de Pizan.* Ed. Renate Blumenfeld-Kosinski, pp. 297–311.

Boffey, Julia. "Richard Pynson's Book of Fame and the Letter of Dido." *Viator* 19 (1988): 339–53.

———. "Wynkyn de Worde and Misogyny in Print." In *Chaucer in Perspective.* Sheffield: Sheffield Academic Press, 1999, pp. 236–51.

Bono, Barbara J. *Literary Transvaluations: From Virgilian Epic to Shakespearean Tragicomedy.* Berkeley: University of California Press, 1984.

Bornstein, Diane, ed. *The Feminist Controversy of the Renaissance: Guillaume Alexis, An Argument Betwixt Man and Woman (1525); Sir Thomas Elyot, The Defence of Good Women (1545); Henricius Cornelius Agrippa, Female Pre-Eminence (1670).* Delmar, NY: Scholars' Facsimiles and Reprints, 1980.

———. "Anti-Feminism in Thomas Hoccleve's Translation of Christine de Pizan's Epistre au Dieu d'Amours." *English Language Notes* 19 (1981): 7–14.

Bossy, Michel-André. "Woman's Plain Talk in *Le Débat de l'omme et de la femme* by Guillaume Alexis." *Fifteenth Century Studies* 16 (1990): 23–41.

Boswell, Jackson, and Sylvia Holton. *Chaucer's Fame in England: STC Chauceriana 1475–1640.* New York: Modern Language Association, 2004.

Braden, Gordon. "Gaspara Stampa and the Gender of Petrarchism." *Texas Studies in Language and Literature* 38.2 (1996): 115–39.

Brant, Sebastian. *The Shyp of folys.* Trans. Alexander Barclay. London: Pynson, 1509. London: J. Cawood, 1570.

———. [*Shyppe of fooles.*] Trans. Henry Watson. London: Wynkyn de Worde, 1509. London: Wynkyn de Worde, 1517.

Brink, Jean R., ed. *Female Scholars: A Tradition of Learned Women before 1800.* Montreal: Eden Press Women's Publishing, 1980.

Brook, Leslie C. "The demandes d'amour in the Chantilly and Wolfenbuttel Manuscripts." *Fifteenth Century Studies* (1997): 222–35.

Bühler, Curt F. "A Survival from the Middle Ages: William Baldwin's Use of the 'Dictes and Sayings'." *Speculum* 23 (1948): 76–80.

Burke, Peter. *Popular Culture in Early Modern Europe.* London: Maurice Temple Smith, 1978. Rev. rpt. Aldershot: Scolar Press, 1994.

Burrow, Colin. "'Full of the Maker's Guile': Ovid on Imitating and On the Imitation of Ovid." *Ovidian Transformations: Essays on the Metamorphoses and Its Reception.* Ed. Philip Hardie, Alessandro Barchiesi, and Stephen Hinds. Cambridge: Cambridge University Press, 1999, pp. 271–87.

Camargo, Martin. *Ars dictaminis, ars dictandi.* Turnhout, Belgium: Brepols, 1991.

Camden, Carroll. *The Elizabethan Woman*. Houston, Tex.: Elsevier Press, 1952: 25.

Campbell, P. G. C. "Christine de Pisan en Angleterre." *Revue de littérature comparée* 5 (1925): 659–70.

Carroll, Berenice. "Christine de Pizan and the Origins of Peace Theory." In *Women Writers and the Early Modern British Political Tradition*. Ed. Hilda L. Smith. New York: Cambridge University Press, 1998, pp. 22–39.

Cartwright, Kent. *Theatre and Humanism: English Drama in the Sixteenth Century*. Cambridge: Cambridge University Press, 1999.

Chance, Jane. "Gender Subversion and Linguistic Castration in Fifteenth-Century Translations of Christine de Pizan." In *Violence Against Women in Medieval Texts*. Ed. Anna Roberts. Gainesville, FL: University of Florida Press, 1998, 161–94.

Chartier, Alain. *Delectable Demaundes, and Pleasaunt Questions, with Their Seuerall Aunswers, in Matters of Loue, Naturall Causes, with Morall and Politique Deuises*. London: John Cawood for Nicholas Englande, 1566. London: T. Creede, 1596; London: B. Alsop, 1640.

———. *La Belle Dame Sans Merci*. Trans. Richard Roos. In *Boke of fame*. London: Pynson, 1526.

———. *Les Demandes Damours, auec les Responces*. [By Alain Chartier?]. Paris: 1550.

Chaucer, Geoffrey. *Here begynneth the boke of fame, made by Geffray Chaucer: with dyuers other of his workes*. London: Pynson, 1526.

———. *The Canterbury Tales*. *The Riverside Chaucer*, ed. Larry D. Benson. 3rd ed. Boston: Houghton-Mifflin, 1987.

———. *The Loue and Complayntes Bytwene Mars and Venus*. Westminster: Julian Notary, 1500.

Cicero, Marcus T. *De optimo genere oratorum*. Trans. H. M. Hubbell. London: Heinemann, 1949.

Cohen, Gustave, ed. *Recueil de farces françaises inédites du XVe siècle ...* Cambridge, Mass: Medieval Academy of America, 1949.

Coldiron, A. E. B. *Canon, Period, and the Poetry of Charles of Orleans: Found in Translation*. Ann Arbor: University of Michigan Press, 2000.

———. "How Spenser Excavates Du Bellay's Antiquitez." *Journal of English and Germanic Philology* 101.1 (January 2001): 41–67.

———. "Journey and Ambassadorship in the Marriage Literature for Mary Tudor (1496–1533)." In *Renaissance Tropologies*. Ed. Jeanne Shami. Pittsburgh, PA: Duquesne University Press, forthcoming.

———."Public Sphere/Contact Zone: Habermas, Early Print, and Verse Translation." *Criticism* 46.2 (2004): 207–22.

———. "Translation's Challenge to Critical Categories." *Yale Journal of Criticism* 16.2 (Fall 2003): 315–44.

———. "Towards a Comparative New Historicism: Land Tenures and Some Fifteenth-Century Poems." *Comparative Literature* 53.2 (Spring 2001): 97–116.
Cole, Mary Hill. *The Portable Queen: Elizabeth I and the Politics of Ceremony*. Amherst: University of Massachusetts Press, 1999.
Collingwood, Sharon. *Market Pledge and Gender Bargain: Commercial Relations in French Farce 1450–1550*. New York: Peter Lang, 1996.
Copeland, Rita. *Rhetoric, hermeneutics, and translation in the Middle Ages: Academic Traditions and vernacular texts*. Cambridge, England: Cambridge University Press, 1991.
Copland, Robert. *Poems*. Ed. Mary C. Erler. Toronto: University of Toronto Press, 1993.
———, trans. *Here Begynneth the Hystory of the Noble Helyas Knyght of the Swanne* … . London: Copland, 1512.
Craik, T.W. "The True Source of John Heywood's *Johan Johan*." *Modern Language Review* 45 (1950): 289–95.
Cressot, Marcel. *Le Vocabulaire des Quinze joyes de mariage d'après le texte de la seconde édition de la Bibliothèque elzévirienne de 1857*. Paris, 1939.
Crotch, W. J. B. *The Prologues and Epilogues of William Caxton*. London: Oxford University Press, 1928.
Crow, Joan. "*Les Quinze Joyes de Mariage* in France and England." *Modern Language Review* 59 (1964): 571–7.
———, ed. *Les Quinze joyes de mariage*. Oxford: Blackwell, 1969.
Crowley, Timothy. "Arms and the Boy: Marlowe's *Aeneas* and the Parody of Imitation in *Dido, Queen of Carthage*." *English Literary Renaissance*, forthcoming.
Davidson, Clifford, and John Stroupe, eds. *Drama in the Middle Ages: Comparative and Critical Essays*. New York: AMS, 1990.
Davis, Lloyd, ed. *Sexuality and Gender in the English Renaissance: An Annotated Edition of Contemporary Documents*. New York: Garland, 1998.
Delany, Shelia. "'Mothers to Think Back Through': Who Are They? The Ambiguous Example of Christine de Pizan." *Medieval Texts and Contemporary Readers*. Ed. Laurie A. Finke and Martin B. Schichtmann. Ithaca, NY: Cornell University Press, 1987. Rpt. In *The Selected Writings of Christine de Pizan*. Ed. Renate Blumenfeld-Kosinski. New York: W. W. Norton and Co., 1997, pp. 312–28.
Deleuze, Gilles, and Félix Guattari. *Kafka: Pour Une Littérature Mineure*. Paris: Éditions de Minuit, 1975.
Derrida, Jacques. *De la Grammatologie*. Paris: Édtions de Minuit, 1967.
Deschamps, Eustace. *Miroir de Mariage. Oeuvres Complètes d'Eustache Deschamps*. Ed. Gaston Raynaud, vol 9 of 11 vols. Paris: Firmin-Didot, 1894.
Desrey, P. "La Genealogie Auecques Les Gestes Et Nobles Faitz Darmes Du … Prince Godeffroy De Boulion." See Robert Copland, trans.

Dolan, Fran. "'Taking the Pencil Out of God's Hand': Art, Nature, and the Face-Painting Debate in Early Modern England." *PMLA* 108.2 (March 1993): 224–39.

Downing, Crystal. "Face Painting in Early Modern England," *PMLA* 109.1 (January 1994): 119–20.

Driver, Martha. "Christine de Pisan and Robert Wyer: *The C. Hystoryes of Troye, or L'Epistre d'Othea Englished*." *Gutenberg Jahrbuch*, 1997: 125–39.

———. *The Image in Print*. London: The British Library, 2004.

Du Bellay, Guillaume. *Fragments de la première Ogdoade de Guillaume Du Bellay, seigneur de Langey*. Ed. V. L. Bourilly. Paris: Société Nouvelle de Librairie et d'Édition, 1905.

Du Bellay, Joachim. *Les Antiquitez; Les Regrets*. Ed. Françoise Joukovsky. Paris: Flammarion, 1994.

Dunbar, William. *The Poems of William Dunbar*. Ed. Priscilla Bawcutt. 2 vols. Glasgow: Association for Scottish Literary Studies, 1998.

Dundes, Alan. "On the Structure of the Proverb." In *The Wisdom of Many: Essays on the Proverb*. Ed. Alan Dundes and Wolfgang Meider. New York: Garland, 1981, pp. 43–64.

Du Pont-Allais, Jean. *Sensuyt la louenge et beaulte des dames*. Toulouse: Nicolas Vieillard, 1535.

Edwards, A.S.G. "Poet and Printer in the Sixteenth Century: Stephen Hawes and Wynkyn de Worde." *Gutenberg Jahrbuch* (1980): 82–8.

Ellis, Sir Henry. *Original Letters Illustrative of English History Including Numerous Royal Letters from Autographs in the British Museum, the State Paper Office and One or Two Other Collections*. London: Dawsons of Pall Mall, 1969.

Faivre, Bernard. *Répertoire des farces françaises: des origines à Tabarin*. Spectateur français. Paris: Imprimerie Nationale Editions, 1993.

———. *Les Farces Moyen Age et Renaissance*. Vol. I, *La guerre des sexes*. Ed. Salamandre. Paris: Imprimerie nationale, 1997.

———. *Les farces Moyen âge et Renaissance, vol II, Dupés et trompeurs*. Ed. Salamandre. Paris: Imprimerie nationale, 1999.

Felberg-Levitt, Margaret. *The Demande d'Amour*. Montreal: CERES, 1995.

———. "Jouer aux demandes d'amour." *Moyen Français* 38 (1996): 93–124.

Fenoaltea, D., and D. Rubin. *The Ladder of High Designs*. Charlottesville: University of Virginia Press, 1991.

Feylde, Thomas, and Wynkyn de Worde. *Here Begynneth a Lytel Treatyse Called the Co[n]traverse Bytwene a Louer and a Jaye*. London: Wynkyn de Worde, 1527.

Firenzuola, Agnolo, and Adriano Seroni. *Opere*. Firenze: Sansoni, 1971.

———. *On The Beauty of Women*, Edited and trans. by Konrad Eisenbichler and Jacqueline Murray. Philadelphia: University of Pennsylvania Press, 1992.

Fitzherbert, John, and Anthony Fitzherbert. *The Boke of Husbandry*. London: Thomas Berthelet, 1548.

Fleig, Arthur. *Der Treperel-Druck der Quinze Joyes de Mariage*. Greifswald: Julius Abel, 1903.
Fleuret, Fernand. "Bibliographie des éditions des Quinze Joies de Mariage." *Les Quinze joyes de mariage*. Paris: Garnier, 1936.
Forhan, Kate Langdon. *The Political Theory of Christine de Pizan*. Burlington, VT: Ashgate, 2002.
———. "Polycracy, Obligation, and Revolt: The Body Politic in John of Salisbury and Christine de Pizan." In *Politics Gender and Genre*: *The Political Thought of Christine de Pizan*. Ed.Margaret Brabant. Boulder, Colo: Westview Press, 1992. pp. 33–52.
Forni, Kathleen. "Richard Pynson and the Stigma of the Chaucerian Apocrypha." *Chaucer Review* 34.4 (2000): 428–36.
Fowler, Alastair. *Kinds of Literature An Introduction to the Theory of Genres and Modes*. Cambridge, MA: Harvard University Press, 1982.
Fox, Allan B. "Chaucer's Prosody and the Non-Pentameter Line in John Heywood's Comic Debates." *Language And Style: An International Journal* 10 (1977): 23–41.
France, Peter, ed. *The New Oxford Companion to Literature in French*. Oxford: Clarendon Press, 1995.
Frank, Grace. "Proverbs in Medieval Literature." *MLN* 58 (1943): 508–15.
Fraser, Russell Alfred. "The Court of Venus." Ph.D. Thesis. Harvard University, 1950.
Galderisi, Claudio. "Stratégie de l'anonymat et saturation mimétique dans Les Quinze Joies de Mariage." *Littératures Classiques* 31 (Autumn 1997): 13–26.
Garcie, Pierre. [Trans. Robert Copland.] *The rutter of the sea, with the hauens, roades, soundings ...* London: Iohn Awdeley, for Antony Kytson, [1573?].
Gay, Jules. *Bibliographie des ouvrages relatifs à l'amour, aux femmes, au mariage* ... 2nd ed. Paris: J. Gay, 1864.
Genette, Gérard. *Les Seuils*. Paris: Éditions des Seuils, 1987.
Gildenhuys, Faith, ed. *The Bachelor's Banquet*. Binghamton, NY: MRTS, 1993.
Gill, J.S. "How Hermes Trismegistus was Introduced to Renaissance England." *Journal of the Warburg and Courtauld Institute* 47 (1984): 222–5.
Gillespie, Alexandra. *Print Culture and the Medieval Author*. Oxford: Oxford University Press, 2006.
Gosynhyll, Edward. *Here begynneth a lyte boke named the schole house of women*. London: T. Petyt, 1541, 1561, 1572. In *The virtuous scholehous of vngracious women*. [London: 1548?].
———. *The prayse of all women, called mulieru[m]pean [in verse]*. [London: W. Middleton, 1542], [1557?].
Green, Karen. "Christine de Pizan and Thomas Hobbes." *Philosophical Quarterly* 44 (Oct 1994): 456–75.
Greene, Thomas M. *Besieging the Castle of Ladies*. Binghamton, NY: Center for Medieval and Early Renaissance Studies, 1995.

Gringore, Pierre. *Le Chasteau d'amours*. Paris: [s.n.], [avant 1500].

———. *Chasteau de Labour*. Trans. Alexander Barclay. Paris: A. Vérard, ca. 1503.

———. *La complainte de trop tard marié* [Texte imprimé]. Paris: [s.n.], 1505.

Guild, Elizabeth. "Women as Auctores in Early Modern Europe." In *The Cambridge History of Literary Criticism III: The Renaissance*. Ed. Glyn P. Norton. Cambridge: Cambridge University Press, 1999, pp. 426–32.

Halasz, Alexandra. *The Marketplace of Print Pamphlets and the Public Sphere in Early Modern England*. New York: Cambridge University Press, 1997.

Hanna, Ralph, and Traugott Lawler, eds. *Jankyn's Book of Wikked Wyves*. Athens: University of Georgia Press, 1997.

Happé, Peter. "Dramatic Images of Kingship in Heywood and Bale." *SEL* 1500–1900 39.2 (Spring 1999): 239–53.

Heft, David. "Proverbs and Sentences in Fifteenth-Century French Poetry." Ph.D. dissertation. New York University, 1941.

———. "Proverbs and Sentences in Fifteenth-Century French Poetry." NY: Washington Square, 1942.

Helgerson, Richard. *Forms of Nationhood: The Elizabethan Writing of England*. Chicago: University of Chicago Press, 1992.

Henderson, Judith. "John Heywood's *The Spider and the Flie*: educating queen and country." *Studies in Philology* 96.3 (Summer 1999): 241–74.

Henderson, Katherine, and Barbara McManus. *Half Humankind: Contexts and Texts of the Controversy about Women in England, 1540–1640*. Urbana and Chicago: University of Illinois Press, 1984.

Henry VIII. *Assertio septem sacramentorum aduersus Martin Lutheru[m]*. London: Pynson, 1521.

Hermans, Theo. "Images of Translation: Metaphor and Imagery in the Renaissance Discourse on Translation." *The Manipulation of Literature: Studies in Literary Translation*. Ed. Theo Hermans. New York: St Martins Press, 1985, pp. 103–35.

Heywood, John. *A mery play betwene Johan Johan the husbande, Tyb his wyfe, and Syr Johan the preest*. London: Rastell, 1533.

———. *Dialogue conteynyng the number of effectuall prouerbes in the Englishe tounge, compact in a matter concernynge two maner of maryages*. London: Berthelet, 1546.

———. *Heywood's Works and Miscellaneous Short Poems*. Ed. Burton A. Milligan. Urbana: University of Illinois Press, 1956.

———. *The Plays of John Heywood*. Ed. Richard Axton and Peter Happé. Cambridge: D. S. Brewer, 1991.

———. *Two hundred Epigrammes, upon two hundred prouerbes, with a thyrde hundred newely added and made* ... London: Berthelet, 1555.

Hicks, Eric, ed. *Le Debat sur le Roman de la Rose*. Paris: Honoré Champion, 1977.

Hindman, Sandra. *Christine de Pizan's "Epistre Othéa": Painting and Politics at the court of Charles VI.* Toronto: Pontifical Institute of Mediaeval Studies, 1986.

Hodnett. *English Woodcuts, 1480–1535; with additions and corrections.* Oxford: Oxford University Press, 1973.

Horace. *Satires, Epistles and Ars poetica*, Trans. H. Rushton Fairclough. London: Heinemann, 1929.

Hubrecht, Georges, ed. See Anon., *La Complainte de Trop tost marie*.

Hull, Suzanne. *Chaste, silent & obedient: English books for women, 1475–1640.* San Marino, Calif: Huntington Library, 1982.

Jerome, Saint. *Admonitio Adversus Iovinianum. Liber I*, Ed. J-P Migne. *Patrologia Latina* 23.

Johnson, Robert C. *John Heywood.* New York: Twayne, 1970.

Jordan, Constance. *Renaissance Feminism: Literary Texts and Political Models.* Ithaca, NY: Cornell University Press, 1990.

Joukovsky, Françoise. "La Querelle des femmes." *Magazine Littéraire* 319 (March 1994): 51–2.

——— ed. See Du Bellay.

Jubainville, M. H. D'Arbois de and M. Francisque André, eds. *Aube: Archives ecclésiastiques, série G. vol 2 of Inventaire Sommaire des Archives Départementales antérieures à 1790.* Paris: Alphonse Picard et Fils, 1896.

Juvenal. *Works.* Ed. George G. Ramsay. Cambridge: Harvard University Press, 1950.

Katz, Richard. *The Ordered Text.* New York: P. Lang, 1985.

Kennedy, Angus J., and Kenneth Varty, eds. *Le Ditié de Jeanne d'Arc.* Oxford: Society for the Study of Medieval Literatures and Language, 1977.

Kittredge, George Lyman. "John Heywood and Chaucer." *American Journal of Philology* 9.4 (1888): 473–4.

Kosta-Théfaine, Jean-François. "The *Proverbes moraulx* de Christine de Pizan." *Le Moyen Français* 38 (1996): 61–78.

Krause, Eberhard. Neue beiträge zu den "XV joyes de marriage." Wangerin: H. Rosenkranz, 1929.

Krier, Theresa, ed. *Refiguring Chaucer in the Renaissance.* Gainesville, FL: University of Florida Press, 1998.

Krontiris, Tina. *Oppositional Voices: Women as Writers and Translators in the English Renaissance.* London & New York: Routledge, 1992.

Kuin, Roger. *Chamber Music: Elizabethan Sonnet Sequences and the Pleasure of Criticism.* Toronto: University of Toronto Press, 1998.

Labalme, Patricia H., ed. *Beyond Their Sex: Learned Women of the European Past.* New York: New York University Press, 1980.

Lacharrière. *La Complainte douloureuse du nouveau marié. Anciennes poésies françaises.* Paris: A. Firmin Didot, 1830.

Lancashire, Ian. *Dramatic texts and records of Britain: a chronological topography to 1558.* Toronto: University of Toronto Press, 1984.

La Tour Landry, Geoffroy de. William Caxton. Ed. and trans. M. Y. Offord. *The Book of the Knight of the Tower*. London: Oxford University Press, 1971.

Lea, Henry C. *A History of Sacerdotal Celibacy in the Christian Church*. 4th ed., revised. London: Watts & Co., 1932.

LeBlanc, Yvonne. "Va lettre va: The French Verse Epistle (1400–1550)." *Speculum* 74.3 (1999): 784–5.

Lefèvre de Ressons, Jean. See Mathéolus.

Le Franc, Martin. *Le champion des dames*. Lyon: s.n., 1485. Paris: Galiot Dupré, 1530. Ed. A. Piaget and E. Droz. Lausanne: Payot, 1968.

Lerer, Seth. *Chaucer and His Readers: Imagining the Author in Late Medieval England*. Princeton, NJ: Princeton University Press, 1993.

Lewicka, Halina. "Un Prénom spécialisé." *Études sur l'ancienne farce française*. Paris: Éditions Klencksieck, 1974.

Lines, Candace. "'To take on them judgements': absolutism and debate in John Heywood's plays." *Studies in Philology* 97.4 (Fall 2000): 401–32.

Łobzowska, Maria. "Two English Translations of the XVth Century French Satire 'Les Quinze Joyes de Mariage'." *Kwartalnik Neofilologiczny* 10.1 (1963): 17–32.

Long, Richard A. "Heywood, Chaucer, and Lydgate." *Modern Language Notes* 64.1 (1949): 55–6.

Lydgate. *The payne and sorowe of euyll maryage*. London: Wynkyn de Worde, ca. 1530.

———. *The Payne and Sorowe of Euyll Mariage*. Trans. J. Lydgate. London: Wynkyn de Worde, 1530.

Mahoney, Dhira. "Middle English Regenderings of Chrsitine de Pizan." in *The Medieval Opus*. Ed. Douglas A. Kelly. Amsterdam: Rodopi, 1996, pp. 405–27.

Malcolmson, Christina. "Christine de Pizan's City of Ladies in Early Modern England." *Debating Gender in Early Modern England, 1500–1700*. New York: Palgrave MacMillan, 2002, pp. 15–35.

Map, Walter. *Here begynneth a lytel treatyse called the dysputacyon or co[m]playnt of the herte thorughe perced with the lokynge of the eye*. London: Wynkyn de Worde [1516].

———. *The Latin Poems Commonly Attributed to Walter Mapes*. Ed. Thomas Wright. London: Camden Society, 1841; rpt. New York: AMS Press, 1968.

———. *Phillis and Flora The sweete and ciuill contention of two amorous ladyes. Translated out of Latine: by R.S. Esquire*. London: W. W[hite] for Richarde Jones, 1598.

Marlowe, Christopher. *The tragedie of Dido Queene of Carthage played by the Children of her Maiesties Chappell*. London: Widdowe Orwin, for Thomas Woodcocke, 1594.

Mathéolus. *Les Lamentations de Mathéolus*. Trans. Jean Lefèvre de Ressons, ed. A.G. Van Hamel, 2 vols. Paris, 1892–1905.

Maxwell, Ian. *French Farce and John Heywood.* Melbourne: University of Melbourne Press, 1946.

Meurier, Gabriel. *Tresor de sentences dorees, dicts, proverbes & dictons communs, reduits selon l'ordre alphabetic Avec le Bouquet de philosophie morale.* Lyon: pour B. Rigaud, 1582.

Mieder, Wolfgang. *International Proverb Scholarship An Annotated Bibliography.* Garland folklore bibliographies, vol 3. New York: Garland Pub, 1982.

Meun, Jean de et Guillaume de Lorris. *Roman de la Rose*, ed. Félix Lecoy. 3 vols. Paris: Champion, 1965–70.

Meyer, Paul. "Note sur le manuscrit offert par Christine de Pisan à Isabeau de Bavière (Musée Britannique Harley 4431)." In *Oeuvres poétiques de Christine de Pisan.* Ed. Maurice Roy, III,.xxi–xxiv. 3 vols. Paris: Firmin-Didot, 1886–1896.

———. [Untitled note]. *Romania* 6 (1877): 499–503.

Minnis, A. J. *Medieval Theory of Authorship*: *Scholastic Literary Attitudes in the Later Middle Ages*, 2nd ed. Philadelphia: University of Pennsylvania Press, 1988.

Miskimin, Alice. *The Renaissance Chaucer.* New Haven, CT: Yale University Press, 1975.

Montaiglon, Anatole. *Receuil de Poesies françoises des XVe et XVe siecles ...* Paris: P. Jannet, 1857, VII, pp. 287–301.

Moret, Philippe. *Tradition et Modernité de l'aphorisme.* Geneva: Droz, 1997.

Mubashshir ibn Fatik, Abu al-wafa. *Dictes or sayengis of the philosophers ...* Trans. Guillaume de Tignonville; trans. from French, Anthony Woodville. Westminster: Caxton, 1477.

Mullini, Roberta. "'Mondict seigneur le légat [...] a faict jouer des farces en francoys au grant appareil': John Heywood e la farsa francese alla corte di Henry VIII." In *Anglistica e ...: Metodi e percorsi comparatistici nelle lingue, culture e letterature di origine europea*, vol I. Ed. Giuseppe Sertoli and Goffredo Miglietta. Trieste, Italy: Università di Trieste, 1999, pp. 227–37.

Neville, William. *Powder and Paint*: *A History of the Englishwoman's Toilet.* London: Longmans, 1957.

Nicholson, R. H. "The State of the Nation: Some Complaint Topics in Late Medieval English Literature." *Parergon* 23 (1979): 9–28.

Norland, Howard. "Formalizing English Farce: *Johan Johan* and Its French Connection." *Comparative Drama* 17 (1983): 141–52; reprinted in *Drama in the Middle Ages*: *Comparative and Critical Essays.* Ed. Clifford Davidson and John Stroupe. New York: AMS, 1990, pp. 356–67.

Obermeier, Anita. *The History of Auctorial Self-Criticism in the European Middle Ages.* Amsterdam: Rodopi, 1999.

Ovidius Naso, Publius. Trans. George Turberville. *The heroycall epistles of Publius Ovidius Naso in Englishe verse.* London: Denham, 1567.

Ozawa, Hiroshi. "The Structural Innovations of the More Circle Dramatists," *Shakespeare Studies* 19 (1980–81): 1–23.

Patterson, Lee. "'For the Wyves love of Bathe': Feminine Rhetoric and Poetic Resolution in the *Roman de la Rose* and the *Canterbury Tales*." *Speculum* 58 (1983): 656–95.

Phillippy, Patricia A. "Establishing Authority: Boccaccio's *De Claris mulieribus* and Christine de Pizan's *Le Livre de la cité des dames*." In *The Selected Writings of Christine de Pizan*. Ed. Renate Blumenfeld-Kosinski. New York: W. W. Norton., 1997, pp. 329–61.

Pilkington, Adrian. *Poetic Effects: a Relevance Theory Perspective*. Amsterdam: J. Benjamins, 2000.

Pizan, Christine de. [*Body of Policy.*] *Here begynneth the booke whiche is called the body of polycye ... To prynces. To nobles and to the people.* London: John Skot, 1521.

———. *Boke of the Cyte of ladyes*. Trans. Bryan Anslay. London: H. Pepwell, 1521.

———. *The Book of Fayttes of Armes and of Chyualrye*. Ed. A. T. P. Byles. London: Oxford University Press, 1932.

———. *C. Hystoryes of Troye [Epistre Othea]*. Trans. R. Wyer. London: Robert Wyer, [1549].

———. *The Selected Writings of Christine de Pizan*. Ed. Renate Blumenfeld-Kosinski. New York: W. W. Norton, 1997.

———. *Ditié de Jeanne d'Arc*. Trans. Renate Blumenfeld-Kosinski, from Angus J. Kennedy and Kenneth Varty, eds. Oxford: Society for the Study of Mediaeval Languages and Literature, 1977.

———. *The Epistle of Othea*. Ed. Curt Bühler. EETS. London: Oxford University Press, 1970.

———. *Epistre Othea*. Ed. Gabrielle Parussa. Geneva: Droz, 1999.

———. *Fayttes of Armes and of chyualrye*. Trans. W. Caxton. Westminster: Caxton, 1489.

———. *Livre du Corps de Policie*. Ed. Robert Lucas. Geneva: Droz, 1967.

———. *Morale Prouerbes of Cristyne*. Trans. Anthony Woodville. Westmestre [sic]: Caxton 1478. Re-edited and printed in *The Boke of Fame*. London: Pynson, 1526. Re-edited by William Blades. London, [Blades, East, & Blades]: 1859.

———. *Poems of Cupid, God of love Christine de Pizan's* Epistre au dieu d'amours *and* Dit de la rose, *Thomas Hoccleve's* The letter of Cupid. Ed. Thelma Fenster and Mary C. Erler. Leiden, E.J. Brill, 1990.

Pompen, Aurelius, ed. *The English versions of the Ship of Fools; a contribution to the history of the early French Renaissance in England*. London: Longmans, Green and Co., 1925.

Pratt, Karen. "Translating Misogamy: The Authority of the Intertext in the Lamentationes Matheoluli and Its Middle French Translation by Jean LeFèvre." *Forum for Modern Language Studies* 35.4 (October 1999): 421–35.

Pratt, Mary Louise. "Criticism in the Contact Zone: Decentering Community and Nation." *Critical Theory, Cultural Politics, and Latin American Narrative*. Ed.

Steven M. Buell, Albert H. LeMay, and Leonard Orr. Notre Dame and London: University of Notre Dame Press, 1993.

Prendergast, Thomas, and Barbara Kline, eds. *Rewriting Chaucer: Culture, Authority, and the Idea of the Authentic Text 1400–1602*. Columbus: Ohio State University Press, 1999.

Prescott, Anne Lake. *French Poets and the English Renaissance: studies in fame and transformation*. New Haven, CT: Yale University Press, 1978.

———. *Imagining Rabelais in Renaissance England*. New Haven, CT: Yale University Press, 1998.

Purkiss, Diane. "Marlowe's *Dido, Queen of Carthage* and the Representation of Elizabeth I." In *A Woman Scorn'd: Responses to the Dido Myth*. Ed. Michael Burden. London: Faber and Faber, 1998, pp. 151–67.

Quilligan, Maureen. *The Allegory of Female Authority*. Ithaca, NY: Cornell University Press, 1991.

———. "The Allegory of Female Authority: Christine de Pizan and Canon Formation."In *Displacements: Women, Tradition, Literatures in French*. Ed. Joan DeJean and Nancy K. Miller. Baltimore, MD: Johns Hopkins University Press, 1991.

Reed, A. W. *Early Tudor Drama, Medwall, the Rastells, and the More Circle*. London: Methuen, 1926.

Reed, Thomas L. *Middle English Debate Poetry and the aesthetics of irresolution*. Columbia: Columbia University, 1990.

Rey-Flaud, Bernadette. *La Farce ou la machine à rire: théorie d'un genre dramatique 1450–1550*. Geneva: Droz, 1984.

Richards, Earl Jeffrey. "Christine de Pizan, the Conventions of Courtly Diction, and Italian Humanism." In *Reinterpreting Christine de Pizan*. Ed. Earl Jeffrey Richards. Athens: University of Georgia Press, 1992, pp. 250–71.

Rigg, A. G., ed. *Gawain on Marriage: The Textual Tradition of the* De coniuge non ducenda *with Critical Edition and Translation*. Toronto: Pontifical Institute of Medieval Studies, 1986.

Roberts-Baytop, Adrianne. *Dido, Queen of Infinite Literary Variety*. Salzburg: Inst. für Englische Sprache und Literatur, 1974.

Roy, Maurice, ed. *Oeuvres poétiques de Christine de Pisan*. 3 vols. Paris: Firmin-Didot, 1886–1896.

Ruggiers, Paul, ed. *Editing Chaucer: The Great Tradition*. Norman OK: Pilgrim Books, 1984.

Saint-Gelais, Octavien. See Anon., "Letter of Dydo to Eneas."

San Pedro, Diego Fernández de. *Petit Traité de Arnalte et Lucenda, autresfois traduit de langue Espaignole en la Françoyse & intituleì l'Amant mal traité de s'amye*. Paris: Sertinas, 1548.

Santucci, Monique. "Pour une nouvelle interpretation des *Quinze joyes de mariage*." In *Le Récit bref au moyen âge*. Ed. D. Buschinger. Amiens: Université de Picardie, 1980, pp. 153–73.

Sébillet, Thomas. *La Louenge des femmes: Invention extraite de commentaire de Panatgruel, sur l'Androgyne de Platon.* Lyons 1551. Ed. Ruth Calder. New York: Johnson Reprint Corp., 1967.

Spenser. *Amoretti and Epithalamion.* London: Ponsonby, 1595.

———. *Complaints Containing sundrie small poemes of the worlds vanitie.* London: Ponsonby, 1591.

Sperber, Dan, and Deirdre Wilson. *Relevance: communication and cognition.* Oxford: Blackwell, 1986.

Stierle, Karlheinz. "*Translatio studii* and Renaissance." In *The Translatability of Cultures.* Ed. Wolfgang Iser and Sanford Budick. Stanford, Calif: Stanford University Press, 1996, pp. 55–66.

Strauss, Barrie Ruth. "The Subversive Discourse of the Wife of Bath: Phallocentric Discourse and the Imprisonment of Criticism." *ELH* 55.3 (Fall 1988).

Strong, Roy C. *The Cult of Elizabeth Elizabethan Portraiture and Pageantry.* London: Thames and Hudson, 1977.

Summit, Jennifer. "The Goose's Quill: The Production of Female Authorship in Late Medieval and Early Modern England." PhD dissertation, Johns Hopkins University, 1996.

———. *Lost Property: The Woman Writer and English Literary History 1380–1589.* Chicago: University of Chicago Press, 2000.

Sultan, Stanley. "*Johan Johan* and Its Debt to French Farce." *JEGP* (1954): 23–27.

Surrey, Henry Howard, Thomas Wyatt, Nicholas Grimald, and Richard Tottel. *Songes and Sonettes, Written by the Right Honorable Lorde Henry Haward Late Earle of Surrey, and Other.* London: Richard Tottel, 1557.

Tchemerzine, Avenir. *Bibliographie d'Éditions originales et rares d'auteurs français des Xve, XVIe, XVIIe, et XVIIIe siècles* ... 10 vols. Paris: M. Plée, 1927.

Theophrastus. *Aureolus Liber de Nuptiis.* Cited in Jerome.

Tilley, Morris Palmer. *A Dictionary of the Proverbs in England in the Sixteenth and Seventeenth Centuries; A Collection of the Proverbs Found in English Literature and the Dictionaries of the Period.* Ann Arbor: University of Michigan Press, 1950.

Tracy, P. B. "Robert Wyer: A brief analysis." *The Library* 6th series 2 (1980): 294–303.

Ulrich, Laurel. *Good Wives Image and Reality in the Lives of Women in Northern New England, 1650–1750.* New York, NY: Knopf, 1982.

Utley, Francis. *The Crooked Rib: An Analytical Index to the Argument about Women in English and Scots Literature to the End of the Year 1568.* Columbus: Ohio State University Press, 1944.

Valerius. See Map.

Venuti, Lawrence. *The Translator's Invisibility A History of Translation.* London: Routledge, 1995.

Vickers, Nancy. "Diana Described: Scattered Woman and Scattered Rhyme." *Critical Inquiry* 8.2 (Winter 1981): 265–79.

Villon, François. *Le Grant Testament*. Ed. Jean Rychner and Albert Henry. Geneva: Droz, 1974.

Virgil, and C. Day Lewis. *The Eclogues, Georgics and Aeneid of Virgil*. London: Oxford University Press, 1966.

Waithe, Mary Ellen, ed. *A History of Women Philosophers: Medieval, Renaissance, and Enlightenment Philosophers, AD 500–1600, II*. Boston: Kluwer Academic Press, 1989.

Walker, Greg. *The Politics of Performance in Early Renaissance Drama*. Cambridge: Cambridge University Press, 1998.

Wall, Wendy. *The Imprint of Gender: Authorship and Publication in the English Renaissance*. Ithaca, NY: Cornell University Press, 1993.

Wallace, C.W. *The Evolution of the English Drama up to Shakespeare*. Berlin: Georg Reimer, 1912.

Wallace, David. *Chaucerian Polity: absolutist lineages and associational forms in England and Italy*. Stanford, CA: Stanford University Press, 1997.

———. *Premodern Places*: *Calais to Surinam, Chaucer to Aphra Behn*. Malden, MA: Blackwell, 2004.

Walters, Lori. "The Woman Writer and Literary History: Christine de Pizan's Redefinition of the Poetic *Translatio* in the *Epistre au dieu d'amours*." *French Literature Series* 16 (1989): 1–16.

Warren, Nancy Bradley. "French Women and English Men, Joan of Arc, Margaret of Anjou, and Christine de Pizan in England, 1445–1540." *Exemplaria* 16.2 (Fall 2004): 405–36.

Watkins, John. *The Specter of Dido*. New Haven, CT: Yale University Press, 1995.

Watson, Henry. [*Here Endeth Ye Hystorye of Olyuer of Castylle, and of the Fayre Helayne*]. London: Wynkyn de Worde, 1518.

Watson, Thomas. *Hekatompathia or Passionate Centurie of Loue*. London: John Wolfe for Gabriell Cawood, 1582.

Westfall, Suzanne. *Patrons and Performance*: *Early Tudor Household Revels*. Oxford: Clarendon, 1990.

Whiting, Bartlett Jere. *Proverbs in Certain Middle English Romances in Relation to Their French Sources*. Cambridge, MA: Harvard University Press, 1933.

———, and Helen Wescott Whiting. *Proverbs, Sentences, and Proverbial Phrases from English Writings Before 1500*. London: Oxford University Press, 1968.

Whitford, Richard. *A werke for housholders or for them ye haue the gydynge or gouernaunce of any company*. London: Wynkyn de Worde, 1530.

Whitney, Isabella. *The Copy of a Letter, Lately Written in Meeter, by a Yonge Gentilwoman*: *to Her Vnconstant Louer With an Admonitio[n] to Al Yong Gentilwomen, and to All Other Mayds in General to Beware of Mennes Flattery* ... London: Richarde Jones, 1567.

Willard, Charity Cannon. "Women and Marriage around 1400: Three Views." *Fifteenth-Century Studies* 17 (1990): 475–84.

Wilson, Frank Percy, and Antoine de la Sale. *The Batchelars Banquet*. Oxford: Oxford University Press, 1929.

Wilson, Katharina M., and Elizabeth M. Makowski. *Wykked Wyves and the Woes of Marriage: Misogamous Literature from Juvenal to Chaucer*. New York: SUNY Press, 1990.

Woodbridge, Linda. *Women and the English Renaissance: Literature and the Nature of Womankind, 1540–1620*. Urbana and Chicago: University of Illinois Press, 1984.

Wright, Louis B. *Middle-Class Culture in Elizabethan England*. Rpt. New York: Octagon Books, 1980.

Index

Note: Page numbers in italics indicate figures.

acrostics, 4, 13, 20, 142, 145–6, 158–65, 171
adultery, 175, 188
Aers, David, xiii
aesthetics, xiii, 3, 5, 6–7, 15. *See also under* books; poetics
Alexis, Guillaume, 17, 78, 80–81, 84
    Interlocucyon with an argument betwyxt man and woman, xiv, 11–12, 15–18, 23, 69–70, 72–4, *73*, 78, *79*, 81, 85–6, 93, 95–8, 101, 111, 131, 142
    Le Débat de l'homme et de la femme, 69, 69n1, 70–71n2, 72, 81, 83
allegorical romance, 14. *See also* romance
L'amant mal traite de samye, 9
anadiplosis, 51
animal imagery, 168
anonymity, 138
Anslay, Bryan, 17, 21n1, 24, 38
    translation of *Livre de la Cite des dames* (Pizan), 17
Anthony, Saint, 175
anticlericalism, 174, 175, 176, 183, 185, 189
antifeminist literature, 1, 21n1, 22, 36–7, 49, 72, 74, 116, 170. *See also* misogyny
Appolonius of Tyre, 9
Aragon, Catherine of, 164
asclepiadic verses, 116n11
Aspasia, 38n36
auctoritas. See authority
Augustine, Saint, 87
    City of God, 34, 36
authority, 24–5, 31, 35, 38, 39, 44–52, 53, 56–65, 124–5. *See also* authorship; women writers
authorship, xv, 5. *See also* authority; women writers
    deauthorization, 21, 24, 26, 38, 60n61

strategies of anonymity, 138
suppression of, 21–2, 37, 54n54, 72, 72n4, 163
Axton, Richard, 18n418, 174–6, 179, 184

Babyngton, Anthony, 31, 38
Badius, J., 96
Baldwin, William, 66
Barclay, Alexander, 12n11, 54n54, 116
    translation of *Chasteau de Labour* (Gringore), 11–12, 11n10, 14, 16, 19
    translation of *Narrenschiff* (Brant), 12n11
Basoches, 189
Bawcutt, Priscilla, 70–71n2, 178n10
Beaute of Women (Anon; imp. Fawkes), xiv, 14, 16, 18, 69–70, 97–112, *99*, 110n30, 146, 201–14. *See also* Dupont-Alais, Jean: *Louenge et Beaulte*
    French imprints of, 100–104
beauty, 14–15, 97–111, *98*, *107*
Behn, Apra, 38
Benjamin, Walter, 44n44
Bersuire, Pierre, 31
biculturalism, 41n41, 191. *See also* cross-cultural contact; mediation; translation
bigamy, 164
Blason des femmes, 18, 99–100n20
Blumenfeld-Kosinski, Renate, 26, 27n16
Boccaccio, Giovanni, 8n8, 71, 87
    De Casibus, 8n6, 8*n*6
    De Claris multieribus, 8n6, 8*n*6
the body, 10, 13–15, 18, 97–111. *See also* beauty
    body odors, 13, 103, 182–3, 182n14
Boethius, 51n52
Boffey, Julia, xii, 57, 57n55, 58n56, 62, 64, 86, 86n14, 92–3, 116, 116n12, 125

The Boke of Fame, 22, 24, 39, 56–7, 57n55, 58, 60, 62, 66n64, *87*, 88–9, 93–4, 193–201
Boleyn, Anne, 164
Bonet, Honoré, *Arbre des batailles*, 26
Bono, Barbara J., 86, 86n14
book burning, 113
books. *See also* paratexts; printers; printing
   aesthetics of, xiii, 3, 5, 6–7, 15
   binding of, xiii
   design of, xiii, 3, 7, 56–7, 59, 62, 62n62, 64
   distribution of, xiii
   illustration of, xiii. *See also* woodcuts
   presentation of, xiii, 2
Bornstein, Diane, xiv, 17, 37, 69n1, 71, 71n3, 72, 74, 84
Bossy, Michel-André, 69n1, 71–2, 83, 83n8
Braden, Gordon, 14n13
Brant, Sebastian, 12n11, 96, 116
   Narrenschiff, 12n11
   Shyp of folys (The Shypp of Fooles), 12–13
Bruges, Louis de, 41
Budick, Sanford, 51n52
Burckhardt, Jacob, 6
Burgundy, xii, 3, 3n1
Burrow, Colin, 119–20
Byblis, 94
Byles, A. T. P., 26

caitiff, 153, 153n12, 157
Camden, Carroll, 107n29
canonicity, xv, 3, 5, 6, 8, 17, 20
   Chaucerian canon, 56–64
   Pizan and, 34, 39, 43, 49, 49n50, 54n54, 56, 57, 57n53, 68
   Pynson and, 57, 57n3
Carroll, Berenice, 26
Cartwright, Kent, xiii, 187, 189–90
Castle of Labour (trans. Barclay), 11–12, 14, 16, 19
catenary structures, 10–11
Caxton, William, xv, 2–3, 9, 17, 21–7, 22n3, 25n7, 27n15, 38–9, 42n42, 44–50, 48n43
   imprint and translation of *Morale*

Prouerbes of Cristyne (Pizan), 24–5, 25n7, 38–68, 42n42, 45n45, *46*
   imprint of *Aeneid*, 25
   imprint of *Dictes and Sayinges of the Philosophres* (Mubashshir ibn Fatik), 54n54, 65
   imprint of *Fayttes of Armes and of chyualrye* (Pizan), 24, 25n9, 26, 36
   presentational strategies of, 44–52
celibacy, 143, 145, 150
censorship, 4, 20, 113, 142. *See also* printers: suppressions by
cento-writers, 70
Chance, Jane, 21, 21n1, 28, 31, 37
chansons d'aventure, 11, 15, 80–81, 83, 95
characters, naming of, 20
Charles V, 27–8, 50–51
Charles VI, 3n429, 43
Charles VII, 27n16, 27*n*16, 88
Charles VIII, 88
Chartier, Alain, 56
   La Belle Dame Sans Merci, 9, 56, 64–5
   Les Demandes damour, 178n10
chastity, 85–97
Chaucer, Geoffrey, 6, 8n, 9, 15, 25, 37, 48–9, 56, 58, 60n61, 65, 119, 121–2, 133. *See also The Boke of Fame*
   Canterbury Tales, 118, 189
   ballade on fortune (Truth), 56
   General Prologue, 118
   Wife of Bath's Prologue, 37, 49
   Wife of Bath's Tale, 8n6, 37, 49, 49n49
   House of Fame, 56–7, 64–5, 121
   Legend of Good Women, 8, 8n6
   Parliament of Fowls, 56
   the *querelle* and, 37
   translation of "Complaint of Mars" (Oton de Graunson), 9
   translation of "Complaint of Venus" (Oton de Graunson), 9
   as translator, 121
   Troilus and Criseyde, 6, 189n25
   "Truth" (ballade on fortune), 56
Chaucerian canon, 56–65
Chaucerian prologues, 122–3n14, 123, 139
Le Chemin de l'hôpital, 12

Chettle, Henry, 96
chevilles, 7
chiastic structure, 51
Cicero, 51n52
class, 10–11, 12, 14–19, 115
clergy, 143, 145, 150, 189. *See also* anticlericalism
clinamen, xiii
closural acrostic, 161
colophons, 15, 22n3, 24, 45, 47, 49, 62, 64–5, 72, 80, 137, 142n2, 146, 160–61, 165–6, 174, 191
Col, Pierre, 35, 42
comic secular drama, 189
Company of Stationers, 2
compilators, 70
"Complaint of Mars," 9
"Complaint of Venus," 9
The complaynte of them that ben to late maryed, 226–35
Complaynt of a louers life, 74, 77, 78
A complaynt of them that be to soone maryed, 12, 19, 141–65, 141n1, 168, 171–2, 215–26. *See also under* Gringore, Pierre
"contact zones," 5
Copeland, Rita, 51n52
Copland, Robert, 1, 3, 12–13, 20, 23, 36, 38, 116, 141–3, 141n1, 142n2, 145–6, 148, 150, 157–9, 159n15, 160–67, 171. *See also* acrostics
    imprint of *Hye Way to the Spittal Hous*, 12, 141
    imprint of Jyl of *Testament* (Jyl of Braintford), 141
    imprint of *Sorrowes That Women Haue When Theyr Husbandes Be Dead*, 141
    printer's interventions of, 158–65
    suppression of Gringore's authorship by, 163
    translation of *The Complaynt of them that be to late maryed* (Gringore), 1, 11, 13, 15, 19, 141–4, 141n1, 142–3, 148, 158–72, 159–61, 163, 165, 171
    translation of *The Fyftene Joyes of Maryage*, xiv, 11–14, 16, 18–20, 36n33, 94, 113–40, 207–14

    translation of Garcie's *The rutter of the sea* (Garcie), 150
    translation of Gringore's *A Complaynt of them that be to soone maryed* (Gringore), 141–65, *147*, 171–2
    versification of *Le Chemin de l'hôpital*, 12
Cornyshe, William, 175, 176n8
cosmetics, 107
courtly literature, 1, 7, 10, 13, 14, 152. *See also* romance
courtship, 10
Crenne, Helisenne de, 38*n*36
"critical tact," 19–20
critique-à-clef, 93
cross-cultural contact, xii–xiii, xiv, 4–6, 41n41. 191. *See also* mediation; translation
cuckoldry, 19, 125, 145, 165, 170, 173–4, 184–6, 186n22, 188–9
Cupid, 119

Davies, John, 54n54
    Epigrams, 113
deauthorization, 21, 24, 26, 38, 60n61. *See also* authority; authorship
de Bretagne, Anne, 163
de Bruges, Louis, 41
De Coniuge non ducenda, 116, 116n11
de France, Jeanne, 163
de Graunson, Oton, 9
Delectable Demaundes, 178n10
Deleuze, Gilles, 41n41
demandes d'amour, 15, 178–80, 178n10, 190
de Meun, Jean, 1
deracination, 22, 38, 40
Derrida, Jacques, *De la Grammatologie*, 89
Deschamps, Eustache, 35, 71n3, 121
    Miroir de Mariage, 35
Desroches sisters, 38*n*36
deterritorialization, 41–2, 41n41
de Worde, Wynkyn, 3, 23, 36, 38, 66, 66n64, 70, 72
    imprint of *The complaynte of them that ben to late maryed* (Gringore), 226–35
    imprint of *Complaynt of a louers life*, 74, *77*, 78

imprint of *A complaynt of them that be to soone maryed* (Gringore), 12, 19, 141–65, 141n1, 168, 171–2, 215–26
imprint of *The Fyftene Joyes of Maryage*, xiv, 11–14, 16, 18–20, 36n33, 94, 113–40, 207–14
imprint of *Interlocucyon with an argument betwyxt man and woman* (Alexis), xiv, 11–12, 15–18, 23, 69–70, 72, *73*, 74, 78, *79*, 81, 85–6, 93, 95–8, 101, 111, 131, 142
imprint of *Prouerbes of Lydgate*, 75
imprint of *Seyings of Salomon and Marcolphus*, 76
Prouerbes of Lydgate, 75
Stans puer ad mensam, 66, 66n64
dialectical structures, xiv, 10–11, 19, 69n1, 97, 111, 143–4, 171, 176. *See also* gender: gender dialectics
Dido, 11n9, 85–97. *See also* imp. Pynson; *Letter of Dydo to Eneas* (Anon)
Dolan, Fran, 107, 107n29, 108
Donawerth, Jane, 38n36, 38*n*36, 52n53, 94, 96, 119, 145, 166, 182n14
Donne, John, 175n4
drama, 190
  comic secular drama, 189
  French drama, 189–90
  Tudor drama, 13, 19, 122, 173, 177, 182n14, 189–90
Driver, Martha, xii, 22, 30n26, 31, 74, 74n6, 136n21, 146, 724n
Du Bellay, Jean, 17n42, 174–5n2
  Antiquitez, 62n62
du Castel, Etienne, 50n51
du Castel, Jean, 40
Dunbar, William
  Ane Tretis of Twa Mariit Wemmen and a Wedo, 178n10
Dupont-Alais, Jean, 98–100n20
  Louenge des dames, 98–100n20
  Louenge et Beaulte des femmes, 98–100
Durling, Nancy Vine, 187n23

early modern literature
  unreadability of, xi, xin1

Edward IV, 45n45
Edward VI, 175
Edwards, A. S. G., xii
Eleanor of Aquitaine, 7
Elyot, Thomas, 71n3
England, 23–4, 37, 41, 70, 84–5, 114–15, 132, 136, 140, 173, 191
  early printing in, 2–4
  Englishness, 65, 131, 139, 148, 161, 163
  France and. *See also* cross-cultural contact
  Tudor context, 19, 23, 25, 28, 34, 37, 37n53, 55, 57, 66, 117, 122, 132, 163, 164, 190
enjambments, 116, 118, 131, 141
epigrams, 19, 62, 67, 113, 176n6
epilogues, 4, 15
Erler, Mary C., 37, 37n34, 141, 159n15
erotica, 110
euphuistic style, 67

Faivre, Bernard, 188
fame, 56–65
farce, 13, 20, 173–4, 176n7, 177, 187–90, 191
La Farce du Pasté. *See also* Heywood, John: *A mery play betwene Johan Johan the husbande, Tyb his wyfe, and Syr Johan the preest*
  compared to Heywood's translation, 177–88
Fawkes, Rycharde, *99*, 100
  imprint of *Beaute of Women* (Anon), xiv, 14, 16, 18, 69–70, 97–112, *99*, 110n30, 146, 201–14
femininity. *See* gender; women
feminist literature, 70, 84–5, 88, 97, 139, 141. *See also under* Pizan, Christine de
Fenster, Thelma, 37, 37n34
Ferguson, Margaret, xii
Feylde, Thomas, *Connaissance d'Amours*, 96
fidelity, 51
Fitzherbert, John, 66–7n66
flatulence, 13, 158
"flocking behavior," xiii
Forhan, Kate Langdon, 28, 29n21
form, xiii, xv, 5. *See also* genre
format allongé, 45, 60

Forni, Kathleen, 57, 57n55, 62
The Foure PP, 179n12
Fowler, Alastair, 67
framing, 15, 81, 143, 171
   commendatory, xiii
   fictional, xiii
le Franc, Martin, *Le champion de dames*, 35
France, 3n1, 28–9, 34n31. *See also* Burgundy
   England and. *See* cross-cultural contact
   Frenchness, 15, 27, 65, 72, 98, 105, 122, 139, 146, 174, 191
   gender in, 7–10
   Great Schism and, 28
   history of, 164–6
Franco-Burgundian literature, xii, 3, 3n1
François I, 28
francophone subculture, 3
Fraser, Russell Alfred, 19
   The Court of Venus, 19
freedom, 150, 168
French drama, 189–90
Frotinus
   Stratagemata, 26
Fulgentius, 31
The Fyftene Joyes of Maryage (imp. de Worde; trans. Copland), xiv, 11–14, 16, 18–20, 36n33, 94, 113–40, 116n33, 140–146, 148–51, 155, 157, 168, 171, 174
   French imprints of, 136–7, 136n31
   French Prologue, 117, 118, 120, 123, 125, 127, 128, 131–2, 135, 139
   the lost epilogue, 137–8
   misogamy and, 137–8
   misogyny and, 137–8
   paratexts to, 207–14
   "The Proheyme of the Auctour," 123–36
   "The Prologue of the Translatour," 117–32
   woodcuts in, 136–7

Gadol, Joan Kelly, xiv
Gager, William, 96
Galderisi, Claudio, 138
Garcie, Pierre
   The rutter of the sea, 150

gender, xi, xiii–xv, 1–4, 6, 7–10, 23, 69–70. *See also* men; women
   in de Worde's *Interlocucyon*, 70–85
   in *Epistre Othea*, 31, 34
   in *La Farce du Pasté*, 177–88
   gender debates, 17, 69–70, 78, 80–83, 83n9, 85, 108, 171. *See also* querelle de la Rose/querelle des femmes
   gender dialectics, 23–4, 34, 38, 143, 171
   gender discourse, 1–2, 4–5, 9, 14, 18, 71, 77, 81, 111–12, 117, 131, 141–2, 156, 164, 191
   gender relations, xi, xiv, 1, 3–4, 3n1, 7, 10, 11–14, 35, 67, 70. *See also* marriage
   readership and, 18, 35, 138–9
   translation and, 4–6, 94, 94n18
   tropes and, 4, 6
gender dialectics. *See also* dialectical structures
genre, xiii, xv, 5–10, 15
georgic mode, 66, 66n66
Gesta Romanorum, 137n22
Gifford, Humphrey, 96
Gillespie, Alexandra, xii, 74
Gladwell, Malcolm, xiii
goliardic verses, 116n11
"good wives," 148–9, 168
Gosynhill, Edward, 71
   Mulierum Paean, 71
   Schole House for Women, 71
Graunson, Oton de, 9
Great Schism, the, 28
Green, Karen, 30n25
Greene, Thomas M., 54n54
Gringore, Pierre, 11n10, 159–64, 166n22
   Chasteau de Labour, 11n10. *See also Castle of Labour* (trans. Barclay)
   Chateau d'Amours, 9
   La complainte de trop tard marie (The Complaynt of them that be to late maryed), 141–4, 158–72
   La complainte de trop tost marié (A Complaynt of them that be to soone maryed), 141–58, *147*
Guattari, Félix, 41n41

Halasz, Alexandra, 2–3, 38
Hanna, Ralph, 143
Hannay, Margaret, 94, 94n18
Happé, Peter, 174, 176, 179, 184, 184n18, 190–91
Hawes, Stephen, 116
Helicon, 94
Hellinga, Lotte, xii
hendecasyllabic lines, 60, 81
Henry IV, 40
Henry V, 27n16, 27n16
Henry VII, 26, 45, 45n45, 56
Henry VIII, 3n431, 28–9, 34n31, 56, 88, 93, 127, 163–4, 175n4
    Seven Sacraments, 127
Heywood, John, 15, 19–20, 54n54, 66, 122, 122n6, 175n4, 176n6, 184n18, 189n25
    authorship of, 176, 176n8
    Dialogue conteyning the number of effectuall prouerbes in the Englishe tounge..., 176n6
    The Foure PP, 179–80n12
    A mery play betwene Johan Johan the husbande, Tyb his wife, and Syr Johan the preest, 11, 13, 16, 19, 66, 173–81, 173–91, 177n9, 179n12
        compared to French original, 177–88
        contexts of, 174–7
        gender in, 177–88
        literary history and, 188–91
        method of lexical naturalization, 181–2, 191
    The Pardoner and the Frere, 177, 189n25
    A Play of Love, 179–80n12
    Play of the Wether, 179–80n12
    translation of *La Farce du Pasté*, 173–91
    use of names, 183–4
    Witty and Witless, 179–80n12
Hindman, Sandra, 34
Hoccleve, Thomas, 21, 21n1, 23, 37
Hodnett, Edward, 105
Horace, 51n52
Howleglas, 66–7n66
Hull, Suzanne, 131

humanism, 19, 58, 58n58, 111, 173n1, 189–91
Hundred Years' War, 3n431, 20, 26, 28, 34n31
Hye Way to the Spittal Hous (imp. Copland), 12, 141
Hymen, 119

imitation, 5
impotence, 1, 13, 15, 19, 115, 141–2, 148, 165, 168, 170, 184
incest, 127, 164, 186
infidelity, 145. *See also* cuckoldry
influence models, 17
intentio auctoris, 146
intertextuality, 5, 6–7
Isabeau de Bavière, Queen of France, 35, 42
Iser, Wolfgang, 51n52
Islip, Adam (imp.), 113
    Bachelars Banquet, 113n2
    The xv Joyes of Marriage, 113n2

James III, 45n45
Jauss, Hans Robert, 122–3
Jerome, Saint, 51, 51n52, 71, 80
John, Duke of Bedford, 40
Jordan, Constance, xiv
Joukovsky, F., 62n62
Juno, 94
Jyl of Braintford, *Testament*, 141

Knyght of the Swanne, 137n22
Krontiris, Tina, 94, 94n18
Kuin, Roger, 19–20, 19–20n15

Labé, Louise, 38n36
Lai de Lanval, 9
Lamentationes Matheoli, 35–6, 36n33, 49, 116, 125n16, 171. *See also* Mathéolus (Mathieu de Boulogne)
Lanyer, Aemilia, 38
Lawler, Traugott, 143
Le Fèvre, Jean, *Livre de Leesce*, 35
le Franc, Martin, *Le Champion de Dames*, 35
Le Noir, Michel, 1n445, 31, 144n5, 146, 148n6, 162, 164
le Noir, Philippe, 26
Lerer, Seth, 58, 122n14

Letter of Dydo to Eneas (Anon; imp.
    Pynson), xiv, 14–18, 69–70, 85–97,
    87, 111–12, 131, 143, 193–201
Lewicka, Halina, 181–2n13, 181n11
liberty, 13, 18, 117, 124–5, 132–3, 135–6,
    138, 139, 141, 150
lineation, 6–7, 15
literary conventions, 10
literary exemplarity, 8
Lobzowska, Maria, 122–3n14
Louenge des femmes, 18
Louis XII, 34, 34n31, 160, 163–4
love, 3, 6, 85–97
low-georgic mode, 66–7n66
Lucas, Robert, 26–7, 27n17, 28n18
Lucrece, 94
Luxembourg, Jaquette de, 40
Lydgate, John, 25, 36, 57, 64–5, 85n13
    Consuio Quisquis Eris, 56
    *The Payne and Sorowe of Euyll
        maryage*, 116
    Prouerbes of Lydgate, 56, 64, 66n64,
        75, 78
    Siege of Thebes, 189, 189n25

"*machine à rire*," 190
Macrobius, 31, 87
Mahoney, Dhira, 21, 22n3
Malcolmson, Christina, 23, 36, 37n35
mal mariée poem topos, 154
manuscript culture, 2, 6, 13, 22, 34n31,
    37n35, 45
Map, Walter, 10, 71, 124–6, 26
marginalia, 25, 100
"marketplace of print," 2–3
Marlowe, Christopher, 96, 113
    Dido, Queen of Carthage, 96
    Elegyes, 113
marriage, 133, 135–6, 150, 168. *See also*
    The Fyftene Joyes of Maryage
    (imp. de Worde; trans. Copland);
    marriage complaints; misogamy;
    specific works
    as captivity, 144
    class and, 12, 115
    disenchantment of, 13
    economics of, 1, 10, 12–13, 18–19,
        114–15, 115n4, 141–2, 144, 151–4,
        156, 165, 170
    imprisonment and, 1, 18, 124, 130,
        132–3, 135, 136n21, 152n4,
        153n12, 168
    late, 165–71
    liberty and, 133, 135–6, 150, 168
    Pauline doctrine and, 85n13, 129, 165
    poverty and, 12, 115, 115n4, 141, 165
    reconfiguration of, 10
    as a trap, 18, 115, 121, 128, 132–3,
        135, 149
    women and, 3, 6
marriage complaints, 11, 215–35. *See also
    The complaynte of them that ben to
    late maryed; A complaynt of them
    that be to soone maryed*
Mary, Queen, 164, 175
masculinity. *See* gender; men
Mathéolus (Mathieu de Boulogne), 1, 10,
    35, 36n33, 42, 71n3, 80, 103, 114,
    124, 125, 125n16, 126, 164, 170
Medea, 94
media experiments, xiii, xiv, 2
mediation, xii–xiii, 15. *See also* cross-
    cultural contact
medieval period
    literature of the, 59
    Renaissance period and, xiii, 2
    translation practices in the, 51n52
mel-sel-fel rhetorical exercise, 111
men, xii–xiv, 86. *See also* gender
    eroticism and, 141
    male antitypes, 171
    male perspective, 97
    male voice, 70–71, 85, 97, 145–6
meter, 7, 60, 62n62, 116n11, 127
methodology, 16–20
Minnis, A. J., 26
mise-en-page, xiii, 4, 7, 15
misogamy, 11–13, 18–19, 110, 113,
    116n11, 135, 137n22, 145, 176n6,
    177, 183, 184, 188. *See also*
    marriage complaints
    antimarital satire, 171, 174, 185
    in *La Farce du Pasté*, 177–88
    in *The Fyftene Joyes of Maryage*, 113–
        40, 137–8, 137n22, 156, 190–91
    French, 145

in Heywood's *A mery play*, 173–91, 176n8
translation and, 173–91
misogyny, 1, 8, 167. *See also* antifeminist literature; women
   bicultural, 191
   classical, 10
   clerical, 80
   French, 145
   in *The Fyftene Joyes of Maryage*, 137–8
   in Heywood, 173–91, 176n6
monarchists, 28
Monk's Tale rhyme, 105–6, 123, 130, 137, 139n27, 143–4, 161
Montaiglon, Anatole, *Receuil de Poesies françoises des XVe et XVIe siecles*, 98–100n20
Montreuil, Jean de, 35
Moralisé, 31
moralités, 189
moralities drama, 190
More, Thomas, 175n4
Morley, translation of *Trionfi*, 6
Morpheus, 119–220
Morse, Ruth, xii
mothers-in-law, 144–5, 157–8
Mubashshir ibn Fatik, Abu al-wafa, *Dictes and Sayinges of the Philosophres* (trans. Woodville), 54n54, 65
Mullini, Roberta, 174–5, 174–5n2
Muses, 94
Myrra, 94
mythography, 31

la nasse (the noose), 115, 124, 130, 132, 144, 149, 156n14, 162. *See also* marriage: as a trap
new historicism, 19–20, 19–20n15
Newman, Karen, xii
Niobe, 94
Norland, Howard, 176–7, 183, 185, 187

occupatio stanza, 101
occupatio topos, 123
octosyllables, 81–2
Olyuer of Castylle, 137n22
originality, 5

orthography, xi, 57, 60, 60n60
ottava rima, 100, 105–6. *See also* Monk's Tale rhyme
Ovid, 10, 86, 92, 113, 119, 120n13
   Heroides, 86, 87, *87*
   "Letter of Dido," 56, 57n55, 64, 86n14
Ozawa, Hiroshi, 179–80n12, 179n12

"pamphlet wars," xiv, 1, 69
paratexts, xii, 10–11, 13, 15–18, 25, 69–70, 81, 86, 158–65, 174, 191. *See also* specific kinds of paratexts
   to *The Fyftene Joyes of Maryage*, 116–17, 120, 122–3, 139–40, 207–15
   in the marriage complaints, 158–65, 171
   paratextual meanings, 4, 23, 30, 45, 72, 88, 97, 138, 142–3, 148
   in Pizan's *Prouerbes moraulx (Moral Proverbs)*, 38–9, 48, 52–6, 65
   visual, 72. *See also* illustration; woodcuts
parodies, 14
Parussa, Gabriella, 34
Pauline doctrine, 85n13, 129, 165
Payne and Sorowe of Euyll Marriage, 137n22
pentameter verse, 7, 14–15, 18, 45, 81, 116–17, 116n11, 137, 139, 143, 149, 174
Pepwell, H., 24, 38
periodization, xiii, xv, 2, 5–6
Petrarchan modes, xiv, xv, 6, 9, 14, 14n13, 15, 108, 180
phallic imagery, 14, 18, 96
Pigouchet, Philippe, 31, *32*
Pitts, Brent A., 125n15
Pizan, Christine de, xiv, 1, 8, 16, 21n1. *See also* Pizan, Christine de, works of
   authority of, 24–5, 29, 31, 35, 38, 44–52, 56–65
   Boccaccio and, 87
   fame and, 56–65
   as a feminist writer, 16–17, 22, 23, 30n25, 31, 34–8
   gender and, 29, 34–8, 42, 51
   as historian, 24, 26, 38
   historical context of her work, 28, 34n31
   as military historian, 24, 26, 38

opinion of the English, 27, 27n16
political theory of, 26–8, 30n25
promonarchical stance of, 28, 30n25
publication of, 9, 9n8
reception of, 21–38, 34n31, 40–44
self-glossing by, 31
as theorist of peace and war, 26–7
Pizan, Christine de, works of
   Cent Ballades, 40n37
   Dit de Poissy, 40n37
   Ditié de Jeanne d'Arc, 27n16, 41
   early printed translations of
      in *The Boke of Fame*, *61, 63*
      Boke of the Body of Polycye, 22, 24, 27, 29, 36
      Boke of the Cyte of ladyes, 23, 24, 36
      The Booke ... called the body of polycye ..., 24
      C. Hystoryes of Troye, vii, 24, 27n16, 29, 30, *33*, 34
      Fayttes of Armes and of chyualrye, 24, 25n9, 26, 36
      Letter of Cupid, 24, 35, 37
      Morale Prouerbes of Cristyne, 24–5, 25n7, 38–68, 42n42, 45n45, *46*
      "Morall prouerbes of Christyne," *61, 63*
   Enseignements moraulx a son fils, 41, 43, 66n64
   Epistre au dieu d'amours, 21, 23, 34–5, 37, 49, 49n50, 69, 69n1
   Epistre Othea, 8n6, 21, 24, 29–30, 31, 34
   Faits d'armes et de chevalrie, 24, 25n9, 26, 36
   Jeux a vendre, 40n37
   La Lamentacion sur les maux de France, 27n16
   L'épître de la déese Othéa [Les Cent Histoires de Troye], vii, 8n6, 21, 24, 27n16, 29–30, 31, *32, 33*, 34
   Livre de la Cite des dames, 17, 21n1, 23n5, 34–6, 37n35, 40n37, 43, 43n43, 49, 87
   Livre du Corps de Policie, 22, 24, 27, 29, 36
   Livre du Duc de vrais amants, 40n37
   Oroyson Nostre Seigneur, 40n37
   Prouerbes moraulx, 16, 24, 38–68, 40, 40n37, 42n42, 44–5, 58n58, 65–8, 66n64
      Caxton's imprint of, 44–52
      as Chaucerian, 56–65
      context of, 52–6
      paratexts and, 52–6
      printers' interventions and, 38–9
Pizan, Tomas de, 50n51
places publiques, 190
Play of Love, 179n12
Play of the Wether, 179n12
plots, 11, 162, 173–4, 176, 179, 184, 189
poesis, 140
poetics, 6–7. *See also* aesthetics
   translators' role in developing, 6–7
poetry, 7–10. *See also specific kinds of poetry; specific kinds of verse*
   of the English Renaissance, 6
   features of, 10–15
   translated, 6–7
point of view, 6–7
Pratt, Karen, 125n16
Pratt, Mary Louise, 5
prefaces, 4
Prescott, Anne Lake, xii, 94, 94n18
"Prieur de Bucy." *See* Alexis, Guillaume
printers, 2–4. *See also* books; translators; *specific printers*
   aesthetic innovations of, xiii, 3, 15
   francophone, 4
   interventions of, xii–xiii, 2, 7, 15, 18, 69–70, 111–12, 158–65. *See also* paratexts
   mediation by, 15
   presentational strategies of, xii–xiii, 2, 38–9, 60, 62, 62n62
   readers and, xv
   self-promotion by, 22
   suppression of authorship by, 22, 54n54, 72n4, 163
   suppressions by, 14, 21–2, 31, 37, 43, 54n54, 72n4, 78, 85n13, 126–7, 129, 163, 190
   technical innovations of, xiii, 2, 7, 111–12
   visual innovations of, 111–12
printing, 2–4. *See also* books; printers; woodcuts

economics of, 2–3, 9, 22, 45, 59, 92
French-Burgundian influence on early printing in England, 2–4
history of, 2–4
manuscript culture and, xiii, 2, 6, 13, 22, 34n31, 37n35, 45
marketplace of, 2–3, 9
printing practices, 22
script and, xiii, 37n35
proems, 15. *See also* prologues
prologues, 15, 18, 26, 30, 30n24, 37, 48, 48n47, 49, 88, 92–5, 104–6, 116n11, 117–28, 122–3n14, 131–3, 135–6, 139, 149, 174, 179
   English, 30, 30n24, 48–9, 48n47, 95, 101, 122
   French, 117–18, 120, 123, 125–8, 131–2, 135, 139, 165–6
promiscuity, 13, 165, 167–8, 184
pronouns, use of universal masculine, 43
provenance, 25, 40–41, 41n39, 53, 100
proverbs, 38–68, 66–7n66
pseudo-stichomythia, 179n12
puns, 13n420, 53, 94, 107, 133, 135, 150, 153, 169n23, 194n18
Purkiss, Diane, 86, 86n14, 96
Pynson, Richard, 3, 9, 14, 17, 25, 38, 44, 56–60, 57n55, 60n60, 62m 64–5, 84, 86, 88, 96
   and the *Calendrier des bergiers*, 74
   imprint of *Letter of Dydo to Eneas*, 85–97, *87*

quaestio tradition, 132, 143
querelle de la Rose/querelle des femmes, 1, 7–10, 15, 17, 23, 34–6, 36n32, 37, 42, 49, 70, 85, 111, 115, 115n9, 164, 167, 170–71
Les Questions diverses, 178n10
Quilligan, Maureen, 24, 43, 43n43, 49n50
Les Quinze Joyes de mariage (Anon). *See also Fyftene Joyes of Maryage* (imp. de Worde; trans. Copland)
Les Quinze Joyes de mariage (Anon), 113, 113n1, 117, 122–3n14

Rastell, John, 19, 175, 175n, 176
Rastell, William, 175n

reader response, 5
readership, 10, 37n35. *See also* reception
   bicultural, 41n41
   English, 18, 21–38, 35, 40–44, 97, 140
   female, 18, 42
   French, 135
   gender and, 18, 34–8, 35, 138–9
   horizon of expectations, 122–3
   nationality and, 135
   printers and, xv
   script *vs.* print, xiii, 37n35
   Tudor, 38, 97, 140
reception, 5, 37. *See also* readership
Redman, I., 66n64
Reed, A. W., 176n8
Renaissance period, 5–6
   English Renaissance poetry, 6
   literature of the, 59
   medieval period and, xiii, 2
   translation practices in the, 51–2
Rey-Flaud, Bernadette, 190
rezeptiongeschichte, 37
rhétoriqueurs, 84, 104, 159, 161
rhyme royal verse, 7, 24, 47–8, 50, 94–5, 116, 116n11, 117, 122–3, 127, 137, 139, 143, 146, 160–61, 165–6, 174, 179, 179n12
rhyme scheme, 83–4, 148n8, 177n9
Rich, Barnabe, 54n54
Richard III, 45n45
Rigg, A . G., 116
Rivers, George, 96
   Heroinae, 96
romance, 7–10, *9*
Roman de la Rose, 8–10, 35–6, 36n38, 37, 49, 96, 152. *See also querelle de la Rose/querelle des femmes*
rondeaux, 179–80
Roy, Maurice, 42n42
Ryghtwyse, John, 96

Saint Gelais, Octavien de, 17, 56, 86
   Épîtres d'Ovide, 90
   S'ensuyt les XXI épistres d'Ovide, 90, *91*
   translation of Ovid's *Heroides VII*, 17, 86, *87*. *See also* imp. Pynson; *Letter of Dydo to Eneas* (Anon)

Salisbury, John of, 40
  Policraticus, 28
Santucci, Monique, 115n5, 117
satire, xiv, 12, 14, 15, 117, 122–3n14, 145, 156, 171, 174, 176, 177, 185, 189, 190
Scrope, Stephen, 21, 21n1, 31
  translation of *Epistre Othea*, 29–30
Sébillet, Thomas, *La Louenge des femmes*, 110
seduction, 8, 13
sexuality, 13, 98, 165–71, 174
  sexual failures, 13. *See also* impotence
  sexual stereotypes, 174
  translation and, 4–6
  women and, 3, 6, 10, 85–97, 165–71
The Seyenges of Salomon and Marcolphus (Anon; imp. de Worde), 18n418, 66n64, 74, 76, 78
shepherd's calendars, 66–7n66, 67
Silvestris, Bernardus, 31
Simpson, James, xiii
Skot, John, 27, 29, 38
sotties, 189, 190
sound effects, 6–7
Spearing, A. C., xiii
Speght, Rachel, 37
Spelman, W., 54n54
Spenser, Edmund, 54n54
  Amoretti, 62n62
  Faerie Queene, 62n62
Stafford. Edward, 28
Stans puer ad mensam (de Worde), 66, 66n64
Stierle, Karlheinz, xii, 51n52
Summit, Jennifer, 21, 21n1
Sychaeus, 87
syllabification, 149
syntax, 6–7

Temple of Bras, 66–7n66
Tertullius, 87
tetrameter verse, 7, 81, 149, 174, 177n9
text-and-exegesis format, 31
textual deterritorialization, 41–2n41
theme, xiii
Theophrastus, 1, 10, 36n33, 71n3, 114
Tignonville, Guillaume de, 35
Tilley, Morris Palmer, 54n54, 63n66
tipping points, xiii

titles, 4, 15
tone, 6–7
topoi, 9, 16, 18, 30, 47, 80, 121, 148, 157, 170–71
Tottel, Richard, 96
  Songes and Sonets, 96
transformational arts, xiii
translation, xii–xiii, 4–6, 51n52, 70, 83, 121–2. *See also* cross-cultural contact; translators
  "contact zones" and, 5
  Englished, 25n7, 40, 50, 117, 224n
  gender and, 4–6, 94, 94n18
  invisible, 72
  medieval *vs.* Renaissance practices, 51n52
  misogyny and, 173–91, 177–8
  periodization and, 5–6
  of poetry, 6–7
  of prose, 6
  sexuality and, 4–6
  tropes and, 121
translatio studii, xii, 51n52
translators, 38, 117–23, 121. *See also* printers; translation; *specific translators*
  female, 94n18
  gender and, 94, 94n18
  interventions of, 111–12
  role in developing poetics, 6–7
Travistsky, Betty, xiv
Trionfi, 6
tropes, 4, 6, 8, 9, 13, 14, 14n13, 51, 121
Troyes, treaty of, 27n16
Tudor drama, 13, 19, 122, 173, 177, 182n14, 189–91
Tudor humanists, 190–91
Tudor, Mary, 163, 164. *See* Mary, Queen
Tudor myth, 70, 86, 88, 93
Tudor readership, 38, 97, 140
Tudors, 28, 117, 122, 163, 164
Turberville, George, 96
  Heroicall Epistles, 96
"two-tradition" paradigm, 190
typefaces, xiii
typography, xi, xii, 16, 26, 31, 45, 59, 62n62, 72, xin1

Utley, Francis, 3, 164

Valerius Maximus. *See* Map, Walter
Vegetius
    De re militari, 26
ventriloquism, 15–16, 19, 21, 25, 51, 145
Vérard, Antoine, 26
verse. *See specific kinds of verse*
verse proverbs, 67
versification, 7
Vickers, Nancy, 14n13
Vieillard, Nicolas, 99–100n20
Villon, François, 83
    Le Grant Testament, 83
Virgil, *Aeneid*, 25, 86–7
virtue, 85–97

Wager, W., 54n54
Walker, Greg, 175n4, 176
Wall, Wendy, xiv
Wallace, C. W., 176n8
Walters, Lori, xiv
war, 26–8
Warren, Nancy Bradley, 88
Wars of the Roses, 117
Watkins, John, 86, 86n14
Watson, Henry, 116
Westfall, Suzanne, 189–90, 190
Whitney, Isabella, 37, 96
    "To an Unconstant Lover," 96
widows, 127, 164
wife-beating, 13, 18n418, 180–181
Williams, Deanne, xii
wisdom literature, 16
Witty and Witless, 179n12
Wolsey, Cardinal, 174
"woman questions," xi, xv, 1, 3–4, 37–8
women, xi–xv, 3–4, 6, 11, 14, 69–70. *See also* gender; marriage; misogyny; *querelle de la Rose/querelle des femmes;* women writers
    agency of, 10, 18, 108
    in *The Beaute of Women*, 97–111
    beauty of, 14–15, 97–111

    bodies of, 13, 14–15, 18, 97–111
    chastity and, 85–97
    clerical treatises on, 8
    in *The Complaynt of them that be to late maryed*, 158–71
    in *A Complaynt of them that be to soon maryed*, 141–58
    debates about, 69–112
    eroticism and, 98, 109–10
    in *Interlocucyon*, 70–75
    in *Letter of Dydo to Eneas*, 85–97
    liberty for, 139
    love and, 3, 6, 85–97
    Pauline doctrine and, 85n13
    as readers, 42
    sexuality and, 3, 6, 10, 85–97, 165–71
    speech of, 10
    as translators, 94n18
    voice of, 15–17, 21, 29, 31, 64, 69, 71, 85–7, 94, 97, 112, 139, 142, 144–58, 171
    widows, 127, 164
    wife-beating, 13, 18n418, 180–181
    woman *vs.* lady, 11, 14
women writers, 24, 38–9, 38*n*36, 54n54. *See also* authority; authorship; Pizan, Christine de
Woodbridge, Linda, xiv
woodcuts, 4, 15, 110, 136–39, 136–7
Woodville, Anthony, 66–7n66
    translation of *Dictes and Sayinges of the Philosophres*, 54n54, 65
    translation of *Morale Prouerbes of Cristyne*, 24–5, 25n7, 36–68, 42n42, 45n45, *46*
Woodville, Elizabeth, 45n45
Woodville, Richard, 40
working-class protagonists, 10–11
writing as flatulence, 158
Wyer, Robert, 3, 30–31, 38, 92, 724n
    translation of Pizan's *C. Hystoryes of Troye*, 33

Ypomédon, 9